THE RELIGIOUS FACTOR

GERHARD LENSKI is Associate Professor of Sociology at The University of Michigan, a co-author of *Principles of Sociology* and a contributor to numerous professional journals. He received his doctorate from Yale University in 1950.

THE RELIGIOUS FACTOR

*A Sociological Study of Religion's Impact
on Politics, Economics, and Family Life*

BY
GERHARD LENSKI

REVISED EDITION

145

ANCHOR BOOKS
DOUBLEDAY & COMPANY, INC.
GARDEN CITY, NEW YORK

The Religious Factor was originally published by Doubleday & Company, Inc. in 1961. The Anchor Books edition is published by arrangement with Doubleday & Company, Inc.

Anchor Books Edition: 1963

To My Parents

PREFACE

During the last decade the subject of religion has received increased attention both in popular and scholarly circles. Much of this attention has been devoted to the recent religious revival and its causes. Relatively little attention, however, has been devoted to the subject which is central in this book: the consequences of religious belief and practice in the everyday life of society. Yet from both the sociological and religious standpoints, these consequences are of crucial importance.

Unhappily, many of the findings of this study will prove disturbing to men of every faith—Protestants, Catholics, Jews, humanists, and positivists alike. We all tend to believe, or want to believe, that our own group is superior to other groups in every way. Yet systematic research invariably reveals glaring discrepancies between the idealized image which we form and hard reality. I take no pleasure in challenging cherished illusions, but at the same time I feel that this can prove beneficial.

I do not expect this book to be the final word on the subject. In fact, it is my hope that it will stimulate further research in this important area. Religion is far too important a matter to be ignored or dealt with superficially, as has been the custom among American social scientists for a generation or more.

In an effort to make this book as readable as possible, I have omitted from the text certain statistical materials which are normally a part of contemporary sociological research reports. However, the necessary materials have been incorporated in Appendix I, and those readers who are especially concerned with tests of significance may find it desirable to read this appendix before beginning Chapter 2.

No study such as the one reported here can ever be undertaken by a single individual. Rather, the co-operative efforts of a substantial number of people and organizations are always involved. Therefore, I wish to take this opportunity to express my sincere appreciation to all who have contributed so much to this study.

My greatest debt is to the Detroit Area Study and its leaders, Professor Ronald Freedman, Chairman of the Executive Committee, and Professor Harry Sharp, Director. In the spring of 1957 Professors Freedman and Sharp invited me to submit a proposal for an investigation of some aspect of the religious situation in Detroit. This was the beginning of the project. During the academic year 1957–58 Professor Sharp not only trained a staff of interviewers and supervised the collection of data, he also provided countless invaluable suggestions on research techniques and procedures. Finally, both men read the original draft of this manuscript and made many valuable criticisms and suggestions.

In the analysis of the data I was greatly aided by financial assistance from three sources. First, I received a grant from the Social Science Research Council which not only freed me from my usual academic responsibilities for two summers, but also made possible the important interviews with the clergy which were conducted separately from the Detroit Area Study. Second, I received a grant from The University of Michigan's Horace H. Rackham Faculty Research Fund which made it possible for me to hire a research assistant and meet other costs involved in the analysis of the data. Finally, I received a fellowship from a special university fund based on a grant from the Ford Foundation which freed me from two thirds of my regular academic responsibilities in the fall semester of the academic year 1959–60, permitting me to prepare the first draft of the manuscript.

Numerous friends and colleagues have provided assistance in other ways, and I wish to express my sincere appreciation to each of them. I especially wish to thank John Leggett for his careful and accurate work as research assistant; Morris

Axelrod and Charles Cannell for their help in obtaining trained personnel for interviewing the clergy; H. M. Blalock for advice on statistical problems; G. E. Swanson, Daniel Miller, Daniel Katz, and Samuel Eldersveld for permission to use data which they gathered in previous years of the Detroit Area Study; and Father Lawrence J. Cross, S.J., and Monsignor Edward J. Hickey for help in the construction and pretesting of interview schedules.

A special word of appreciation is due to those who read the first draft of this manuscript and offered many insightful and helpful criticisms. In addition to Professors Freedman and Sharp, these were Professors J. Milton Yinger, Albert F. Wessen, and Gibson Winter, and Mrs. Mavis Cavendish.

I also wish to express my appreciation to the staff and graduate students of the Detroit Area Study who contributed much to this study not only through their diligence in interviewing and in coding data, but also through many valuable suggestions at the time the interview schedule was being constructed. In addition to Professor Sharp, the staff included John Leggett, Donald Halsted, Aida Tomeh, and Mrs. Martin David. Members of the student group were Thomas Bakker, Nancy Bonte, Aage Clausen, Edward Cummings, John Dennis, Paul Eberts, Allan Feldt, John Gilmore, Bruce Hackett, Constance Hill, Suzon Karon, Wayne Kiyosaki, Carolyn Lewis, Jacquelyn Love, Jean Mann, Alexander Matejko, John Musial, Marvin Olsen, Robert Richards, Jr., Judith Samonte, Gary Sampson, Martha Sandoz, William Smit, Paul Smith, K. S. Srikantan, David Street, Lorraine Tiss, Mattieu Van Hunsel, Margaret Vandenbosch, Laurence Weiner, and Robert Yesner.

Finally, I wish to express my appreciation to my wife for the countless ways in which she has aided me in carrying this study through to completion. I could not begin to enumerate here all the many things she has done to aid me in this work.

Because so many people have contributed so much to this study, I found it impossible to use the first person singular form of the pronoun in writing this book. To say that I found this or that seemed a misrepresentation of the facts. Hence the use of the pronoun "we." This is no affectation: it is an honest statement of fact. However, while many have contributed much to this book, the final decisions have all been mine, and thus also the final responsibility.

GERHARD LENSKI

August 1960

PREFACE TO REVISED EDITION

I have had neither the time nor the opportunity to undertake an extensive revision at this time. However, I have endeavored to revise a number of specific areas in an attempt to clarify my point of view. I have also added a number of footnote references to relevant studies that have appeared since publication of the original edition.

As I stated in the preface to the original edition, it was my hope that this book would stimulate increased research in this area; it seemed far too important both from the theoretical and applied standpoints to be neglected as it has been. I must confess that I am pleased to see already signs of increased activity—frequently in reaction to findings or interpretations set forth here. I had no illusions then, and I have none now, that this book will be the final word on the subject of religion's influence on secular institutions.

In the various reviews of this book, a number of criticisms have been made, most of them well taken. There are, however, several which seem, in my opinion, not so well taken, but important enough to deserve at least brief comment.

First, one reviewer has criticized my failure to take account of ethnic differences within the Catholic group. This criticism is well taken in the sense that at the present time there are clearly differences within the Catholic group linked with ethnicity. I have not explored these in great detail because it seems clear that with increasing intermarriage across ethnic lines, these differences will disappear and a common American Catholic subculture will emerge. Thus the design of this study was oriented to the future rather than the past. Some have also argued that Detroit Catholics are so different from American Catholics generally with respect to ethnicity that generalization from this community is dangerous. A recent check which I made indicates that whereas 53 per cent of American Catholics in a national sample of the Survey Research Center indicated a Northwest European background, the same was true of 44 per cent of Detroit Catholics in the 1958 Detroit Area Study.

Second, several men have criticized my failure to take account of denominational differences within the Protestant group. Ironically, it had been my intention when I began my analysis of the data to include a chapter on this subject. Unhappily, I found so few differences—which I felt I could prove to the satisfaction of other sociologists—had their origin in denominationalism that I eventually abandoned the effort. There *are* differences as I point out in Appendix III, but those which can be shown to be statistically significant almost without exception vanish with controls for class or region of birth. For example, Baptists are the least likely to be Republicans—but this is simply because so many of them are southern-born. If controls do not destroy relationships, then they produce irregular relationships which make me fearful of drawing conclusions, especially when there is no theoretical rationale for them.

Finally, another critic has raised the question of whether this study really has much to say about religion's influence on daily life. By this he means that most of the differences between groups described here are not ones with which the groups, and especially their professional leadership, are greatly concerned. As an ordained seminary professor (as well as a professional sociologist) he finds this disturbing. While it is certainly true that this study has left many stones unturned, and perhaps too many that are of special relevance to church leaders, it seems to me that it can prove of great practical value by serving as a reminder that religious organizations have many consequences which their leaders never intended, and of which they may even be unaware. (It is my impression that church leaders often have only a very limited grasp of the nature of the influence religious groups exert on the average man or on society at large.) Too often they fail to recognize the very human character of the groups they lead and the influence they exert; too often they exaggerate (though unintentionally) the role of the Divine in these groups. For those who are committed to the Judaic-Christian tradition, this is ironic, since one of the basic themes running through the whole of the Bible is God's struggle against religion—or more precisely, man-made, popular, and official religion.

GERHARD LENSKI

June 1962

CONTENTS

THE RELIGIOUS FACTOR

Chapter 1

INTRODUCTION TO THE STUDY

God is concerned with the whole of men's lives: on at least this one point all the churches agree. He is not merely the Lord of the Sabbath, but is equally concerned with men's activities the other six days of the week: their work, their play, their politics, their family life.

But how does this doctrine work in practice? Does a man's religious commitment *really* influence his everyday actions, especially a man who lives in the highly secularized environment of the modern American metropolis? Is there *really* a difference between the believer and the unbeliever in the market place or in the voting booth? Does the *type* of religious commitment make a difference: do the actions of Protestants differ from those of Catholics and Jews in the fields of politics, economics, and family life? If so, are these differences due to the influence of their religion, or to something else?

This book reports the findings of a study designed to provide answers to some of these questions. The study was carried out in the Midwestern metropolis of Detroit, fifth largest community in America today, and probably eleventh largest in the world. Here, by means of personal interviews with a carefully selected cross-section of the population of the *total* community (i.e., suburbs as well as central city), we sought to discover the impact of religion on secular institutions. Strictly speaking, the findings set forth in this volume apply only to Detroit. However, in view of the steady decline of localism and regionalism in America during the last century, it seems likely that most of these findings could be duplicated by similar studies in other communities. This is a matter to which we shall return later in this chapter.

I. BACKGROUND OF THE STUDY

(The basic problem with which this study is concerned, the influence of religion on secular institutions, has long been debated by laymen and scholars alike.) One school of thought denies that religion has any significant influence on politics, economics, or other important secular areas of modern society. This view has gained considerably in popularity during the last century and is very evident in the many social science textbooks which largely ignore religion, apparently thinking it irrelevant to the problems at hand. For example, in a leading textbook on American politics, published as recently as 1958, there are only minor scattered references to religion, none of which suggest that religion is, or could be, a factor of importance on the contemporary American political scene.[1] What is even more significant, none of the major reviewers of this book thought this omission deserving of comment.

By contrast, a second school of thought asserts that religion has been, and continues to be, a force in human history. For example, many of the proponents of this point of view maintain that American civil liberties rest ultimately on the foundation provided by the Judaic-Christian conception of the nature of man. Others, in a more critical vein, see religion as a force fostering superstition and retarding the progress of science.

This lack of consensus is hardly surprising in view of the limited amount of serious, systematic research devoted to the problem. Less systematic sociological research has been devoted to religion than to any other major institution of our society. Particularly lacking are studies of the *interrelations* between modern religious institutions and other basic institutional systems.

Positivism and economic determinism

For those familiar with the history of sociology, there are obvious reasons for this neglect. Sociology is essentially a

[1] V. O. Key, *Politics, Parties, and Pressure Groups* (New York: Thomas Y. Crowell, 1958, 4th edition). Otherwise this is an excellent textbook.

child of the French Enlightenment, and from its inception was committed to the positivist view that religion in the modern world is merely a survival from man's primitive past, and doomed to disappear in an era of science and general enlightenment. From the positivist standpoint, religion is, basically, institutionalized ignorance and superstition.[2]

While still in its formative years sociology was also strongly influenced by the theory of economic determinism. For the economic determinist, the economic institutions of society are the ultimate source of all social change.[3] Changes in all other social institutions represent nothing more than adjustments to prior changes in the economic institutions on which they are dependent for their very existence.

Neither positivism nor economic determinism was conducive to sustained sociological research in the field of religion, since both theories viewed religion as a negligible force in the modern world. Furthermore, both tended to provide solutions, not problems, and research flourishes only where the existence of unsolved problems is recognized.

Durkheim and Weber

It was not until the early twentieth century that any serious challenge to either of these two systems of thought developed within sociology. The challenge, when it finally came, was raised chiefly by two men: the German sociologist Max Weber, and his French contemporary, Emile Durkheim. Shortly after the turn of the century each of these men published a major work concerned with the place of religion in

[2] Properly speaking, the positivists applied this generalization only to *traditional* religion. Some, like Comte, sought to establish a new religion of Humanity, which would perform the socially useful functions of traditional religions. However, since this new religion never found acceptance except among a small minority, our description of their view seems only a slight overstatement, at least so far as the implications for research are concerned.

[3] Except, of course, change originating in the physical environment, or outside the social system. From the standpoint of the economic determinists, such change would normally be "filtered" into the social system through the economic institutions of society, since they would be the first to adjust to the changed environment.

human society, which brought them into sharp conflict with the older sociological viewpoints.

In *The Elementary Forms of Religious Life*, Durkheim opposed the positivists with a provocative analysis in which he argued that the roots of religious belief and practice lie in the very fabric of society itself and in the nature of human interrelations, not in ignorance and superstition as the positivists maintained. The religion of primitive man is the symbolic expression of his awareness of the social system on which he depends not only for the material necessities of life, but for psychic necessities as well. According to Durkheim, the religious man who feels dependent upon some external moral power is not the victim of an hallucination. Such a power exists, in the form of society itself. In short, religious institutions embody in symbolic form some of the most profound insights of men. Far from being an unfortunate survival from man's primitive past, they are an integral and necessary element in any stable social system. The form which religious symbols take may change, but there is something basic underlying the forms, and this basic element is destined to survive so long as human societies continue.

About the same time, Weber offered an equally significant challenge to the economic determinists.[4] In his famous essay, *The Protestant Ethic and the Spirit of Capitalism*, he sought to demonstrate that without the Protestant Reformation modern Western capitalism would never have developed.[5] This form of economic enterprise, according to Weber, is unique in human history, since the driving force behind it is not the spirit of greed (for men have always been avaricious) but a spirit of *dedication and commitment to work*. For Weber, the "spirit of capitalism" is distinguished by three main characteristics:

(1) a conviction that work is a worthwhile activity in its

---

[4] For an excellent summary and analysis of the work of Weber, see Reinhard Bendix, *Max Weber: An Intellectual Portrait* (Garden City: Doubleday, 1960), Parts I and II, or Talcott Parsons, *The Structure of Social Action* (New York: McGraw-Hill, 1937), Part III.

[5] *The Protestant Ethic and the Spirit of Capitalism*, translated by Talcott Parsons (New York: Charles Scribner's Sons, 1958).

own right, and not merely as the means to material comfort or wealth;

(2) a belief that economic judgments should be made on purely rational grounds, without regard to traditional criteria;

(3) a distaste for personal indulgence.

Once established, Weber argued, capitalism can be expected to be self-perpetuating; but the critical problem is to discover its origin in precapitalist society. Only by discovering the source of the spirit of capitalism can we discover the source of modern capitalism itself.

Weber found this source in Protestantism in general, and more especially in Calvinism and Puritanism. (He saw the spirit of capitalism as an unintended by-product of these important religious movements, which contained in their theology the seeds of a radical reorientation of men's thinking concerning economic activity.) For example, for the followers of Luther and Calvin, work was to be viewed not as a penalty for sin, but rather as a means of glorifying God. For Calvinists and Puritans, self-indulgence was among the most deadly sins. For Calvinists and Puritans, and later for Methodists as well, life was not to be lived on a day-to-day basis; rather, God demanded a rationalized, unified system of life and the elimination of magic as a means to salvation. In these and other ways, Protestantism laid the foundation for the emergence of the spirit of capitalism.[6] Thus, economic institutions are *not* the uncaused cause of all social change. Rather they are part of a complex social system in which change may originate at various points, with significant consequences for all other parts of the system.

Weber was careful to point out that he was not trying to replace economic determinism with a theory of religious determinism, nor was he even denying the tremendous importance of economic institutions in the process of social

[6] Weber conceded that prior to the Protestant Reformation, isolated individuals had exhibited the spirit of capitalism, but he maintained that this was not enough to permit the emergence of capitalism as a dominant economic system. The dominance of capitalism presupposes whole groups of men committed to the spirit of capitalism, and prior to the Reformation this was lacking. Ibid., p. 55.

change. His goal was simply to challenge what he regarded as the unrealistic and oversimplified theory of social change advocated by the economic determinists and to suggest a more adequate alternative.[7]

While the work of Durkheim and Weber has generated much discussion and debate, unfortunately it has led to little systematic, empirical research. Furthermore, most of the work that has been done has been limited to investigations of problems of an historical character, with all of the attendant methodological difficulties.[8] There have been no major studies of the problems raised by the theories of Durkheim and Weber as they apply to the modern metropolitan community. As a result we do not know much more today about the influence of religious institutions on secular institutions in modern society than was known half a century ago.

[7] Throughout his career Weber was greatly concerned with this important problem which he attacked by means of a broadly comparative study of China, India, ancient Israel, and Western Europe. Originally published as *Gesammelte Aufsätze zur Religionssoziologie* (Tübingen: J. C. B. Mohr, 1920–21), 3 volumes, these materials are now available in English translation as follows: (1) *The Protestant Ethic and the Spirit of Capitalism*, op. cit.; (2) *From Max Weber: Essays in Sociology*, trans. by H. H. Gerth and C. Wright Mills (New York: Oxford University Press, 1946), Part III; (3) *The Religion of China*, trans. by H. H. Gerth (Glencoe: The Free Press, 1951); (4) *The Religion of India*, trans. by H. H. Gerth and Don Martindale (Glencoe: The Free Press, 1958); and (5) *Ancient Judaism*, trans. by H. H. Gerth and Don Martindale (Glencoe: The Free Press, 1952).

[8] See, for example, Ernst Troeltsch, *The Social Teachings of the Christian Churches*, trans. by Olive Wyon (London: Allen & Unwin, 1931), 2 vols.; Werner Sombart, *The Jews and Modern Capitalism*, trans. by M. Epstein (London: T. Fisher Unwin, 1913); R. H. Tawney, *Religion and the Rise of Capitalism* (New York: Harcourt, Brace, 1926); Amintore Fanfani, *Catholicism, Protestantism, and Capitalism* (London: Sheed and Ward, 1951). For an interesting new study, see David S. Landes, *Religion and Enterprise: The Case of the French Textile Industry* (forthcoming).

[9] At the present time G. E. Swanson is engaged in a study of the relevance of Durkheim's theory to the contemporary religious scene, and is utilizing materials from the Detroit Area Study. A monograph based on this study should be forthcoming in the next several years.

Weberian theory and the present study

From its inception this study was designed with the Weberian controversy in mind. No one who has read Weber's analysis of the historical significance of religion for economics can help wondering what relevance his theory has for the contemporary scene. Are the major religious groups in America today the carriers of distinctive economic ethics? Do the economic values and actions of Protestants and Catholics in mid-twentieth-century America differ as much as Weber suggests they did in post-Reformation Europe? Are Protestants more inclined to view their work as a sacred calling? Do they practice the pattern of worldly asceticism Weber identified with the Puritans and Pietists of an earlier era?

Since Weber's concern was with the origins of the capitalist system, he has little to say explicitly about religion's role in a mature capitalist society. What he did say tended to be brief asides rather than carefully developed analyses.[10] However, his basic theoretical position strongly suggests that here, as in all other types of societies, religion is a factor to be reckoned with. Underlying the whole of his writings on the sociology

---

[10] See, for example, *The Protestant Ethic*, op. cit., pp. 55 and 72. Here Weber specifically rejects the hypothesis that Protestantism is a *necessary* condition for the *survival* of capitalism (though elsewhere, as in Chapter I, he indicates that significant differences in the economic ethics of religious groups persist). He states that a mature capitalist society will possess its own institutionalized arrangements for educating and selecting individuals to perform the various functions required by the system, so that assistance from the churches will no longer be required.

In conceding the irrelevance of religious institutions to the survival of capitalism, Weber seems to have supposed that capitalism represents the end product of economic evolution. It apparently did not occur to him *at this point* that capitalism might have to contend with a revival of anti-capitalistic values and might ultimately be destroyed or substantially modified, and that the outcome of this struggle might be profoundly affected by non-economic factors such as religion.

Actually, however, it is unfair to examine Weber's views on this matter too closely since it is evident from the context of his remarks that his chief purpose in making them was to define the limits of his own problem and thereby avoid entanglement in what he regarded as a very different problem: that of determining the conditions necessary for the survival of capitalism.

of religion we find two basic postulates which point to this conclusion. First, he assumes that every major religious group develops its own distinctive orientation toward *all aspects of life,* and that these orientations profoundly influence the daily actions of its adherents and hence the institutional structure of society.[11] Second, Weber assumes that these orientations are partially independent of the social situation of the group.[12] On the basis of these postulates we would expect differences between religious groups in mature capitalist (or even post-capitalist) societies as well as in precapitalist societies. And we would expect them not only in economic behavior, but in political behavior, family life, and all other areas of human activity. Furthermore, we would expect these differences to be more than mere reflections of the differences in the economic situations of the religious groups.

Theories of urbanism and the present study

While Weberian theory leads one to expect religion to have a significant effect on secular institutions in contemporary America, other theories point to a different conclusion. This is true not only of positivism and economic determinism; it is equally true of the theories of urbanism.

During the last century and a half the Western world has undergone a dramatic transformation. In 1800 the people of

11 While Weber is noted chiefly for his analysis of the impact of religious institutions on *economic* institutions, it is clear that he believed they influenced *all* of the major institutional systems of society. For example, in a number of places Weber speaks of the impact of Christian groups on the kinship system, undermining its traditional position of centrality in human affairs. See, for example, *The Religion of China,* op. cit., pp. 236–37, or Weber, *The City,* translated by Don Martindale and Gertrud Neuwirth (Glencoe: The Free Press, 1958), pp. 102–3. Elsewhere he speaks of the impact of religion on art, science, government, and education (*The Protestant Ethic,* op. cit., pp. 13–17, 168, 249, etc.).

12 It is this second assumption which brings Weber sharply into conflict with the economic determinists. They are very willing to grant the first of his assumptions, but regard the differences between religious groups as mere reflections of differences in their economic situation. For a more detailed discussion of this point, see *From Max Weber,* op. cit., pp. 267–70, or Bendix, op. cit., especially Chapter 8.

Western Europe and the United States were predominantly agrarian, and scattered among thousands of small towns and villages. Today they are largely city dwellers, increasingly concentrated in a small number of massive metropolitan centers. As long ago as 1950, nearly one third of the American population was concentrated in fourteen great metropolitan communities, each with a population of a million or more. There is every indication that this trend will continue for years to come.

This trend is significant for our study, because urban living produces a distinctive way of life.[13] Among the many important features of urbanism, two deserve special attention in the present context, since both suggest that, in the modern metropolis, the influence of religion on secular institutions is substantially reduced, or even eliminated altogether.

To begin with, urban conditions bring people of diverse backgrounds into constant and close association with one another. More than that, they find that they are obliged to co-operate in the production of goods and services, the maintenance of law and order, and a variety of other tasks essential to the well-being of the total community. As a consequence they find it necessary to ignore the differences which divide them, at least while they are engaged in those activities requiring co-operation. Eventually, what began as a mere *modus vivendi,* or temporary arrangement for specific situations only, becomes generalized into a basic value applicable to all kinds of situations. In short, norms of *tolerance* and *secularism*[14] inevitably arise in urban centers. Norms peculiar to one religious group or another are de-emphasized, leaving

---

[13] See, for example, Louis Wirth, "Urbanism as a Way of Life," *The American Journal of Sociology,* 44 (1938), pp. 1–24; Georg Simmel, "The Metropolis and Mental Life," in *The Sociology of Georg Simmel,* trans. by Kurt H. Wolff (Glencoe: The Free Press, 1950), pp. 409–24; Pitirim Sorokin and Carle C. Zimmerman, *Principles of Rural-Urban Sociology* (New York: Holt, 1929). In large measure all of the modern theories of urbanism are derived from the pioneering work of Ferdinand Tönnies, entitled *Gemeinschaft und Gesellschaft.* This volume has now been translated into English by Charles P. Loomis under the title *Community and Association* (London: Routledge and Kegan Paul, 1955).

[14] Secularism is used here in the sense of religious neutrality.

a common core of moral norms which are shared by all the various faiths represented in the community.

The second characteristic of urbanism which suggests that religious institutions may have little impact on secular institutions is the pronounced tendency toward *specialization* and *compartmentalization.* Specialization in the work of both individuals and organizations has been carried to a level undreamed of in simpler communities. As specialization increases, people tend to view life less and less as a unified whole, and more and more as a series of discrete parts relatively unrelated to each other. Thus, in the modern metropolis work and family life tend to become two distinct aspects of life, a sharp contrast with the situation in agrarian communities, or even in urban communities of an earlier era.

Similarly, religion becomes increasingly a highly compartmentalized activity rather than an integral part of the daily round. The more compartmentalized religion becomes, the less influence we should expect it to have on secular institutions. One of the main channels for exercising influence, the membership of the faithful in secular organizations, can no longer be used. Transformation from within (such as Weber was concerned with) ceases to be a possibility in a world of persons accustomed to thinking of religion in compartmentalized terms. In such a situation, religious organizations can only influence secular organizations through pressure-type tactics from without.

If this view of urbanism is valid, one can only conclude that, while Weberian theory may have had validity in other times and places, it is largely irrelevant to the secularized, specialized, and compartmentalized modern metropolis.

A decade ago few sociologists doubted the basic tenets of the classical theory of urbanism, but today the situation is changing. Research during the last decade has made it increasingly evident that, while the rise of the modern metropolis has certainly led to many radical changes in behavior, there are also many striking evidences of continuity with traditional ways of life which prevailed in simpler communities of an earlier era. For example, recent research has shown that kinship roles in particular, and primary-type relationships (i.e., close or intimate social relations) in general, have proven far more resistant and durable than earlier urban theorists ever imagined they could be.[15]

The traditional view of urbanism as it affects religion has recently been questioned by several writers. Most notable among these is Will Herberg. In his provocative essay, *Protestant-Catholic-Jew,* Herberg asserts that urban conditions of life promote what we shall here call *communal* religion, as contrasted with *associational* religion.[16] According to the classical theories of urbanism, religion in the modern metropolis becomes a highly specialized aspect of life. The church itself becomes a highly specialized formal association, and ceases to be a nucleus around which a variety of social relationships is organized, as in the typical agrarian community. Herberg suggests, however, that the very impersonality of so much of modern life creates in individuals a need for communal relationships, broader than the family, but narrower than the total society.

Earlier in American history ethnic groups served such a function, and individuals were able to enjoy this sense of communal identification and participation as members of the German, Polish, Italian, or other ethnic colonies established in this country. Today such groups are rapidly disintegrating, but many of the needs they served continue to be felt. In this situation, Herberg argues, Americans are turning increasingly to their religious groups, especially the three major faiths, for the satisfaction of their need for communal identification and belongingness. In brief, the specialization and compartmentalization inherent in the urban way of life drive men to transform their religious groups from narrow, specialized associations into groups which are more communal in character.[17]

In view of the increasing recognition of the elements of continuity between the patterns of life in the modern metropolis and in the simpler communities of an earlier era, we can be

[15] See Morris Axelrod, "Urban Structure and Urban Participation," *American Sociological Review,* 21 (1956), pp. 13–18, or Floyd Dotson, "Patterns of Voluntary Association Among Urban Working Class Families," ibid., 16 (1951), pp. 687–93.

[16] Garden City: Doubleday, 1956.

[17] This is a rather free translation of Herberg's views, and tends to make explicit ideas which are left implicit in much of his discussion of the subject.

less confident of the irrelevance of Weberian theory in the modern setting. On the contrary, recent changes in the sociological theory of urbanism are almost all of such a nature as to *increase* our expectation that religious institutions have a significant impact on secular social institutions. In the last analysis, however, the issue can only be settled by systematic, empirical research.

II. DESIGN OF THE STUDY

The sample survey

For purposes of studying vast and sprawling social organizations such as the modern metropolis, sociologists have developed a new research technique known as the *sample survey*. This technique involves three basic elements: (a) interviews, (b) with a representative cross-section of the population being studied, (c) utilizing a standardized schedule of questions.

In these interviews individuals are questioned concerning their attitudes, values, beliefs, and patterns of action. The interview thus becomes a substitute for direct observation of the behavior of individuals. This is a substitution which sociologists are somewhat reluctant to make since it introduces an opportunity for error, but it is invaluable for financial and other reasons. By interviewing a person the researcher can acquire in a matter of minutes information about his behavior which would require hundreds of hours of direct observation. Furthermore, even if one could afford to spend such vast quantities of time in observing the behavior of a single individual, this would be impossible for practical reasons. Few people would be willing to be subjected to sustained scrutiny over an extended period of time, even scrutiny of their more public behavior. The more private aspects would be totally closed to social research. Hence, sociologists feel that the advantages gained far outweigh the possible losses.

One of the most critical steps in developing a sample survey is the selection of the cross-section, or sample of persons, to be interviewed. Since it is impossible to interview each and every resident in a modern metropolis, it is imperative that those who are interviewed be as representative of the total population as possible. One simply cannot meet a representative cross-section of Detroiters by standing on a downtown corner and stopping those who pass by, or even by going from door to door in a series of neighborhoods. A truly representative cross-section can be contacted only by following the most rigorous procedures of selection.

Several different sampling procedures are employed by sociologists for this purpose. The procedure followed in this study is one known as *probability sampling,* the most accurate and also the most expensive method. It provides every adult resident of the community with an equal opportunity of being interviewed.[18] Repeated tests have shown that when probability sampling techniques are employed properly, it is possible to determine the characteristics of a population of several million on the basis of interviews with as few as six hundred persons, with errors of no more than a few percentage points in most instances. *Table 1* illustrates how accurate carefully designed probability samples can be. Despite the fact that the various Detroit Area Studies were based on samples of but seven hundred to a thousand households, the results differed very little from those obtained by the U. S. Census in interviews in over a million households.

The success of a sample survey also depends greatly on the construction of the interview schedule. Questions must be worded in such a way that their meaning is clear and unambiguous to even the most uneducated member of the community. The wording of the questions must *not* suggest that there is a "right answer," or one which the interviewer expects from any self-respecting respondent. Furthermore, it is important that the questions deal with matters with which respondents are reasonably familiar, since experience has shown that people tend to answer questions even if they know nothing about the matter, provided they can do so without obviously betraying their ignorance. In order to insure comparability of responses, interviews in this study were standardized.

[18] Persons interested in obtaining a detailed description of the sampling procedures used in the 1958 Detroit Area Study should write to the Detroit Area Study, Department of Sociology, The University of Michigan, Ann Arbor, Michigan, for "The Sample Design for the 1957–58 Detroit Area Study," mimeographed paper #1443.

Table 1

COMPARISON OF FINDINGS OF U. S. CENSUS (1950) AND
DETROIT AREA STUDIES (1952–1956): MAJOR OCCUPATIONAL
GROUP FOR WORKERS IN THE DETROIT AREA*

	1950 Census	Detroit Area Studies:				
Occupational group		1952	1953	1954	1955	1956
Professional, technical, and kindred workers	9%	9%	9%	9%	10%	9%
Managers, proprietors, and officials	9	10	10	11	9	8
Clerical, sales, and kindred workers	22	21	18	19	19	19
Craftsmen, foremen, and kindred workers	19	20	20	23	19	17
Operatives and kindred workers	27	26	29	23	27	30
Service workers including private household	9	10	9	10	11	12
Laborers	5	3	4	4	4	3
Not reported	1	1	1	1	1	2
Total	101%	100%	100%	100%	100%	100%

* SOURCE: Harry Sharp, *A Social Profile of Detroit/1956* (Ann Arbor: Detroit Area Study, 1957), p. 76.

That is to say, the same wording was used in all interviews, and questions were asked in the same order. Unless this is done, all the gains which result from the careful selection of a cross-section of the populace might easily be lost. The interview schedule used in the present study may be found in Appendix II.

Finally, the success of the sample survey depends upon the training of the interviewers. They must learn to see their job as that of eliciting as accurately as possible an extensive body of information from total strangers. The fact that interviewer and respondent are strangers makes this a great deal easier. Individuals are generally willing to give strangers, especially professional interviewers, information which they would not give to casual acquaintances or sometimes even to close friends. However, to create the right atmosphere the interviewer must be trained to cultivate a somewhat businesslike and detached manner. At the same time he must appear friendly and sympathetic to the views of the respondent, for it is especially important that the interviewer should never express, or even suggest that he may feel, any objection to the respondent's values or distaste for his behavior. Given a carefully selected sample of respondents, a properly designed interview schedule, and adequately trained interviewers, it is possible to obtain with considerable accuracy and at reasonable cost a picture of many facets of the life of massive social organizations such as the modern metropolis.

THE DETROIT AREA STUDY

As is evident, modern survey research usually requires the co-operative efforts of a considerable number of people and is likely to be most effective when handled by some permanent organization with previous experience and technical knowhow. Fortunately, such an organization was available for the present study: the Detroit Area Study, a facility of the Department of Sociology of The University of Michigan. This organization was established in 1951 for the dual purpose of training graduate students in survey research and of providing faculty members with a research instrument suitable for the study of the modern metropolitan community.[19]

The Detroit Area Study was headed by a director, Dr. Harry Sharp, aided by four research assistants. This staff works with a different member of the faculty each year in the investigation of some problem which he has selected for study. The problems dealt with vary greatly from year to year. (Prior to 1958, the year of the present study, research centered chiefly on politics and family life.[20])

[19] For a more detailed description of the Detroit Area Study, see Ronald Freedman, "The Detroit Area Study: A Training and Research Laboratory in the Community," *The American Journal of Sociology*, 59 (July 1953), pp. 30–33. Professor Freedman was the moving force behind the establishment of the Detroit Area Study and its first director.

[20] These earlier studies have resulted in a large number of publications, many of which are in scholarly journals. However, among those more readily available to the general public, the following may be noted: Daniel R. Miller and Guy E. Swanson, *The*

For each study certain facilities of the Survey Research Center of the University are also utilized. Of vital importance is the work of the sampling section, headed by Professor Leslie Kish.

THE 1958 SURVEY

For purposes of the present study, a sample of 750 Detroiters was selected to be interviewed during the first quarter of 1958. Letters were sent these persons explaining in very general terms the nature of the study and asking their co-operation.[21] Shortly thereafter the interviewer came to their home and either interviewed the person selected or made an appointment for an interview at a later date. Of the 750 persons originally chosen, interviews were completed with 656, yielding a completion rate of 87 per cent. This is considered to be an excellent rate by experts.

The 13 per cent with whom interviews were not obtained were a very heterogeneous group. Some were too senile to be interviewed. A number could never be found at home despite repeated visits at all hours of the day and evening. A few others could not be interviewed owing to language difficulties (though this number was held to a minimum owing to the presence of a Polish-speaking interviewer). Finally, 8 per cent of those originally chosen refused to grant an interview.

A careful study of these non-respondents revealed that they were very similar to the respondents with respect to race, sex, employment status, type of dwelling unit, and marital status. The only distinctive feature of the non-respondents was their age: a somewhat disproportionate number of them were 60

Changing American Parent (New York: Wiley & Sons, 1958); Robert O. Blood and Donald Wolfe, *Husbands and Wives* (Glencoe: The Free Press, 1960); Morris Janowitz, Deil Wright, and William Delany, *Public Administration and the Public: Perspectives Toward Government in a Metropolitan Community* (Ann Arbor: Bureau of Government, 1958); and Samuel J. Eldersveld, *Political Affiliation in Metropolitan Detroit* (Ann Arbor: Bureau of Government, 1957).

[21] This letter merely informed them that a study was to be made of attitudes and opinions of Detroiters on various subjects. No indication of the specific nature of the study was given.

years of age or over.[22] This means that conclusions based on the responses of older people are slightly less reliable than those based on younger and middle-aged persons. This limitation has little bearing on the conclusions of this study, since very few are based solely or primarily on the responses of older people.

The interviews themselves were largely uneventful, though in one instance an elderly man in our sample had a heart attack shortly before the interview and the interviewer had to render first aid and call the ambulance. Most interviews proved to be pleasant experiences for both interviewer and respondent, judging from the postinterview evaluation by the interviewers. Forty per cent described their rapport with the respondent as "excellent," another forty per cent as "good," and only two per cent as "poor" or "very poor." Several respondents even wrote to Dr. Sharp, the director, expressing their pleasure at having been selected.

In addition to the interviews with the cross-section of Detroiters, a series of special interviews were conducted during the summer of 1958 with a sample of Detroit clergymen. This was done because of the special significance of religious leaders for this study and also because the small number of clergy in the community made it unlikely that more than one or two would be interviewed in the regular cross-sectional sample. The clergymen interviewed were those serving a sample of the churches attended by the 656 Detroiters in the basic cross-sectional sample. A list was made of the churches which these respondents reported attending, and from this list every third church was selected and the head pastor interviewed. The response was extremely good. The completion rate for clergy interviews was also 87 per cent, yielding 127 completed interviews.[23]

[22] Harry Sharp and Allan Feldt, "Some Factors in a Probability Sample Survey of a Metropolitan Community," *American Sociological Review*, 24 (October 1959), pp. 650–61. Over a three-year period the response rate was 78 per cent among persons aged 60 and over; among younger persons it was 87 per cent.

[23] The number of clergy interviewed would have been greater than 127 except for the fact that in a good number of instances members of the cross-sectional sample attended the same church.

Types and degrees of religious commitment

Since the basic concern of this study was with the effect of religious commitment on daily life, one of the first problems was to identify and define the various types of religious commitments. We found it necessary to distinguish between two basic types. The first of these involves the commitment of individuals to a *socio-religious group*. The second involves commitment to a type of *religious orientation* which transcends socio-religious group lines. We shall examine each of these in turn.

SOCIO-RELIGIOUS GROUP MEMBERSHIP

In religion, as in all other phases of human activity, men are social beings. That is to say, in their religious activities men constantly relate themselves to others. Religious activity stimulates social interaction and group organization, with the result that the religious life and activity of individuals comes to be organized in terms of a variety of religious groups.

Religious groups in the modern metropolis are a much more complex form of social organization than has generally been recognized. Far too often American sociologists have regarded them as merely one more type of specialized, formal association[24]—the counterpart of the corporation, the labor union, the Kiwanis club, or the PTA—except, of course, that the religious group is viewed as far less influential than most since it brings its members together for only an hour a week, and even then attracts but a minority of the population.

This view corresponds with certain obvious facts, but ignores others. It is the truth, but not the whole truth. The crucial fact which it ignores is that religious groups are basically *endogamous* (that is, group members normally marry

[24] See, for example, Leonard Broom and Philip Selznick, *Sociology* (Evanston: Row, Peterson, 1955), pp. 440–41. See, also, Harry M. Johnson, *Sociology: A Systematic Introduction* (New York: Harcourt, Brace, 1960), Chapter 16, where the discussion of religious groups is in terms of an associational-type group. Most other basic texts also seem explicitly or implicitly to equate the church with the religious group, at least in the modern metropolis. This same pattern may be found in Thomas F. Hoult's recent volume, *The Sociology of Religion* (New York: Dryden, 1958), pp. 152–68.

others within their group),[25] with the result that interaction among members of a family normally involves interaction among members of the same religious group. The more deeply people have internalized the norms, or standards, of their group, the more their actions reinforce similar tendencies in other members of their family. In short, family groups (when religiously homogeneous) tend to function as subunits of the larger and more inclusive religious group.

This is not to say that Catholic families, for example, are *merely* subunits of the Catholic Church, any more than we would say that American families are merely subunits of American society. However, just as American families are subunits of our society, reinforcing by rewards and punishments those societal standards which they adopt for their own, so, too, religiously homogeneous families serve as subunits of the religious group, reinforcing its norms.

A second fact of major importance is that one's earliest years, so crucial in the development of personality and in the establishment of behavior patterns, are normally spent in the family group. Furthermore, during this period the child's chief relations are with his mother, whose contacts outside the socio-religious group are normally far more limited than those of the father.

A third fact of some importance is that friendly cliques (the other major type of primary group in our society) also tend to be religiously homogeneous. When this is true, these groups likewise tend to function as subunits of religious groups.

Collectively these facts are of great importance. They show that religious groups cannot be thought of merely as formal associations even in the modern metropolis. The system of social relationships which constitute each of the major religious groups in our society involve much more than the limited number of highly specialized and relatively impersonal relationships to which the associations give rise (e.g., relationships between priest and parishioner, Sunday school teacher and pupil, etc.). In addition to these there are a vast number of very generalized, highly personal, and very basic social

[25] We shall present evidence in the next chapter to show that both families and friendly cliques tend to be religiously homogeneous.

relationships (such as those between friends or between the members of a family) which constitute an integral part of every religious group. *In short, religious groups are communal as well as associational groups. Hence our analysis must take account of religious communities, or subcommunities, as well as religious associations.*[26]

[26] This distinction between communities and associations has long been a major concern in sociological theory, but its relevance for systematic research has hardly begun to be exploited. Ferdinand Tönnies' volume, *Gemeinschaft und Gesellschaft,* op. cit., has been the most important single work clarifying the distinction. According to Tönnies, associations (*Gesellschaften*) arise out of the desire of men to attain specific, but limited, ends without regard for the affective character of the social relationships required by their collective effort. Ties of cordiality and friendship are unnecessary in an association. In fact, those participating may even be personally hostile toward one another. By contrast, communities (*Gemeinschaften*) arise out of the natural attraction of like-minded persons for whom the social relationships established are an end in themselves, and not merely the means to some other end. Tönnies believed that there are no pure communities or associations in the real world, since all human groups contain elements of both. However, the relative proportions of communal and associational traits vary greatly from group to group, with important consequences for the life of men.

Other early sociologists were also aware of this important distinction. Max Weber made frequent use of it in his writings, borrowing directly from Tönnies. Durkheim's distinction between mechanical and organic solidarity was clearly a comparable distinction.

In most of the early literature on this subject, the major emphasis was on the decline of communal social relationships and the growth of associational relationships in modern society. The latter were typically seen as subversive of the former and hence there was a tendency for this important theoretical distinction to be taken over by the "professional viewers with alarm"—much to the detriment of modern sociological theory and research. It was not until Roethlisberger and Dickson's important study, *Management and the Worker* (Cambridge, Mass.: Harvard University Press, 1939), that it was discovered that formal associations not only do not necessarily destroy communal relationships, but may even give rise to them. Slowly, as the implications of this important study have come to be recognized, the full potential of Tönnies' concepts have begun to be apparent. One of the major aims of this study is to demonstrate the value of these concepts as tools for enhancing our understanding of the nature of religious groups, the role

To include both the communal and associational aspects of religious groups, we shall refer to them in the future as socio-religious groups. By using this somewhat cumbersome and less familiar term we hope to direct attention to three things. First, the groups we shall examine are more than associations. Second, their subcultures reflect the experience and influence of the subcommunities *as well as* the associations, which means that these subcultures ought never be interpreted as merely by-products of, or derivations from, theology. Third, in Detroit race as well as religion defines the boundaries of group membership, a fact of crucial importance in the case of Protestantism.

In the metropolitan community of Detroit there are at present four major socio-religious groups, plus several minor ones. The major ones are, in order of size:

1.	White Protestants	41 per cent
2.	White Catholics	35 per cent
3.	Negro Protestants	15 per cent
4.	Jews	4 per cent

The remaining 5 per cent of the population is made up of persons with no religious preference, and of Eastern Orthodox, Negro Catholics, and a very small number of Moslems and Buddhists. The membership of individuals in these groups was determined simply on the basis of their response to a question asking for their religious preference and on the basis of their race.

It may seem surprising that the Protestant population has been divided by race rather than denomination. This was done for the simple reason that the denominational groups within Detroit Protestantism no longer constitute self-contained socio-religious groups to any great degree, while the racial groups do. Both the religious and secular activities of Protestants in Detroit are highly segregated along racial lines. The two populations usually worship separately, and marriage and other primary-type relations seldom cut across the racial line. By contrast, there is a great amount of intermarriage among Protestants of different denominations, and with

they play in human societies, and the means by which they are able to play this role.

even greater frequency ties of friendship cut across denominational lines. Furthermore, there is a considerable movement
back and forth across denominational lines within each racial
group. The 1958 survey revealed that in only about one third
of the Protestant families were both husband and wife
lifelong members of the same denomination (Q. 34, 146–
47).[27] In all the other cases either the husband or wife, or
both, had previously belonged to a different denomination.
The limited importance attached to denominational loyalties
is also emphasized by the fact that roughly half the Protestants in our sample said they would like to see their denomination merge with one or more other Protestant groups (Q.
82). Finally, our data revealed very few significant differences
among Protestant denominations which did not reflect differences in the class position or regional background of individual
members (for some of the evidence on this point, see Appendix III, *Table 55*). For all these reasons we have treated
Protestantism as a unit, except as it is divided along racial
lines.

DEGREE OF GROUP INVOLVEMENT

In studying the influence of membership in a group on the
actions and attitudes of individuals, one expects to find differences related to *the degree of their involvement*. The greater
the degree of a man's involvement in a group, the greater its
influence on him. Hence, for example, when we compare
Protestant and Catholic patterns of voting in elections, we
should expect to find greater differences between highly involved Protestants and highly involved Catholics than between "marginal" members of the two groups. (While Weber
does not mention this point explicitly in his analysis of the
formation of the spirit of capitalism, it is clear that he viewed
this development as arising out of the actions of highly committed and involved Calvinists and Puritans.)

In view of the dual character of religious groups already
noted, involvement must be viewed as at least a two-dimen-

---

[27] Q. is an abbreviation for "Question." Here and elsewhere
throughout this book this type of notation refers to the specific
question in the interview schedule on which the discussion is based.
The interview schedule is printed in full in Appendix II.

sional phenomenon. We can speak of the involvement of the individual in either the association or the subcommunity, and one is not a simple mathematical function of the other.

As a measure of the degree of an individual's involvement in the *associational* aspect of his socio-religious group we have used the frequency of his attendance at corporate worship services. Owing to the small size of the sample and the constant need for controlled comparisons (i.e., comparisons between persons with similar characteristics relevant to the problem at hand), most of the comparisons involve only two categories: (a) those who attended worship services every week, plus those who attended services two to three times a month and also some church-related group at least once a month; (b) all others. The former will be referred to as those "actively involved" in the churches, the latter as the "marginal members" of the group.

Communal involvement has been measured in terms of the degree to which the primary relations of an individual (i.e., his relations with friends and relatives) are limited to persons of his own group. In the course of the interview, data were obtained about the religious preference of each respondent's spouse, and also about the proportion of his relatives and close friends who were of the same faith. These data were used to divide the members of each socio-religious group into two categories: (a) those who were married to someone of the same socio-religious group, and who also reported that all or nearly all of their close friends and relatives were of the same group; (b) the remainder of the population.

While there is usually some relationship between associational involvement and communal involvement, it is an extremely limited one. Using the Tau_b measure of statistical association developed by Goodman and Kruskal, the coefficients of association between communal and associational involvement ranged from .00 for the white Catholic group to .03 for the white Protestant group. This means that if one attempted to predict the degree of communal involvement of white Protestants on the basis of their associational involvement (or vice versa), one would succeed only 3 per cent more often than a person who attempted to predict without this information.[28] For those familiar with the Pearsonian r, it may be noted that Tau_b is roughly equal to r^2. Hence, in terms of this more familiar measure the coefficients vary from .0 to .1, again indicating almost no relationship.

RELIGIOUS ORIENTATIONS

To properly assess the influence of religious commitments, it is also necessary to study the influence of different religious orientations. In the religious tradition of the Western world, various types of religious orientations have competed with one another, each emphasizing a different facet of the Judaic-Christian heritage. Among the more prominent are mysticism, devotionalism, asceticism, ceremonialism, doctrinal ortho-doxy, millennialism, and ethicalism. Sometimes individuals emphasize one orientation to the almost total exclusion of the others; sometimes several orientations are cultivated simul-taneously. Over the years the relative importance of these orientations has shifted many times as one, then another, gained the ascendancy, but all survive to the present day.

There is good reason for believing that different religious orientations lead to different patterns of thought and action in the secular realm. For example, we would hardly expect to find enthusiasm for political reform among millennialists, but we might expect to find it among ethicalists.[29] Hence these orientations are of concern to us in this study.

[28] More precisely stated, a coefficient of .03 means that this is the degree to which predictions would be improved if one knew the distribution of respondents in terms of one variable and both sets of marginals, over prediction based merely on a knowledge of one set of marginals. See Leo Goodman and William H. Kruskal, "Measure of Association for Cross Classifications," *Journal of the American Statistical Association*, 49 (1954), pp. 732–64. See also H. M. Blalock, *Social Statistics* (New York: McGraw-Hill, 1960), pp. 232–34.

[29] The problem of causality is more difficult here than where group membership is involved. Membership in the major socio-religious groups normally is handed down over many generations, and thus cannot be thought of as the consequence of secular pat-terns of thought and action with which it is linked. Religious orientations, by comparison, seem less stable (though we have no good evidence on this). Hence, it is possible to argue with equal plausibility that they can be either cause or consequence of the

In the present study it did not prove practical to investigate the influence of all the many orientations found in the rich and complex Judaic-Christian tradition. Rather, we limited our investigation to two orientations which seemed most likely to be related to the problem at hand. These are *doctrinal orthodoxy* and *devotionalism*.[30]

By *doctrinal orthodoxy* we refer to that orientation which stresses intellectual assent to prescribed doctrines. Those who are *orthodox*, therefore, are those who accept the prescribed doctrines of their church; the *heterodox* are those who deviate from these intellectual norms to a greater or lesser degree.[31]

By *devotionalism* we mean that orientation which emphasizes the importance of private, or personal, communion with God. The term "pietism" might have been used with equal propriety, but since it carries certain evaluative overtones, it seemed wiser to use the less familiar term. We measured the degree of a person's commitment to this orientation by the frequency with which he prayed and the frequency with which he sought to determine God's will when he had important decisions to make.

In short, devotionalism is a more active, behavioral type of religious orientation, especially when compared with doctrinal orthodoxy, which is an extremely passive, intellectual orientation.

---

secular patterns with which they are linked. Since our data do not permit us to resolve this issue, we shall proceed on the assumption that the flow of influence works in both directions, but we shall be chiefly concerned with explaining why particular orientations produce the peculiar consequences they do (or seem to).

[30] In a very real sense our measure of associational involvement may be thought of as being also a measure of a special type of religious orientation. It might be labeled the *collectivist* orientation since it stresses essentially the importance of collective, or corporate, worship. To avoid confusion, we shall speak of our measure of associational involvement as though it were merely a measure of involvement, but the reader should be alert to its significance as a measure of a distinctive type of religious orientation as well.

[31] It should be noted that this conception of orthodoxy differs considerably from the traditional Jewish understanding of the term, where orthodoxy was essentially conformity to prescribed patterns of action. This should not cause difficulty, however, since the Jewish group is too small for *intra*group analysis of this type.

These two orientations were selected for several reasons. First, on *a priori* grounds they appeared to contrast, or even conflict, with one another. Second, both seemed to be widely accepted by modern Americans. Third, both seemed to be potentially important. These expectations were fully justified, as will become evident. The concept of religious orientations proved a valuable tool in analyzing the impact of religion on daily life. Especially valuable was the demonstration that orthodoxy and devotionalism are not merely two alternative measures of "religiosity" as is so often imagined. On the contrary, they are separate and independent orientations (the Tau_b value was only .05), and each has its own peculiar consequences for the behavior of individuals.

Secular institutions studied

Since the aim of this study was to discover what impact different types of religious commitment have on the secular institutions of the community, it was necessary to gather a considerable body of information about the daily lives of the Detroiters we interviewed. Our questions dealt with three major areas of secular activity: (1) economic behavior; (2) political behavior; and (3) family life.

We shall frequently have to consider the implications of findings in one area for our understanding of another. However, this is only to be expected, since it is a fundamental axiom of sociology that human societies are social systems, which is to say that the constituent elements of any society are inevitably interrelated and interdependent. It is this *systemic* view of society which distinguishes the sociological view of political and economic behavior from that of the more narrowly circumscribed disciplines of political science and economics.

The problem of causation

In attempting to establish the nature and extent of the influence exerted by religious institutions on economic, political, and kinship institutions, we necessarily become involved in the analytically treacherous problem of *causation*. Causal relationships are difficult to prove rigorously in the social sciences. In most cases our data only permit us to say that there is a certain pattern of association between two or more phenomena: an increase in A is associated with a decrease in B.

This is especially true when data are obtained by sample surveys. At the most we can only assert that certain types of phenomena regularly precede others in a temporal sequence, as in the case of the finding that those who grew up in families headed by a father working in a factory have on the average lower incomes than those who grew up in families headed by a physician or lawyer. This cannot be proven to be a causal relationship, although all relevant social theories point to the conclusion that it is.

Men have to organize their thinking about social phenomena in causal terms. But in this field we cannot rigorously prove causality, and so we must find alternative standards for deciding whether the conception of cause and effect can properly be used at all in a given instance. At the present time, two standards are generally accepted. First, a causal inference should be reasonable and logical in the light of theory. Second, there should be no evidence contrary to the causal hypothesis. That is, there should be no evidence of the absence of an association between the two variables involved. Neither should there be any evidence that the presumed cause occurs later in time than the presumed effect.

The model of social change on which the present study is built is a model of multiple causation, and therefore stands in sharp contrast to the model of the economic determinists. Because human societies are social systems, or units made up of interrelated parts, changes in any one part normally affect other parts. Thus, changes in religious institutions affect political, economic, kinship, and other secular institutions, just as changes in any of the others affect religious institutions. However, we assume that no one institutional system is the sole initiator of social change, as the economic determinists have claimed for economic institutions.[32]

While this model of change and causation is not as neat and simple as that of the economic determinists, modern scholarship and research increasingly support it. It may be

[32] For an excellent discussion of this problem see J. Milton Yinger, *Religion, Society, and the Individual* (New York: Macmillan, 1957), p. 296.

well to spell out two of its implications for the present study. In the first place, *no attempt is being made to substitute religious determinism for economic determinism.* Clearly religious institutions themselves are continually affected by developments in the other major institutional systems of society, as will become evident in the analysis which follows. Second, while we shall often mention the influence of religious institutions on secular institutions, we shall never suggest that such influence is a *sufficient* cause by itself of the phenomena involved. At most we seek to establish that these influences are a *necessary* cause of certain patterns observed in secular institutions—that is, other influences may also be at work, but without the influence of the religious factor, these patterns would not retain their present character in its entirety.

III. AN INTRODUCTION TO DETROIT

Before concluding this introductory chapter, let us examine the setting of the study: the metropolitan community of greater Detroit. While in certain respects Detroit is a fairly typical metropolitan center, in others it is not so typical. In order to make an intelligent judgment as to how far our findings can be generalized, some familiarity with the community setting is essential.

History of the community

Detroit is much older than most communities in the Midwest, with permanent settlement dating from 1701. Of special significance is the fact that its initial settlement was by the French, rather than the British; as a consequence, Detroit was a Catholic community throughout most of its early history. In this respect Detroit most closely resembles St. Louis and New Orleans among the major metropolitan centers in the country.

Throughout the eighteenth century Detroit remained a small military and trading post. As an indication of the roughness of life in the early years, Cadillac, the founder of the community, is reported to have commented, "When with wolves, one learns to howl."

French rule in Detroit ended in 1760 when the British

assumed control of the area. Great Britain ceded the territory to the United States in 1783, but owing to the reluctance of the British to withdraw and the opposition of the Indians, American control of Detroit was not established until 1796.

Until the early nineteenth century the community remained predominantly French in culture. The first Catholic parish, St. Anne's, was established in 1703, and remained the only church in the community for over a hundred years. The first civilians of British or American stock to settle there seem to have come in the early 1790s, but it was not until nearly two decades later that the first Protestant church was established in the area. This was a Methodist church founded in 1810 in River Rouge, now one of Detroit's suburbs. First Presbyterian Church, the oldest Protestant church in Detroit proper, was not completed until 1820, though the congregation was established several years earlier.

As one indication of the continuation of French influence, it is interesting to note that in 1823 the parishioners of St. Anne's parish succeeded in electing their pastor as a delegate to Congress in an election which was apparently fought along ethnic and religious lines. Their pastor, Father Gabriel Richard, was one of the outstanding figures in the early history of the community, and was instrumental in founding The University of Michigan.

During the 1820s and 1830s transportation to the West improved, and a heavy migration of New Englanders and New Yorkers began, leading to a decline in French influence. In 1830 the population of Detroit was still only 2200, but by 1840 it had leaped to 9000, and by 1850 to 21,000. The French were soon reduced to a small minority, and in Detroit today those of French extraction constitute only 4 per cent of the total population. This figure would be even smaller were it not for some movement in more recent years of new migrants from Quebec and France.

In the 1830s Detroit began to take on increasingly the cosmopolitan character which it possesses today. Along with the migration of New Englanders and New Yorkers of Yankee stock came the beginnings of German and Irish immigration. In the 1850s the first Jewish congregation was established. After the Civil War immigration from eastern Europe became

increasingly heavy, particularly from Poland. Since World
War I migration from the rural South has been especially
heavy. The result is that today Detroit is an extremely cosmopolitan community, with no single ethnic group predomi-
nating. The largest single ethnic group today is the British,
who constitute roughly 19 per cent of the total population.[33]
Next are the Negroes, who total 17 per cent. They are followed by the Germans and Poles, each of whom constitute
approximately 11 per cent, and then the Irish, representing
about 10 per cent. The French, Italians, and Jews each constitute about 4 per cent of the population. The remaining 20
per cent is divided among several dozen ethnic groups and
persons of mixed background.

After 1830 Detroit grew rapidly. From 1830 to the Civil
War the population more than doubled every ten years, so
that by 1860 the total exceeded 45,000. From 1860 to 1900
the pace slackened somewhat with the increase per decade
ranging from 40 to 75 per cent, but by 1900 the population
totaled 285,000. From these figures it can be seen that even
before the rise of the auto industry, Detroit was a thriving
and expanding community.

The first two automobiles appeared on the streets of Detroit in 1896, both built locally. This marked the beginning
of an important new era. At a fairly early date Detroit manufacturers gained the upper hand in the new industry, and an
increasing proportion of the national automobile industry became concentrated in the community. As a result a new era of
very rapid population growth ensued, with the population of
the metropolitan community passing the million mark by
1920. Since that time the depression of the 1930s and the
recession of the middle 1950s, combined with progressive
decentralization of auto production, have slowed the *rate* of
population growth. Even so, by 1960 the metropolitan community numbered 3.7 million persons. Or, to put the matter
in a different perspective, *by 1960 the population of this community was larger than that of 34 of the 50 states.*

[33] These figures are based on the responses of individuals in
our 1958 survey to the question, "What is the original nationality
of your family on your father's side?"

Detroit today

Among the major metropolitan centers of this country Detroit is unique in the degree to which its economy is dependent on a single industry. All other cities with a population over one million, with the exception of Washington, D.C., have a much more diversified economy. Hence, the sharp decline in the market for automobiles, combined with a major shift to automation during the period covered by this survey, had serious repercussions in the community, most notably in the form of widespread and sustained unemployment.

Heavy dependence on the automobile industry is related to other distinctive characteristics of the community. For one thing, industrial or factory workers form an unusually high proportion of the population. Again, Detroit tends to be a one-union town to a degree that is unusual among metropolitan centers. Finally, this whole constellation of characteristics is related to the fact that wages in Detroit are among the highest in the nation.

Because of this peculiar economic structure, political lines are generally drawn rather sharply in the community, except in municipal and school board elections which are nonpartisan by law. In state and national elections Detroit Democrats and Republicans tend to be far apart in their thinking. With strong support from the United Auto Workers Union and from the Negro minority, Democrats take a vigorous stand for welfare-state programs and civil rights. With equally strong support from management, Republicans take their stand for classical capitalism, or perhaps more accurately, in opposition to Democratic proposals to expand welfare services. The ideological lines dividing the two parties seem to be drawn more sharply in Detroit (and in the state of Michigan generally) than in most other segments of the country. However, the uniqueness of the political situation in Michigan can easily be, and has often been, exaggerated.

The religious scene in present-day Detroit is best described as generally placid and unexceptional. Detroit is not, and has never been, a national religious center in any sense of the term and has produced few nationally known religious leaders. Its most prominent religious leader in recent years was probably the late Edward Cardinal Mooney, who was noted chiefly for his able administrative leadership within his own arch-diocese. In Protestant circles there have been a few outstand-ing preachers, of whom Henry Hitt Crane of Central Method-ist Church has probably been the most prominent in recent years. Reinhold Niebuhr once served a congregation in De-troit, but his national reputation can hardly be attributed to this fact.

Seminaries with a national, or even a regional, orientation frequently serve as bases for prominent religious leaders. But in Detroit there are no Protestant or Jewish seminaries at all, and the chief Catholic seminaries seem primarily oriented toward the local archdiocese and its needs.

The absence of nationally visible religious leaders does not mean, however, that the cause of religion suffers. On the contrary, the churches are generally well attended, and at least the institutionalized aspects of religion flourish. The majority of the clergy of all faiths seem to be vigorous, hard-working men, skilled in what they take to be their major task: that of building their own parish or congregation. Here and there one can even find experimentation and the development of new types of programs. Both the Presbyterians and the Episcopalians in Detroit support experimental programs de-signed to develop new techniques for coping with the prob-lems the churches must face in the rapidly changing metropo-lis.

There is one notable exception to the current pattern of religious placidity. This is the ferment created by certain bi-zarre and radical cults on the fringe of the Negro Protestant group. The most interesting of these from the sociological standpoint is an organization called the Muslim Holy Temple of Islam which was founded in Detroit in 1931 by Elijah Poole.[34] Like the majority of Detroit Negroes, Poole is a mi-grant from the South. He is also the son of a Baptist minister. The doctrine which he preaches is black supremacy and ha-

[34] Despite its name, this group can hardly be classified as a Moslem sect. The name seems to have been used to emphasize the group's rejection of Christianity, which they regard as a white man's religion. For a description of this group, see C. E. Lincoln, *The Black Muslims in America* (Boston: Beacon Press, 1961).

tred for the white race (especially the Jews) combined with a stern asceticism. His official temple creed asserts: "There is no good in white men. All are the children of the devil." The present membership of the "Black Muslims" is estimated at 70,000 scattered through 29 cities, and is concentrated chiefly in the lowest stratum of the Negro subgroup. The growth of this movement in Detroit has been quite limited, but the degree to which it has succeeded indicates a level of intergroup tension with dangerous potentialities.

In its economics, politics, ethnicity, and religion, Detroit most closely resembles Cleveland, Pittsburgh, Buffalo, and Chicago. In common with these communities, Detroit is noted for heavy industry, high wages, a large industrial population, a large proportion of eastern European immigrants of peasant background, and a rapidly growing Negro minority recently arrived from the rural South. Among the major metropolitan centers it bears least resemblance to New York and Washington, both of which differ markedly in terms of economics, ethnicity, and religion, and, in the case of voteless Washington, in terms of politics as well.

Despite these local peculiarities it seems probable that most of our findings in Detroit can be generalized and applied to other major metropolitan centers throughout the country, with the possible exception of the South. This appears likely for two reasons. In the first place, the issues we investigated are basically national in character, and not local. Advances in transportation and mass communication mean that people all over the country are nowadays subject to similar pressures and influences. Local and even regional peculiarities have been progressively eroded. More and more the nation is becoming a political, economic, religious, and social unit. Secondly, Americans are becoming more and more mobile. *Of those now living in greater Detroit, nearly two thirds were born elsewhere.* More than half were born outside of Michigan, and therefore outside the sphere of Detroit's direct influence, and within the orbit of some other metropolitan center. This constant movement of population also hampers the development of regional peculiarities, and promotes the homogeneity of the national population.

In the last analysis, however, the only sure test of the generalizability of the findings of a study based on a single community can come from similar studies conducted elsewhere. For this reason, throughout this book references will be made (usually in footnotes) to earlier studies which have dealt with similar problems elsewhere. In this way the reader will be better able to judge to what degree the findings of this study are unique to Detroit, and to what degree they may apply to other communities.

Chapter 2

THE FOUR SOCIO-RELIGIOUS GROUPS

Let us now turn to our *dramatis personae*, the four major socio-religious groups. There are a number of questions which should be answered before we examine the secular institutions of the community. In the first place, how do the groups compare with one another in terms of vitality? Related to this is the question of trends: are they holding their own in a highly urbanized setting such as Detroit, or are they declining as the positivists of the last century predicted? Second, how strong are doctrinal orthodoxy and devotionalism among present-day Detroiters? How are these religious orientations distributed among the groups? Third, what of the relations between one group and another? What do the members of each group think about the other three? Finally, how do our four groups fit into the structure of the larger community? How are they distributed geographically and how are they distributed in the class system? These are the questions which we shall seek to answer in this chapter.

I. STRENGTH OF GROUP TIES

The pattern at present

When one examines the four major socio-religious groups in Detroit in the light of our distinction between the association and the subcommunity, it quickly becomes evident that each is a distinctive type of social organization. The Jewish and Catholic groups present the sharpest contrasts, so let us examine them first.

THE JEWISH GROUP

{In the case of Judaism we are confronted with a group in which the religious associations have been seriously weakened.} In a recent analysis of church attendance in the Detroit area by Harold Orbach (based on six of the first seven sample surveys of the Detroit Area Study), it was found that only 12 per cent of the Jews (N=192)[1] reported regular weekly attendance at synagogue or temple.[2] Another 20 per cent reported attending at least once a month, and 56 per cent only on High Holy Days, or a few times a year. Twelve per cent did not attend at all.[3]

On the basis of such evidence one might conclude that the ties binding the individual to the group are very weak. However, the 1958 survey indicates that while the (associational bond is weak in the Jewish group, the *communal* bond is extremely strong.) In fact, available evidence indicates that the communal bond in the Jewish group is as strong, or stronger, than in any other group. For example, it was found

[1] This symbol (N=192) means that the percentage cited in the same sentence is based on 192 cases. Similar notations will be found throughout the book, since such information is necessary if one is to calculate statistical significance and the probability that the differences reported are due to sampling error (see Appendix I). When, however, percentages are based on certain standard subgroups in a single study, the value of N is not given in the text, but is reported in *Table 51* of Appendix I.

[2] Harold L. Orbach, "Aging and Religion," *Geriatrics*, 16 (October, 1961), pp. 530–40. This approach may well underrate the strength of associational ties among Jews, since in the original design of this study, there was insufficient recognition of the number and strength of *secular* Jewish associations.

[3] In a study of the Jewish group in an eastern seaboard city of 130,000, only 22 per cent reported attending synagogue at times other than High Holy Days. See Marshall Sklare and Marc Vosk, *The Riverton Study: How Jews Look at Themselves and Their Neighbors* (New York: The American Jewish Committee, 1957), p. 11. In Washington, D.C., 25 per cent reported attendance at least once a month. See Stanley Bigman, *The Jewish Population of Greater Washington in 1956* (Washington: The Jewish Community Council of Greater Washington, 1956), p. 100. These figures suggest that Detroit Jews are *more* active in synagogue than Jews on the East Coast.

that *all* of the Jewish respondents in our sample who were married (N=24) were lifelong Jews married to a lifelong Jewish spouse.[4] When asked what proportion of their close relatives were Jewish, 96 per cent said that all or nearly all were Jewish. When asked the same question about their close friends, 77 per cent reported that all or nearly all were Jewish. Such evidence makes it clear that while the ties binding individual Jews to their religious associations have been seriously weakened in modern times, the ties of communalism remain strong. If our sample is at all reliable, the great majority of Detroit Jews find most of their primary relationships within the Jewish subcommunity.

THE CATHOLIC GROUP

The white Catholic group presents a very different picture in every respect. On the basis of Orbach's six-year survey, it appears that more than 70 per cent of Detroit Catholics (N=2374) attend Mass at least once a week and only about 5 per cent fail to attend at all. While there may be some measure of exaggeration in these figures,[5] it is certain that the ties

---

[4] In the special interdecennial sample survey of 1957 the Bureau of the Census included a question on religious preference. One of the findings of this census was that over 96 per cent of all American Jews are married to persons currently professing to be Jews. For Catholics the comparable figure was 89 per cent. For all Protestants, both Negro and white, the figure was nearly 96 per cent. U. S. Bureau of the Census, *Current Population Reports: Population Characteristics,* Series P-20, No. 79 (February 2, 1958); see especially Tables 6 and 7. In interpreting these figures it must be kept in mind that Protestants are much more likely to marry Protestants merely because of chance, since 66 per cent of all Americans aged 14 and over are Protestants, while this is much less likely for Catholics and Jews, who constitute only 26 and 3 per cent of the population respectively.

[5] Those conducting sample surveys found long ago that there is some tendency for respondents to exaggerate their good qualities and minimize their poor qualities when being interviewed. Such exaggerations usually tend to be minor in character rather than blatant misrepresentations or falsification. In studies more concerned with relative than with absolute frequencies of various types of behavior, such misrepresentations do not present a serious problem since there is reason for believing that exaggerations occur in roughly the same *proportions* throughout the population.

(binding the individual to the nuclear association are far stronger in Catholicism than in Judaism.)

In the case of communal ties, the situation is exactly reversed. Catholics are far more inclined than Jews to marry and establish other intimate personal relationships outside their group. Sixteen per cent of the Catholic respondents in the 1958 survey reported that they were currently married to a non-Catholic. In addition still others had contracted marriages with non-Catholics who ultimately became Catholics, or themselves left the Catholic Church as a consequence of marrying a non-Catholic, so that 30 per cent of all those who were raised as Catholics married someone who was raised a non-Catholic.

In view of the high rate of intermarriage between Catholics and non-Catholics, it is hardly surprising that a substantial minority of Catholics have a significant number of close relatives who are non-Catholics. Whereas 96 per cent of the Jews reported that all or nearly all of their close relatives were Jewish, only 79 per cent of the Catholics reported that all or nearly all of their close relatives were Catholics. There was an even more pronounced discrepancy with respect to ties of friendship. Whereas 77 per cent of the Jewish respondents reported that all or nearly all of their close friends were Jewish, the comparable figure for Catholics was only 44 per cent.

On the basis of such data we can see that Judaism and Catholicism represent two distinct types of socio-religious groups in the modern metropolis. In the Jewish group communal ties predominate, and ties with religious associations are extremely weak. In the Catholic group the relationship is reversed, though it would be an exaggeration to say that Catholic communal ties are weak.

THE WHITE PROTESTANT GROUP

In the white Protestant group still another pattern emerges. The proportion of white Protestants who attend worship services regularly falls far below the Catholic figure, though not nearly so low as in the Jewish group. In Orbach's six-year survey it was found that roughly one third of the white Protestants in Detroit (N=2887) attend worship services every Sunday. Slightly more than 20 per cent attend from one to three times a month, and 14 per cent never attend. The remaining third attend occasionally.

(In communal solidarity and strength, however, white Protestants closely match white Catholics) Whereas 84 per cent of the white Catholics who were married reported that their spouse was of the same faith, 86 per cent of the white Protestants made the same statement. Whereas 70 per cent of those who were raised Catholics married someone raised a Catholic, 73 per cent of the white Protestants married someone raised a Protestant. Seventy-nine per cent of the white Catholics and 76 per cent of the white Protestants reported that all or nearly all of their close relatives were of the same faith. Finally, 44 per cent of the white Catholics reported that all or nearly all of their close friends were of the same faith; the corresponding figure for white Protestants was 38 per cent.

Judging from such evidence, it appears that the white Protestant group is the least cohesive of the three white socio-religious groups. It lacks the very strong communal bond of the Jewish group, and it lacks the very strong associational bond of the Catholic group. In terms of the *relative* strength of these two bonds, however, the white Protestant group resembles the Jewish group a bit more than the Catholic group since the communal bond seems to be somewhat stronger than the associational bond. However, this resemblance should not be exaggerated; the differences are still very real.

THE NEGRO PROTESTANT GROUP

(In the Negro Protestant group the communal bond is extremely strong, owing to the discriminatory practices of whites.) As Drake and Cayton noted in their book on Chicago Negroes, race relations in the North and South differ chiefly in the area of secondary relationships, or the more impersonal, contractual relationships.[6] In the South these are segregated, in the North they are integrated. In the realm of primary relationships—intimate relations of kinship and friendship—segregation tends to be the rule in the urban North almost as much as in the rural South. (Of necessity, therefore, the overwhelm-

[6] St. Clair Drake and Horace R. Cayton, *Black Metropolis* (New York: Harcourt, Brace and Co., 1945), Chapter 6.

ing majority of Negroes in Detroit marry other Negroes, and find their intimate personal relationships with others of their own race.) Counterdiscrimination by Negroes themselves is also a factor.

While data were not obtained on these matters in the 1958 survey, it seems safe to estimate that not less than 98 per cent of Detroit Negroes are married to others of their race and also find their *close relatives* limited to their own race. With respect to *close friends*, it seems that an estimate of 90 to 95 per cent being limited to others of the Negro race would not be far wide of the mark.[7]

To some extent the estimates above exaggerate the degree to which Negro Protestants associate with other Negro Protestants, since a small minority of the Negro population consists of Catholics, non-believers, and adherents of non-Christian cults. However, since these groups constitute no more than about 10–12 per cent of the Negro population, their influence is not great. Furthermore, most of these Negro minorities seem to share in the subculture of the dominant Negro Protestant majority.[8]

(While the associational bond in the Negro Protestant group is not nearly so strong as the communal bond, it is nevertheless stronger than in any of the other socio-religious groups except the white Catholic.)Nearly 40 per cent of Negro Protestants (N=1030) attend worship services every Sunday, and more than three quarters attend at least once a month. Negro Protestants were tied with white Catholics in having the smallest percentage of persons who have completely divorced themselves from the nuclear religious associations. Only 5 per cent never go to church.[9]

[7] These estimates are based primarily on conclusions derived from the author's personal contacts with Negro students from the Detroit area attending the University of Michigan. Also it may be noted that in the 1958 Detroit Area Study, only 1 interracial marriage was discovered in nearly 550 marriages.

[8] For example, Orbach's study of church attendance, op. cit., shows that the church-attendance patterns of Negro Catholics are virtually identical with those of Negro Protestants, and stand in sharp contrast to the much more regular attendance of white Catholics.

[9] The smallness of this figure for all four groups seems to indi-

SUMMARY

For a summary of the evidence so far we may turn to *Figure 1*, which shows that each of our four groups possesses a distinctive combination of communal and associational attributes. Of the four, the white Protestant group seems to be the least cohesive, but is obviously in no danger of dissolution.

Figure 1

RELATIVE STRENGTH OF ASSOCIATIONAL AND COMMUNAL BONDS IN THE FOUR MAJOR SOCIO-RELIGIOUS GROUPS

Socio-religious Group	Strength of bonds:	
	Associational	Communal
Jews	Weak	Strong
White Catholics	Strong	Medium
White Protestants	Medium	Medium
Negro Protestants	Medium	Strong

One final bit of evidence concerning group cohesion and solidarity was obtained when we asked Detroiters whether they thought any of their friends or relatives would try to discourage them, or would be at all disturbed or unhappy, if they attempted to join another faith (Q. 75, 75a, 87, 87a, 100, 100a). Judging from the vigor of the responses, it is clear that desertion of one's native group is regarded as closely akin to treason in many circles. For example, when a young Jewish housewife was asked whether her friends and relatives would try to discourage her from changing her faith she replied: "Yes—they'd kill me. My mother is very religious." In answer to the same question a young Catholic man said succinctly: "I'd get hung." A Lutheran housewife, a convert from Catholicism, described in some detail the vigorous efforts her friends and relatives made to dissuade her.

Nearly two thirds of all Detroiters stated that they thought their friends and relatives would try to discourage them if

cate that for the overwhelming majority of persons who identify with one or another of the groups, the nuclear religious associations are of some importance, no matter how slight.

they attempted to join another group. The percentages in each group expecting this were as follows:

White Catholic	81 per cent
Jews	72 per cent
White Protestants	60 per cent
Negro Protestants	24 per cent

Those who said that no one would attempt to discourage them were then asked whether they thought any of their friends or relatives would be at all unhappy or disturbed if they made such a change, since even this kind of mild response would be something of a restraining influence. In the four major groups, an additional 10 per cent indicated that such a reaction was likely. In other words, fully 72 per cent of the total membership of these groups expected some objection if they sought to shift their allegiance. Omitting the Negro Protestants and taking the three white groups together, 82 per cent, or more than four fifths, expected *some* type of sanction. Broken down by groups, the figures were as follows:

Jews	96 per cent
White Catholics	87 per cent
White Protestants	75 per cent
Negro Protestants	28 per cent

These figures again suggest that whatever the Jewish group lacks in associational vitality is more than compensated for by the strength of the communal bond.[10]

Social change and associational vitality

Since social arrangements are constantly changing in modern industrial societies, a static, structural view is never wholly adequate. Unless we discover the basic changes which are occurring and the reasons for them, our views quickly become out-of-date and irrelevant.

[10] In a study of an unnamed eastern seaboard community of 130,000 it was found that only 2 per cent of the Jewish parents interviewed had no objection to their children marrying a Gentile. Sklare and Vosk, op. cit., p. 33.

RELIGIOUS REVIVAL?

In recent years much has been written about a "religious revival" in America.[11] The exact nature of this revival has been much debated, but the consensus of most observers seems to be that the social climate in America has changed in some way so that Americans are more interested in religion and more willing to give religious speakers and writers a serious hearing.[12] Beyond this, the experts disagree. Some maintain that America is currently undergoing a powerful and important religious revival of a serious nature. Many more see the revival as, at best, a superficial wave of religiosity. Still others assert that it involves nothing more than a quickening interest in religion—but an interest devoid of commitment except in a minority of cases.

HERBERG'S THESIS

Of all the many discussions of this subject, Will Herberg's essay, *Protestant-Catholic-Jew*, contains the most penetrating insights.[13] As noted previously, Herberg argues that religious groups are becoming a more important feature of American life owing to basic changes in the nature of American society itself. For years America was the land of the immigrant, and so long as immigrants continued to pour into this country, the ethnic group provided them with an essential anchorage, a meaningful subcommunity in an increasingly impersonal mass society. While the ethnic churches and synagogues enjoyed an honored position in these groups, religious loyalties were generally less powerful than ethnic loyalties. This is indicated

[11] It should be noted here that the 1959 Detroit Area Study directed by G. E. Swanson was focused specifically on this subject and will be reported in detail in a forthcoming monograph. Here we shall attempt no more than a limited examination of this subject since it is not a matter of major concern.

[12] Even on this point there is not complete agreement, as shown by the recent article of Seymour M. Lipset, "Religion in America: What Religious Revival?" *Columbia University Forum* (Winter 1959). In this article Lipset marshals a considerable body of evidence to support his thesis that "by far the most striking aspect of religious life in America is not the changes which have occurred in it—but the basic continuities it retains."

[13] Op. cit.

by the cleavages which separated Italian from Irish Catholics, German from Swedish Lutherans, and German from Polish Jews.

But, Herberg says, when the children of the immigrants reached maturity, a large number dissociated themselves from the ethnic subcommunity. It stood for something foreign and alien, and this "second generation" wanted above everything else to be a hundred per cent American. (In rejecting the ethnic subcommunity, the second generation was obliged to reject also the church with which the subcommunity was inextricably linked. Hence, as the second generation became more numerous, interest in religion tended to decline.)

However, Herberg argues that in recent years the second generation has begun to die off and the rising third generation does not need to strive to be American and to shed foreign and alien ways. It *is* American in every respect. Hence it can afford the luxury of reviving cultural patterns and loyalties abandoned by the second generation. In particular, it can afford to return to the church of its fathers.

This development is not only possible, but probable since, with the disintegration of the old ethnic subcommunities, Americans have a growing need for some *new* group to serve as an anchorage in modern society. Increasingly this anchorage is supplied by the religious groups. It is they who now provide the essential reference point from which the individual can relate himself to a mass society which, otherwise, threatens to reduce him to a statistical digit.

THE EVIDENCE RELEVANT TO HERBERG'S THESIS

In the 1958 Detroit Area Study we endeavored to test certain aspects of Herberg's theory, hoping not merely to check its validity but more especially to discover what is actually happening to the strength of the associational bond in the several socio-religious groups. (Basically our findings confirm Herberg's thesis that the Americanization process is linked with the recent strengthening of religious associations, but several important modifications are necessary to make it conform to existing facts.)

Among both white Protestants and white Catholics, the third generation (unless otherwise indicated, this includes fourth and subsequent generations as well) was more active in the churches than the second generation, as Herberg predicted (see *Table 2*). However, our evidence did not support his hypothesis that the second generation is less active in the churches than the first. Only in the Jewish group was this tendency evident. Among white Protestants there was no difference in frequency of church attendance between these two generations, while among Catholics the second generation showed a marked increase in attendance over the first. Instead of the pattern of decline and return which Herberg speaks of, *our data suggest a pattern of increasing religious activity linked with increasing Americanization.* It should be added that further tests revealed that these differences are not a function of the age differences between the generations.[14]

Table 2

PERCENTAGE OF RESPONDENTS REPORTING WEEKLY ATTENDANCE AT WORSHIP SERVICES, BY IMMIGRANT GENERATION, REGION OF BIRTH, AND SOCIO-RELIGIOUS GROUP

	PERCENTAGE ATTENDING SERVICES EVERY WEEK*				
Immigrant Generation	Non-southern White Catholics	White Protestants Non-southern	Southern-born	Non-southern Jews	
First	58 (36)	23 (30)	— (0)	18 (11)	
Second	79 (105)	23 (57)	— (5)	0 (13)	
Third plus	85 (66)	34 (101)	22 (45)	— (0)	

* The figures in parentheses refer to the number of cases in each cell.

A second qualification to be made in Herberg's theory concerns intrasocietal migration. Southern-born white Protestant migrants to Detroit are no more active in the churches than first- or second-generation immigrants from abroad, even though in many cases they are sixth-, seventh-, eighth-, or more, generation Americans. (See *Table 2.*)

The explanation for this seems to be that the transition from the semirural South to a modern metropolitan community is

[14] This conclusion is further supported by Orbach's finding, op. cit., that, except among Jews, church attendance varies little from one age category to another.

in many respects a change comparable to that experienced by a first-generation immigrant from abroad. The metropolis is a new world filled with unfamiliar institutions. The established white Protestant churches seem strange and unfamiliar by rural southern standards, and hence not especially attractive. A few congregations have been organized which seek to recapture the spirit and flavor of the rural, southern congregations, but such efforts are, at best, only partially successful. In short, activity in city churches seems most frequent among those who are not only the most Americanized but also the most urbanized. Since the trend is definitely towards a more Americanized and more urbanized population, it seems likely that these developments should strengthen the churches.

Of special interest here are the results obtained in 1958 when Detroiters were asked about *changes* in church attendance "during the last ten or fifteen years" (Q. 40). On the surface these data suggest anything but a religious revival. Thirty-seven per cent reported that they were attending church (or synagogue) less often than they had, while only 24 per cent reported an increase.

However, when responses to this question were classified by the immigrant generation of the respondent, a very different pattern emerged. Among first-generation immigrants from abroad and first-generation migrants from the South, there was a net loss to the churches of 24 per cent.[15] Among second- and third-generation immigrants the net loss dropped to a mere 3 or 4 per cent. But when the southern-born were excluded, *the churches enjoyed a net gain of more than 5 per cent among fourth-, or more, generation Americans.* In short, insofar as there is evidence of a religious revival in Detroit at the present time, this revival seems concentrated in the most urbanized and Americanized segments of the population. *Table 3* gives a more detailed picture of this trend.

[15] In other words, those reporting a decline in attendance minus those reporting a gain equaled 24 per cent of the total number of respondents in the category.

Table 3

NET GAINS AND LOSSES IN INDIVIDUAL CHURCH ATTENDANCE
REPORTS FOR LAST TEN OR FIFTEEN YEARS, BY IMMIGRANT
GENERATION, REGION OF BIRTH, AND SOCIO-RELIGIOUS GROUP,
IN PERCENTAGES

	NET PERCENTAGE GAIN OR LOSS*				
Immigrant Generation	Non-southern White Catholics	White Protestants Non-southern	Southern-born	Non-southern Jews	
First	0 (36)	−20 (30)	— (0)	−27 (11)	
Second	+2 (104)	−5 (57)	— (5)	−31 (13)	
Third	+4 (49)	−6 (48)	— (4)	— (0)	
Fourth plus	+18 (17)	+2 (53)	−32 (41)	— (0)	

* The figures in parentheses refer to the number of cases in each cell.

One might suppose that these relationships are merely reflections of the upward movement of the children and grand-
children of immigrants in the class system. In other words,
the greater amount of religious activity observed among
members of the third and fourth generations could be due
merely to the fact that they are more often found in the middle class than members of the first and second generations.
However, this was not the case. *Table 4* indicates, when we
hold constant the class position and socio-religious group of
Detroiters, those in the third generation still attend church
more often than those in the first and second generations.[16]

[16] Recently two studies have been made of the relationship
between immigrant generation and frequency of church attendance, using data gathered in *national* samples collected by the
Survey Research Center of The University of Michigan. In a paper entitled "Religion and Politics: The 1960 Election" (unpublished as yet), Philip Converse reports a positive correlation between
degree of Americanization and church attendance for both Catholics and Protestants (p. 27). This pattern holds up even when
controls are introduced for ethnicity among the Catholics. This
finding is of importance since there has been some reason for thinking that the basic relationship might be simply a reflection of the
stronger commitment of Irish and other Northwest European
Catholics to their church together with the fact that Irish and
other Northwest European immigration reached its peak a genera-

Table 4

PERCENTAGE OF NON-SOUTHERN WHITES ATTENDING CHURCH EVERY SUNDAY, BY SOCIO-RELIGIOUS GROUP, CLASS, AND IMMIGRANT GENERATION

Socio-religious Group:	First and Second Generations		Third and Later Generations	
Class	Per cent	N	Per cent	N
White Catholics				
Middle class	77	52	88	32
Working class	71	87	82	34
White Protestants				
Middle class	30	33	38	60
Working class	19	27	27	41

THE TRANSFORMATION OF THE CLASS SYSTEM

Another major consideration in any attempt to assess trends in associational involvement is the progressive transformation of the occupational and class structures of American society. For some years the proportion of the male, urban, labor force in white-collar, or non-manual, positions has been slowly increasing with increasing mechanization and automation. Furthermore, not only has the middle class been increasing in size relative to the working class, but its social standards are

---

tion or two before the immigration from South and East Europe.

Bernard Lazerwitz has made a more extensive analysis of this same problem, using two national samples (neither of which is the same as Converse's) containing 3411 cases. Among white Protestants he found 30 per cent of the first generation reported regular church attendance compared with 35 per cent of the second generation and 39 per cent of the third. For Catholics the comparable figures were 69, 70, and 77 per cent; for Jews, 13, 9, and 8 per cent. Thus the overall national patterns are basically the same as those in Detroit. However, when certain socio-economic controls were applied, the *Catholic* pattern proved unstable. In a number of instances Herberg's pattern of decline and return emerged, though even with these controls, third-generation Catholics reported higher rates of regular church attendance a bit more often than the first generation. See Lazerwitz, "The 'Three Generation' Hypothesis: An Investigation of Findings By Herberg and Lenski" (unpublished paper to be read at American Sociological Association meetings, 1962).

permeating the working class more and more with each passing year, thanks to the growing influence of the mass media. As a result, an ever increasing number of people who are objectively manual workers think and act like the middle class. This is especially true of the upper stratum of the working class: skilled and supervisory workers. Therefore, those religious associations which are more successful in appealing to the middle classes should find the proportion of the total population actively involved in their organizations increasing in coming years. Conversely, those which have more appeal for the working classes may well experience some decline.

(In all but the Jewish group the evidence indicates rather clearly that the middle classes are more highly involved in religious associations than the working classes)[17] Among white Catholics, 74 per cent of the working class claimed to attend Mass every week, but among the middle class the figure was 82 per cent. For white Protestants, the corresponding figures were 23 and 32 per cent respectively, and for Negro Protestants 28 and 38 per cent.

In the case of the Jewish group the percentage of persons attending synagogue every week was greater in the working class than in the middle class, but owing to the limited number of cases in the 1958 sample the difference could have been

[17] The greater involvement of the middle classes in religious associations has been found uniformly in other years of the Detroit Area Study, and in numerous other studies both in this country and abroad. See, for example, E. R. Wickham, *Church and People in an Industrial City* (London: Lutterworth Press, 1957); Emile Pin, S.J., *Pratique Religieuse et Classes Sociales dans une Paroisse Urbaine Saint-Pothin à Lyon* (Paris: Éditions Spes, 1956); A. B. Hollingshead, *Elmtown's Youth* (New York: Wiley, 1949); or Robert and Helen Lynd, *Middletown* (New York: Harcourt, Brace, 1929). Much has been written about the alienation of the working class from the churches, but the fact is often overlooked that the working class participates in *all types* of associational activity far less than the middle class. The only formal associations which have managed to win the active participation of any significant proportion of working-class people seem to be the churches, the unions, and in some countries, workingmen's political parties and clubs. On the whole, working people have limited their voluntary social relationships to those of an informal, primary type much more than the middle class. In particular, they have limited such relationships to those built on the foundation of kinship. See Dotson, op. cit.

due to sampling error. In an effort to determine whether the Jewish group actually differed from the other groups in this respect, data from the 1952, 1953, and 1957 samples were also examined and the results combined with those from the 1958 sample. Of the 68 middle-class Jewish respondents in these four samples, none reported attending services at synagogue or temple every Sabbath, though 19 per cent of the 26 working-class respondents did so. These figures suggest that the Jewish group may differ from other groups in this respect.

Once again changes in attendance during the last ten or fifteen years (Q. 40) are of special interest. Among *middle-class* whites of all groups who were *neither* first-generation immigrants *nor* southern-born, a *net gain* of 8 per cent in church attenders was indicated (N=168). Among comparable working-class whites a *net loss* of 6 per cent was reported (N=171). The greatest gains were found among middle-class whites of the fourth or later generations (excluding again the southern-born). In this category there was a *net gain of 26 per cent* in church attenders.[18]

Such evidence suggests that the declining size of the working class and its increasing permeation by middle-class values will result in a rise in the percentage of persons active in the churches. This important trend therefore is likely to reinforce the influence of the Americanization and urbanization trends noted previously.[19]

[18] This figure is surprisingly high in view of the fact that more than three quarters of the 39 respondents in this category were white Protestants and less than one quarter white Catholics. As we have already seen, increased religious activity was reported much more often among Catholics than among Protestants, so that this figure would not be expected in a category dominated by Protestants.

[19] In this connection it should be noted that the growth in numbers and influence of the middle class and the trend toward Americanization and urbanization both exercise an influence on church attendance partly independent of the other (see *Table 4*). Among white Protestants, class seemed to be a bit more important than Americanization; among Catholics the opposite was true.

RISING LEVEL OF EDUCATION

A fourth social trend which promises increased associational involvement for at least the white Protestant and Catholic churches is the rising level of educational attainment. Among the white Protestants in our sample who had attended college, 41 per cent reported regular weekly attendance at worship services. Only 25 per cent of those with a high school education or less reported regular attendance. For Catholics the comparable figures were 86 and 74 per cent respectively. Among Negro Protestants and Jews the opposite pattern was indicated, but the number of college-trained persons in these groups was so small that extreme caution must be exercised in generalizing from the sample.[20]

WORKING WIVES AND MOTHERS

Finally, one of the important trends in contemporary American society is the increasing tendency of married women to work outside the home. This is one development which could have serious consequences for the Protestant churches, both white and Negro. In both groups working wives were much less often active in the churches. Among white Protestant married women who were not employed, 36 per cent reported weekly attendance at services (N=97). By contrast, only 17 per cent of the working wives reported weekly attendance (N=35). Among Negro Protestant wives the comparable figures were 56 and 35 per cent (Ns=32 and 17). Among Catholics the wives who did not work were slightly more active in attendance than those who did, but the difference was negligible. Since in the majority of American families the wife and mother plays the key role in stimulating religious interest and activity, this trend is one which cannot be ignored.[21]

[20] We are not the first to discover this positive relationship between formal education and church attendance, but the differences reported in other studies have not usually been quite so large. See, for example, *The Catholic Digest*, 17 (December 1952), p. 5, or Michael Argyle's reference to Gallup poll data, *Religious Behavior* (Glencoe: The Free Press, 1959), p. 44.

[21] A recent paper by Bernard Lazerwitz reports no difference in church attendance between women in the labor force and those who are not. "Some Factors Associated with Variations in Church

RELEVANCE OF TRENDS FOR THE CHURCHES

Putting together the various bits and pieces of evidence, we find that none indicate a decline in associational involvement among white Catholics, and several point to the opposite conclusion. (The increasing Americanization of the population, the growth of the middle class, the permeation of the working class by middle-class values, and the rising level of education are all likely to cause an increase in the proportion of Catholics regularly attending Mass.)

Prospects for the white Protestant churches are less clear-cut than for the Catholic churches. They should gain from the Americanization of the population, but not so much as the Catholics. The urbanization of the recent southern migrants and their children should benefit Protestantism far more than Catholicism, but these benefits may well be offset by continuing migration from the South. Protestantism should gain more than Catholicism from the rising level of education, since college-trained white Protestants are more than half again as likely as those with less education to be regular churchgoers, whereas among Catholics the differential is approximately eight to seven. One important development, however, is likely to work against any major increase in associational involvement—this is the trend toward increasing employment of women outside the home. The fact that, among white Protestants, working wives are so much less active could be a serious matter. (Considering the combined influence of *all* these factors, it seems likely that there will be some increase in the proportion of white Protestants in Detroit attending church regularly during the next generation, but this increase should be somewhat less than the Catholic increase.)

Our data indicate less optimistic predictions for Negro Protestants and Jews. Negro Protestant churches stand to gain nothing from the Americanization of the population, though the urbanization of the population could benefit them *in the*

Attendance," *Social Forces*, 39 (May 1961), pp. 301–9. His data are based on three national samples of the Center. Unfortunately, Lazerwitz provides no controls for marital status, region, race, community size, or other factors which might be involved.

long run. In the short run, the continued migration of southern Negroes to northern cities seems likely to depress the rate of associational involvement. The growth of the Negro middle class might well benefit the Negro Protestant churches, but unfortunately available evidence strongly indicates that the Negro group may be the last to benefit from the transformation of the American economy. If the pattern of working wives becomes more common, this will hurt the Negro churches, and our data also suggest that the rising level of education may have the same effect. In short, the evidence indicates that in the next generation the percentage of Negro Protestants attending church regularly may well decline.

Finally, we come to the Jewish group. Almost all available evidence indicates a substantial decline in synagogue and temple attendance except on High Holy Days. Those who now attend services regularly at other times are largely concentrated among the older, less educated, foreign-born, working-class members of the group. For example, in Detroit Orbach found that only 3 per cent of those under 40 reported regular attendance compared with 28 per cent of those over 60. More recently Lazerwitz found that in a national sample only 6 per cent of those under 35 attended regularly compared with 25 per cent of those over 50.[22] While these differences may be partly a reflection of life-cycle patterns, it seems hard to believe that there will be a four- to nine-fold increase in the proportion of the present generation of young Jewish adults participating regularly in temple services. The synagogues and temples of Detroit could be virtually deserted in another generation, except on High Holy Days, if current trends are not reversed. However, in view of the strong communal ties uniting the members of this group (and probably also the secular associational ties) the group seems in little danger of assimilation or disintegration.

Social change and the subcommunities

As the present condition of the Jewish group indicates, it is not safe to infer the strength of communal ties from the strength of associational ties. Neither is it safe to infer trends in one from trends in the other. These two types of group

[22] Lazerwitz, *Social Forces,* 39 (May 1961), p. 304.

involvement are sufficiently independent of one another for each to require separate analysis.

Since endogamy is the backbone of socio-religious communalism, changes in relevant attitudes or behavior are especially important in assessing trends in communalism. One of the questions we asked everyone was whether they thought it wiser for members of their group to marry within the group (Q. 72, 84, and 97). The overwhelming majority of white respondents said that it *was* wiser. This was true of 92 per cent of the Jews, 81 per cent of the Catholics, and 75 per cent of the Protestants.

When the views of Detroiters were analyzed by immigrant generation, age, and class, those segments of the population which are growing in relative size were *more* committed to the principle of endogamy than those which are declining. For example, 80 per cent of the third-generation Americans thought it wiser for people to marry someone of their own faith, compared with 73 per cent of the first and second generation.[23] Similarly, 83 per cent of the middle class, but only 66 per cent of the working class, shared this belief.

What people say they believe is one thing, while what they do is sometimes something else. Hence we were especially interested in the incidence of mixed marriages as related to class and generation. Virtually all of the mixed marriages involved white Protestants and Catholics, so we focused our attention on these.

One of our important findings was that it is most unwise to assume that spouses who are *currently* of the same faith were *always* of the same faith. Although 85 per cent of the white Protestants and Catholics in our sample reported that they and their spouse were of the same major faith (i.e., Protestantism or Catholicism), a check of their religious background revealed that only 68 per cent had been reared in the same faith. In other words, one fifth of the now homogeneous marriages had been contracted by persons raised in different faiths. For this reason it seemed necessary to study two aspects of mixed marriages: (a) are more marriages being con-

[23] If age is used as the criterion, 74 per cent of those under 35 years of age favored endogamy compared with 63 per cent of those aged 50 and over.

tracted among persons raised in different faiths than was true in the past? and (b) are more married couples currently of differing faiths than was true in the past?

Using immigrant generation as the measure, we found no significant difference in the frequency with which mixed marriages had been contracted, but there seemed to be a trend with respect to the persistence of religious differences after marriage. Among first- and second-generation, northern-born Americans, 17 per cent reported that their spouse was currently of a different faith (N=213), but among third-generation respondents the comparable figure was only 11 per cent (N=143). In other words, *the more Americanized the individuals, the greater the probability that mixed marriages will lead to the conversion of one partner or the other, and that religious unity will eventually be established within the nuclear family.*

The communalistic tendency to limit friendships to one's own group was neither increasing nor declining in Detroit. The evidence indicated only that restrictive tendencies of this type are fairly stable and present patterns are likely to continue for the foreseeable future.

Summary

By way of summarizing all of the foregoing data, it appears that the major social trends of our time tend to strengthen both the associational and communal aspects of the two major socio-religious groups: the Catholic and white Protestant. As a minor qualification to this statement we should note that this strengthening apparently does not extend into the area of friendship, but is limited to marriage and kinship. In the case of the two smaller groups, the Negro Protestants and Jews, the nuclear associations seem to be weakened by current trends, but the data do not tell us how the subcommunities are being affected.

However, more important than any of these more specific conclusions is the general conclusion suggested by the evidence as a whole: contrary to the views and predictions of nineteenth-century positivists, *traditional religious groups continue to be viable and vigorous organizations.* What is more, they promise continued viability and vigor in the foreseeable future.

II. RELIGIOUS ORIENTATIONS

Embedded in the institutional structure of both Judaism and Christianity are a variety of religious orientations which have, to some degree, competed and contended with one another. As noted in Chapter 1 we have limited our analysis here to two of the more important of them: doctrinal orthodoxy and devotionalism.

Doctrinal orthodoxy

For our measure of doctrinal orthodoxy we have relied on the responses of Detroiters to six questions. These were:

1. Do you believe there is a God, or not? (Q. 42)

2. Do you think God is like a Heavenly Father who watches over you, or do you have some other belief? (Q. 43)

3. Do you believe that God answers people's prayers, or not? (Q. 44)

4. Do you believe in a life after death, or not (Q. 45); if so, do you also believe that in the next life some people will be punished and others rewarded by God, or not? (Q. 45a)

5. Do you believe that, when they are able, God expects people to worship Him in their churches and synagogues, *every* week, or not? (Q. 46)

6. Do you believe that Jesus was God's only Son sent into the world by God to save sinful men, or do you believe that he was simply a very good man and teacher, or do you have some other belief? (Q. 52)

Because the Jewish group was too small for intragroup analysis of this type, these questions were designed for classifying Christians only. Christians were classified as orthodox if they asserted that they believed in a God who watched over them like a Heavenly Father, who answered prayers, and who expected weekly worship, if they believed that Jesus was God's only Son, and if they believed in punishments and rewards in a life after death. If an individual expressed uncertainty or unbelief with respect to *any* of these items he was

Note definition of orthodox and unorthodox

classified as unorthodox. In many of the preliminary tabulations distinctions were made between the more unorthodox and the less unorthodox, but in the end we decided that the size of the sample made it impractical to extend the analysis to more than a simple dichotomy between the orthodox and unorthodox.

The reader may wonder why we used such a rigorous definition of orthodoxy. We generally decided on strict definitions *whenever* we were faced with the problem of where to divide such basic variables, and the reasoning behind this decision was as follows. If there are differences between people with more or less of a given characteristic, it seemed likely that the most meaningful differences appear between those who are most committed and the remainder of the population. Furthermore, it is when individuals are strongly committed to something that we can best judge the influence of the commitment on their lives. It therefore seemed wiser to define our more orthodox category so as to include only those who took the orthodox position on *all* items.

As might be expected, doctrinal orthodoxy proved more frequent among Catholics than among Protestants. Sixty-two per cent of the Catholic respondents took an orthodox stance on all items, compared with only 38 per cent of the Negro Protestants and 32 per cent of the white Protestants.[24] Most of the heterodox accepted the majority of the six basic doctrines. Only 10 per cent of the white Protestants, 4 per cent of the white Catholics, and 2 per cent of the Negro Protestants rejected more than half of them.

Devotionalism

The second basic religious orientation we sought to isolate was that which values direct, personal communication with God through prayer and meditation, and which seeks divine direction in daily affairs. To establish an index of devotionalism, we utilized answers to two questions: Question 44b on the frequency with which the respondent engaged in prayer, and Question 55 on the frequency with which he sought to

[24] For a detailed breakdown on the responses of members of the different groups to each of these questions, see Appendix III, *Table 56.*

determine what God wanted him to do when he had important decisions to make.

Detroiters were ranked high in devotionalism if (a) they reported praying more than once a day, plus asking what God would have them do either *often* or *sometimes,* or if (b) they reported praying once a day, but *often* asking what God would have them do. Using this measure, 68 per cent of the Negro Protestants were ranked high in devotionalism. The comparable figures for white Catholics and Protestants were 47 and 29 per cent respectively. It may be noted that doctrinal orthodoxy was somewhat more common than the devotional orientation among Catholics, while the reverse proved true among Negro Protestants. In the case of the white Protestant group these two orientations were more nearly balanced in strength.

One of the striking findings of this study was the limited nature of the relationship between these two orientations. Using the Tau_b measure of association, a coefficient of only .05 was obtained. In terms of the more familiar Pearsonian r, this same relationship would produce a coefficient of approximately .23. Both measures indicate the modest character of the relationship, and emphasize the necessity for differentiating between the various elements of what is so often subsumed under the single heading, "religiosity."

Trends in orthodoxy and devotionalism

Earlier in this chapter we sought to discover whether the communal and associational aspects of religious group organization are gaining or declining. The same question should also be raised about our two important religious orientations.

(Among white Catholics, the evidence suggests a trend toward increased devotionalism and increased doctrinal orthodoxy) Comparing more recent immigrants with those who were more Americanized, the latter were more often active devotionally *and* doctrinally orthodox than the former.[25] Class data suggest that devotionalism increases the farther up the social scale one goes; but orthodoxy is not affected by changes in status. Thus the transformation of the class system

[25] See Appendix III, *Table 57,* for statistical details underlying the generalizations in this section.

should increase the general measure of Catholic devotionalism, but have little effect on Catholic orthodoxy. The data on education suggest that the rising level of education will have little or no effect on either orientation.

Among white Protestants, current social trends should have the effect of somewhat weakening both orientations. The doctrinally orthodox were more numerous among the southern-born, first- and second-generation immigrants, working-class people, and the less well educated. Since all of these groups are likely to decline in the future, heterodoxy is likely to increase, barring some major change originating in the churches themselves. It looks as though white Protestant devotionalism will also decline, but the differences between the classes suggest that the transformation of the class system might be a force counteracting this trend.

Earlier in this chapter we found that attendance at white Protestant churches will probably increase, but we are now saying that there may be a decline in the proportion of those same congregations committed to such basic orientations as orthodoxy and devotionalism. On first inspection this combination of developments may seem improbable. Surely such trends cannot move in opposite directions.

This, however, is very close to what Herberg had in mind when he stated his now familiar paradox that Americans are becoming more religious while at the same time becoming more secular (Despite attending the churches more frequently, their thoughts and values are less often derived from distinctly religious (in the sense of associational) sources and more often derived from secular sources) In short, a transcendental faith is gradually being transformed into a cultural faith. Contrary to Herberg, our data do not suggest that such a fate is likely to overtake American Catholicism in the foreseeable future, but they do suggest that American Protestantism has already moved far in this direction, and is continuing to move further.

In the Negro Protestant group, just as in the white Protestant group, there is likely to be a decline in both doctrinal orthodoxy and in devotionalism in the next generation. Every indicator, without exception, points to a decline, and in all but one instance (out of six), to a rather pronounced decline.

Throughout this discussion of future trends we have spoken entirely of trends resulting from changes in the structure of American society, ignoring changes which might originate from ferment within the churches themselves. Obviously, however, organizations, like organisms, change in response to both external and internal forces.[26] For example, a powerful movement of spiritual revitalization might suddenly sweep through one of our groups in response perhaps to internal stresses created by the numerous contradictions between the ideals and practices of the churches. We cannot rule out this possibility. However, movements of this nature are not common, and if they should develop in the Protestant churches, they would be confronted with secular social trends pushing powerfully in the opposite direction. Hence, even if such movements were to develop, the probabilities of their success are not impressive. (Detroit Protestantism seems in some danger of becoming what Richard Niebuhr and others have referred to as a "cultural religion.") That is to say, it is in danger of becoming a religion which has lost its transcendental character. Perhaps this is too sweeping an inference to draw from our limited data on orthodoxy and devotionalism, but the fact remains that Protestant church attendance is increasing while at the same time *both* orthodoxy and devotionalism are declining.[27] This strongly suggests that such a trend is under way. We might add that the pages of history are replete with the ruins of cultural religions which have had the misfortune of subsequently encountering transcendental religions.

III. INTERGROUP IMAGES

In a pluralistic society, interrelations among the various subgroups are of major concern to everyone. Some measure of intergroup conflict and tension seems inevitable so long as divisions remain, though these are not necessarily a threat to the stability of the social system and its chances for survival.

[26] See Chapter 8, Section II, for a more detailed discussion of this point.
[27] Others report the same trend. See, for example, Peter Berger's damning indictment of contemporary American Protestantism, *The Noise of Solemn Assemblies* (Garden City: Doubleday, 1961).

Peaceful patterns of intergroup relations frequently develop. Controversies between groups can become "institutionalized" —that is, their expression can be confined to well-defined and socially acceptable channels; the present popular emphasis on interfaith and interracial discussion is an example. However, as events since World War II in India, Lebanon, and Palestine indicate, conflicts between socio-religious groups contain a potentiality for disruptive violence unmatched by any other kind of intrasocietal conflict, with the possible exception of those based on class differences.

It may seem unnecessary to refer to such unpleasant possibilities in a study of an American community. By and large, socio-religious groups in this country have achieved a peaceful pattern of relationships, and in our highly secularized environment the threat of internecine strife seems remote indeed. Yet even here violence has not been wholly eliminated from the scene, and intergroup conflicts have not been wholly institutionalized. The struggle between the Negro and white groups provides the clearest example. Large numbers in both groups seem ready to "man the barricades," and organizations like the White Citizens' Councils and the Black Muslims have little difficulty in recruiting supporters. Even in the case of Jewish-Gentile relations, violence erupts occasionally, as in bombings of Jewish synagogues. Finally, it may be well to note that while violent attacks on Catholics are not a part of the current scene, anti-Catholic riots and mob violence were not infrequent in nineteenth-century America.

These remarks are not designed to paint a dismal picture of intergroup relations in America, but only to serve as a reminder that popular optimism often fails to reckon with the strength of the passions which communal loyalties and antagonisms can arouse. Here, as elsewhere, the potentiality for intergroup strife and violence exists.

Our aim in this section is to explore relationships among the groups at the level of the ordinary member. To accomplish this, we tried to discover what kind of *image* each of the groups has formed of the others. How do white Catholics look to white Protestants, and *vice versa*? What general characteristics do Negro Protestants attribute to Jews? Such images contain many facets, three of the more important being group tolerance, group honesty, and group power. We could not rely on any simple question to elicit the necessary data, and each respondent was therefore asked a series of questions. For example, Protestants were asked:

1. Compared with Protestants, do you think Catholics as a whole are more tolerant, as tolerant, or less tolerant of the religious beliefs of other people? (Q. 76)

2. Compared with Protestants, do you think Catholics as a whole are more fair, as fair, or less fair in their business dealings? (Q. 77)

They were then asked a more general question about the power of Catholics:

3. Do you feel that Catholics have been trying to get too much power in this country, or not? (Q. 78)[28]

The same three questions were then repeated with comparisons made between Protestants and Jews.

When interviewing Catholic or Jewish respondents we used the same wording in the first two questions, simply reversing the names of the groups. On the question of power, a change in wording was introduced because historically Protestants have been the holders of power in American society. For Catholics and Jews the question was worded:

Do you feel that Protestants have too much power in this country today, or not? (Q. 90 and 107)

Of the three questions, the one dealing with power is probably the best indicator of serious tensions. Excessive power in one group invariably appears to other groups as a direct threat; it frightens them and frequently creates a predisposition to defend themselves in every possible way, including extralegal methods. By contrast, the belief that another group is lacking in tolerance or honesty may create ill will, but is less likely to lead to physical conflict.

Unfortunately, in the planning stage of this study the need for differentiating between Negro and white Protestants was not so evident as it later became. Hence, parallel questions

[28] These questions were adapted from the earlier *Catholic Digest* Survey.

concerning white images of the Negro Protestant group were not obtained. However, we did question white respondents about their attitudes on integrated schools and living in the same neighborhood with Negroes. These data leave something to be desired from the standpoint of comparability, but nevertheless they give us a valid insight into the white image of the Negro group.

An unusually large number of Detroiters were unwilling to commit themselves on the questions about the tolerance, fairness, and power of other groups. Combining the responses to all of these questions, it was found that nearly one quarter were noncommittal. This was far above the average for other questions in the interview (typically 1 to 5 per cent).

There are two alternative explanations for this. The large number of noncommittal responses may reflect a judicious suspension of judgment by many Detroiters who realized they could not form valid judgments on such matters merely on the basis of personal experience. On the other hand, many people with strongly critical views of other groups may simply have been reluctant to sound "prejudiced" in front of a stranger—a stranger, moreover, who was taking notes on everything they said. The noncommittal response provides the perfect solution to their problem.

Undoubtedly there were some instances of each of these two possibilities, but since Detroiters were generally willing to express opinions on a great variety of other subjects, the second hypothesis is probably the explanation in the majority of cases. This conclusion is also supported by the judgments of the interviewers.

White Protestants

Of all the groups, the white Protestants enjoyed the most favorable image in the eyes of others (see *Table 5*).[29] That is to say, Catholics have a more favorable image of Protestants than of Jews, and Jews have a more favorable image of

[29] We are assuming here that when Catholics and Jews make generalizations about "Protestants" they are usually thinking in terms of *white* Protestants. As noted previously, it would have been desirable to have made a racial distinction in these questions, but this need was not anticipated in advance.

Table 5

PERCENTAGE EXPRESSING FAVORABLE IMAGE OF VARIOUS SOCIO-RELIGIOUS GROUPS WITH RESPECT TO TOLERANCE, BUSINESS FAIRNESS, AND POWER, BY SOCIO-RELIGIOUS GROUP

Group Passing Judgment	PERCENTAGE EXPRESSING FAVORABLE IMAGE* REGARDING:									Mean
	Religious Tolerance			Business Fairness			Power			
	of Prots.	of Caths.	of Jews	of Prots.	of Caths.	of Jews	of Prots.	of Caths.	of Jews	
White Protestants	—	30	49	—	71	47	—	49	56	50
Negro Protestants	—	44	49	—	64	39	—	63	44	51
White Catholics	60	—	54	78	—	45	68	—	58	61
Jews	65	31	—	62	68	—	73	65	—	61
Mean	63	35	51	70	68	44	71	59	53	56

* Responses were defined as favorable if the out-group was rated as equal with, or better than, the in-group in tolerance and fairness, and if the out-group was said not to be trying to get (or not having) too much power.

Protestants than of Catholics. On each of the three criteria (religious tolerance, business fairness, and power), at least 60 per cent of both Catholics and Jews expressed approval of the white Protestants.

Although they were the least criticized, white Protestants were the most critical of other groups. As *Table 5* indicates, they were especially critical of Catholics on the grounds of religious intolerance. They were least critical in the case of Catholic business practices.

To understand why Protestants were so often critical of other groups, but so seldom criticized themselves, it is necessary to remember that historically the United States has been a Protestant nation, in the sense that its culture and institutions were molded mainly by Protestants, and therefore inevitably expressed their viewpoints and values. As other groups have come into this country they have been at least partially assimilated to the Protestant-dominated secular culture. This means that they tend to judge Protestants by standards which are at least partially Protestantized, and therefore judge them more favorably than they judge other groups.

Also, Protestants have been the traditional holders of power. The continuance of this tradition is not likely to alarm other groups, providing only that their exercise of power allows aggressive and ambitious members of the newer groups to rise. In a society with democratic political institutions, and economic institutions which are becoming increasingly bureaucratized, such opportunities seem considerable. Hence, members of the newer groups are not overly critical or fearful of Protestant power.

From the Protestant standpoint, however, the situation looks quite different. Increasingly positions of power are being occupied by people whose commitment to traditional American standards, particularly those with a distinctively Protestant flavor, is not certain. Their rise may well lead to a transformation of the traditional institutional system; hence they are to be feared.

This reasoning is supported by a comparison of Lutheran responses with those of other white Protestants on the questions concerning the power of Catholics and Jews. Intra-Protestant denominational comparisons normally revealed no appreciable differences, but this was one of the exceptions. Among Lutherans (N=66), 59 per cent said that Catholics are not trying to get too much power in this country today; for all other white Protestants (N=192) the figure was 45 per cent. Two thirds of the Lutherans said Jews are not trying to get too much power, compared with slightly over half of the other Protestants.

One might suppose that these variations are due to differences in class position, but this is not the case. There is no appreciable difference in the class distribution of Lutherans and other white Protestants. Forty-seven per cent of the Lutherans are in the middle class compared with 44 per cent of all other white Protestants. The important fact seems to be the relatively recent immigrant status of Lutherans compared with other Protestants. Because they are more recent immigrants, they are less likely to feel that their traditional powers are being threatened by the advances of Catholics and Jews.

It also seems significant that white Protestants single out *different* characteristics of Catholics and Jews for criticism. They are twice as likely to criticize Jews for unfairness in business practices as for religious intolerance. This parallels the fact that the chief threat to Protestant power from the Jewish group is in the *economic* area. In the case of the Catholics, the situation is exactly reversed. They are criticized often for religious intolerance, but seldom for unfair business practices. Again, it seems more than coincidence that Catholic successes have been greater in the political than in the economic arena; hence any tendencies toward religious intolerance are more of a threat when found in this group.[30]

That white Protestant criticisms and fears are not wholly without foundation is indicated by certain other findings of this study. For example, nearly half of the white Catholic

[30] In this connection it is significant to note that on the question dealing with the power of the Jewish group, Protestants frequently complained that they have too much power financially, but not politically. By contrast, a number of references were made to Catholic power as a political threat. For example, when questioned about the power of Catholics, a Congregationalist housewife asked the interviewer, "Do you mean politically? I feel it [the Catholic Church] is basically a political organization."

respondents in the 1958 sample said that they did not feel that the ministers of other churches should be allowed to teach publicly (as on the radio) things that are contrary to Catholic teaching (Q. 95). Another 10 per cent expressed uncertainty on this matter. Such widespread rejection of the American tradition of freedom of speech in such a large subgroup is bound to become known to white Protestants and cause fear and distrust. In this connection it is significant that nearly as many *Catholics* said that Catholics are *less* tolerant in religious matters than non-Catholics as said the reverse.[31]

White Catholics

Catholics were much less critical and fearful of white Protestants than the latter were of them. However, it is interesting to note that Catholic criticisms of Protestants roughly paralleled Protestant criticisms of Catholics. Both groups were most critical of the other in the area of religious tolerance, and least critical in the area of business practices (see *Table 5*).

Catholics were consistently more critical of the Jews than of the white Protestants. This difference was especially marked in the area of business practices.

The most favorable image of the Catholic group was held by the Negro Protestant group. On all three items Negro Protestants were less critical of Catholics than either white Protestants or Jews. In fact, the only item on which any sizable number of Negro Protestants criticized the Catholic group was religious tolerance. The favorable image which Negro Protestants have formed of the Catholics is undoubtedly related to the strong stand the Catholic hierarchy has taken for racial integration. The fact that Catholic schools and churches have often been among the first to be integrated has not escaped the attention of the masses of Negro Protestants.

A further indication of the high regard which Negro Protestants have for the Catholic group appears in their responses to the question of what church they would join if they joined

---

[31] Eighteen per cent of Catholics said that Protestants were less tolerant than Catholics in religious matters, but 15 per cent said they were more tolerant. In their judgment of Jews, the comparable figures were 21 and 12 per cent.

any other (Q. 118). Slightly over 30 per cent said they would join the Catholic Church.[32] By contrast, only 12 per cent of the white Protestants gave this response.

The Jewish group was much more critical of Catholics than the Negro Protestants were. In fact, they were nearly as critical as the white Protestants. Like both Protestant groups, the Jews most often criticized Catholics on the grounds of intolerance.

Jews

Of the three major white groups, the Jewish group was the most often criticized, and at the same time, the least critical of others. We have already noted the images which Jewish respondents had of other white groups, and the images which these other groups had of them. The Jews were somewhat less critical of the Protestants than were the Catholics, and they were also somewhat less critical of the Catholics than were the Protestants. This relatively favorable image was reciprocated by the white Protestants but not by the Catholics, who were much more critical of the Jews than of the Protestants.

The Negro Protestants resembled the Catholics far more than the white Protestants so far as their image of the Jewish group was concerned. This image was a highly critical one: in the frequency with which criticism was expressed it was second only to the white Protestant image of the Catholic group. Like other groups, Negro Protestants were most critical of Jewish business practices.

Throughout the critical comments of Gentiles, both white and Negro, certain themes constantly recurred. First, "the Jews are not trying to get power; they already have it." Second, "their power is economic and financial, not political." Third, "the Jews are less fair in their business dealings than non-Jews."

These views can be seen illustrated in a variety of com-

[32] It seems likely that some of the less well-educated misunderstood this question. Following as it did on the heels of the series of questions calling for comparisons of Protestants, Catholics, and Jews, some Protestant respondents may have thought the interviewer was asking if they were to become either Catholic or Jewish, which they would choose.

ments made by Detroiters in response to our questions about Jews. For example, an elderly, self-employed Presbyterian craftsman said:

> Sure the Jews are less fair. I know from my own experience. It's because they've been subjugated so long. But they're pretty sly.

He went on to say:

> They're not trying to get power, but they have it because they have money.

A Catholic cab driver was more blunt. He said:

> The Jews grab whatever they can.

A small Negro painting contractor was unsure whether or not the Jews are trying to get too much power. He explained:

> They've got power already. But I don't think it's an organized effort. It's their belief to own property, and this makes them more powerful.

A young Catholic housewife told us:

> I think Jews are very tricky, some of them, though some are as straight as can be.

On the whole, though, she made it clear she felt that Jews are less fair than Catholics in their business dealings. By contrast, a young Baptist housewife stated that she believed that Jews are as fair as Protestants in their business dealings, but she added as an afterthought:

> But Jews do try to take advantage a little.

It is interesting to speculate about why Gentiles, both white and Negro, are so critical of Jewish business ethics. These attitudes are frequently dismissed as mere prejudice, but such a view of the problem seems far too superficial. As noted previously, there is a marked selectivity in the negative imagery of all of the groups. Different groups are criticized for different things, which suggests that more than mere ignorance and ill will are at work. To some degree, at least, these unfavorable images reflect real attributes of the groups involved.

In the case of the Jewish group, it seems significant that to such a large degree its contacts with Gentiles occur in the context of the merchant-customer relationship. A study based on the 1952, 1955, and 1956 Detroit Area Studies combined revealed that nearly half of the Jewish family heads were self-employed compared with only 9 per cent of the rest of the population.[33] This same study indicated that Jews were even more heavily concentrated in the ranks of retail merchants a generation earlier.

These facts seem important because the merchant-customer relationship normally involves conflict, and, for the customer, tension and anxiety as well. The fact that the merchant is far more familiar with the merchandise and with exchange relationships generally puts the customer at a distinct disadvantage. In this situation the merchant's definition of proper conduct and ethical behavior is likely to differ considerably from the customer's, regardless of the socio-religious commitments of the individuals involved. In a word, practices which customers define as dishonest are frequently not so defined by merchants.

Any group which meets the world primarily (or even frequently) in the role of merchant is likely to be regarded, and not wholly without reason, as untrustworthy in business dealings. For contemporary American Jews the problem is further aggravated because their businesses are generally small and family-owned, easily identifiable with the Jewish group. Customers who have unpleasant experiences with Jewish businessmen (or professional men) are easily able to generalize from their immediate experience with one man to the whole group. The Catholic and Protestant groups are far less vulnerable in this respect since the businessmen among their members are much more likely to be employees of some large, bureaucratized enterprise. The economic ethics of such concerns and their employees may be no better than those of

---

[33] David Goldberg and Harry Sharp, "Some Characteristics of Detroit Area Jewish and Non-Jewish Adults," in Marshall Sklare, ed., *The Jews: Social Patterns of an American Group* (Glencoe: The Free Press, 1958), p. 112.

small merchants, but ownership and control of most modern corporations is so diffuse or so hidden as to defy popular identification with any particular group. Injured customers of such a company are therefore less prone to generalize their unpleasant experiences to some particular socio-religious group. Hence, sharp business practice by Gentiles seems less likely to generate a negative image of the group to which they belong.

Negro Protestants

In interviews with white Detroiters we asked three questions concerning the Negro group: first, should white and Negro students attend the same or separate schools (Q. 25)? second, would they be "at all disturbed or unhappy" if a Negro with the same income and education moved into their block (Q. 26)? third, if they said they would be, or if they were uncertain, what would make them disturbed or unhappy (Q. 26a)? This last question proved especially valuable in discovering the images which whites had of Negroes.

Far more whites were worried about integrated *neighborhoods* than about integrated *schools*. Only one third expressed a preference for segregated schools, but slightly more than half said they would be disturbed or unhappy if a Negro with comparable education and income moved into their neighborhood. Middle-class Detroiters were more concerned about integrated neighborhoods, while working-class Detroiters were more concerned about integrated schools.

Of the three white socio-religious groups, Catholics were the most likely to be disturbed by Negroes moving into their neighborhood, with 58 per cent expressing this view. White Protestants followed closely, with 53 per cent. Among the Jews, only 19 per cent said that they would be disturbed or unhappy.[34]

In answer to the follow-up question about their reasons for being disturbed or unhappy, some people simply stated that

---

[34] Differences were greater in the middle than in the working class. In the former, 67 per cent of the Catholics, 56 per cent of the Protestants, and only 16 per cent of the Jews said they would be disturbed or unhappy. In the working class the figures were 52, 50, and 25 per cent respectively.

their own property values would decline, and they could not afford to take a loss, or did not wish to. In some cases there was no indication that the individual himself held an unfavorable image of the Negro group. For example, a self-employed Jewish craftsman told us:

> The property value goes down. Someone who has saved for a lifetime to buy a decent place has to sell and loses half of his investment.

A Canadian-born Baptist factory worker said:

> Sure I'd be disturbed, but not because of the people themselves. I don't want to be financially whittled down, but I don't think I'm any better than the nigger.

On the other hand, some responses clearly indicated an unfavorable image. For example, a Methodist subcontractor in the building business said:

> Seventy-five per cent of them are not very far from the jungle in temperament or habits.

A Catholic widow in her forties who was planning to move because Negroes were moving into her neighborhood at that very time said:

> They just destroy the whole neighborhood. They neglect everything. Their way of life is so different from ours.

A more unusual explanation was offered by a successful Italian Catholic businessman. He said he would be disturbed and explained his feelings this way:

> Pride. My prestige would be hurt living in the same neighborhood.

An older Lutheran factory worker summed up a sentiment which we heard many times from workingmen:

> It's all right to work with 'em, but I don't believe in living with 'em.

Approximately two fifths of the white Catholics and Protestants in Detroit gave answers which clearly indicated a negative image of the Negro group. By contrast, only one eighth of the Jews did so. A similar pattern was observed on the question concerning the schools. Here, a third of the Catholics and Protestants expressed a preference for segregated schools, but only 8 per cent of the Jews. It is especially ironic that the Jewish group, toward which the Negro Protestants were least favorably disposed (as we observed earlier), was the group which had the most cordial attitude toward them, while the Catholic group, toward which they were much more favorably disposed, was so much more critical of them.

The subcommunities, the churches, and intergroup images

Though the churches have often been accused of fostering intergroup tension and hostility, our evidence indicates that actually the subcommunities are the primary source of this in Detroit at present. As may be seen in *Table 6*, those who were most involved in the subcommunities were a good bit

Table 6

PERCENTAGE OF DETROITERS EXPRESSING FAVORABLE VIEWS OF SOCIO-RELIGIOUS GROUPS OTHER THAN THEIR OWN, BY SOCIO-RELIGIOUS GROUP, DEGREE OF COMMUNAL INVOLVEMENT, AND DEGREE OF ASSOCIATIONAL INVOLVEMENT

Type of Involvement: Degree of Involvement	PERCENTAGE OF FAVORABLE VIEWS BY:[a]		
	Catholics	White Prots.	Negro Prots.
Involvement in Subcommunity			
Highly Involved	49	45	—[b]
Other	62	54	—[b]
Involvement in Church			
Highly Involved	55	53	55
Other	60	50	51

[a] The percentages shown in this table are the means of responses to all questions dealing with intergroup images; they include all questions concerning Jews, Catholics, Protestants, and Negroes.
[b] In the interview no data were gathered concerning interracial ties of kinship and friendship; hence it did not prove practical to analyze the Negro Protestant group in terms of degree of communal involvement. Furthermore, casual observation indicates that relatively few Detroit Negroes have many primary group ties extending beyond the bounds of their socio-religious group.

less likely to express favorable views of other groups than those who were not so involved.

By contrast, involvement in the churches had much less effect on images of other groups. In fact, in the case of Protestants, both Negro and white, those who were more active in the churches were a bit *more* likely to express favorable views of other groups than those who were less involved.[35]

These findings, like many to be reported in future chapters, underline the need for differentiating between the communal and associational aspects of socio-religious groups. They point up the fact that while socio-religious subcommunities are derivative from, and dependent on, religious associations (at least in modern societies), they are not mere appendages whose characteristics are dictated by the associations. On the contrary, the influence of the subcommunity on its members may be quite different from that of the religious association with which it is linked.

A word on terminology

Before concluding this discussion of intergroup images, a word must be said about the relationship between our cumbersome phrase, "unfavorable group image," and the briefer, more familiar term, "prejudice." Many social scientists would undoubtedly equate the two, but on the basis of the evidence, this step seems neither wise nor justified. Strictly speaking, the term "prejudice" denotes an *unreasonable* viewpoint. As we have attempted to show, the evidence indicates that some, at least, of the unfavorable group images observed in this study are not wholly unreasonable. To lump all unfavorable group images under the single heading of "prejudice" may well prejudice the outcome of any serious analysis of the subject.

This subject of prejudice and unfavorable group images is much more complex than is often recognized. There is much about the unfavorable images which socio-religious groups form of each other which is quite reasonable, provided only

[35] Robert C. Angell reports a similar finding in his 1956 Detroit Area Study. See "Preferences for Moral Norms in Three Problem Areas," *American Journal of Sociology*, 67 (May 1962), p. 659. His data deal only with white images of the Negro group.

that one accept certain basic value postulates shared by members of the group. All human judgments rest ultimately on the foundation of value postulates which are untestable and accepted finally on grounds of faith. Given differing postulates and differing patterns of action among groups, unfavorable images are bound to arise. Sometimes a group may allow its values to distort its *perceptions,* in which case there are grounds for speaking of "prejudice." Often, however, it seems that the unfavorable images arise simply because different groups are committed to different values and therefore act differently and are judged accordingly. To equate this with negative images based on *distorted perceptions* can only confuse the discussion of the subject.

In many cases the term "prejudice" has been used by social psychologists and sociologists more as a weapon than as a scientific tool. Often the label has been pinned on group images which social scientists, with their own distinctive values, find offensive. Comparable images which they find congenial are ignored. Hence, most modern analyses of prejudice normally contain a discussion of the prejudiced views which southern whites have of Negroes, but rarely a discussion of the prejudiced views which northern liberals have of southern whites. Nevertheless, striking similarities may be observed, and could serve as a fruitful basis for achieving a better understanding of this whole complex problem.

Unfortunately, the very use of this term "prejudice" stands in the way of the development of a more adequate understanding of the problem. "Prejudices" are something that the other fellow has. By utilizing the more inclusive, and less polemical term, "unfavorable group image," a more adequate view of this subject might well be attained.

IV. DISTRIBUTION OF THE GROUPS IN THE COMMUNITY

Since its original settlement in 1701, the community of Detroit has spread out in every direction, except where prevented by the Detroit River and Lake St. Clair. Today it is roughly twenty miles from the point of original settlement on the river to the outer edges of suburban municipalities such as Birming-

ham to the northwest, Livonia and Wayne to the west, or
Trenton to the south. In the expansion of the community,
the municipality, or political entity, of Detroit has been unable to keep pace. As a result, the community is now divided
into a hodgepodge of local governments, each of which
jealously fights to preserve its own autonomy.

The distribution of population in present-day Detroit is far
from random: one need only drive through the residential
sections of the community to observe the pattern of racial
segregation. The demarcation lines are not perfectly drawn,
but the residences of the great majority of whites are separated from those of the great majority of Negroes. Certain
residential areas are also noted for their heavy concentration
of groups such as Jews, Poles, and Hungarians. In an earlier
era there were also areas noted for their concentrations of
Irish, French, Italians, and Germans.

Religion and residence

While the decline of the ethnic groups has facilitated residential intermingling among the socio-religious groups, systematic analysis reveals that still today the latter are unevenly
distributed in most sections of the community. In our analysis
we divided the community into twelve major areas which
have emerged as spontaneous and unplanned by-products of
the growth of the metropolis. Seven of the twelve areas are
within the city of Detroit proper, with four lying west of
Woodward Avenue (the dividing line between the east and
west sides of the city), and three lying east of it (see
Figure 2). Two of these areas constitute "the inner city."
This is the oldest section of the city, and traditionally its
center. Surrounding the inner city is an area we have labeled
"the middle city." We have included here the municipalities
of Hamtramck and Highland Park, which are totally sur-
rounded by the municipality of Detroit. As the city expanded
beyond the bounds of the inner city during the nineteenth
and early twentieth centuries, this was the new area of settlement. Both the inner city and the middle city have been divided into an eastern and western half, with Woodward Avenue serving as the dividing line, except where Highland Park

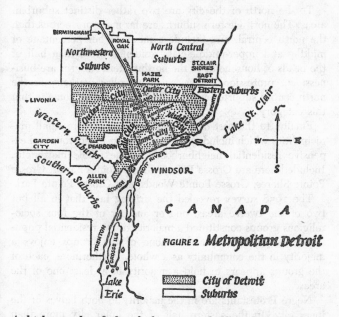

FIGURE 2. *Metropolitan Detroit*

City of Detroit
Suburbs

(which was classified with the western half) spills over Woodward Avenue.

Beyond the middle city is an area we have called "the outer city," which lies on the northern and western boundaries of the city. It is the area of most recent settlement *within* city boundaries. It has been divided into three areas as shown in *Figure 2*, two being west of Woodward Avenue, and one east.

The outlying suburbs are divided into five areas. To the south is a tier of municipalities and townships extending from the Detroit River to the western limits of the community. These southern suburbs include a number of municipalities along the river which are almost as old as Detroit itself. These were once independent communities, but with the great expansion of Detroit in the twentieth century, have gradually been absorbed into the metropolis. To the west of the city is a large suburban area including the municipalities of Dearborn, Livonia, and Garden City. This area has enjoyed most of its growth and development in the last several decades.

To the north of the city are two rather distinct suburban areas. The northwestern suburbs are far more prosperous than the north central, and include a much higher percentage of middle- and upper-middle-class residents. More than half of the heads of households in the northwestern suburbs are businessmen, professional men, or white-collar workers; in the north central suburbs only a little over a quarter come within this category.

Finally, to the east of the city are a number of small municipalities which include some of the most prosperous and expensive residential neighborhoods in the whole metropolis. Included here are Grosse Pointe, Grosse Pointe Farms, Grosse Pointe Shores, Grosse Pointe Woods, and Grosse Pointe Park.

The 1958 survey revealed the striking fact that in all but two of the twelve areas, one or another of the four socioreligious groups constituted a majority of the residential population, despite the fact that none of the groups enjoys a majority in the community as a whole. Furthermore, each of the groups appears to hold a majority in at least one of the areas.

Negro Protestants are in the majority in both halves of the inner city. In the eastern half of the inner city more than three quarters of the population are members of this group.

Despite the large size of their group, white Catholics form a majority in only two of the areas: the southern suburbs and the outer east side of the city of Detroit. In the middle east side of the city Catholics still constitute a plurality, but owing to the steady movement of Negroes into this area they no longer have a majority. Historically Catholics formed a majority on most of the east side of the city of Detroit. Still today Catholics outnumber white Protestants on the east side by a better than three-to-two margin.

The Jewish group is the most concentrated geographically. All of the Jewish respondents in the 1958 sample lived west of Woodward Avenue, and one third of them lived in the relatively small central section of the outer city just west of Woodward Avenue, in which Jewish residents appear to constitute a majority of the population. The remainder of the Jewish respondents in our sample were all located in four nearby areas (i.e., the northwestern and western suburbs, and the western portions of the middle and outer city areas).

White Protestants constitute a majority in the western portion of the outer city and in all of the suburban areas except the southern. In most of these areas their majority is small, but in the northwestern and north central suburbs the margin is more sizable. In the north central suburbs 70 per cent of the respondents in the 1958 survey identified themselves as white Protestants, while in the northwestern area 60 per cent did so.

Of the four major socio-religious groups, white Protestants rank with Catholics as the most widely scattered and the least concentrated. The relative degree of residential concentration of the four groups can best be seen in the Tau_b measure of association between area of residence and socio-religious group. The coefficients for the several groups were as follows:

Jews	.39
Negro Protestants	.37
White Protestants	.10
White Catholics	.07

The fact that the coefficient for the Jewish group was even higher than for the Negro Protestants is especially remarkable since Negroes are so severely limited in their choice of residential areas both by finances and by out-group hostility. The Jews are somewhat less limited than the Negroes by out-group hostility, and, as we shall see, are much less limited by finances than any other group. One can only conclude that the magnitude of this coefficient is one more indication of the strength of the communal spirit in this group.[36]

Religion and the class system

Differences in the geographical location of groups in a community are usually linked to differences in their location in the *class structure* of the community. Detroit is no exception to the general rule.

The heavy concentration of the Negro Protestant popula-

[36] For similar evidence based on a recent study of Montreal, see O. D. Duncan, "Residential Segregation and Social Differentiation," *International Population Conference*, Vienna, 1959.

tion in the least desirable residential sections is clearly a reflection of their position in the class structure. As shown in
Table 7, no other group has such a large percentage of its
family heads concentrated in the working class and so few in
the middle class.[37] More than two thirds of all Negro family
heads are in *the lower half of the working class.* No other
group has more than a quarter of its members in this class.

Table 7

PERCENTAGE OF RESPONDENTS IN VARIOUS CLASSES, BY SOCIO-
RELIGIOUS GROUP

Socio-reli-gious Group	Upper-middle[a]	Lower-middle[a]	Upper-working[b]	Lower-working[b]	Total	N[c]
Jews	43	30	9	17	99	23
White Protestants	19	25	31	25	100	259
White Catholics	12	27	35	25	99	220
Negro Protestants	2	10	19	69	100	94

[a] Upper-middle-class respondents are those in families in which the family
head was a businessman, a professional man, a clerk, or a salesman, and himself
had an income of $8,000 or more in 1957. Those in families whose head was
in a similar occupation, but earned less than $8,000, were classified as lower-
middle class.
[b] Upper-working-class respondents are those in families in which the head was
a manual worker or service worker who himself earned at least $5,000 in 1957.
Those in families whose head was in a similar occupation, but earned less than
$5,000, were classified as lower-working class.
[c] The income of the family head was not reported in 28 cases, and hence the
Ns shown here are slightly lower than the total Ns for each of these groups.

The group in the community which is best off economically
is clearly the Jewish group. Almost three quarters of its members are in the middle class, and nearly half in the upper-
middle class.[38] Differences between white Protestants and

[37] As we are using the term here and elsewhere throughout this
study, the term "middle class" refers to professional men, proprie-
tors, managers, officials, clerks, and salesmen and their families.
The term "working class" refers to foremen, manual workers, and
service workers and their families. For a justification and explanation of this division, see Seymour M. Lipset and Reinhard Bendix,
Social Mobility in Industrial Society (Berkeley: University of Cali-
fornia Press, 1959), pp. 14–17, 165–71, 180–81, and 289.
[38] Lest it be supposed that the small number of cases on which
this generalization is based makes it unreliable, it should be noted

white Catholics are generally quite small except that the white Protestants are half again more numerous than white Catholics in the upper-middle class. However, we have some reason for thinking that sampling error in the 1958 survey may have caused some overestimate of the proportion of Catholics in the middle class and some underestimate of their proportion in the working class, since in previous years the figure for middle-class Catholic families was usually closer to one third than to two fifths.[39]

These data concerning the relationship between socio-religious group membership and class position are of crucial importance for the interpretation of the findings set forth in the chapters which follow. Most of the forms of secular activity which we shall examine in Chapters 3 to 7 are linked with class position in some way. Because of this we shall constantly find it necessary to limit our comparisons between socio-religious groups to individuals in the same class. Failure to do this could only result in confusing the impact of the class system and the system of socio-religious groups.

---

that other surveys, both national and local, yield similar results. In the Goldberg-Sharp study based on three separate Detroit Area Studies, it was found that 40 per cent of Jewish family heads reported an annual income of $7000 or more compared with 16 per cent of non-Jewish families (op. cit.). Lazerwitz reports 54 per cent of Jews outside New York having a total family income of $7500 or more. "Jews in and out of New York City," *Jewish Journal of Sociology*, 3 (1961), p. 256.

[39] See Goldberg and Sharp, ibid., p. 112, for summary figure for the 1952, 1955, and 1956 samples combined. The largest discrepancy between their findings and those of the 1958 sample involve the Catholic group where there was a difference of 6 percentage points in the proportion in the middle class. For Negro Protestants there was a difference of 4 points, for white Protestants, 1 point, and for Jews the figures were identical.

Chapter 3

RELIGION AND ECONOMICS

Since Weber first drafted his controversial essay on the Protestant Ethic, revolutionary changes have overtaken the economies of Western nations. Though private enterprise is far from dead, these nations have clearly passed beyond the stage where capitalistic principles dominate the operation of the economy.[1] Even in the United States, which so often prides itself on being the last bastion of capitalism, capitalist institutions are hedged about with countless new arrangements designed to protect the masses of citizens against the consequences of the unchecked operation of a free enterprise system. Nowhere are these newer arrangements more evident than in the modern metropolis.

How have these changes affected the relationship between religion and economics? What role does religion play in the new economic order? Do Protestants rise more rapidly in the economic world than Catholics, as Weber claimed was once true? What is the position of the Jewish group in our modern economy? If socio-religious group membership makes a difference, is it because of the influence of the *churches* or the *subcommunities*? What influence do devotionalism and doctrinal orthodoxy have on economic behavior? These are the questions which we shall seek to answer in this chapter.

[1] See Karl Polanyi, *The Great Transformation: The Political and Economic Origins of Our Times* (New York: Rinehart, 1944).

I. SOCIO-RELIGIOUS GROUP MEMBERSHIP AND ECONOMIC BEHAVIOR

Vertical mobility

For many years following Weber's publication of his essays on the Protestant Ethic and the spirit of capitalism, it was generally accepted that Protestants were more successful than Catholics in the competition for economic advancement. The chief question debated was whether the Protestant advantage was *because of Protestantism, or in spite of it*.[2]

More recently, however, several scholars have challenged the assumption that Protestants are more successful than Catholics, at least when opportunities for advancement are equal. In the first of these studies, Mack, Murphy, and Yellin concluded that they are not.[3] Their study was based on questionnaire responses obtained from a sample of salesmen, engineers, and bank officials. These authors concluded that there were no statistically significant differences between Catholics and Protestants in either actual occupational advancement or aspirations for advancement. However, a careful analysis of their data indicates that their conclusion is not warranted so far as actual movement is concerned.[4] On the contrary, statistically significant differences did exist, demonstrating that Protestants were upwardly mobile more often than Catholics.

[2] See, for example, Tawney, op. cit.

[3] Raymond Mack, Raymond Murphy, and Seymour Yellin, "The Protestant Ethic, Level of Aspiration, and Social Mobility," *American Sociological Review*, 21 (June 1956), pp. 295–300.

[4] The authors divided their sample into six subsamples, each of which was analyzed separately and chi square values computed. When this is done, the normal (and proper) procedure is to add the chi square values and also the degrees of freedom, since the samples involved are independent tests of the same proposition. Also, a one-tail test should be used when testing a theory which predicts not merely the existence of differences but also their direction (as with Weberian theory). Had these things been done, the chi square value for father-son mobility would have been 14.2 with 6 degrees of freedom. A one-tail test shows that the differences which they found would not occur because of sampling error more than two times in a hundred, or well below the accepted limits for rejecting the null hypothesis.

In a more recent discussion of the same subject, Lipset and Bendix also report finding no differences between the rates of mobility of Catholics and Protestants, using a national sample of American men interviewed in connection with the 1952 presidential election.[5] However, their analysis of these data is somewhat cursory, and therefore their conclusions cannot be accepted at face value. Especially serious is their failure to control for the size of the community in which their respondents were raised. As they later demonstrate, this has a significant effect on mobility, with those raised in larger cities being more successful economically than those raised in small towns and on the farms.[6] This is important because census data show that while less than a quarter of the white Protestants in this country live in communities of 250,000 or more, more than half of the Catholics do.[7] Thus the Protestants in their sample competed under a severe handicap.

FINDINGS OF THE 1958 SURVEY

Our evidence from the 1958 Detroit Area Study survey is consistent with the actual findings of the Mack, Murphy, Yellin study, and indicates that white Protestant men rise further in the class system than Catholics. As is evident in *Table 8*, when white Protestants were compared with Catholics who began life at the same point in the class system, the former rose to (or stayed in) the ranks of the upper-middle class more often than the latter.[8] At the opposite extreme, Catholics wound up in the lower half of the working class more often than Protestants three out of four times. Differences were especially marked among the sons of middle-class men and farmers.

Unfortunately, there were not enough Jewish males in our sample to permit analysis, but the heavy concentration of

---

[5] Lipset and Bendix, op. cit., pp. 48–56.

[6] Ibid., pp. 204–13.

[7] U. S. Bureau of the Census, op. cit., Table 3.

[8] The probability that the predicted pattern would occur in four independent subsamples merely because of sampling error is less than .07. Here, and elsewhere in this book, binomial probabilities will be given in footnotes. For tests of the statistical significance of differences between two specific percentages, see the tables in Appendix I.

Table 8

OCCUPATIONAL LEVEL OF WHITE MALE RESPONDENTS, BY FATHER'S OCCUPATION, AND RELIGION, IN PERCENTAGES (1958 SURVEY)

Respondent's Occupational Level	Middle Class*		Upper-Working Class		Lower-Working Class		Farmer	
	C	P	C	P	C	P	C	P
Upper-middle Class	40	59	22	31	16	18	20	39
Lower-middle Class	28	14	15	7	18	5	0	0
Upper-working Class	20	27	48	38	21	42	40	30
Lower-working Class	12	0	15	24	45	34	40	30
TOTAL	100	100	100	100	100	99	100	99
Number of Cases	25	22	27	29	38	38	15	23

* Sons of lower-middle-class fathers were combined with sons of upper-middle-class fathers because the number of the former was insufficient to permit separate analysis and because the relative proportions of males at the two class levels were the same for Catholics and Protestants in the 1958 sample.

Jews in the middle class, and even the upper-middle class, found in all recent studies, including our own, indicates their rapid rise in the economic system.[9] Only a generation or two ago a substantial proportion of American Jews were manual workers.

In the case of Negro Protestants, our findings were hardly surprising. The great majority were sons of either farmers or semiskilled and unskilled workers. Their sons remain concentrated in the ranks of the semi- and unskilled. Of the 19 Negro Protestant sons of farmers, only 2 had escaped from the lower half of the working class. Among the 16 sons of lower-working-class fathers, only 3 had risen.

To a considerable degree this lack of mobility is due to white hostility and resistance, though this is probably not a sufficient explanation. Other groups, such as the Japanese, Chinese, and Jews, have gotten ahead despite opposition.

[9] In addition to the findings of our own study cited in Chapter 2, see Sklare, op. cit., Part 2, and Bigman, op. cit., pp. 29–31. See also census data from 1950 on the incomes of the Russian-born, who are largely Jewish.

This suggests that we must look for other factors if we are to explain fully the economic failure of Negro Protestants in Detroit and other northern metropolitan centers.

WELLER'S FINDINGS

Concurrent with the present study, and related to it, Neil J. Weller carried out an intensive analysis of vertical mobility among the most urbanized and Americanized segments of the white Catholic and Protestant groups.[10] His study was based on an analysis of 1100 white, male Catholics and Protestants raised in American communities of 25,000 or more in states north of the Mason-Dixon line. These men were interviewed in Detroit Area Study surveys from 1952 to 1958.

Weller's findings, based on six separate samples, are essentially the same as those obtained in the 1958 survey (see *Table 9*).[11] The chief differences occur among the *sons of upper-working-class fathers*. The 1958 data suggest that Protestants with this background are more likely than Catholics to arrive at both of the extremes in the class system, while his data suggest the opposite conclusion. This is a relatively minor inconsistency when compared with the general similarity in findings.

Because of the size of his sample, Weller was able to introduce into his analysis certain controls which were not possible in the 1958 data alone. For example, he introduced an important control for *ethnicity* to see if it was possible that the relative lack of success of Catholics in the job world might reflect economic discrimination against persons of southern or eastern European background. Such a hypothesis seemed

[10] Neil J. Weller, *Religion and Social Mobility in Industrial Society* (unpublished doctoral dissertation, The University of Michigan, 1960).

[11] It should be noted that the data reported in *Table 8* are included in *Table 9* as well. If one eliminates these overlapping data from his table and examines the eight independent samples (four from 1958, four from the other years), it may be seen that in 7 out of the 8 possible comparisons Protestants have risen to the ranks of the upper-middle class more often than Catholics. The probability of this occurring by chance is less than .04. The same probability holds with respect to decline to the ranks of the lower half of the working class.

Table 9

OCCUPATIONAL LEVEL OF WHITE MALES BY FATHER'S OCCU-
PATIONAL LEVEL AND BY RELIGION, IN PERCENTAGES (DETROIT
AREA STUDY SURVEYS: 1952–1958)

Respondent's Occupational Level	FATHER'S OCCUPATIONAL LEVEL							
	Upper-Middle Class		*Lower-Middle Class*		*Upper-Working Class*		*Lower-Working Class*	
	C	P	C	P	C	P	C	P
Upper-middle Class	32	49	28	38	28	27	16	26
Lower-middle Class	22	20	22	30	10	13	11	7
Upper-working ·Class	20	17	22	25	31	40	39	36
Lower-working Class	26	14	28	7	31	20	34	31
TOTAL	100	100	100	100	100	100	100	100
Number of Cases	99	157	36	40	202	205	276	162

Source: Weller, ibid, Table 10.

plausible in view of the much greater concentration of such
persons in the Catholic population. Weller's analysis demonstrated clearly, however, that this was not the explanation for
Catholic-Protestant differences. With both ethnicity and class
origins held constant, white Protestants advanced further on
the average in the job world than Catholics in all of the seven
possible comparisons.

Taking advantage of the size of his sample, Weller also
examined the important question of trends to see if there was
any evidence that Catholic-Protestant differences are declining
in magnitude. His analysis of this question was based on comparisons of the younger men (under forty) in his sample with
the older. His basic finding was that differences between Catholics and Protestants were equally great in the two age categories, and, if anything, were slightly larger among the
younger men. In short, Weller's data provide no support for
the hypothesis that Catholic-Protestant differences in this area
are declining.

On the basis of such evidence as is now available, it appears
that in the modern American metropolis socially significant
differences exist in the rates of mobility among the four major

socio-religious groups.) The Jewish group seems clearly to be the most successful, with white Protestants second, Catholics third, and Negro Protestants fourth. The only evidence to the contrary is the Lipset-Bendix study, which suggests that there is no difference between the Catholic and white Protestant groups. However, as noted previously, this evidence is based on a very limited analysis of the data.[12]

The fact that the Negro group ranks last and the Catholic group next to last suggests that success depends simply on economic opportunity, which in turn depends on the social acceptability of a group to the economically dominant white Protestants. However, the marked success of the Jewish group clearly indicates that the problem is more complex, for if this hypothesis were correct, Catholics should have been far more successful than Jews. Furthermore, in countries where Catholics were originally economically dominant (as in Latin America), we would expect Catholics to be more successful on the average than Protestants, but this does not seem to have been the case. In short, we are led to search for other factors if we are to develop a more adequate theory to account for these differences.

[12] Recent analyses of data gathered in two separate national surveys of the Survey Research Center of The University of Michigan appear to confirm one conclusion based on data from the Detroit area, namely, that Protestants are more likely to rise to the ranks of the upper-middle class than Catholics, even when level of origin is held constant. The first, by Elton Jackson and Harry Crockett, Jr., is entitled, "Occupational Mobility in the United States" (unpublished paper read at American Sociological Association meetings, 1962). The second, by Harold Organic, is a doctoral dissertation at The University of Michigan. The Jackson-Crockett sample reveals larger Catholic-Protestant differences than Weller's Detroit sample, but differences in the Organic sample are smaller than in Weller's. This suggests that Detroit may be reasonably typical of the urbanized sections of the non-southern parts of this country, at least in this respect (both recent analyses were limited to white males from the urbanized, non-southern parts of the country). In the two samples there were nine independent subsamples based on the class level of the respondents' fathers. Of these, Protestants were ahead in seven, and one ended in a tie. The mean net Protestant advantage was ten percentage points. Neither of these studies indicates, however, that there are any appreciable Catholic-Protestant differences in mobility to other levels in the class system.

Work values

As a first step in this direction, we were led to examine the responses of Detroiters to a series of questions we asked concerning the relative importance of various work-related values. Each person interviewed was asked to rank the following in order of their importance in a *man's* job:

1. High income
2. No danger of being fired
3. Working hours short, lots of free time
4. Chances for advancement
5. The work is important and gives a feeling of accomplishment

Each of these, we believed, represented a separate and distinct basis for evaluating jobs and careers. The last alternative is closest to the Protestant Ethic as conceived by Weber; it stresses both the worth of the work and the personal satisfactions it can afford. The first alternative, in contrast, stresses only the *extrinsic* satisfactions linked with work—the paycheck. In much of the current literature on the Protestant Ethic, this, together with a desire for advancement, is conceived to be the essence of the Protestant Ethic.[13] While it is undoubtedly futile at this late date to try to "purify" sociological usage, it may at least prove worthwhile to call attention to these two divergent conceptions of the Protestant Ethic. Of our five alternatives, the fifth best expresses the classical Weberian understanding of the term, the first the current popular understanding, while the fourth occupies the middle ground between them. A concern for chances for advancement is consistent with both the classical and current usages.

The third alternative on our list was designed to express a view completely in opposition to any conception of the Protestant Ethic. The second was designed with the same purpose, but in retrospect it seems somewhat less in conflict with the Weberian definition than it seemed at first, since it does express a desire to work.

[13] See, for example, William H. Whyte, *The Organization Man* (New York: Simon & Schuster, 1956).

If our interpretation of the relation of these five values to Weberian theory is correct, it is amazing how strong a hold the Protestant Ethic, in the classical sense, has on all segments of the American population. Nearly half of those we interviewed ranked the fifth alternative first, and two thirds selected either the fourth or fifth alternatives. In contrast, only 4 per cent ranked "short hours" first.

When we divided Detroiters by class, we found, as expected, that the strength of the Protestant Ethic varies directly with class level. In the lower half of the working class, only a third ranked the fifth alternative first; in contrast, three quarters of the upper-middle class ranked it first. Members of the lower-middle class were the most likely to choose a chance for advancement as their first choice; members of the upper-middle class were the least likely. All of the other three values found their greatest popularity in the lower-working class and the least support in the upper-middle class. Thus it seems that while the Protestant Ethic is a pervasive influence in American life, it finds its greatest support in the middle, and more especially in the upper-middle, class.

When we explored the relationship between vertical mobility and these five work values, we expected to find that upwardly mobile men would lay great stress on chances for advancement. To our surprise we found that *downwardly* mobile men were the most likely to rank advancement first. Half of them chose this alternative compared with less than a third of the upwardly mobile men and about a quarter of the non-mobile men. The first choice of the upwardly mobile men was "work which is important and gives a feeling of accomplishment." *In brief, both our analysis of the distribution of work values by class and of their relationship to vertical mobility indicated that this fifth alternative stands in a very special relationship to occupational success.*

Building on this finding, we turned next to the problem of how socio-religious group membership was linked to these values. Perhaps the most striking finding was that all three white groups rank the fifth alternative at the top of their list. The percentages ranking this alternative first were as follows in each of the four major groups:

White Protestants	52 per cent
Jews	48 per cent
White Catholics	44 per cent
Negro Protestants	24 per cent

The application of controls for the class position of respondents and of their parents, and for the education of respondents had two chief effects. First, it reduced (but did not eliminate) the difference between the Negro and white groups. Second, it revealed that the differences between white Protestants on the one hand and Jews and Catholics on the other are greater among the better educated and in the middle classes than among the less well educated and the working classes.

If Jews and Catholics were less likely than white Protestants to value "work which is important and gives a feeling of accomplishment," they were more likely to value chances for advancement and high income. The percentages placing these two values first were as follows:

Jews	45 per cent
White Catholics	40 per cent
Negro Protestants	40 per cent
White Protestants	31 per cent[14]

These findings appear to confirm the belief that there are two different though related systems of work values which are often confused by being given the same label, "the Protestant Ethic." Both undoubtedly are capable of motivating men to work hard and achieve, but the nature of the motivation is not the same, and one would expect other differences to follow from this. White Protestants seem clearly to display the classical pattern of the Protestant Ethic more often than members of the other three groups. However, Jews and Catholics are more likely to display those qualities which today are commonly regarded as exemplifying the Protestant Ethic. Al-

[14] A recent study by Father Andrew Greeley reports similar differences among 1961 college graduates. On the basis of a national sample, he reports Jewish graduates were the most likely to express an interest in "making a lot of money." Catholics ranked second, Protestants third. *The Influence of Religion on the Career Plans and Occupational Values of June 1961 College Graduates,* unpublished doctoral dissertation, University of Chicago, 1962.

though there is clearly a difference between these two systems
of work values, it would be a great mistake to suppose that
they are antithetical to one another. Clearly they are not;
those who rate income and chances for advancement high in
their hierarchy of values usually rate the intrinsic satisfactions
high also, and vice versa. This suggests that perhaps the best
way to conceive of their relationship is to think of them as
variations on a basic theme, rather than as two distinct
themes.

If we take this view, it seems clear that it would be difficult
to explain the relative success of Jews and white Protestants
in terms of differences in this area. Perhaps some small part
of the relative success of members of these two groups can be
attributed to their greater valuation of the intrinsic satisfactions to be found in work, but the percentage differences involved are so small that we must look elsewhere for the major
part of the explanation.

Attitudes toward work

In Weber's classic essay on the Protestant Ethic, an entire
chapter is devoted to a discussion of Luther's doctrine of "the
calling." It was Weber's contention that this important Protestant doctrine played a major role in the formation of the
spirit of modern capitalism. Luther insisted that all worthwhile
occupations are equally important in the sight of God, and
that God calls some men to serve Him as cobbler, farmer, and
magistrate, just as He calls others to serve Him as minister or
priest. In this way he reoriented his followers' thinking about
work and its importance in life. For those Protestants who
took Luther's doctrine of the calling seriously, secular vocations provided a vehicle for service to God just as much as
religious vocations. Work was no longer merely a means for
earning the necessities of life; it was one of the major means
by which men might serve God. Hence, a man did not labor
as little as possible, as he might when confronted with a task
that was merely difficult and unpleasant. Rather, he worked
as hard as possible.

As Weber pointed out, the doctrine of the calling came to
be modified in the Calvinist tradition, and subsequently un-
derwent still further modification at the hands of Deists such

as Benjamin Franklin. However, the important point, Weber argues, is that, beginning in the sixteenth century, those in the Protestant tradition were trained to take a very different view of work from those raised in the Catholic tradition. Catholics continued to regard work primarily as a necessary evil; a consequence of Adam's fall and a penalty for sin. By contrast, Protestants came to view it as an opportunity for serving God, or, in the Deist version, for building character.[15]

To date almost nothing has been done to explore the relevance of Weber's thesis for the world of work in contemporary

[15] As illustrative of the difference, compare the following statements of Martin Luther and St. Thomas Aquinas. Luther writes: "Your work is a very sacred matter. God delights in it, and through it he wants to bestow his blessing on you. This praise of work should be inscribed on all your tools, on the forehead and the face that sweat from toiling. For the world does not consider labor a blessing. Therefore it flees and hates it. . . . But the pious, who fear the Lord, labor with a ready and cheerful heart; for they know God's command and will. Thus a pious farmer sees this verse written on his wagon and plow, a cobbler sees it on his leather and awl, a laborer sees it on wood and iron: 'Happy shalt thou be, and it shall be well with thee.'" Ewald Plass, ed., *What Luther Says: An Anthology* (St. Louis: Concordia Publishing Co., 1959), Vol. III, p. 1493, or see Roland Bainton, *Here I Stand* (New York: Abingdon-Cokesbury, 1950), pp. 233–34, where examples from Luther's table talk are cited. Compare these with St. Thomas' explanation of the four reasons for work: "Manual labor is directed to four things. First and principally to obtain food; wherefore it was said to the first man: 'In the sweat of thy face shalt thou eat bread' . . . Secondly, it is directed to the removal of idleness whence many evils arise . . . Thirdly, it is directed to the curbing of concupiscence, inasmuch as it is a means of afflicting the body . . . Fourthly, it is directed to almsgiving. . . . It must, however, be observed that under manual labour are comprised all those human occupations whereby man can lawfully gain a livelihood, whether by using his hands, his feet, or his tongue." *The Summa Theologica of St. Thomas Aquinas*, translated by the Fathers of the English Dominican Province (London: Burns Oates & Washbourne, 1932), II–II, Q. 187, 3.

While two swallows do not make a spring, the quotations cited above seem typical of the references to man's labor found in the two writers. Even more interesting are their treatments of Adam's banishment from the Garden of Eden. St. Thomas mentions only the unpleasant consequences; Luther takes the view that labor would be even more satisfying than it is, had it not been for Adam's sin.

American society. In what may be the only study with evidence on this subject, Melville Dalton found that, in one industrial plant which he studied, white Protestant machinists worked harder and produced more than Catholics in comparable jobs.[16] He found that Catholics were much more likely than Protestants to deliberately restrict output.

In our present study we have no work records such as Dalton used. Instead, we are obliged to rely on the expressions of attitudes toward work supplied by Detroiters in interviews in their homes. However, while our evidence is inferior to Dalton's in this respect, we have the advantage of a much broader and more representative sample.

In an effort to gain some insight into the influence of religion on job performance, we asked each of the men we interviewed the following question:

> Some people tell us that they couldn't really be happy unless they were working at some job. But others say that they would be a lot happier if they didn't have to work and could take life easy. How do you feel about this? (Q. 5)

We then asked:

> Why is that? (Q. 5a)

On the basis of their responses to these two questions, each of the members of our sample was placed in one of three categories. First there were those who expressed a *positive* attitude toward work. That is to say, they valued work for its own sake, or for the intrinsic rewards it provides. In this group also were those who rejected a life of ease because they regarded it as immoral. As a Baptist engineer expressed it:

> Man must have a purpose in life and something to occupy his mind. I get great satisfaction from my work.

A Lutheran businessman put it this way:

> Man wasn't made to be idle. The happiest people I know are very active. Man is happiest when he is creating

16 Melville Dalton, "Worker Response and Social Background," *The Journal of Political Economy,* 55 (1947), pp. 323-32.

something or loving something. It is an inherent trait in man to want to see something he has created.

A Jewish craftsman put the matter much more simply when he said:

I like to work.

A Negro Baptist welder told us:

It just isn't right if you're not working.

All of the men cited above said that they would not be happy unless they were working. However, there were others who gave the same answer to the first question, but in explaining why, indicated that work itself had no positive attraction for them. Rather, they found the alternatives even less attractive, or in some instances they indicated that they would go on working because they liked extrinsic rewards linked with work. These we classified as persons with a *neutral* attitude toward work.

The answer of a Catholic postal clerk is typical of a large number of such responses. He said that he would be unhappy not working, but when asked why this was, he said:

I wouldn't want to just loaf. I guess I'd want to do something, but it wouldn't have to be a job. (Why is that?) You'd get bored doing nothing.

Or, as a Lutheran photoengraver expressed it:

I'd rather work. It's a healthier life. Otherwise I'd always be boozing it up.

A Catholic high school science teacher said he didn't care if he worked or not, providing he had enough money to take care of himself.

Some people, however, made it clear that they would quit their jobs immediately if they were financially independent. Their *negative* attitude toward work was highly evident. For example, a Lutheran optician said:

I feel I could take life easy if I had enough money. Traveling or gardening would be nice.

A Catholic insurance adjuster told us:

I have a certain nature which likes to lay around without doing anything—maybe it's inborn laziness.

Jewish males were the most likely to express a positive attitude toward work, with 42 per cent indicating this. White Protestants ranked second with 30 per cent, Negro Protestants third with 24 per cent, and Catholics last with 23 per cent.

One might suppose that the difference between white Protestants and Catholics simply reflects Old World influences and the peculiar cultural heritage of recent Catholic immigrants, who are often of peasant stock. However, this did not seem to be the case. Catholics who were northern-born, third-generation Americans were much more likely to have a *negative* attitude toward work than were first- and second-generation immigrants (36 vs. 14 per cent).[17] By contrast, among northern-born white Protestants, the more Americanized were a bit more likely to have a *positive* attitude toward work (30 vs. 24 per cent).[18] While the latter difference may well be due to sampling error, the difference involving Catholics does not seem to be. On the basis of such evidence we can only infer that Protestant-Catholic differences in this area involve much more than mere differences in degree of Americanization and urbanization. In fact, Americanization and urbanization appear to increase, rather than reduce, differences between these two major socio-religious groups.[19]

We found an even more striking and important difference between white Protestants and Catholics when we analyzed attitudes toward work with class position held constant. Among Protestants, positive attitudes toward work were *more* frequent and negative attitudes *less* frequent among men holding *more* responsible positions than among men in *less* responsible positions. Among Catholics this relationship was *reversed*,

[17] There were 22 men in the former category and 69 in the latter.

[18] There were 40 men in the former category and 37 in the latter.

[19] Unfortunately, there were too few Jewish males and too few northern-born Negro males in our sample to permit us to extend our analysis of the effects of urbanization and Americanization to these groups.

as shown in *Table 10*.[20] To sum up, *it appears that Protestantism is conducive to more positive attitudes toward those positions in society which are more demanding (and also more rewarding), while Catholicism is conducive to more positive attitudes toward the less demanding (and hence less rewarding) positions.* This could well be an important factor contributing to the differences in economic success noted previously.[21]

This last finding suggests, however, that more is involved than just the Protestant doctrine of the calling. If Protestants have a more positive attitude toward work than Catholics solely because of their commitment to this doctrine, this difference ought to be evident *at all class levels*. But this is not the case among manual workers. This suggests that something more than this doctrine is involved. Just what this "something more" is will become apparent both in the pages which follow and in Chapter 5 when we examine the interrelations between religion and family life.

[20] Unfortunately, once again there were so few Jewish male respondents, and so few Negro Protestant males in white-collar positions that it was not possible to extend this analysis to them.

[21] Professor Charles Westoff of New York University informed me that he has found similar differences between white Protestant and Catholic men in their degree of commitment to work. His findings are based on interviews with 1165 young couples living in seven of the eight largest metropolitan centers in this country, and reflect responses to a battery of nine questions. His differences persisted both when the class position and educational attainments of the respondents were controlled. It also seems significant that these differences were more marked among middle-class men than working class, and among college-educated men than those lacking this. However, contrary to my findings, he found a positive correlation between commitment to work and level of responsibility among Catholics (though the correlation was not as high as among Protestants). The other important difference involved the Jewish respondents. With class position controlled, middle-class Jewish males ranked between white Protestants and Catholics, while working-class members of the group showed the least commitment to work. For details of this study see Charles Westoff, Robert G. Potter, Philip Sagi, and Elliott Mishler, *Family Growth in Metropolitan America* (Princeton, N. J.: Princeton University Press, 1961). However, the findings cited here have not yet been published.

Table 10

PERCENTAGE OF MALE DETROITERS HOLDING POSITIVE, NEU-
TRAL, AND NEGATIVE ATTITUDES TOWARD WORK, BY CLASS,
AND SOCIO-RELIGIOUS GROUP

S-r. group: Class*	ATTITUDE TOWARD WORK:				N	Positive Minus Negative
	Positive	Neutral	Negative	Total		
White Protestants:						
Upper-middle	36	52	12	100	25	24
Lower-middle	32	57	11	100	19	21
Upper-working	23	56	21	100	39	2
Lower-working	30	33	37	100	27	—7
White Catholics:						
Upper-middle	19	56	25	100	16	—6
Lower-middle	18	57	25	100	28	—7
Upper-working	18	64	18	100	38	0
Lower-working	33	48	19	100	21	14

* Both classes are divided here on the basis of the income of the family head. In the middle class the dividing line is $8,000; in the working class it is $5,000.

Religion and the labor movement

In the modern world, labor unions are an institutionalized expression of a very distinctive set of values which have gained wide acceptance in recent times. Above all, they embody the concern of wage laborers with security in a world dominated by the free labor market, where neither legal nor moral ties bind workers to their jobs in any enduring fashion. The unions also express the workers' concern with problems of wages, hours, and working conditions and their commitment to the collectivist approach in solving these problems.

In many respects the values for which the unions stand are in opposition to the values embodied in the "Protestant Ethic" and the "spirit of capitalism." For example, the Protestant Ethic and the spirit of capitalism stress the intrinsic satisfactions which could, or should, be gained from work; but the unions have usually acted on the premise that work is a necessary evil, and the less of it, the better. The Protestant Ethic encourages men to strive to do their very best; the unions have sought to replace the standard of excellence with the standard of seniority as the basis for hiring and firing. In short, the union movement has sought to replace the situation where a few men enjoy the benefits of their commitment to work and their personal excellence with a situation where the masses can enjoy greater security, and sometimes even prosperity.

Because unions symbolize such a distinctive set of economic values, they afford a useful point of reference for the social analyst. By observing the attitudes of people toward unions, we can infer much about their economic values.

In Detroit today the overwhelming majority of manual workers are union members. This is largely because a few giant corporations dominate the labor market. Manual workers in these corporations have been successfully organized, and union shops have been established which compel most manual workers to become union members shortly after they are employed.

At the other end of the scale—among business and professional men—the unions have made little headway. Between these extremes lies the lower-middle class: the level of the lower-white-collar worker, the clerk, and the salesman. It is at this level, and only at this level, that any large number of Detroiters are free to choose whether or not to join a union. They are therefore ideal subjects for our present inquiry.

Slightly over a quarter of the male workers in the lower-middle class in Detroit are union members. White Catholics in the lower-middle class are far more likely to become union members than are white Protestants. Thirty-eight per cent of the former, but only 15 per cent of the latter belonged to unions.[22] Unfortunately, there were not enough Negro Protestant or Jewish males in this class to extend the comparison to them.

Among manual workers there were, as expected, no significant differences in the percentages of men who were union members in each of the three larger socio-religious groups.

[22] We used here the responses of housewives concerning their husbands as well as the responses of the men, so that we might have more cases. The percentages are based on 27 Catholics and 33 Protestants.

In each group approximately three quarters were union members.

(Mere membership in a union is not a particularly reliable indicator of men's economic values. Far more important are their attitudes toward unions and union policies, and their degree of activity in union affairs. Using such indicators, we can discover the individual who is forced against his wishes to become a member of a union, and who shares none of its goals or values. We can also use such indicators to identify those individuals who, while not members of any union, share the basic values of the trade union movement.)

In the 1957 Detroit Area Study several questions were asked which are relevant here.[23] In one of these, union members were asked how often they attended union meetings. Negro Protestants reported attending "all" or "most" meetings more often than either Catholics or white Protestants. The percentage in each group saying they attended all or most meetings was as follows:

Negro Protestants	29 per cent	(24 cases)
White Catholics	26 per cent	(46 cases)
White Protestants	17 per cent	(65 cases)

A second question asked of these men was how much interest they had in their union. Seventy-five per cent of the Negro Protestants described themselves as "strongly" interested in their union. By contrast, only 52 per cent of the Catholics and 42 per cent of the Protestants were "strongly" interested.

On still another question the men were asked whether their union took stands on controversial political issues, and if so, whether they generally agreed with its stand. The great majority of Negro workers were unaware that their union took stands on controversial political issues, so it was not possible to use this question as a measure of their support of union values. Comparing white Catholics and Protestants, however, a substantial difference was noted. While 88 per cent of the Catholics expressed support for their union's position on con-

[23] These and other data from the 1957 Detroit Area Study were made available to the author through the courtesy of Professors Daniel Katz and Samuel J. Eldersveld, who were jointly the chief investigators that year.

troversial issues, only 63 per cent of the white Protestants did so. In short, *these measures indicate that while white Protestant workers may be union members with roughly the same frequency as Catholic or Negro Protestant workers, they are less supportive of the union program and of the values for which the unions stand.*

In the 1952 survey of the Detroit Area Study one additional question was asked which is very relevant to our present subject. In that year half of those interviewed were asked whether they believed that the majority of members of the CIO would agree with them on controversial political issues of an economic nature (such as those involving price controls and National Health Insurance, issues which were then in the news). They were also asked whether they believed that the majority of businessmen would agree with them on these same issues. As shown in *Table 11*, white Protestants were the most likely to expect businessmen to agree with them, and the least likely to expect members of the CIO to agree with them. These patterns held good in the middle class as well as the working class.

Table 11

PERCENTAGE EXPECTING TO FIND MAJORITY OF BUSINESSMEN, OR MAJORITY OF MEMBERS OF THE CIO, AGREEING WITH THEM ON CONTROVERSIAL POLITICO-ECONOMIC ISSUES, BY SOCIO-RELIGIOUS GROUP AND CLASS (1952 SURVEY)

Class: S-r. group	Percentage expecting to find majority of CIO members agreeing with them	N	Percentage expecting to find majority of businessmen agreeing with them	N
Middle Class:				
White Protestants	33	34	73	44
White Catholics	50	24	57	37
Jews	(88)	8	64	11
Working Class:				
White Protestants	70	56	51	69
White Catholics	89	44	45	49
Negro Protestants	90	29	47	32

These data are especially valuable since they indicate more precisely the nature of the white Protestant objection to unionism revealed in the 1957 and 1958 surveys. (The unions deviate too much from the traditional pattern of middle-class economic values with which businessmen have long been identified, and with which the Protestant Ethic is linked.) Quite clearly, working-class Protestants have an affinity for middle-class economic values, while middle-class Catholics have an affinity for working-class values. Our data indicate that the pull of working-class values on the middle-class Catholics is somewhat stronger than the pull of middle-class values on the working-class Protestants.

Similar findings have recently been reported by Glantz as a result of his study of a sample of white Philadelphians in 1952.[24] In this study Philadelphians were asked whether they agreed or disagreed with six partisan statements, three taken from the publications of the National Association of Manufacturers, three from publications of the CIO. Respondents were classified into three groups on the basis of their answers: those who were (a) business-oriented; (b) labor-oriented; and (c) indeterminate. Among middle-class respondents 41 per cent of the Protestants, but only 21 per cent of the Catholics, were classified as *business*-oriented. Among working-class respondents 43 per cent of the Catholics, but only 28 per cent of the Protestants, were classified as *labor*-oriented.

Self-employment: the entrepreneurial spirit

Historically, those who sought to get ahead usually went into business for themselves. As the names of Henry Ford and Andrew Carnegie attest, great fortunes could be amassed by the talented and ambitious. While few enjoyed the success of these men, many others became wealthy and prosperous following the time-honored formula of "striking out on your own."

Today, however, the situation is different. With the growth of giant corporations, the modern entrepreneur is forced more

[24] Oscar Glantz, "Protestant and Catholic Voting Behavior in a Metropolitan Area," *Public Opinion Quarterly*, 23 (Spring 1959), pp. 73–82.

and more into the field of retail commerce where competition is severe and bankruptcies frequent. (The most promising fields today for those who wish to be self-employed are in the professions, especially law and medicine; but even here the large firm is gaining ground at the expense of the small private practice.)

In view of these changes in the organization of economic activity, one might well expect to find no differences among socio-religious groups so far as the frequency of self-employment is concerned. However, this is not the case. Nearly half of the 27 male heads of Jewish families in the 1958 survey were self-employed. By contrast, only 7 per cent of the male heads of non-Jewish families were self-employed. Similar findings were reported by Goldberg and Sharp on the basis of their analysis of the 1952, 1955, and 1956 surveys.[25] In other studies of Washington, D.C. and New York City, approximately one third of the Jewish males were found to be self-employed, which, while somewhat lower than the figure for Detroit, is still well above the figure for non-Jews in these cities.[26]

(Scholars are generally agreed that the high rate of self-employment found in the Jewish group represents a traditional Jewish response to Gentile discrimination.) Barred from employment and advancement in many business firms dominated by Gentiles, Jews have been forced into occupations where they are not dependent on the good will of others. Despite these limitations, Jews have been extremely successful, as we have seen.

Differences between white Protestants and Catholics were generally quite small, *until an effort was made to limit comparisons to persons raised in similar settings.* When comparisons were based on all employed males, 8 per cent of the Catholics and 10 per cent of the Protestants were found to be self-employed. However, when immigrant generation and region of birth were held constant, larger differences emerged. Among first- and second-generation immigrants, Protestants were twice as likely to be self-employed as Catho-

[25] Op. cit., p. 112.
[26] Bigman, op. cit., p. 27, and Ben B. Seligman, "The Jewish Population of New York City: 1952," in Sklare, op. cit., p. 102.

lics (15 vs. 8 per cent). Among third-generation Americans raised outside the southern states, Protestants were three times as likely to be self-employed (12 vs. 4 per cent).[27] Similar results were obtained when Detroiters were asked if they had ever been self-employed at any time in their lives. (Protestant men were twice as likely as Catholics to report that at some point in their careers they had been self-employed.) In short, it appears that even in the bureaucratized modern metropolis there are real and significant differences among the major socio-religious groups in the degree to which they value occupational independence and autonomy, with the Jews ranking first, white Protestants second, and Catholics third.)

Belief in the possibility of success

Linked with any system of values one typically finds a set of *beliefs about the nature of man and the world* which complement the values and give them sense and meaning. Such is clearly the case here. (Those who support the values embodied in the spirit of capitalism typically maintain that adherence to such values brings success.) Typically they argue that those who work hard and do their work well are bound to rise and win recognition. The Horatio Alger myth is a classic example.

In the 1952 survey two questions were asked to determine whether individuals accepted a *modified* version of certain elements contained in the Horatio Alger myth. These questions were:

1. Some people think that the children of workingmen have little chance of becoming well-to-do and important businessmen, while other people think they have a good chance. How much chance do you think they have these days of becoming well-to-do and important businessmen?

[27] Among first- and second-generation immigrants there were 39 Protestants and 71 Catholics; among members of the third generation there were 42 Protestants and 24 Catholics. No comparison of the southern-born was possible since no Catholic males were southern-born. Of the 23 southern-born white Protestants, only one was self-employed. In addition to the persons cited above, there were 16 Catholics and 11 Protestants for whom the necessary data on immigrant generation were not available.

2. Some people say that the men who are getting to be important people in the community are getting there *mainly* because of their family connections. Which do you feel is more important—a person's own ability or his family connections?[28]

As might be expected, the middle class was more likely than the working class to believe in the availability of opportunities for workingmen's sons and in the importance of ability. For this reason we again had to limit comparisons between the socio-religious groups to persons in the same class.

As predicted, white Protestants were more inclined than others to believe that the sons of workingmen have good chances for advancement (see *Table 12*). This was true on both class levels. On this question there was little difference between Jews and Catholics in the middle class, and little difference between Catholics and Negro Protestants in the working class.

Table 12

PERCENTAGE BELIEVING WORKINGMEN'S SONS HAVE GOOD CHANCES FOR ADVANCING AND THAT ABILITY RATHER THAN FAMILY CONNECTIONS ARE THE MAIN FACTOR IN SUCCESS, BY SOCIO-RELIGIOUS GROUP AND CLASS (1952 SURVEY)

Class: Socio- religious Group	Percentage believing workingmen's sons have good chances to advance	Percentage believing ability more important than family connections	N
Middle Class:			
White Protestants	73	89	120
Jews	59	90	22
White Catholics	61	71	83
Working Class:			
White Protestants	62	82	200
White Catholics	51	70	164
Negro Protestants	52	66	62

On the second question, white Protestants and Jews both expressed great confidence in the value of ability. Catholics

[28] Emphasis in original question.

and Negro Protestants, by contrast, were more often critical of this traditional article of faith.

On first inspection one might suppose that the responses of the four groups to these two questions were simply reflections of the degree of discrimination each encounters in its struggle for advancement. White Protestants rarely encounter racial or religious discrimination in employment; Negro Protestants encounter more than anyone else. Hence the difference in outlook.

Such a view greatly oversimplifies the problem as shown by the fact that there is no appreciable difference in the views of Negro Protestants and Catholics despite numerous indications that job discrimination against Negroes is far, far greater than that against Catholics. Similarly, if attitudes were merely reflections of objective conditions in the job market, we would expect Jews to be more pessimistic than Catholics. Yet neither of these relationships was found. (Jews have much more confidence in ability than Catholics, and Catholics have little more than Negro Protestants.) These findings indicate that such attitudes are partly independent of the extent of objective discrimination against groups. Whatever their origin, lack of confidence in ability and in chances for upward mobility almost certainly inhibit many Catholic youths who might otherwise rise in the system.

In the 1958 survey we also asked a question designed to discover to what degree beliefs about the nature of God stimulated or inhibited efforts to get ahead. The question was:

> Do you think that God is more pleased when people try to get ahead, or when people are satisfied with what they have and don't try to push ahead? (Q. 50)

White Protestants were, as expected, the most likely to perceive God as desiring to see men get ahead. Negro Protestants were the most likely to perceive God as desiring men to be content with what they have.[29] Among the three white

[29] Judging from comments made by respondents, this proved to be a difficult question for many to answer. Many said, "God is pleased to see men try to get ahead, providing they don't hurt others in the process."

groups, differences were quite small, with 60 per cent of the white Protestants, 58 per cent of the Jews and 55 per cent of the Catholics seeing God as favoring efforts to get ahead. Among Negro Protestants the figure dropped to 33 per cent. The utilization of class controls did not change the ordering of the groups except that middle-class Negro Protestants were comparable with middle-class whites in the frequency with which they perceived God as endorsing men's strivings.

It is noteworthy that the biggest differences between white Catholics and Protestants occurred at the higher class levels, where, as we have seen before, Catholics seem to do least well, and seem least well-adjusted. Among college-trained persons in middle-class families where the head of the family earned $8000 or more per year, 85 per cent of the white Protestants (N=20) perceived God as endorsing striving, but only 62 per cent of the Catholics (N=13) shared this belief. When we used college education alone as the criterion, 79 per cent of the white Protestants (N=42), but only 66 per cent of the Catholics (N=41) believed God endorses striving. These data further support our earlier image of the higher status Catholic as one who lacks many of the values and beliefs appropriate to his status, and whose children may therefore become downwardly mobile with greater frequency than the children of his non-Catholic peers.

Spending and saving

Shifting from the economics of production to the economics of consumption, we inquired into the manner in which families use their income. To what degree is it saved and transformed into capital? How much of it is utilized for the purchase of consumable goods in general, and luxury goods in particular?[30]

[30] The questions used in this section of the study were developed in consultation with Professors George Katona and James Morgan of the Consumer Finance Studies section of the Survey Research Center of The University of Michigan. On their advice, attitudinal rather than behavioral questions were used in this area because they reported that they have found the attitudinal data highly correlated with the behavioral, and less likely to destroy rapport with the respondent.

INSTALLMENT BUYING

Early in the 1958 interviews we asked Detroiters whether they thought that it was a good or bad idea to buy things on the installment plan (Q. 8) and why they felt as they did (Q. 8a).

Some endorsed the idea wholeheartedly. For example, a Catholic steelworker said:

> If we waited until we got enough money to buy things, then there wouldn't be any business. That's why this country is so well off.

Or, as an optimistic Presbyterian housewife expressed it:

> It's the American way of life.

Others, however, were less sure that installment buying is good for either the individual or the nation. A Negro Presbyterian in the painting and contracting business said:

> Most people have a tendency to overspend themselves. This is bad for the individual and bad for the economy.

A Baptist businessman with a large income said:

> I look at things as an investment. The average cost of installment buying is too high.

Or, finally, a Negro janitor's wife explained her opposition to installment buying in this way:

> At first the businessmen have sugar in their mouths, but when you can't pay they curse you. I don't like it.

Detroiters were sharply divided in their views on the subject. Forty-six per cent thought it a good idea, 38 per cent disapproved. Criticism of installment buying was most often expressed by Jews, 56 per cent of whom thought it unwise. White Protestants ranked second with 44 per cent disapproving, Catholics third with 40 per cent, and Negro Protestants last with 35 per cent.

One striking finding was that among Catholics disapproval of installment buying is more frequent among newer immigrants than among the more Americanized, whereas just the opposite is true among Protestants (*Table 13*). These data point to the conclusion that once again the two major economic groups are diverging rather than converging in economic attitudes and behavior (see also *Attitudes toward work*).

Table 13

PERCENTAGE OF NON-SOUTHERN-BORN DETROITERS DISAPPROVING OF INSTALLMENT BUYING, BY SOCIO-RELIGIOUS GROUP, IMMIGRANT GENERATION, AND CLASS

Socio-religious Group: Immigrant Generation	CRITICAL OF INSTALLMENT BUYING:			
	Middle Class		Working Class	
	Per cent	N	Per cent	N
White Protestants:				
Third generation	38	60	51	41
1st and 2nd generations	34	32	42	53
White Catholics:				
Third generation	35	31	35	34
1st and 2nd generations	41	51	39	84

The reasons which Detroiters gave for disapproving of installment buying also revealed differences, especially among members of the working class. (White Protestants were much more likely to disapprove because they felt it morally wrong, or because they felt it harmed a person's character and was likely to establish a pattern of financial irresponsibility.) Thirty per cent of the working-class white Protestants, but only 18 per cent of the working-class Catholics, and 9 per cent of the working-class Negro Protestants, disapproved on these grounds.

BUDGETING

Immediately after the question on installment buying, we asked our respondents whether they kept careful records of how much they spent on things (Q. 9 and 9a). We were especially interested to discover if Protestants were more likely than Catholics to budget family expenditures. In the light of Weber's discussion of Puritan character, we expected that such differences would exist.

(Actually, however, Catholics proved a bit more likely than white Protestants to keep detailed family budgets, though the difference between the groups was negligible) (15 vs. 13 per cent). Apparently very few families keep detailed budgets, and the majority keep no financial records at all. The only group keeping detailed financial records with any frequency was the Jewish group. A quarter of the Jewish respondents reported keeping family budgets, but even in this group slightly more than half kept no records of any kind.

SAVINGS

Next we turned to the subject of savings. (First we asked respondents whether or not they had a savings account, owned government bonds, or saved in any other way (Q. 10). The overwhelming majority of our white respondents said they did.) Ninety-six per cent of the Jews, 85 per cent of the white Catholics, 83 per cent of the white Protestants, but only 35 per cent of the Negro Protestants reported savings.

This told us little, however, about the extent or regularity of savings in the several groups. We did not feel that we could ask people directly how large their savings were, since some would be unable to answer and others might be seriously annoyed by such a question.[31] Instead, we relied on a

---

[31] Such a question was asked in the 1960 survey (a study of white males, aged 21–55 in the lower-middle and upper-working classes) and substantial differences were found between white Protestants and Catholics even when income was held constant. For example, of those earning $6000–$9999 per year, 27 per cent of the Protestants (N=112) but only 7 per cent of the Catholics (N=154) reported savings in excess of $5000. In the same category 46 per cent of the Protestants and 16 per cent of the Catholics reported savings of $2000 or more. Among those with incomes of $10,000–$13,000 a year, 54 per cent of the Protestants (N=37) and 41 per cent of the Catholics (N=39) reported savings of $5000 or more. See Ronald Johnstone, "The Protestant Ethic in a Modern Metropolis" (mimeographed paper, Detroit Area Study, 1960). These data were obtained from Harold Wilensky's study of labor and leisure, and will be fully reported in his forthcoming book, *The Middle Mass* (Glencoe: The Free Press).

series of questions concerning their attitudes toward saving. These questions were:

1. Do you think every family should save a part of its income every month, or not? (Q. 11)

If they answered "Yes" to this question, we then asked:

2. How important do you feel this is—should people save even if it means doing without some things they could really use, or should they save only when they can do it without trouble? (Q. 11a)

3. Why do you feel saving is important? (Q. 11b)

(Virtually everyone agreed that families should save a part of their income every month. But when we moved to the second question it became clear that many feel that people should not try to save if this means they must deprive themselves of things they can use.) Only half of Detroiters took the stern view. Jews were the most likely to favor doing without things in order to save, with 58 per cent expressing this view. Slightly less than half of the members of the other three groups shared this view. In other words, except for the Jewish group, differences were negligible.

It was not until we reached the third question that larger differences began to emerge. To begin with, we observed moderate differences in the *number* of reasons Detroiters gave to support the view that saving is important. While this may have depended partly on the extent of their formal education, it seems likely that it is also related to the intensity of feeling on the subject.[32]

Jewish respondents were the most likely to offer multiple reasons for believing saving important. One third of them did so. White Protestants ranked second with 28 per cent, Catholics with 19 per cent, and Negro Protestants fourth with 11 per cent offering multiple reasons. When class controls were introduced, the chief effect was to reduce the differences in

[32] The latter is strongly suggested by the fact that there were noteworthy differences between the three white socio-religious groups in the number of reasons they gave why saving is important (see the next paragraph), yet differences in extent of formal education among the groups were very small (see Chapter 6).

the middle class between Jews and white Protestants and between Catholics and Negro Protestants. Among middle-class respondents 37 per cent of the Jews and 36 per cent of the white Protestants and 23 per cent of both Catholics and Negro Protestants gave multiple reasons. Among working-class respondents the pattern was much the same as in the total sample.

Among working-class respondents, there were interesting variations in the types of reasons they advanced for believing that saving is important. Some saved to attain some *major long-range goal* such as the purchase of a home, higher education for their children, or security later in life, while others were only concerned with short-range needs and emergencies. Twenty-two per cent of the working-class white Protestants cited some long-range goal. This figure was even higher (by a small margin) than that for any of the middle-class groups. By contrast, only 11 per cent of the working-class Catholics and 7 per cent of the working-class Negro Protestants said they were saving to attain some major, long-range goal.

The relevance of this difference for our earlier findings concerning vertical mobility can hardly be exaggerated. Higher education is expensive, especially at the better colleges and universities. For families with low incomes, it is imperative that a program of savings be instituted years in advance of the time children attain college age.

In view of these data on savings, it seems more than coincidence that, among persons from working-class families, nearly twice as many white Protestants as Catholics have attended college. Among the sons and daughters of workingmen, 16 per cent of the white Protestant respondents but only 9 per cent of the Catholics had attended college. The importance of college attendance as a means of social advancement is revealed by the fact that among white Protestant and Catholic children of workingmen, those with at least some college training were more than two and a half times as likely to rise to the ranks of the middle class as those whose education did not go beyond high school (78 vs. 29 per cent).

Summary

Before turning to the second major section of this chapter, it may be profitable to review our findings up to this point. (In this first section we have sought to discover in what ways and to what degree the major socio-religious groups differ in economic attitudes, beliefs, values, and behavior.) While the magnitude of the differences has varied considerably, the pattern has been strikingly stable. (On the great majority of variables either the Jews or the white Protestants have ranked first with the other ranking second, the Catholics have usually ranked third, and the Negro Protestants fourth.) With considerable regularity the Jews and white Protestants have identified themselves with the individualistic, competitive patterns of thought and action linked with the middle class, and historically associated with the Protestant Ethic or its secular counterpart, the spirit of capitalism. By contrast, Catholics and Negro Protestants have more often been associated with the collectivistic, security-oriented, working-class patterns of thought and action historically opposed to the Protestant Ethic and the spirit of capitalism.

These findings recall the debate between Weber and Sombart earlier in the century concerning the role of the Jews in the creation of the spirit of capitalism.[33] Sombart suggested that everything Weber ascribed to Puritanism might with equal justice be ascribed to Judaism, and probably in greater degree.[34] In fact, Sombart suggested that Puritanism was essentially a modified form of Judaism, and that Judaism was an earlier and historically more important source of the spirit of capitalism.

Weber vigorously rejected this hypothesis, maintaining that Judaism merely gave rise to "speculative pariah-capitalism," or "financial capitalism," while Puritanism gave rise to "bourgeois capitalism" with its distinctive elements of ethical universalism, the shattering of the extended family system, the rationalization and depersonalization of economic relationships, and so forth. In other words, Weber believed Judaism produced a sterile form of capitalism which lacked

[33] Sombart, op. cit.; Weber, The Protestant Ethic, op. cit.
[34] Sombart, ibid., pp. 191–92.

that potentiality for revolutionizing the social order which he believed inherent in bourgeois capitalism.

It is not our purpose in this study to attempt to unravel the difficult historical problem of the origin of the capitalist spirit. Our concern is with the relationship between religion and "the spirit of capitalism" today. Regardless of whether Protestantism or Judaism is the progenitor of modern capitalism, both faiths currently develop in their adherents attitudes, values, beliefs, and behavior patterns which are in keeping with the spirit of capitalism to a greater degree than those developed by Catholicism. Regardless of whether one accepts or rejects Weber's view that Judaism was incapable of generating the modern capitalist system, it seems clear that the Jewish subculture greatly facilitates the rise of individuals in an established capitalist system.

One final point should be noted here. Frequently when comparisons were limited to third-generation Americans raised in the North, differences between socio-religious groups proved more pronounced than similar comparisons involving the total sample. This suggests that the differences may not stem *merely* from lingering cultural traditions of the past, but that conditions of life in the modern metropolis may actually generate, or magnify, differences between socio-religious groups. This is a rather startling finding, quite contrary to the predictions of most students of the urban community, who constantly stress the homogenizing tendencies of the metropolis and metropolitan institutions. If the findings of this study are valid, it looks as though this sweeping generalization, so long an integral part of the theories of urbanism, may well require critical re-examination. Evidently, when men who have been trained from early childhood in different social systems and have internalized differing sets of values are exposed to common stimuli, the result does not have to be convergence in attitudes, values, or behavior. Apparently the stimuli may activate tendencies which previously lay dormant, and thus produce larger, instead of smaller, differences in behavior.

II. GROUP INVOLVEMENT AND ECONOMIC BEHAVIOR

Associational involvement

One question is immediately raised by our findings concerning differences in economic thought and action among the several socio-religious groups. Have *the churches* contributed to these differences, or are they the result of other influences? Are the churches as irrelevant and uninfluential in the economic realm as many people think, or do they play a role in shaping and molding economic attitudes, values, beliefs, and behavior?

This is not an easy question to answer, but as a first step we shall compare those members of each of the groups who were *more* actively involved in their church with others in the same group who were *less* actively involved.[35] If the churches do contribute to these differences between socio-religious groups, we would expect that the greater the degree to which white Protestants are involved in their churches, the more likely they will be to display the individualistic, competitive, rationalistic patterns of thought and action identified with the Protestant Ethic and with the middle class. Similarly, we would expect that the more Catholics and Negro Protestants are involved in their churches, the more they will display the collectivistic, security-oriented, anti-entrepreneurial working-class patterns of thought and action. If, however, the churches are irrelevant and have no effect on economic behavior and attitudes, we would expect to find no noticeable differences between those members of a given group who attend their church regularly, and those who do not, when other relevant factors are controlled.

ECONOMIC SUCCESS AND ASSOCIATIONAL INVOLVEMENT

In examining the relationship between involvement in the churches and vertical mobility, we found that upwardly mobile men (i.e., middle-class sons of working-class or farmer

[35] Unfortunately, owing to the small number of Jewish respondents, such comparisons were not possible in this group.

fathers) were more likely to be regular church attenders than non-mobile men, in both the middle and working classes. Among white Protestants 38 per cent of the upwardly mobile men (N=19) were regular church attenders compared with 31 per cent of the non-mobile middle-class men (N=16) and 16 per cent of the non-mobile working-class men (N=62). Among Catholics 78 per cent of the upwardly mobile (N=27), 76 per cent of the non-mobile middle class (N=17), and 58 per cent of the non-mobile working class (N=52) reported regular church attendance.

While these figures suggest that church attendance may be conducive to upward mobility we cannot ignore the possibility that active involvement in the churches may be a *consequence*, rather than a *cause*, of vertical mobility. The high level of involvement among the upwardly mobile may simply represent conformity, or even overconformity, to middle-class norms.

In an effort to resolve this problem, we examined the relationship between vertical mobility and the religious situation in the home in which these respondents were raised. This was possible since we had gathered data on the religious commitments of respondents' parents (Q. 36 and 38) as well as on the respondents themselves.

When we compared white Protestants raised in working-class families in which both parents were highly religious with those raised in working-class families in which this was not true, we found a notable difference in the percentage who had risen to the middle class.[36] Among the 43 children of devout working-class or farm parents, 51 per cent had risen to the ranks of the middle class. By contrast, only 31 per cent of the 102 children of other working-class and farm parents had been as successful.

When we divided these respondents by sex and by class background (working class vs. farm), the same pattern

[36] The parents of a respondent were classified as highly religious if (a) the respondent reported attending worship services every week and if he further stated that *both* his mother and father were at least as religious as he, or (b) if the respondent reported that he attended worship services less than once a week but at least once a month, and that *both*, of his parents were *more* religious than he.

emerged in *all four* subsamples. The pattern was more pronounced among women than among men.[37] The class background of respondents apparently had no effect on the relationship.

Not only were the children of devout Protestant parents more likely to be upwardly mobile, they were also somewhat less likely to be downwardly mobile. Of the 16 children of devout parents in business or the professions, 38 per cent were downwardly mobile, compared with 47 per cent of the 15 children of less devout parents. While this difference is too small to be statistically significant, it is worthy of note in view of the evidence on upward mobility.

These data strongly indicate that the relationship of the individual white Protestant to his church *antedates* upward mobility. Thus, while it is plausible to argue that this relationship is merely due to the attraction which church membership and activity have for the successful middle-class Protestant, the causal relationship seems to operate more often in the opposite direction. This is not to deny that to some degree there is a two-way flow of influence. As a result of modern research, social theorists are becoming more aware of the fact that in human affairs influence normally operates on *two-way* streets with some traffic moving in each direction. Hence, positive correlations between variables frequently reflect mutual reinforcement rather than a simple relationship where one variable is the cause and the other the effect. However, this is not to say that the flow of traffic on all streets is equally heavy in both directions. On the contrary, quite often most of the traffic moves in one direction. In the present instance our data indicate that a high degree of involvement in the white Protestant churches more often stimulates upward mobility than the other way round.

In the case of Catholics the situation seems quite different. Using the same mode of analysis, we found that 31 per cent of the sons and daughters of devout Catholic workers and farmers had been upwardly mobile (N=84). Of the children of less devout Catholic workers and farmers, 39 per cent

[37] Among men there was a percentage difference of 13 points; among women it was 29 points.

had been upwardly mobile (N=38). In short, there was either no relationship, or a negative relationship between the commitment of Catholics to their church and the economic success of their children. Once again this pattern was more pronounced among women than among men.[38]

When the sons and daughters of Catholic professional men and businessmen were studied, it was found that those raised in devout families were somewhat more likely to be downwardly mobile than those raised in less devout families (64 vs. 50 per cent). Since there were only 14 persons in each of these categories, the difference was too small to be statistically significant, though noteworthy because of its similarity to our other findings.

On the basis of these data it appears that involvement in the Catholic Church does not have the same consequences as involvement in the white Protestant churches. At best it seems to be irrelevant to mobility, and at worst, something of a hindrance. The relationship between upward mobility and *current* church attendance among Catholics therefore appears to be a result of the influence of mobility on attendance rather than the reverse, as appears to be the case among white Protestants. The fact that upwardly mobile sons and daughters of working-class and farm parents are more faithful in their attendance at Mass seems to reflect conformity, or overconformity, to the standards of their new social peers rather than the influence of childhood socialization.

OTHER TYPES OF ECONOMIC BEHAVIOR

These conclusions were reinforced by our analysis of the relationship between associational involvement and economic attitudes, beliefs, values, and behavior of other types. On the overwhelming majority of the questions asked, white Protestants who were active in the churches were more likely to take a stand consonant with the spirit of capitalism than were marginal members of the group. Among middle-class Protestants, this pattern was observed in 12 out of 14 questions where comparisons were possible; among members of the

---

[38] Among men there was a difference of 3 percentage points; among women 14 points.

working class, the pattern was observed on 14 out of 17 questions.[39]

The situation among Catholics proved to be quite different. Our data indicate that involvement in the Catholic Church is *not* conducive to commitment to the spirit of capitalism. There is either no relationship, or perhaps even a slight negative relationship. Comparisons among middle-class Catholics were possible on 14 questions, and on only 6 did the active churchgoers express views consonant with the spirit of capitalism more often than the marginal members. Among working-class Catholics this same pattern was observed in only 5 out of 13 comparisons.[40]

On 12 questions our sample included enough active and inactive members of both socio-religious groups in both classes for uniform comparisons to be made. *Table 14* gives some indication of the average magnitude of the differences involved. At both class levels there is a steady progression from the active Catholics to the active Protestants, with the percentage of responses consonant with the spirit of capitalism steadily increasing. White Protestants who are active in the churches are nearly half again as likely to take stands consistent with the spirit of capitalism as those active in the Catholic Church.

It is not practicable to examine in detail each of the patterns of response for both socio-religious groups at both class levels for all of the many items. However, there are some differences among the items which deserve special attention. In the first place, involvement in the white Protestant churches is quite clearly associated with some measure of hostility toward the labor unions. For example, 34 per cent of the Protestant male workers who rarely if ever attend church (N=64) reported being strongly interested in the unions in the 1957 survey, but only 17 per cent of the irregular church-

[39] The reason for the difference between the classes in the number of questions was that several of the items were asked only of union members and there were not enough middle-class union members to make comparisons possible.

[40] It was not possible to make three of the comparisons made among white Protestant workers because there were so few Catholic workingmen who were *both* inactive in the church and also union members.

Table 14

MEAN PERCENTAGE OF RESPONSES ON 12 ITEMS CONSONANT WITH THE SPIRIT OF CAPITALISM,* BY SOCIO-RELIGIOUS GROUP, DEGREE OF ASSOCIATIONAL INVOLVEMENT, AND CLASS

Socio-religious Group: Degree of associational involvement	Middle Class: Per cent	N	Working Class: Per cent	N
White Protestant: active	53	43	40	33
White Protestant: marginal	45	74	35	116
White Catholic: marginal	40	17	31	35
White Catholic: active	38	74	29	101

* The items included are: (1) positive attitude toward work; (2) disagreement with majority of CIO members on controversial issues; (3) agreement with majority of businessmen on controversial issues; (4) believe workingmen's sons chances of advancement good; (5) believe ability more important than family connections; (6) believe God loves those who strive; (7) now self-employed; (8) ever self-employed; (9) disapproves of installment buying; (10) keeps budget; (11) gives multiple reasons for saving; (12) has long-range goals for saving.

goers (N=23) and 4 per cent of the most active churchgoing workers (N=25) shared this interest. In the 1952 survey 55 per cent of the active churchgoing Protestant members of the working class (N=20) believed that most members of the CIO would disagree with them on controversial political issues, but only 35 per cent of the irregular participants from this group (N=20) and 28 per cent of the marginal members who rarely attended (N=50) shared this view. Finally, in the 1958 survey we found that none of the active, middle-class, Protestant men (N=16) had joined a union, but 19 per cent of the marginal members of the group had (N=31).

A second area of noteworthy differences involves self-employment. Whereas 31 per cent of the active, middle-class, white Protestant men (N=16) were self-employed, this was true of only 6 per cent of the marginal members (N=31). In the working class the difference was much smaller, the comparable figures being 8 and 5 per cent (Ns=12 and 57). Also noteworthy is the fact that marginal members of the white Protestant churches were much more likely to have shifted out of self-employed positions into the ranks of those hired by others. Whereas 62 per cent of those active middle-class, white Protestant males who had ever been self-employed were still self-employed at the time of the interview in 1958, the same was true of only 19 per cent of the marginal members of the group. Among members of the working class the comparable figures were 30 and 22 per cent.

Involvement in the white Protestant churches was also strongly associated with the belief that ability is more important than family connections in getting ahead, with agreement with businessmen in controversial economic and political issues, and, among working-class people, with a critical view of installment buying.

There were, however, two important questions which produced *no* evidence that involvement in the white Protestant churches strengthened commitment to behavior patterns usually associated with the spirit of capitalism. First, we found no evidence that involvement in the white Protestant churches intensifies aspirations for advancement.[41] When respondents were asked to choose between chances for advancement, high income, economic security, and other items, marginal members of the group were as much concerned with advancement as the more active members. This is consistent with our earlier finding that there are no appreciable differences between Protestants and Catholics in this respect.

Second, and more surprising, we found no evidence that involvement in the churches increases the frequency of positive attitudes toward work on the part of men. On the contrary, those who were marginal to the churches seemed a bit more likely to hold a positive attitude toward work than were those who were more active. This again suggests that the Protestant churches have allowed the doctrine of the calling to be neglected.[42]

[41] At least this was true when men and women were combined. For men alone a small relationship was observed with 29 per cent of those active in the churches ranking a chance for advancement ahead of all other criteria, compared with 23 per cent of the marginal members of the group.

[42] Contrary to this finding, Westoff found a positive relationship between commitment to work and involvement in the Protestant churches. This was especially evident among men in the working class. He found no such relation among Catholic men. See footnote 21, page 97 above.

As *Table 14* indicates, differences between marginal and active Catholics were generally small. A few, however, were large enough to deserve comment. At both class levels active Catholics were more likely to believe that God prefers to see men strive to get ahead rather than rest content with what they have. This indicates that involvement in the Catholic Church does not reduce aspirations. Active working-class Catholics were also more likely than marginal members to rank chances for advancement higher in their hierarchy of job-related values. Finally, active working-class Catholics were much less often critical of installment buying than were marginal members, and active working-class Catholic males were much less likely to have a positive attitude toward work than were marginal males. Over-all, there were not many substantial differences, and most of them occurred when the active Catholics were *less* committed than marginal Catholics to standards associated with the spirit of capitalism.

One of the more surprising findings in this area concerned the Negro Protestant churches and their relationship to the spirit of capitalism. We had expected that involvement in the Negro Protestant churches would be *negatively* linked with commitment to the spirit of capitalism, since the group as a whole lacked a strong commitment. However, such was not the case. Those who were active in the Negro Protestant churches were *more* likely to express views consonant with this spirit than were marginal members. On 10 out of 15 questions this relationship was observed. On the 12 items used in *Table 14*, 30 per cent of the responses given by the active, working class, churchgoers were consistent with the capitalist spirit, but the same proved true of only 24 per cent of the responses of the marginal members.

A comparison of these figures with the corresponding figures for *working-class* white Catholics and Protestants is extremely interesting. Active Negro Protestant churchgoers actually show a higher frequency of responses compatible with a capitalist orientation than active Catholics. Furthermore, the difference between active and marginal members within the Negro Protestant group is greater than the difference within the white Protestant group, indicating that the Negro Protestant churches exercise an even stronger influence than the white Protestant churches. If Negro Protestants in Detroit do not generally exhibit as strong a commitment to the spirit of capitalism as members of other groups, this is not because of the influence of the churches—it is *in spite of* their influence.

These findings are especially significant in view of the very different social situation of the Negro and white Protestant groups. If we were to adopt the position of the economic determinists, we would inevitably predict that Catholics would occupy a position intermediate between that of white and Negro Protestants so far as economic thought and action are concerned, since both historically and currently the economic situation of American Catholics has been intermediate between that of Negro and white Protestants. Our findings indicate, however, that the common elements of the Protestant tradition shared by these latter groups constitute a very real factor in the situation. Despite the marked economic differences which still divide white Catholic and Negro Protestant workers, the two groups are currently quite similar in their basic economic values. This suggests that if and when the objective differences in economic status are reduced, Negro Protestants will come to resemble white Protestants in economic beliefs, values, attitudes, and actions more closely than Catholics because of the influence of their churches.

Communal involvement

When we examined the interrelations between vertical mobility and the involvement of white Protestants and Catholics in their subcommunities, we found that a *high* degree of communal involvement was consistently linked with a *low* rate of vertical mobility. Those who were highly involved in their socio-religious subcommunities were less likely *either* to have risen *or* to have fallen in the class system than were those who were more marginal to the group. This pattern was especially marked for Catholics.

Among Catholic sons and daughters of workingmen and farmers, only 22 per cent of those who were highly involved in their subcommunity at the time of the 1958 survey (N=67) had risen to middle-class status. By contrast, 38 per cent of those who were less highly involved (N=97) had been upwardly mobile. Among Catholic sons and daughters of middle-class fathers, only 21 per cent of those highly involved in their subcommunity (N=14) had fallen to the ranks of the working class, as against 36 per cent of those who were less involved (N=39).

Among white Protestant sons and daughters of workingmen and farmers, 34 per cent of those highly involved in their subcommunity (N=61) had risen to middle-class status. The corresponding figure for the less highly involved (N=153) was 37 per cent. Among white Protestant sons and daughters of middle-class fathers the comparable figures for downward mobility were 22 and 34 per cent (Ns=18 and 32).

These figures again pose the difficult problem of causality: is a high rate of vertical mobility a *cause* or a *consequence* of the separation of individuals from their socio-religious subcommunity? Unfortunately, this time our data do not permit us to settle this important question. On logical grounds it seems possible that a high rate of mobility may be both cause and consequence of such separation, but one can build a somewhat stronger case for the thesis that mobility causes a weakening of communal ties than for the opposite thesis.

On one point, however, the findings seem clear. When considering vertical mobility the *differences* between the two subcommunities are much less important than their *similarities*. In other words, it is the relationship of the individual to *some* subcommunity, rather than his relationship to a *specific* subcommunity which is important. This is especially true when we are considering probabilities of downward mobility. It seems to matter little whether an individual is highly involved in the Catholic or the white Protestant subcommunity, as long as he is highly involved in some subcommunity.

When the relations between degree of communal involvement and other aspects of economic behavior were examined, no differences of any magnitude could be found in either the white Protestant or Catholic groups.[43] This suggests that the

[43] Among middle-class white Protestants, those who were highly involved in the white Protestant subcommunity gave responses 45 per cent of which were in conformity with the standards of the spirit of capitalism compared with 42 per cent conformity among those less highly involved. Among working-class white Protestants

churches, rather than the subcommunities, are the primary source of the differences in economic behavior between these two major groups.

III. RELIGIOUS ORIENTATIONS AND ECONOMIC BEHAVIOR

When the relationships between religious orientations and economic behavior were examined, evidence indicated that devotionalism is linked with upward mobility and also with many of the patterns of thought and action associated with the spirit of capitalism. This was not true, however, in the case of doctrinal orthodoxy. Our data indicate that this type of religious orientation was not linked either with upward mobility, or with most of the elements associated with the spirit of capitalism.

Devotionalism

Among white Protestant and Catholic sons and daughters of workingmen and farmers, 37 per cent of those who ranked high in terms of devotionalism had been upwardly mobile (N=134), compared with 31 per cent of those who ranked low (N=232). At the same time, of the respondents raised in *middle-class* families, only 29 per cent of those who ranked high in terms of devotionalism were *downwardly* mobile (N=42), compared with 33 per cent of those who ranked low (N=58). In other words, those ranking high in terms of devotionalism were slightly more successful than those ranking low. This pattern was observed despite the fact that Catholics were somewhat more numerous among those ranking high. Hence there is no reason to believe that this relationship is an artifact of our earlier finding that Catholics are generally less mobile than Protestants.

Noteworthy differences were also observed when other as-

---

the comparable figures were 32 and 30 per cent, for middle-class Catholics 37 and 35 per cent, and for working-class Catholics 29 and 28 per cent. The questions involved here differ slightly from those which served as the basis for *Table 14*, since we had no data on communal involvement for any survey except that conducted in 1958.

pects of economic behavior were examined. The largest of
these differences appeared in connection with the attitudes
toward work of middle-class males. Those ranking high in
terms of devotionalism (both white Protestants and Catholics)
were twice as likely to express a positive attitude toward work
as those ranking low (41 vs. 21 per cent: Ns=27 and 58).
Those ranking high were also noted for their criticisms of installment buying, their tendency to save for long-range goals,
and their use of budgets. There were, however, no differences
to speak of with respect to aspirations for advancement,
record of self-employment, or number of reasons given for
believing saving important. On the question of whether God
prefers to see men strive to advance themselves or be content
with what they have, those ranking high in terms of our measure of devotionalism were a bit more likely to believe that God
prefers to see men be content.

Doctrinal orthodoxy

By contrast with our finding concerning the relationship between mobility and devotionalism, we found that the *less*
orthodox white Protestants and Catholics were somewhat more
likely to have risen in the class system than those who were
more orthodox. However, the difference was small and could
well be due to sampling error. What is important in this instance is the fact that doctrinal orthodoxy and devotionalism
are clearly something more than two interchangeable indices
of "religiosity." Men's religious commitments clearly take different forms, even within a given group, and these variations
seem linked with variations in secular behavior. Especially
intriguing is the evidence that *these commitments, or orientations, seem able to transcend group loyalties and thus produce similarities in behavior among members of different
groups who share a common orientation.*

On most of our measures of economic behavior and attitudes we could find no difference linked with variations in
degree of orthodoxy. There was, however, one notable exception. This involved men's attitudes toward work. Here a strong
relationship was observed. Among white Catholics and Protestants, those who were not so orthodox were twice as likely to
express a positive attitude toward work as the more orthodox

(33 vs. 16 per cent: Ns=66 and 60). In this area the contrast between doctrinal orthodoxy and devotionalism was extremely pronounced, with the two orientations seeming to pull men strongly in opposite directions.

The problem of causation

These findings, especially those involving the relationships between devotionalism and economic behavior, again pose the difficult problem of causation. Which is cause, and which effect?

Economic determinists always have a ready answer to such questions. However, our earlier findings concerning the relationship between vertical mobility and socio-religious group membership make one skeptical of the fundamental tenets of their theory. Furthermore, all of the differences in economic behavior associated with differential commitment to these two religious orientations are differences which we established *with the class positions of respondents held constant.* In other words, if people committed to the devotional orientation are more often advocates of the spirit of capitalism, this cannot be explained simply on the grounds that they are more often members of the middle class while those who lack this commitment are more often members of the working class.

On the basis of our data we cannot assert positively that the religious orientations to which a man is exposed, and to which he becomes committed, actually influence his actions in the economic field. Nevertheless our findings create a strong suspicion that this is in fact the case. If religious ideas and beliefs have any impact at all on economic behavior, it seems reasonable to suppose that the differences in ideas and beliefs associated with the various religious orientations are not without consequences. This is a subject which deserves far more attention than it has yet received.[44]

[44] From the beginning of this study, the examination of the influence of religious orientations on secular institutions has been secondary to our concern with the role of socio-religious groups in daily life. Thus in both the design and analysis of the data it has not been possible to explore this area as fully as it deserves. In future research in this area it is to be hoped that a systematic effort will be made to determine the types of religious orientations dominant in the childhood experience of individuals, since only when

IV. ECONOMIC DETERMINISM
RE-EXAMINED

On the basis of the evidence presented in this chapter it seems safe to conclude that religion makes a difference in the behavior of men in the realm of economic activity. We should not exaggerate the magnitude of this influence, but neither should it be minimized. If there is any single variable which might be regarded as a key factor influencing economic behavior, this is surely class position. Therefore it is significant that, on the whole, differences between *socio-religious groups*, with class controlled, are not much smaller than differences between *classes*, with socio-religious group controlled.

As we have seen, religion makes a difference in several respects. Not only are there differences among the several socio-religious groups, but important differences also frequently exist *within* each group, depending upon the degree and type of religious involvement of the individual and the type, or types, of religious orientation which he has adopted. As a general rule, *commitment to the spirit of capitalism:*

(1) is especially frequent among white Protestants and Jews;

(2) is much less frequent among Catholics and Negro Protestants, even when position in the class system is held constant;

(3) is positively linked with regularity of church attendance among Protestants, both Negro and white;

(4) is negatively correlated with communal involvement both among white Protestants and Catholics;

(5) is linked with a high level of devotionalism in all three of the larger socio-religious groups: Catholic, white Protestant, and Negro Protestant;

(6) stands in no consistent relationship to degree of doctrinal orthodoxy.

To assert that religion is a factor influencing the economic

one has established the anteriority of religious orientations can one handle adequately the important problem of causality.

attitudes and actions of men raises ultimately the question of *why* this should be so. Two major schools of thought present themselves at this point. On the one hand (as we noted earlier) there are those who look for an explanation in terms of factors *external* to the religious groups, such as their location in the class structure. By contrast, the second school focuses on the attributes of the religious groups themselves, especially their theology, and seeks to find the explanation there.

The critical difference between these two schools of thought lies in their basic premises. Members of the first school assume that all systems of thought are mere epiphenomena, shaped and molded by economic forces in particular, and social conditions in general. Members of the second school assume that ideas are something more than this. They believe that the origin and subsequent development of ideas are governed to some degree by their own immanent principles, and to attempt to treat social conditions as the sole cause and explanation of systems of thought is to be guilty of the fallacy of reductionism.

The data obtained in this study do not permit us to prove or disprove either of these theories, but they do shed some light on the problem, and therefore it may be well to reconsider the issues in the light of our evidence.

Much of the evidence turned up in this study fits in well with the theory that social conditions determine systems of thought. For instance, it seems more than coincidence that white Protestants are the most likely to express commitment to the spirit of capitalism, followed by white Catholics and Negro Protestants in that order. This constellation of values which we have labeled "the spirit of capitalism" might well have been called "the middle-class ethic," or perhaps even "the upper-middle-class ethic." In other words, our data indicate that members of an economically advantaged group think and act in a manner appropriate to members of an economically advantaged group, and conversely, members of a disadvantaged group, such as the Negro Protestants, think and act in a manner appropriate to their social situation.

Admittedly, working-class white Protestants tend to think and act like middle-class people almost as often as middle-class Catholics. However, this may be explained on the grounds (that a man's behavior is conditioned as much by the social situation of the group to which he belongs as by his own personal situation.) For example, many of the attitudes and actions of *middle-class* Catholics in our society represent *working-class* responses to life because of the historic position of the Catholic group as a whole in American society. Historically, the overwhelming majority of Catholics have been members of the working class. Even more important, throughout American history the majority of *leaders* in the Catholic group have been persons raised in the working class. By contrast, the white Protestant group has always had a higher percentage of members in the middle class. Even though the majority of white Protestants may not have been raised in the middle class, the majority of their leaders probably have since leaders are normally recruited from higher status levels than other members of the group.

The marked differences in economic behavior between white and Negro Protestants might also be cited as strong evidence to support the first thesis described above: that the social conditions in which a group finds itself, rather than its theology, determine the economic attitudes and actions of its members. The theological positions of these two groups are not very different, yet there are marked differences in the economic behavior of their members. Similarities in theology obviously cannot account for differences in economic behavior.

While one cannot deny that there are real and important links between the social situation of individuals and groups and their economic behavior, this is not to say that these differences in social situation are the whole (or even the chief) explanation for the differences in economic behavior. Far too many difficulties present themselves for one to accept such a view.

To begin with, if such a view is valid, why should there be a relationship between degree of devotionalism and commitment to the spirit of capitalism when the social situations of individuals are held constant? Yet within the limitations set by the size of the sample with which we are working, this seems to be the case. When we hold constant the class position both of individuals and of the socio-religious group to which they belong, differences persist between those who are strongly devotionalistic and those who are not.

A second finding which raises difficulties for the strict "environmentalist" view is that commitment to the spirit of capitalism varies with degree of involvement in Protestant churches, *both* Negro and white. If it varied with associational involvement in the white Protestant churches only, one might argue that associational involvement was a subtle measure of the individual's involvement in an organization dominated by members of the middle class—and therefore only a measure of his exposure to middle-class values. But this is clearly not the case where involvement in the Negro churches is concerned. Since the Negro churches are overwhelmingly made up of working-class people, one would expect involvement in these churches to reinforce *working-class* values, according to any logical derivation from environmentalist theories. As Marx pointed out more than a century ago, class consciousness is stimulated by interaction among persons whose position in the class structure is comparable. Yet we found that such interaction as occurs among members of the working class within the context of the Negro Protestant churches in Detroit facilitates and stimulates identification with economic values long linked with the *middle class*.

A third finding which raises difficulties for the environmentalist position is the remarkable similarity in economic values between the Negro Protestant and white Catholic members of the working class. As we have already noted, the Negro Protestants are disproportionately concentrated in the lower half of the working class when judged by income and occupation. White Catholics are much more evenly distributed (see *Table 7*, page 80). Furthermore if one considers the economic situation of *the group* rather than that of *the individual*, the differences become even more pronounced: a much larger percentage of the members of the Catholic group are members of the middle class. Even so, Negro Protestants differ very little from Catholics in the frequency with which they express commitment to the spirit of capitalism. In fact, when comparisons are limited to the active churchgoers among the working-class members of the two groups, Negro Protestants rank somewhat ahead of white Catholics in this respect. While the

differences between Negro and white Protestants may reflect
the influence of social conditions on economic values, the
similarities between Negro Protestants and white Catholics
seem to indicate that economic values are shaped by something more than economic conditions alone.

Yet another difficulty which confronts the environmentalist
is that of accounting for the phenomenal success of the Jewish
group and their strong commitment to most elements of the
capitalist spirit. Starting as poor immigrants fifty or seventy-
five years ago, the members of this group have advanced to
the point where they are in Detroit, and probably throughout
the country as a whole, the most prosperous of the major
socio-religious groups. They have far outdistanced the Catholics who came to this country a generation or two earlier,
and have even moved ahead of the white Protestants who
originally dominated the positions of privilege in this country.

We cannot account for these successes merely by saying
that the Jews were a minority group subject to discrimination
and therefore challenged to work harder than other groups.
Other minorities have been confronted with similar situations
without responding in this fashion. One may invoke their
urban background in Europe as a factor contributing to their
success. Without denying its influence, we are led to ask why
urban experience has not had a greater effect on the Catholics
in this country. The great majority of Catholic immigrants
settled in urban centers while the Protestants have been
heavily concentrated in the rural areas. Yet three generations
of urban experience seem to have done little to stimulate
Catholic commitment to the spirit of capitalism. In fact, in
many respects Catholic commitment to this system of values
seems higher among first- and second-generation immigrants
(more often of rural background) than among members of
the third generation (typically of urban background). In
brief, the urban experience of the Jews in Europe would seem
at best a necessary cause, but never a sufficient cause for their
economic behavior.

In view of the evidence available both from this study and
elsewhere it appears that the strict environmentalist position,
which explains economic behavior solely in terms of the social
situation of the individual and the group, is untenable. This

is not to deny that social conditions, and especially those of an economic nature, are powerful forces influencing such behavior. However, other factors also exercise a significant influence. Notable among these are the belief systems, or ideologies, to which men subscribe: phenomena whose existence seems limited, but not determined, by the social conditions to which their originators and subsequent proponents are exposed. This is a subject to which we shall return in the final chapter when we have all of the relevant evidence in hand.

Chapter 4

RELIGION AND POLITICS

3 4

In the modern world the boundary between economics and politics has become quite blurred. As the economic systems of nations have become increasingly complex, making men more and more dependent upon vast impersonal economic forces which no single individual or private group can control, men have increasingly shifted the responsibility for crucial economic decisions to agencies of government.

Even in our own nation, which frequently prides itself on being a staunch defender of capitalism, this trend is very apparent. During the last half century we have moved far from the earlier *laissez-faire* system in which economic developments were left largely to the free play of the market and to the decisions of men of property. More and more the operations of the market and the decisions of those who administer private capital are hedged about with restrictions designed to prevent abuses and to protect the more vulnerable segments of society. However, this trend has been contested every foot of the way, and still today Americans are far from agreed on the extent to which governmental intervention in the economy should be carried.

I. SOCIO-RELIGIOUS GROUP MEMBERSHIP AND POLITICAL BEHAVIOR

Republicans and Democrats

Since the depression of the 1930s, this controversy has been organized largely along party lines. The Democrats (in the North) are the chief proponents of increased governmental controls over the economy, and the Republicans the chief opponents of such proposals. This has been especially true in the state of Michigan where during the 1950s the Democratic Party was headed by Governor G. Mennen Williams, an outspoken liberal, and the Republican Party was dominated by men associated with the Taft, or conservative, wing of that party. In Michigan, perhaps more than in most states, recent campaigns have been waged on ideological grounds, and the positions of candidates on major issues thoroughly discussed.

For this reason, the party affiliations of Detroiters are especially valuable as indicators of their basic economic and political outlooks. The Democratic Party is strongly linked in their minds with the principles of the welfare state, and with the political programs and ideals of the labor unions. The Republican Party is just as strongly linked with the entrepreneurial outlook, with the historic spirit of capitalism, and with the political programs and ideals of the business interests of the state.

This is clearly reflected in the responses which Detroiters gave us in the 1958 survey to our questions about their political preferences and their reasons for them. After asking them whether they considered themselves Republicans or Democrats (Q. 15), we went on to ask the great majority who held such a preference (89 per cent) *why* they held it (Q. 15b). The majority of the answers dealt with exactly this issue of the role of government in relation to economic institutions and groups. The following are illustrative of the comments made by Detroiters. A Presbyterian engineer stated that he was a Republican. When asked why, he explained:

> I like the Republicans' attitude toward the individual, and toward individual enterprise. The Democrats are synonymous with the labor unions. They're like a wolf pack.

A young Catholic man employed as a stock handler in a large department store said:

> I am a Democrat because I am a workingman and history shows us the Democratic Party has always helped the workingman.

A Baptist enlisted man stationed at a Nike base justified his Republican preference this way:

I'm against what the union is trying to do to the automobile manufacturers. I'm for business and against the unions.

A Lutheran woman working as a bookkeeper for a contractor said she was a Republican because:

I hate griping workingmen who don't do anything for themselves—they're Democrats.

A Negro janitor who preferred the Democrats said:

A rich man who is born rich don't know how the poor people feel. The Republicans don't consider this.

A young Methodist clerk working for a cement company said:

I'm a Republican because I'm on management's side.

A Polish Catholic man who supervised a parking lot was also Republican. When asked why, he said:

Possibly because I'm anti-union. Most unions are Democratic. The Republican Party is capitalistic.

A Lutheran businessman said:

I think the Republican Party is less for the dole system. It's more for the old "stand on your own two feet" philosophy. They run the government in a more businesslike manner.

But a Negro Baptist janitor said:

I never done no good under the Republican Party.

A Catholic wife of a machinist explained her preference by saying:

It seems like the Republicans are too much for the big capitalist.

Her view was shared by a Lutheran credit manager for a retail appliance firm, even though he did not share her values. He said he was a Republican and justified his preference by saying:

The Republicans are more willing to help business people.

Or, finally, a Lutheran factory worker put it this way:

The Democrats are for the poor people and I'm one of the poor ones. Probably if I had a million dollars I'd be a Republican too.

In various forms this same theme came up over and over again in our interviews.

The 1952 survey conducted by the Detroit Area Study obtained evidence bearing even more directly on this subject. Respondents were asked what they felt the Republican Party stood for, and what they felt the Democratic Party stood for. Listed below in order of frequency are the most frequently cited opinions of Detroiters concerning what the Republican Party stands for:

1. For the rich and upper classes
2. For big business and special interests
3-4. For free enterprise
3-4. Against the workingman
5. For conservatism
6. For the good of the country
7-8. For the workingman
7-8. For isolationism, America first
9. For higher tariffs
10-11. Against waste and too much spending
10-11. For lower tariffs

More than 60 per cent of the responses fell in the first two categories.

The image which Detroiters had of the Democratic Party was quite different, as the following list indicates. As before, the items are in order of the frequency with which they were cited.

1. For the little man, or the common man
2. For labor or the workingman
3. For liberalism
4. For everybody, or for the majority of people
5. For more federal control
6. For spending

    7–8. For socialism
    7–8. For higher taxes
    9–11. For full employment
    9–11. For planning ahead
    9–11. For the Catholics

Once again more than 60 per cent of the responses were classified in the first two categories. Similar results were obtained in the 1957 survey. These data confirm the conclusion suggested by the 1958 survey: the two major political parties are linked in the minds of Detroiters with the class struggle in America and with the struggle between two opposed social philosophies or ideologies.

Detroit, like many of the metropolitan centers of this country, is strongly pro-Democratic. Even in the sweeping Eisenhower victories of 1952 and 1956, Detroit Democrats returned sizable majorities for Stevenson—clearly a consequence of their party loyalties. By combining the findings of the 1957 and 1958 surveys, we found that only 27 per cent of the residents of the community regarded themselves as Republicans, while 51 per cent regarded themselves as Democrats. The remaining 22 per cent identified themselves as independents, though as the 1958 survey revealed, one third of these persons were willing to express a preference for the Democratic Party if pressed (Q. 15a), while only one fifth expressed a preference for the Republican Party. In short, the Democrats enjoyed a considerable advantage.

Religion and party preference

Of the four major socio-religious groups, white Protestants were by far the strongest supporters of the Republican Party. In fact, they were the only group with a Republican plurality. On the basis of the 1957 and 1958 surveys it appeared that 40 per cent of the members of this group were Republicans and 36 per cent Democrats. The remainder, 23 per cent, classified themselves as independents, or persons without any party preference. Catholics ran a distant second so far as support of the Republican Party was concerned. Nineteen per cent of the white Catholics in these two samples classified themselves as Republicans, 57 per cent as Democrats, and the remaining 24 per cent as independents or persons without any party preference. Negro Protestants ran a close third with 15 per cent identifying as Republicans, 69 per cent as Democrats, and 16 per cent as independents. Jewish respondents were the least likely to say they were Republicans, and the most likely to say they were independents. Two per cent called themselves Republicans, 67 per cent Democrats, and 31 per cent independents.

As *Table 15* reveals, there were marked differences in party preference between middle- and working-class Detroiters. Party preference is certainly linked with class position, but this by no means accounts for the relationship between party preference and socio-religious group membership.

Table 15

PARTY PREFERENCE BY CLASS AND SOCIO-RELIGIOUS GROUP FOR THE 1957 AND 1958 SURVEYS COMBINED, IN PERCENTAGES

Class: Socio- religious Group	Republican	Democrat	No Preference or Independent	Total	No. of Cases
Middle Class:					
White Protestants	54	23	23	100	259
White Catholics	30	40	30	100	172
Negro Protestants	13	45	42	100	31
Jews	3	64	33	100	36
Working Class:					
White Protestants	30	48	23	101	365
White Catholics	13	67	20	100	307
Negro Protestants	16	72	12	100	193
Jews	0	75	25	100	12

One of the striking facts revealed by this table is the rather substantial percentage of Republicans among Negro Protestant workers, a figure which is higher than that for either Jewish or Catholic workers. Considering the depressed economic position of this group this figure seems surprisingly high. A more detailed analysis of the 1958 data revealed the explanation: without exception, all of the Negro Protestants who were Republicans were born south of the Mason-Dixon line. This indicates rather clearly that such support as the

Republican Party currently receives from Negro Protestants is a survival of the Lincoln heritage, and the identification of the Great Emancipator with the Republican Party. As one older Negro woman put it in explaining why she was a Republican:

> I've always been taught that's why we're free and that they [the Republicans] stood more for equality.

If the presence of large numbers of southern-born persons in Detroit[1] inflated the percentage of Republicans among Negro Protestants, it had the opposite effect among white Protestants. Among southern-born white Protestants (N=44), only 27 per cent identified themselves as Republicans, whereas 54 per cent of the other white Protestants (N=149) did so. In Detroit there are so many southern-born white Protestants whose pattern of voting is *not* based on economic issues that their presence may well have caused us to *under*estimate the degree of difference in economic attitudes and values between white Protestants and other socio-religious groups. As these southern whites and their children become assimilated into the white Protestant churches and subcommunity they will probably gravitate toward the Republican Party, just as the southern-born Negroes and their children have gravitated toward the Democratic Party.

RELIGION: CAUSE OR CORRELATE OF PARTY PREFERENCE?

Many studies have shown that white Protestants are more likely to be Republicans than are Catholics, even with class controlled.[2] However, one may well argue that socio-religious

---

[1] Twenty-two per cent of the respondents in the 1958 survey reported that they were born in one of the southern states.

[2] See, for example, Paul F. Lazarsfeld, Bernard Berelson, and Hazel Gaudet, *The People's Choice* (New York: Columbia University Press, 1948), or Bernard Berelson, Paul F. Lazarsfeld, and William McPhee, *Voting*, op. cit., pp. 61–69. See also S. M. Lipset, P. F. Lazarsfeld, A. Barton, and J. Linz, "The Psychology of Voting: An Analysis of Voting Behavior," in G. Lindzey, ed., *The Handbook of Social Psychology* (Cambridge: Addison-Wesley, 1954), Vol. II, pp. 1124–70 for an excellent summary of the relevant literature. For an excellent recent study of St. Louis, see Scott Greer, "Catholic Voters and the Democratic Party," *Public Opinion Quarterly*, 25 (1961), pp. 611–25.

group membership does not influence party membership, but is merely a correlate of party membership. It is sometimes maintained that since Catholics (and Jews as well) are more recent immigrants, they gravitated to the Democratic Party because the older native American group so completely dominated the Republican Party. Hence, it is said, the relationship between religion and party affiliation today is merely an accidental by-product of the pattern of immigration to this country and the fact that the earlier immigrants were chiefly Protestants and the later immigrants chiefly non-Protestants. Furthermore, since party affiliation is so much a matter of family tradition, this relationship which developed in the nineteenth century has been carried over into the twentieth century, creating a misleading correlation between religion and party affiliation.

This is a highly plausible hypothesis. To test it we asked our respondents about the political affiliation of their fathers (Q. 16). We then attempted to determine whether, when the father's political affiliation is controlled, Protestants are still more likely than Catholics to be Republicans.

This we found to be the case regardless of whether we examined the children of Republican fathers, Democratic fathers, or fathers with no party preference.[3] Among the white Protestant children of Republican fathers, 87 per cent were themselves Republicans (N=63). By contrast, only 56 per cent of the Catholic children of Republican fathers were still Republicans (N=16). Among children of Democratic fathers, the percentage differential between the two groups was not so great, though the ratios were about the same. Whereas 21 per cent of the white Protestant children of Democratic fathers (N=73) now regarded themselves as Republicans, only 15 per cent of the Catholic children (N=94) had made this shift. The most marked difference was observed among

[3] We utilized the political preference of the *father* in this analysis because previous research has demonstrated that in the overwhelming majority of American families the members share a common political affiliation, and furthermore, that in most families the father has the greatest influence on political thought and action. See Angus A. Campbell, Gerald Gurin, and Warren Miller, *The Voter Decides* (Evanston: Row, Peterson and Co., 1954), and Lazarsfeld, et al., ibid.

the children of fathers who had no party preference. Fifty per cent of the white Protestant children (N=26) became Republicans, but only 19 per cent of the Catholic children (N=36).[4]

One might suppose that these differences merely reflect differences in the class level of either the fathers or their children. Such is not the case, however, as a careful inspection of the data revealed. There were three comparisons in which it was possible to hold constant the class level of the respondent and his or her father, and the father's party preference as well, and still have at least ten cases of both Catholics and Protestants. The percentage of persons in each of these categories who had become Republicans is shown in *Table 16*. In each instance the white Protestants were from two to four times as likely to have become Republicans as their Catholic counterparts. From this we can only conclude that religion is something more than an accidental correlate of party affiliation produced by the conditions of immigration in nineteenth-century America. These data strongly suggest that religious affiliation is an important factor influencing the party affiliation of present-day Americans.

Table 16

PERCENTAGE OF RESPONDENTS HAVING A PARTY AFFILIATION WHO ARE REPUBLICANS, BY SOCIO-RELIGIOUS GROUP, CLASS LEVEL OF RESPONDENT'S FATHER, FATHER'S POLITICAL PREFERENCE, AND CLASS LEVEL OF RESPONDENT

Class level of father: Father's party preference: Class level of respondent	White Protestants Per Cent	N	White Catholics Per Cent	N
Working-Democrat-Middle	46	13	19	21
Working-Democrat-Working	8	36	2	46
Working-No preference-Working	33	12	7	14

[4] Similar findings were reported by Berelson, et al., who reported that in Elmira, New York, only 13 per cent of the Protestant sons of *Republican* fathers defected to the opposite party compared with 66 per cent of Protestant sons of *Democratic* fathers. For Catholics the comparable figures were 44 and 26 per cent respectively, indicating that more than an accidental relation is involved. Op. cit., pp. 132–34.

TRENDS IN PARTY PREFERENCE

Here, as elsewhere, we are led to speculate about future trends. Are the political preferences of each socio-religious group becoming *more* or *less* pronounced with the passage of time? In the one previous study which raised this question, evidence was found which indicated that differences between Catholics and white Protestants are declining.[5] Differences in party preference proved to be greatest among the oldest respondents in that survey, and least among the youngest.

The data from the 1958 survey in Detroit suggest a different trend. If one divides white Protestants and Catholics (other than those born in the South) by age, it is true that the largest difference between the two groups occurs among those persons aged 50 and over (39 percentage points). However, the smallest difference occurs in the group in the middle age range, those from 35 to 49 years of age (23 points). Among those under 35 the difference between the two groups becomes somewhat larger once again (26 points). In other words, our evidence suggests a trend which has either come to an end, or perhaps even reversed itself.

On first inspection it looks as if the findings of these two studies cannot be reconciled and we must fall back on the unsatisfying hypothesis that the differences reflect the fact that two different communities were studied. However, a careful examination of the evidence suggests a more likely hypothesis. The Elmira study was conducted ten years prior to our own. This means that most of the young adults interviewed in our own survey represent a generation which was too young to have been interviewed about political matters in 1948. Those who were from 21 to 30 years of age when our study was conducted in 1958 were only 11 to 20 years of age in 1948. More than that, some of those in our survey who were 31 to 34 years of age in 1958 would have been in college or in the armed forces in 1948. In short, the Elmira study did not tap more than a small fraction of the age cohort represented by our youngest respondents. This means that our middle age category should be compared with the

[5] Ibid., pp. 69–71.

youngest age category in the Elmira study, and our oldest age category with their middle age category.

When this is done, a consistent pattern emerges. For persons born from the late nineteenth century to the middle 1920s, events conspired to produce a political homogenization of white Protestants and Catholics. On this point both studies agree. For persons born since the middle 1920s, however, the trend seems at the least to have been halted, and possibly even reversed. At least this is indicated by the 1958 Detroit Area Study survey; the Elmira study has no evidence on this point.

THE 1956 VOTE

An analysis of the voting patterns of Detroiters in the 1956 presidential and gubernatorial elections revealed little that was surprising. As expected, Eisenhower won a substantial number of votes among independents and Democrats in all the major socio-religious groups. His largest gains seemed to come in the Jewish group (this was surprising), where he received 35 per cent of the vote ($N=40$) as revealed by the 1957 and 1958 surveys, despite the fact that only 2 per cent of the Jews with a party preference described themselves as Republicans. In short, there was a shift of 33 points in the Jewish group. Among white Catholics there was a shift of 19 points; among white Protestants 16 points; among Negro Protestants the shift was only 6 points. In the gubernatorial election, voting was much more nearly along the lines of party preference.

Catholic candidates and the vote

One subject which has been much discussed, but little studied, is the influence of the candidacy of Catholics for high public office on the voting behavior of both Catholics and non-Catholics. In an effort to find out how much effect this might have, we compared the voting behavior of Detroiters interviewed in the 1952 survey in the two previous elections: the 1948 presidential election and the 1950 gubernatorial election. These elections provided an excellent basis for comparison, since the two Republican candidates were strikingly similar in political outlook and personality, and so were the two Democrats. The only difference was that in the 1950 gubernatorial election the Republican candidate, Harry Kelly, was a Catholic. Like Thomas E. Dewey, he was a middle-of-the-road, moderately conservative candidate. Like Dewey, he lacked a colorful personality. Like Dewey, he was running against an ardent Fair Dealer who did have a colorful personality. And like Dewey, he was running against an incumbent seeking re-election. His opponent was Governor G. Mennen Williams, then seeking his second term in office. Williams, like Truman, possesses a special knack for irritating right-wing Republicans and has been repeatedly subjected to sharp and vigorous criticism. By comparing the vote for Dewey with the vote for Kelly, with the class level of respondents controlled, we can get some insight into the effect of Catholic candidacy on voting behavior.

As *Table 17* indicates, Kelly's candidacy seems only to have influenced the voting behavior of white Catholics and Protestants. So far as one can judge, it had no effect on Negro Protestants and Jews, though the number of cases involved and the strong Democratic commitment of the members of both of these groups makes a generalization of this

Table 17

PERCENTAGE OF NON-SOUTHERN-BORN RESPONDENTS VOTING IN THE 1948 PRESIDENTIAL AND 1950 GUBERNATORIAL ELECTIONS WHO VOTED FOR DEWEY AND FOR KELLY, BY SOCIO-RELIGIOUS GROUP, AND CLASS

Class: Socio-religious Group	1948 Election: Dewey Per cent Rep.	N	1950 Election: Kelly Per cent Rep.	N
Middle Class:				
White Protestants	60	75	51	75
White Catholics	40	58	43	49
Jews	13	15	15	13
Working Class:				
White Protestants	28	93	22	81
White Catholics	5	87	10	81
Negro Protestants	0	16	0	13

nature somewhat tenuous. *Table 17* indicates that not only are white Protestants inclined to avoid voting for a Catholic candidate, but at the same time, Catholics are somewhat more likely to throw their votes his way, though the former response was more common in 1950 than the latter.

On the whole, the degree of vote shifting linked with the religious affiliation of candidates seems to have been small in Michigan in 1950, but almost no publicity was given to Kelly's religion by the mass media, and it did not become an issue openly discussed. Where the subject is more openly discussed, as in Kennedy's candidacy for the Presidency in 1960, larger differences become evident. The *Detroit News* poll published June 26, 1960, showed that over half of the Catholics who said they would vote for Vice President Nixon if he were opposed by Governor Stevenson, Senator Johnson, or Senator Symington indicated that they would switch to the Democratic ticket, if the Democratic candidate were Senator Kennedy. Among Protestants the comparable figure was approximately 5 per cent.[6]

The fact that Senator Kennedy had more support among Protestants than any of the Protestant candidates for his party's nomination is ample evidence of the substantial measure of general popularity and respect he had won by this stage in the campaign. However, the marked contrast in the degree of appeal which Kennedy had for Catholics as compared with Protestants testifies to the political potency of socio-religious group loyalties when these are publicized.[7]

Voter turnout

Although there were marked differences in the parties for which members of the different socio-religious groups voted,

---

[6] *The Detroit News,* June 26, 1960, p. 6-B.

[7] In a recent analysis of the 1956 Congressional elections it was found that over 10 per cent of Catholic voters shifted their votes from party to party to support Catholic candidates, regardless of whether these candidates ran on the Republican or Democratic tickets. See Angus A. Campbell, Philip Converse, Warren Miller, and Donald Stokes, *The American Voter* (New York: Wiley & Sons, 1960), pp. 319–20.

the differences in *frequency of voting* were small and generally unimportant. Such differences were a bit larger in the middle class than in the working class. Among members of the middle class, Negro Protestants and Jews in the 1958 survey reported having voted in the 1956 gubernatorial elections more often than white Protestants or Catholics. Ninety-two per cent of the middle-class Negro Protestants and 89 per cent of the Jews reported voting in that election as compared with 85 per cent of the white Protestants and 79 per cent of the Catholics. Among members of the working classes the turnout was much less, and the differences among the groups quite small. Sixty-nine per cent of the white Protestant workers, 68 per cent of the Catholics, and 66 per cent of the Negro Protestants claimed to have voted in that election.[8] Turnout figures for the presidential election were almost identical, except that a handful of respondents reported having voted in the latter election but not in the former.

Partisanship

In Detroit citizens vote under a system of partisan elections in state and national contests, but local contests are conducted on a non-partisan basis. Hence, Detroiters have ample opportunity to compare and contrast these two procedures. Non-partisanship in municipal elections has worked greatly to the advantage of the economically conservative forces in the community, since it has permitted them to control city hall in a community long noted as one of the strongholds of political liberalism. Consequently, liberal leaders in Detroit have recently begun agitating for a return to the partisan system in municipal elections.

In the 1952 survey half the respondents were asked three questions bearing directly on this matter:

[8] These findings cast some doubt on the "cross-pressures" hypothesis that individuals subjected to opposing political pressures tend to avoid voting. On the basis of this hypothesis one would expect middle-class Catholics and Jews and working-class white Protestants to vote less often than others at their class level. Except for the middle-class Catholics, our data fail to conform to this hypothesis. For a detailed discussion of this hypothesis, see S. M. Lipset, *Political Man: The Social Bases of Politics* (Garden City: Doubleday, 1960), pp. 203–16.

1. You know that in Detroit, city officials run for office as individuals, not as Republicans or Democrats. Do you think this is good for the city or bad?

2. Of course, we do have political parties like Republicans and Democrats for the state and national government. Do you think having political parties is good or bad for the country as a whole?

3. Do you think that the Democratic and Republican Parties stand for the same things or different things?

As might be expected, respondents who identified themselves as Republicans were more likely to favor non-partisan elections in Detroit. Eighty-nine per cent of the Republicans (N=80) compared with 79 per cent of the Democrats (N=262) favored non-partisan elections. On the other two questions differences between Republicans and Democrats were negligible.

Socio-religious group proved a much better discriminator on most of these questions. As *Table 18* indicates, white Protestants were most in favor of a non-partisan system, and least in favor of a party system, in state and national government. Furthermore, they were most likely to say that the

Table 18

BELIEFS OF RESPONDENTS CONCERNING THE VALUE OF PARTISAN ELECTIONS, AND CONCERNING SIMILARITIES IN WHAT THE PARTIES STAND FOR, BY CLASS, AND SOCIO-RELIGIOUS GROUP, IN PERCENTAGES

Class: Socio-religious Group	Favor non-partisan elections	Believe parties good	Believe parties alike	No. of Cases *
Middle Class:				
White Protestants	85	77	41	51–60
White Catholics	76	86	25	25–28
Working Class:				
White Protestants	89	74	53	76–87
White Catholics	86	78	40	63–74
Negro Protestants	62	95	22	20–23

* The number of cases varies slightly from one question to another owing to variations in the number of "don't know" and "not ascertained" responses.

two parties really stand for the same thing. By contrast, Negro Protestants were most likely to say that the parties stand for different things, and that partisan elections are good and non-partisan elections bad.

It is not difficult to account for these different attitudes toward political partisanship. Clearly, white Protestants are more likely to feel that partisan elections work to their disadvantage while Catholics and Negro Protestants feel this way about non-partisan elections. In part, this is a reflection of the political leanings of the groups, but there is a definite tendency for these differences to persist even when one controls for party preference, indicating a more general bias that goes beyond the immediate partisan advantages involved.

As the answers to the third question indicate, white Protestants are more inclined to take an *integrative* view of American society, denying the importance of social conflict. Catholics, and to an even greater degree Negro Protestants, tend to deny the integrative view and emphasize the *conflict* view. Many students of the sociology of knowledge have long maintained that groups in power tend to adopt integrative ideologies, while groups which are denied power tend to adopt conflict-type ideologies.[9] While our data do not support this hypothesis as it applies to the two classes, they do support it so far as the socio-religious groups are concerned. White Protestants are clearly the group with the greatest measure of power and authority in the community, while Negro Protestants are at the opposite pole. Thus, white Protestants are the most likely to adopt the integrative view, and Negro Protestants the least likely.

Attitudes toward the welfare state

In any complex society where there are only two political parties, party affiliation can never be a reliable indicator of the total range of political attitudes of individuals or of groups. Because of the multiplicity of political issues, and because these issues divide men in so many different ways, one

[9] For a recent, persuasive statement of this hypothesis, see Ralf Dahrendorf, *Class and Class Conflict in Industrial Society* (Palo Alto: Stanford University Press, 1959).

inevitably finds people with divergent viewpoints on a given issue rallying under the same party banner. Simultaneously, one finds people sharing the same viewpoint on a given issue affiliated with different political parties. Because it is impossible for mass parties such as the Republicans and Democrats to achieve internal unity on all important issues of the day, it is desirable to look behind party preferences and examine the attitudes of group members on specific issues.

In so doing, however, we run a calculated risk. Many individuals have never seriously considered many of the issues confronting American society, yet when questioned about them in an interview are likely to voice some opinion, no matter how hastily arrived at. Obviously such opinions are likely to be somewhat random or hit-and-miss. The more obscure the issue, the more pronounced this randomizing effect which blurs the evidences of group influences on individual thought and action.[10] For this reason we tried to confine our questions to issues of some importance. Nevertheless, it is clear that to some degree the randomizing effect has been at work, especially on issues not currently "in the news."

The first of the issues with which we dealt was the critical issue of how broad the powers of government should be in contemporary American society. This is, of course, the issue which is central to all arguments for and against the modern welfare state. To discover how our respondents viewed this subject, we asked:

[10] To illustrate how this phenomenon operates, one might imagine two groups which influence their members in diametrically opposed ways on a given issue, with the result that all of the individuals in Group A who have given serious thought to the issue are in favor of policy X, while all of the members of Group B who have given the matter thought are opposed to this policy. If, however, half of the members of each group have not given thought to the matter prior to the interview, and respond on the spur of the moment and in completely random fashion, with half favoring policy X and half opposing it, when the analyst relates group membership to attitudes toward policy X, he will find that only 75 per cent of the members of Group A are in favor of this policy, and that 25 per cent of the members of Group B are also in favor of it. In short, spur-of-the-moment decisions made while the interview is in progress cause one to *underestimate* the divergence between groups.

Some people say the government should do more than it has in connection with problems such as housing, unemployment, education, and so on. But others say the government is already doing too much along these lines. *On the whole,* would you say that what the government is doing now is too much, about right, or not enough?[11] (Q. 14)

We expected that white Protestants would be most inclined to say that the government was doing too much, and that members of other groups would be more inclined to say the government was not yet doing enough. If a given respondent said he felt the government was not yet doing enough, we then went on to ask him the following question:

Would you like to see the government go so far as to take over and run the big industries in this country such as the railroads, or the steel industry, or would you not be in favor of this? (Q. 14a)

Among our sample as a whole, only 8 per cent said that they felt the government is already doing too much. From comments made by respondents it seems clear that the inclusion of education in the question confused the issue for many people. A number told us that they thought the government was doing too much in areas such as public housing, but not enough in the area of education. Such persons were classified as responding that on the whole the government is now doing what it should do, neither too much, nor too little. Forty-five per cent believed the government is not yet doing enough; the remainder either said that the *status quo* is satisfactory, or that they were uncertain. In answer to the second question, 7 per cent of the total sample said they would like to see the government run the big industries, and another 5 per cent said they were uncertain. The other 33 per cent who had previously stated that they felt that the government was not yet doing enough in areas such as housing, unemployment, and education, indicated that nevertheless they were opposed to the nationalization of basic industries.

[11] Emphasis present in interview schedule.

As *Table 19* reveals, white Protestants were the most likely to feel that the government is already intervening more than it should in our economy, and they were the least likely to favor nationalization of basic industries. Especially noteworthy was the low percentage of white Protestant members of the *working* class who were favorably disposed to, or even uncertain about, the idea of nationalizing basic industries. This idea found even less favor with them than it did with *middle*-class members of the other three socio-religious groups.

Table 19

PERCENTAGE OF RESPONDENTS EXPRESSING SELECTED ATTITUDES TOWARD GOVERNMENTAL INTERVENTION IN THE ECONOMY IN THE 1958 SURVEY, BY SOCIO-RELIGIOUS GROUP, AND CLASS

Class: Socio-religious group	Govt. doing too much	Prefer status quo	Govt. not doing enough: Oppose nat'l'n.	Favor or uncertain re nat'l'n.	Total	No. of Cases
Middle Class:						
White Protestants	16	49	34	1	100	110
White Catholics	14	40	39	7	100	85
Negro Protestants	8	50	33	8	99	12
Jews	0	35	47	18	100	17
Working Class:						
White Protestants	8	44	42	6	100	130
White Catholics	5	33	40	23	101	115
Negro Protestants	1	32	26	41	100	78

Catholics ranked second both in the frequency with which they said that the government has already moved too far towards the welfare state, and in the infrequency with which they favored the nationalization of industry. Negro respondents ranked third in both respects, and, among middle-class respondents at least, the Jews ranked fourth. In fact, *middle*-class Jews were more likely to express the view that the government is doing too little than were *working*-class members of either the white Protestant or Catholic groups.

Since our control for differences in the class position of respondents does not completely control for differences in income, education and family background, we sought to determine whether these other factors might account for some of the differences between groups. To do this we set up simultaneous controls for the class level of the respondent, the class level of his parents, his education, and the income of the head of the family in which he currently lived. Needless to say, with such stringent controls the number of cases in each comparison was very small. However (as shown in *Table 20*), when comparisons were limited to those cells in which there were at least five persons in each group, it was found that Catholics still were more likely to favor broadening governmental powers than were white Protestants in nine out of ten comparisons.[12] But what is even more significant, the magnitude of the differences was greater than when the simple class control was used in *Table 19*. The mean difference between white Protestants and Catholics was only 13 percentage points in the former table, but in *Table 20* it is 23 points, or nearly twice as great (figures are based on the percentage favoring broader governmental powers).

As a further check on these relationships we examined data from the 1952 and 1957 surveys which bear on this same problem. In the 1952 survey, for example, half of the respondents were asked whether they thought it was a good thing for the government to play a bigger part in dealing with problems like "unemployment, education, the extension of social security, and so on." In the same survey they were also asked how they felt on the subject of price controls: should they be strengthened, should they be eliminated, or should they be retained as they were at the time? Finally, they were asked whether they favored a system of National Health Insurance operated by the government. At the time, this subject, like the subject of price controls, was much in the news. In the 1957 survey respondents were again questioned about their views on governmental aid in the area of

[12] The probability of this occurring by chance in nine out of ten *independent* samples is slightly over .01.

medical care. This time, however, the question was phrased a bit differently, and they were asked whether they thought the government should help people get doctors and hospitals at low cost.

Table 20

PERCENTAGE OF RESPONDENTS FEELING THAT THE GOVERN-
MENT IS NOT DOING ENOUGH WITH RESPECT TO HOUSING,
UNEMPLOYMENT, EDUCATION, AND SIMILAR MATTERS, BY
SOCIO-RELIGIOUS GROUP, CLASS, CLASS ORIGINS, EDUCATION,
AND INCOME OF FAMILY HEAD

Class level of R: *Class origin of R:* *Education of R:** *Income of family head*	White Protestants		White Catholics		Negro Protestants	
	%	N	%	N	%	N
Mid-Mid-Coll-$8,000 plus	29	14	38	8	—	0
Mid-Mid-H.S.-$8,000 plus	13	8	60	5	—	0
Mid-Wkg-H.S.-$8,000 plus	50	12	57	7	—	1
Mid-Wkg-H.S.-$5,000-7,999	35	17	60	20	—	0
Mid-Wkg-H.S.-$0-4,999	0	5	33	6	—	2
Wkg-Mid-H.S.-$5,000-7,999	60	5	50	6	—	2
Wkg-Wkg-H.S.-$5,000-7,999	51	39	56	43	67	6
Wkg-Wkg-H.S.-$0-4,999	46	37	63	27	89	18
Wkg-Frm-H.S.-$5,000-7,999	30	10	67	6	60	5
Wkg-Frm-H.S.-$0-4,999	23	14	87	8	58	26

* The abbreviation H.S. refers to persons with a high school education *or less.*

As *Table 21* indicates, there was considerable stability in the patterns of responses to these questions dealing with various proposals for the extension of governmental powers. For example, in the ten comparisons among groups, with class controlled, white Protestants proved to be the most opposed to any expansion in the powers of government in eight instances, and in the other two ranked second in degree of opposition. At the other extreme, Negro Protestants proved to be the most favorably disposed toward increased governmental powers in four of the six comparisons in which they were involved, and tied for this position in one other instance. The Catholic group rather consistently occupied an intermediate position. Of the ten comparisons in which it was

Table 21

PERCENTAGE OF DETROITERS FAVORING EXPANSION OF GOVERNMENTAL POWER IN VARIOUS AREAS, BY CLASS AND SOCIO-RELIGIOUS GROUPS (DATA FROM 1952, 1957, AND 1958 SURVEYS)

Class: Socio-religious Group	1952 Survey		1957 Survey				1958 Survey			
	Per cent favoring greater governmental powers in unemployment, education, and social security	Per cent favoring stronger price controls	Per cent favoring National Health Insurance	N	Per cent favoring government aid in medical care	N	Per cent favoring greater governmental powers in housing, unemployment, and education	N	Mean percentage consistent with welfare state philosophy	N
Middle Class:										
Wh. Prots.	57	41	20	57	42	125	35		39	110
Wh. Caths.	65	66	52	49	62	79	46		58	85
Jews	83	58	67	12	38	16	65		62	17
N. Prots.	—	—	—	4	94	16	41		—	12
Working Class:										
Wh. Prots.	82	70	57	99	69	193	48		65	130
Wh. Caths.	86	71	50	78	79	152	63		70	115
N. Prots.	91	71	80	37	90	99	67		80	78

involved, it ranked second in seven, and in only three instances occupied either of the extreme positions.

The Jewish group was the most erratic, though usually it was very favorably disposed toward the principle of the welfare state. The only serious exception to this pattern occurred in the 1957 survey, and this may reflect nothing more than sampling error. In short, data from these other surveys confirm the conclusions based on the 1958 survey.

The Jewish advocacy of the welfare state deserves special attention. In Chapter 3 we saw that the Jewish group had an affinity for certain classical capitalistic patterns of thought and action, and enjoyed remarkable success within the context of the capitalist system. One would therefore expect them to be staunch supporters of *laissez-faire* capitalism, and vigorous opponents of the welfare state, much as the white Protestants are. Yet this is clearly not the case. This curious combination of traits deserves closer examination.

As many differences as there may be between capitalism and welfare statism, both systems have one important element in common—both involve *rational*, rather than *traditional*, forms of organization. In capitalism the locus of rationality lies in the business enterprise, while in the welfare state it lies in the governmental system. Hence, the modern Jewish advocacy of the welfare state is not a rejection of rationality, but rather the rejection of one type of rational organization in favor of another more inclusive, and more extreme, form.

This, then, leads us to ask the question of *why* Jews should prefer welfare statism (or democratic socialism) to classical capitalism. The answer here seems to be that under the capitalist system it has become evident to Jews that economic victories do not insure status victories.[13] The successes of the Jews in capitalist societies have not won them comparable social recognition and acceptance. On the contrary, despite their remarkable successes, even the wealthiest Jews frequently find themselves excluded from private clubs and organizations by their economic peers, and from high administrative posts in many corporations dominated by Gentiles.

[13] See Max Weber's discussion of the distinction between class and status in *From Max Weber*, op. cit., pp. 189–94.

Hence, despite their success, American Jews have not developed any sense of solidarity with the American economic elite, and have, in fact, reacted against this elite, their political values, and the social institutions on which they depend.

Democratic socialism, from its inception, has contained a strong utopian element which holds out the promise of social justice to all. It is a form of social organization which promises almost all of the advantages of capitalism, but none of its disadvantages. Based on rational principles, it promises rewards (both material and psychic)· in proportion to the ability of individuals to contribute to its rationally defined goals. It promises that these rewards will be based on universalistic criteria of performance, rather than particularistic criteria of status group membership. Hence, it has a strong appeal for American Jews.[14]

Undoubtedly there are other factors involved in the Jewish commitment to the welfare state. This historic Jewish concern with social justice has surely contributed to this end,[15] but had the Jews been accepted fully into the inner circles of the American economic elite, would their concern with social justice be any greater than that which motivates wealthy Gentiles? One cannot help wonder whether the Jewish commitment to social justice would, under such circumstances, express itself in anything more pronounced than generous private contributions to charity.[16]

Foreign affairs

Having discussed domestic issues, we may now turn to a second major focus of contemporary American politics: the area of foreign affairs. The crucial problem here is that of

[14] The fact that democratic socialism promises a more general application of universalistic criteria of evaluation than found in capitalism is undoubtedly a major factor promoting Jewish support. All available evidence indicates that American Jews are highly resentful of discriminatory practices which ignore their abilities and judge them solely on the grounds that they are Jews.

[15] See Lawrence H. Fuchs, "Sources of Jewish Internationalism and Liberalism," in Marshall Sklare, op. cit., pp. 595–613.

[16] Undoubtedly the persecutions of Jews abroad in the last generation have also served as a stimulus keeping alive Jewish concern for social justice and reform.

defining the role of the American government in relation to other nations.

We asked a series of questions designed to reveal the degree to which Detroiters were concerned with such matters, and their views on them. The questions were as follows:

1. How much thought have you given to world problems —things such as our country's relations with England, France, Russia, and other countries? (Q. 27)

2. Some people say we are spending too much to help other countries and we shouldn't spend a penny abroad except when we have to in the interest of national defense. Do you agree with them or not? (Q. 28)

3. Do you think it was a good idea, or not, for the United States to join the United Nations? (Q. 29)

4. If a workable plan could be developed for a single government for the whole world, would you like to see the United States join it, or not? (Q. 30) Why is that? (Q. 30a)

In general, differences between the four major socioreligious groups were minor. In only two instances were differences of any magnitude found. First, less than 40 per cent of the Negro Protestants favored foreign aid when this is not required in the interests of national defense, while half of the members of other groups did so. Second, Jews were the most likely to endorse the United Nations and the idea of world government. For example, 70 per cent of the Jews, but only 55 per cent of the members of other groups, said they favored American participation in a world government. Or, all of the Jews, but only 90 per cent of the members of other groups, thought American participation in the UN a good thing.

The lack of support for foreign aid among Negro Protestants seems clearly linked with their group's economic difficulties. Negroes in Detroit tend to feel that this country has serious problems at home and should deal with these before attempting to solve the world's problems.

The Jewish tendency toward internationalism is something which has been noted many times before by friends and foes alike.[17] As the victims of nationalistic enthusiasm in count-

---

[17] See, for example, Lawrence H. Fuchs, *The Political Behavior*

less countries for centuries, Jews have naturally developed a distrust of nationalism, and have come to pin their faith on international institutions as the only practical alternative. Our findings in this area, therefore, are hardly surprising.

But more important than these differences is the remarkable uniformity in outlook on international issues found among the four major socio-religious groups. In no other major area of political behavior were differences generally so small and agreement so great.

Civil rights: freedom of speech

A third important area of political controversy involves the issue of *civil rights*. How broadly should the Bill of Rights be interpreted? What rights should, and what rights should not, be guaranteed to American citizens? Should the right of free speech be extended to Communists, Fascists, and others who desire to destroy the traditional structure of American society, or should it be limited only to those willing to work within the framework of American democratic institutions? Or, in a somewhat different area, should Negro children be permitted to attend the same schools as white children, or should they be assigned to segregated schools? Finally, should the coercive power of the law be used to support standards of morality which are not generally shared by the American people, as in such areas as gambling, drinking, birth control, and so forth? These are questions which have repeatedly confronted us in recent years, and they seem likely to remain a source of controversy for years to come.

On the subject of freedom of speech, we asked Detroiters four questions. These were as follows:

1. In our country the Constitution guarantees the right of free speech to everyone. In your opinion, does this include the right for someone to make speeches criticizing what the President does? (Q. 21)

2. In your opinion, does the right of free speech include the right for someone to make speeches against religion? (Q. 22)

---

of American Jews (Glencoe: The Free Press, 1956), or the essays by J. O. Hertzler and Talcott Parsons in Isaque Graeber and S. H. Britt, eds., *Jews in a Gentile World* (New York: Macmillan, 1942).

3. In your opinion, does the right of free speech include the right for someone to make speeches in favor of Fascism or dictatorship? (Q. 23)

4. In your opinion, does the right of free speech include the right for someone to make speeches in favor of Communism? (i.e., speeches only) (Q. 24)

The first of these practices was the only one which the majority of Detroiters felt was protected by the Bill of Rights. Even then, one quarter of our respondents answered that they did not feel that the right of free speech covered criticism of presidential actions. In general, conservatism in this area was linked with limited education, advanced age, and a rural background. However, even among those who had attended college, one eighth did not believe that criticism of presidential actions was a right guaranteed by the Constitution.

Comparing the four major socio-religious groups, one finds several noteworthy differences, especially in the middle class (see *Table 22*). White Protestants were generally the most likely to adopt a liberal interpretation of the Bill of Rights; Negro Protestants the least likely. Comparing the two largest

Table 22

PERCENTAGE OF DETROITERS EXPRESSING BELIEF THAT VARIOUS PRACTICES ARE PROTECTED BY THE BILL OF RIGHTS, BY CLASS AND SOCIO-RELIGIOUS GROUP

Class: S-r. Group	PERCENTAGE BELIEVING SPECIFIED PRACTICE PROTECTED:				N	Mean
	Criticism of President	Attacks on Religion	Fascist Speeches	Communist Speeches		
Middle class:						
Wh. Prots.	88	65	53	46	117	63
Jews	89	53	47	37	19	57
Wh. Caths.	77	52	43	34	92	52
N. Prots.	77	54	23	23	13	44
Working Class:						
Wh. Prots.	69	40	35	33	150	44
Wh. Caths.	70	40	32	32	138	44
N. Prots.	46	28	30	27	87	33

groups, middle-class white Protestants were from one quarter to one third more likely than middle-class white Catholics to adopt the liberal position on all except the issue of criticism of presidential actions. Among members of the working class, no difference was observed between white Catholics and Protestants, though Negro Protestants were a good bit more likely than either of these groups to adopt a conservative position.[18]

As students of American politics have long recognized, members of the middle and upper classes are much more likely to have the financial means, intellectual skills, and social contacts required to influence governmental institutions. Hence, their attitudes and values tend to be far more influential than those of the working class. Differences in attitudes toward freedom of speech among persons of middle-class status are therefore likely to be far more important than similarities among members of the working class. For this reason, the differences observed between the two very large middle-class groups, white Catholics and Protestants, may be very important. One should not exaggerate these differences, since they are of modest proportions, but neither should one minimize them. These are differences which could well have important consequences for the formation of public policy.

One might suppose that these differences are due to factors other than religion which remain uncontrolled in *Table 22*. In particular, education suggests itself as a possible alternative explanation: if middle-class Catholics are less well educated than middle-class Protestants, this might account for the difference. To check this possibility we compared the 34 middle-class Catholics in our sample who had a college education with their 45 white Protestant counterparts. Not only was there no reduction in the magnitude of the differences between the two groups, but on the question dealing with religion there was a substantial increase. Whereas 80 per cent of the college-trained, middle-class, white Protestants took the liberal position on this question, only 59 per cent of their

[18] Robert C. Angell reports a similar pattern of findings based on his analysis of the 1956 Detroit Area Study. See "Preferences for Moral Norms in Three Problem Areas," *American Journal of Sociology*, 67 (May 1962), pp. 650–60.

white Catholic counterparts shared this view. On the other three questions the size of the difference remained the same. From this evidence we can only conclude that variations in degree of education are not the explanation for the difference in attitudes toward freedom of speech observed between middle-class white Catholics and Protestants—despite the fact that attitudes on this subject are clearly influenced by the extent of an individual's education.

A second explanation of the difference might be that relatively more of the Catholics in the middle class are first- and second-generation immigrants. While it is true that this is the case, and also that first- and second-generation immigrants are less committed to the principle of freedom of speech than those who are more Americanized, it does not follow that this is the explanation for Catholic-Protestant differences in the middle class. When we controlled for immigrant generation, the mean difference between middle-class Catholics and Protestants decreased to 7 percentage points for third- (or more) generation Americans. These figures do involve a drop compared with the figure shown in *Table 22* when immigrant generation was not controlled (the figure there was 11 points), but it is significant that when immigrant generation is controlled, there is *no evidence that the groups are converging.* On the contrary, there is a slight hint that the trend may be in the opposite direction.

On the surface the findings of our study appear to differ from those of an important earlier study of this subject made on a national scale. The results of this study (conducted by Professor Stouffer of Harvard, and sponsored by the Fund for the Republic) appeared to indicate that there were no differences between Catholic and Protestant attitudes toward freedom of speech.[19] However, in his analysis Stouffer failed to separate Negro and white Protestants. Had we not separated these two groups, we would have come to the same conclusion as he. The simple fact is that even when one controls for both class and education, Negro and white Protestants differ considerably in their views on freedom of speech, and

[19] Samuel A. Stouffer, *Communism, Conformity, and Civil Liberties* (Garden City: Doubleday, 1955), p. 143.

an indiscriminate mixing of the groups blurs the important differences between white Catholics and Protestants.

Stouffer's analysis also fails to take proper account of other important differences between the major faiths. To begin with, the average level of education of American Jews is substantially higher than that of Protestants and Catholics, as shown by various national surveys. Since education is so highly correlated with liberalism in the realm of civil rights, it seems unwise to draw conclusions about the relative liberalism of the three groups without such a control.

Second, and perhaps even more important, there are major differences in the geographical distribution of Protestants, Catholics, and Jews. Jews are heavily concentrated in the urbanized, eastern section of the country, which is the most liberal part of the nation. Catholics are also heavily represented in this section. Protestants, on the other hand, are heavily concentrated in the rural sections of the country and in the South, the centers of civil rights conservatism.

One might be tempted to postulate a cause-and-effect relationship as a result of such findings, attributing the conservatism of the rural areas and South to the influence of Protestantism, but other evidence makes it clear that the matter is not so simple. When controls are introduced, and comparisons limited to persons similarly situated with respect to region and community size, the pattern shifts. For example, as Stouffer's own figures indicate, among persons living in the North, Protestants prove more liberal than Catholics (and this despite the absence of any control for community size). Thus it appears that Stouffer's analysis of the religious problem must be regarded as incomplete, and his conclusions questionable.

Civil rights: the rights of minority groups

A second aspect of the problem of civil liberties concerns the extension of the full rights and privileges of American citizenship to various minority groups. One of the most controversial issues today revolves around the efforts of northern liberals to integrate public schools, especially in the southern states. However, not even all northerners subscribe to the principle of racial integration in their own communities. Substantial resistance to integration in the North is revealed by our 1958 survey. One third of the white respondents said white and Negro children should attend separate schools (Q. 25). An additional 5 per cent were uncertain.

White Protestants and Catholics were the most likely (34 per cent) and Jews the least likely (8 per cent) to advocate segregated schools. These figures are partly a reflection of the differing percentages of southern-born whites in the various groups. Fifty-five per cent of the southern-born whites favored segregated schools, compared with only 30 per cent of those born elsewhere. Since 90 per cent of the southern-born whites were Protestants, this obviously affected the percentage of Protestants favoring segregated schools. When the comparison is limited to those born outside the South, the three groups rank as follows in terms of the percentage of persons advocating segregated schools:

White Catholics	33 per cent (N=215)
White Protestants	27 per cent (N=210)
Jews	8 per cent (N= 26)

The differences between Catholics and Protestants were greater among those in the middle class and those with a college education than among persons in the working class and those with no more than a high school education.

Civil rights: the legislation of morality

A great deal of public controversy in the area of civil liberties springs from the divergent conceptions of morality prevailing in various groups within the population. Each group has a tendency to seek the sanction of law for it own distinctive standards, with the result that bitter controversies often ensue. To explore this problem, we designed a series of questions relating to areas in which we expected to find divergent moral standards. We then followed each of these questions with a second question designed to determine whether individuals upholding a controversial standard felt that it should be enforced by the government. Needless to say, this is a most important aspect of the larger problem of civil liberties.

We explored five basic areas of moral controversy in this connection: (1) gambling; (2) moderate drinking; (3) birth control; (4) divorce; and (5) Sunday business activity. With respect to each of these we asked Detroiters whether "from the moral standpoint [the practice in question] is always wrong, usually wrong, sometimes wrong, or never wrong."

As even a cursory examination of *Table 23* reveals, the major religious groups differ substantially in their views of these five practices. Protestants are the most strongly opposed to gambling and drinking; Catholics to birth control, divorce, and Sunday business. On this last item, however, differences between Protestants and Catholics are relatively small. The Jewish group is the least critical of drinking, divorce, and Sunday business, and relatively uncritical also of gambling and birth control. On the whole, the patterns are what one would expect in the light of public pronouncements by leaders of the various groups.

One notable surprise was the finding that a large percentage of the Negro Protestants, especially those in the working class, oppose birth control on moral grounds. Why they take this position is not altogether clear, but one authority in this area, Professor Ronald Freedman, has suggested to us that many working-class Negroes with limited education may be confusing birth control with abortion. While we could find no direct evidence of this in the records of the interviews, we did find ample evidence that many working-class Negroes did not understand what birth control is. On a number of occasions interviewers made a marginal notation indicating that they were not at all sure that the respondent understood the question. In one instance a Negro Baptist janitor said birth control is always wrong, but then added, "What do that mean?"

If it was surprising to find so many Negro Protestants opposing birth control, it was also surprising to find so many white Catholics favoring it. Only three fifths of the Catholics interviewed were willing to say that birth control is always or usually wrong from the moral standpoint. Here again there is the possibility that some misunderstanding occurred. Some Catholics may have thought the question included the practice of the rhythm method, which has found conditional approval on the part of Catholic leaders. Perhaps these persons answered that birth control is only "sometimes wrong," but this seems somewhat unlikely. Even if one takes the rhythm

Table 23

PERCENTAGE OF DETROITERS EXPRESSING THE VIEW THAT VARIOUS PRACTICES ARE ALWAYS OR USUALLY WRONG FROM THE MORAL STANDPOINT, BY CLASS AND SOCIO-RELIGIOUS GROUP

Class: Socio-religious Group	PERCENTAGE BELIEVING PRACTICE ALWAYS OR USUALLY WRONG:					
	Gambling	Moderate Drinking	Birth Control	Divorce	Sunday Business	N*
Middle Class:						
White Protestants	50	21	8	34	58	117
White Catholics	17	10	63	66	63	92
Jews	32	5	21	11	17	19
Negro Protestants	77	23	25	38	54	13
Working Class:						
White Protestants	55	25	22	35	51	150
White Catholics	39	12	56	63	62	138
Negro Protestants	67	25	48	25	57	87

* The Ns shown here are the totals for each category. In a very small number of instances responses were not ascertained and these cases were omitted in the calculation of percentages. The total N is listed here, as in other complex tables of this type, to avoid the addition of four or more columns of figures.

method into account, a proper Catholic response to this question would seem to be that birth control is usually wrong, since it is clear that the majority of Americans who engage in this practice do not rely on the rhythm method.

Judging from comments made by Catholics who amplified their views on birth control, it is clear that many, if not most, of those who did *not* condemn it were thinking in terms of the forbidden methods. For example, a young Catholic housewife who never attends Mass any more said:

It's against my religion, but I believe in it.

A young Catholic man working in his parents' store told us:

I was brought up to believe it's wrong, but personally I don't believe this.

There was also the case of an Irish policeman who attended Mass every Sunday, and who had been married for fifteen years but had no children. Although he answered all of the other questions, he refused to answer this one. In short, our evidence suggests that most Catholics understood our question as referring to those methods of birth control which are condemned by their church.

The questions dealing with drinking and gambling were especially interesting since they were among the handful of questions in the whole study which uncovered sharp differences *within* the white Protestant group. Only 25 per cent of the Episcopalians said gambling was always or usually wrong from the moral standpoint. By contrast, more than half of those in other groups opposed it. On the question of drinking, both Lutherans and Episcopalians diverged from the rest of the Protestant group. Only 7 per cent of the Lutherans and 12 per cent of the Episcopalians said that moderate drinking is always or usually wrong. By contrast, 46 per cent of the Baptists and 41 per cent of the Methodists were opposed to drinking even in moderation.

In this study we were less concerned with differences in moral standards than with the implications these differences have for the political life of the nation. As noted previously, differences in moral standards frequently give rise to serious political controversies. Those who oppose a given practice as being immoral frequently seek the support of legal sanctions, while others who do not share their views fight to prevent this. Conflicts which arise out of struggles of this type are frequently bitter and protracted.

To determine how prone Detroiters are to seek governmental sanction for controversial moral norms, we asked all those who said that gambling, moderate drinking, birth control, or Sunday business were "always" or "usually" wrong, whether the government should have laws against this practice (Q. 119a, 120a, 121a, and 122a). As an inspection of *Table 24* reveals, no group has a monopoly on the tendency to seek governmental support for its moral standards. Men of every faith seem inclined to do this with considerable frequency. However, this is hardly surprising since conformity to basic moral norms is usually assumed to be a prerequisite to order and stability in human society. The problem arises, of course, because people cannot agree in their definitions of morality. Some define gambling as gross immorality, while others condone it. Some define the use of certain methods of limiting family size as gross immorality, while others define the failure to plan and limit family size as immoral. Some define racial segregation in schools as a breach of basic morality, while others with equal fervor view integration as immoral.

We found that middle-class white Protestants are the least likely to seek governmental support for standards of morality in which they believe, and working-class Negro Protestants the most likely. Although our data tell us nothing directly about *why* this should be, much can be inferred from a knowledge of American history. Throughout the history of this country minority groups have repeatedly won rights and privileges through governmental action. This has been especially true of the Negro group, which has probably gained more in this way than any other group. Often governmental action has succeeded where appeals to individual conscience have failed. As a consequence, Negro Protestants in particular seem to have developed a faith in the efficacy of governmental action, and perhaps simultaneously some distrust of reliance on individual ideals.

Table 24

PERCENTAGE OF THOSE DETROITERS WHO BELIEVE VARIOUS PRACTICES ARE ALWAYS OR USUALLY WRONG FROM THE MORAL STANDPOINT WHO BELIEVE THAT THE GOVERNMENT SHOULD HAVE LAWS TO FORBID THE PRACTICE, BY CLASS AND SOCIO-RELIGIOUS GROUP

Class: Socio-religious Group	PERCENTAGE OF THOSE BELIEVING SPECIFIED PRACTICE IS WRONG WHO FAVOR GOVERNMENTAL RESTRAINT:*								Mean
	Gambling		Moderate Drinking		Birth Control		Sunday Business		
	Per cent	N	Per cent	N	Per cent	N	Per cent	N	
Middle Class:									
White Protestants	61	56	26	23	(11)	9	48	65	37
White Catholics	67	15	(50)	8	15	53	75	52	52
Negro Protestants	70	10	—	3	—	3	(57)	7	—
Working Class:									
White Catholics	71	51	33	15	32	72	62	82	50
White Protestants	67	82	64	33	21	33	68	75	55
Negro Protestants	76	58	45	20	60	40	76	46	64

* This question was not asked in the case of divorce.

The clergy and politics

One of the frequent sources of political controversy, especially in Latin nations, has been the involvement of the clergy directly in the electoral process. In these countries the clergy have often given vigorous support to certain candidates and parties, usually the more conservative, and have in the process won the enmity of large segments of the population.

In this country the clergy have been less actively involved in politics, and as a result no anti-clerical tradition or anti-clerical party has developed. But even here the issue is not wholly dead.

To discover what Detroiters thought should be the proper role of the clergy in politics, we asked the following questions:

1. Do you think that religious leaders ought to take a *public* stand on questions such as whether white and colored children should go to the same schools? (Q. 59)

2. Do you think religious leaders ought to take a *public* stand on questions such as whether the government should provide doctors and medical care for people? (Q. 60)

3. Do you think religious leaders ought to take a *public* stand for or against some candidate for public office? (Q. 61)

The first two questions were designed to discover whether individuals thought the clergy should take a stand on political issues, with moral implications, while the third was concerned with candidates rather than issues.

No significant differences were found among the three *white* groups on these questions. In all three groups roughly half the members believed the clergy should take a stand on the issue of racial integration in the schools, about a third thought they should do this in the case of "socialized medicine," but only one white Detroiter in eight thought they should take a stand for or against candidates for public office.

Negro Protestants took a very different view. Roughly three quarters believed that the clergy *should* take a stand on the two issues, and nearly half felt that they should even take a stand on candidates.

The uniqueness of the Negro Protestant response to this question is probably due to the fact that for decades the Negro clergy were the chief spokesmen for the Negro group. They were not only the religious leaders of the group; they were simultaneously its political leaders. If they were silent, who would speak for the Negro group? Today the situation is changing. More and more other leaders are emerging, but until this process has fully run its course American Negroes are likely to continue to look to their clergy for political leadership more than most other groups.[20]

Attitudes toward the American system of government

Finally, we sought to discover how religion affects attitudes toward the American system of government. To this end we gathered data relevant to two facets of the problem. First, how has religion affected the attitude of Americans to the principle of government by law, not by men? Second, how has religion influenced the reactions of men to the day-by-day operation of our democratic institutions?

It is doubtful if anything is more basic to the American political system than the principle that ours is a government of laws, not of men. However, in an era of international tension, when the speed and efficiency of government action are so very important, there is a temptation to sacrifice the slower and more cumbersome rule of law for the speedier and more efficient rule of men.

To find out how strongly Americans are committed to the rule of law, and what role (if any) religion plays in this commitment, we asked Detroiters to look ahead to the 1960 presidential election and tell us whether they would prefer "a man who gets things done by never letting governmental rules and regulations stop him, or one who takes longer to get most things done, but generally abides by the rules and regulations" (Q. 19). In the total sample, 16 per cent expressed a preference for the man who would not let rules stand in his way, but 75 per cent expressed a preference for the man who respected the rules. The remainder were uncertain.

We found that the socio-religious group to which an individual belonged was not a major factor influencing his re-

20 In the 1961 mayoralty election in Detroit, the Negro Protestant clergy organized for political action and played a major role in unseating the incumbent mayor.

sponse to this question. Jewish respondents were the most likely to prefer the man who ignores the rules and gets things done, but even among the members of this group, only 22 per cent expressed such a preference. White Protestants and Catholics ranked second with 16 to 17 per cent favoring the efficient man. We were somewhat surprised to find that Negro Protestants were the least attracted by such a candidate, with only 13 per cent expressing such a preference. In retrospect, however, this pattern of response seemed a bit less surprising. Repeatedly throughout this study the evidence indicated that Negro Protestants express an unusually high regard for rules. As we have just seen, they were the most ready to attempt to legislate morality. They were also the most likely to say they would pay the fine resulting from a parking ticket even if they knew they could safely avoid paying it (Q. 13 and 13a).[21]

While socio-religious group membership had only a limited influence on people's attitudes toward the value of rules in government, it had a very definite influence on their beliefs about the effectiveness of American democratic institutions— at least as far as we could judge by their evaluations of the performance of public officials.

One of the questions we asked was whether respondents agreed or disagreed with the statement that "Most public officials are not really interested in the problems of the average man" (Q. 32). By themselves, responses to this question do not tell us too much about attitudes toward public officials *per se*. One might disagree with this statement simply because one feels that most people, whatever their occupation, are not really interested in the problems of other people. To separate these two factors, it proved necessary to examine this question simultaneously with another one. In the second question respondents were asked whether they agreed or disagreed with the statement: "Most people don't really care what happens to the next fellow" (Q. 124). When a man

[21] On the question of whether they would pay a fine resulting from a minor traffic violation if they knew they would not get caught, 72 per cent of the Negro Protestants, 63 per cent of the white Protestants, 61 per cent of the Catholics, and 31 per cent of the Jews reported they would pay the fine regardless.

agreed with the first proposition while disagreeing with the second, we felt that his critical view of public officials probably represented something more than a critical view of mankind generally. It was our belief that this pattern of response might properly be regarded as reflecting dissatisfaction with the way our democratic institutions are functioning in actual practice.

If this interpretation is correct, members of the Jewish group were the most likely to be critical of the current operation of our political system. Forty-three per cent of those Jewish respondents who disagreed with the proposition that most people don't care about others, agreed with the proposition that most public officials are not interested in the average man. The comparable figure for Negro Protestants was 35 per cent, for white Catholics 28 per cent, and for white Protestants only 20 per cent. Class differences were negligible, and controlling for class had no appreciable effect on these figures.[22]

Socio-religious groups as status groups

These findings suggest once again that our four socio-religious groups tend to be "status groups" in the sense in which Weber employed the term. That is to say, they are groups which are differentiated in terms of social honor, and where honor and respect are denied to a particular group, its members tend to react critically toward the social system as a whole, its key institutions, and their leaders.

Thus, it appears that *American radicalism derives at least as much from the "status group struggle" as it does from the more familiar class struggle.* In other words, *the denial of equal honor and respect to all socio-religious groups may be as powerful a factor in stimulating political discontent as the denial of economic advantages and political authority.* This will become even more evident in the next section of this chapter as we examine the influence of communal ties on political behavior.

[22] Kenneth Feigenbaum and Rolland Wright reported similar differences between Catholics and Protestants and Negroes and whites in the Detroit area in a paper read at the March 1962 meetings of the Michigan Sociological Society.

II. GROUP INVOLVEMENT AND
POLITICAL BEHAVIOR

Having completed our intergroup comparisons in the realm of politics, we turn to the intragroup comparisons. Once again our first concern will be with the significance of the individual's relationship to his church and subcommunity, and with the significance of variations in the degree of his involvement in each.

Party preference and associational involvement

When examining the party preferences of Detroiters we found that the Republicans enjoyed a plurality among the white Protestants, but in the other three groups the Democrats had the advantage. This suggests that a preference for the Republican Party may be positively correlated with degree of involvement in the white Protestant churches, but a high level of involvement in the other churches will be linked with a preference for the Democratic Party. Those who are more active in a group usually conform to the norms of that group more faithfully than do marginal and peripheral members.

As *Table 25* indicates, this expected pattern was found among members of both Protestant groups. Among white Protestants, the proportion of Republicans varied *directly* with degree of involvement in the churches; among Negro Protestants it varied *inversely*.[23] Because of the tendency for white Protestant churchgoers to identify with the Republican Party, Republicans were as numerous as Democrats among *working-class* white Protestants who were active churchgoers. This was the *only* instance of a working-class group in which the Democrats did not outnumber the Republicans at least two to one. Among Catholic and Negro Protestant members of the

[23] In an analysis of a national sample of respondents interviewed after the 1952 presidential election it was also found that churchgoing white Protestants were more likely to vote Republican and less likely to vote Democratic than nominal Protestants. See Morris Janowitz and Dwaine Marvick, *Competitive Pressure and Democratic Consent* (Ann Arbor: Bureau of Government, Institute of Public Administration, 1956), p. 27.

Table 25

PARTY PREFERENCE BY CLASS, SOCIO-RELIGIOUS GROUP, AND DEGREE OF ASSOCIATIONAL INVOLVEMENT FOR THE 1957 AND 1958 SURVEYS COMBINED, IN PERCENTAGES

Class: Socio-religious Group: Associational Involvement		Republican	Democrat	No Preference or Independent	Total	No. of Cases
Middle Class:						
White Protestants:	high	59	22	19	100	116
	low	50	24	26	100	143
White Catholics:	high	33	38	29	100	142
	low	17	48	34	99	29
Negro Protestants:	high	6	50	44	100	18
	low	25	33	42	100	12
Working Class:						
White Protestants:	high	40	39	21	100	95
	low	26	51	23	100	267
White Catholics:	high	14	66	20	100	228
	low	8	70	23	101	77
Negro Protestants:	high	10	72	18	100	68
	low	18	73	8	99	123

working class, Democrats outnumbered Republicans from four to one to almost nine to one.

As we noted earlier, white Protestants born in the South tend to retain their traditional regional loyalty to the Democratic Party, thus blurring to some degree the political differences between white Protestants and other groups. We were especially interested to see, therefore, how this might influence the relationship between degree of associational involvement and political preference among white Protestants. As shown in *Table 26*, region of birth greatly influenced the party preferences of active, churchgoing white Protestant workers. Those raised in the northern states were strongly Republican, while those raised in the South were strongly Democratic. This difference seems clearly a by-product of the separation, or segregation, of southern migrants from the

Table 26

PARTY PREFERENCE AMONG WORKING-CLASS WHITE PROTES-
TANTS, BY REGION OF BIRTH AND DEGREE OF ASSOCIATIONAL
INVOLVEMENT FOR THE 1958 SURVEY, IN PERCENTAGES

Region of Birth: Associational Involvement	Republican	Democrat	No Preference or Independent	Total	No. of Cases
Non-southern:					
High	52	13	35	100	23
Low	15	52	33	100	81
Southern:					
High	0	80	20	100	10
Low	23	57	20	100	35

northern-born in the white Protestant churches of Detroit. On
the whole, the southern-born attend separate churches from
the northern-born and this undoubtedly perpetuates patterns
of behavior peculiar to southern Protestantism. In view of this
separation, it seems more than coincidence that the Democratic Party enjoys its greatest support in the white Protestant
group among the active churchgoers who are of southern
origin. This seems to be yet another instance in which the
more active members of the group conform to group norms
more faithfully than marginal members.

THE INTEGRITY ISSUE

The most puzzling feature of our evidence is that active
churchgoing Catholics tend to be Republicans more often,
and Democrats less often, than marginal Catholics (see *Table
25*). We found this especially odd because Democrats outnumber Republicans three to one in the Catholic group as a
whole, and generally those members of a group who are more
highly involved in its activities conform more closely to its
norms. Here the reverse obtains.

This relationship cannot be explained by saying that the
Catholic Church stimulates commitment to the values inherent in the spirit of capitalism with which the Republican Party
is so strongly linked. As shown in Chapter 3, degree of asso-

ciational involvement in the Catholic Church is unrelated to commitment to these values. We must therefore ask: With what other values is the Republican Party identified in the minds of Detroiters? Do any of these values make the party more attractive to active Catholics than to marginal Catholics?

There is a considerable body of evidence that many people think of the Republican Party as the party most concerned with *the morality and integrity of public officials*. It seems significant, for example, that when respondents in the 1957 survey were asked what type of candidate they would like to see run in the next presidential election, 56 per cent of those who said they wanted a man of integrity, or a moral or religious man, were Republicans, although only 40 per cent of the total responding were Republicans. In short, the Republican Party seems to attract individuals who are greatly concerned with the integrity of public officials to a greater degree than does the Democratic Party.[24]

This view is also supported by data gathered in the 1958 survey, when we asked respondents to give some thought to the type of man they would like to see serve as the president of this country succeeding Eisenhower. We confronted them with several "forced choice" questions, one of which was worded as follows:

Would you prefer a man who bases his campaign on his belief in God and the American way of life, or one who bases his campaign on a discussion of political and economic problems? (Q. 18)

Sixty per cent of Detroiters expressed a preference for the man who based his campaign on his belief in God and the American way of life. Only 23 per cent favored the man who based his campaign on a discussion of political and economic problems (a finding which may do much to explain the ease

[24] A decade ago Julian Woodward and Elmo Roper reported finding in a national sample that Republicans were much more likely than Democrats to react to the personal characteristics of U. S. Senators, but they could not explain why this should be. See "Political Activity of American Citizens," *American Political Science Review*, 44 (December 1950), p. 881. Our analysis suggests an explanation for their finding.

with which Eisenhower defeated Stevenson in two successive elections). The remainder of the population was undecided.

When these data were related to the voting preferences of Detroiters and to their involvement in the churches, two important facts emerged. In the first place, those who voted for both Eisenhower and Cobo in the 1956 elections, or in other words, those who were "consistent Republicans," were much more likely to favor a man who based his campaign on his belief in God and the American way of life than were those who voted the straight Democratic ticket of Stevenson and Williams. Seventy per cent of the "consistent Republicans" (N=118) expressed a preference for a candidate who based his campaign on his belief in God and the American way of life, but only 56 per cent of those who voted for both of the Democratic candidates (N=159) shared this view.

Our second finding of importance was that degree of involvement in the churches is positively correlated with a preference for a man who bases his campaign on these beliefs. Among white Protestants, 71 per cent of the active churchgoers expressed this preference, compared with 58 per cent of the marginal members. Among Catholics the corresponding figures were 62 and 48 per cent. Among Negro Protestants they were 83 and 70 per cent. These data further support the hypothesis that the Republican Party has tended to capture the symbols of religion and personal morality, and therefore has a special attraction for active churchgoers, including Catholics as well as Protestants.

Other evidences of this relationship were also noted in the 1957 survey. For example, it was observed that the integrity of the two most prominent Democratic candidates in the 1956 election (Stevenson and Williams) was questioned more often than was Eisenhower's. Sixteen per cent questioned Stevenson on these grounds, 5 per cent questioned Williams, but only 2 per cent questioned Eisenhower. By contrast, 23 per cent cited Eisenhower as a man of integrity, but only 10 per cent cited Stevenson, and 6 per cent Williams. Unfortunately, comparable data were not gathered concerning the Republican candidate for governor, but it seems noteworthy that neither of the Democratic candidates remotely approached Eisenhower by this criterion. While admittedly these are but three out of thousands of candidates put forward by the two major parties in recent years, it seems significant that the two Democratic candidates should have their moral integrity questioned so much more often than the one Republican candidate for whom we have evidence.

It is our impression that in the period since the 1930s at least, the Democratic Party has chosen to make its primary appeal to the nation on the grounds of *economic issues*—a stand which has had a strong appeal for workingmen, and in times of economic crisis for members of the lower-middle classes as well. While the Republicans have also taken a stand on these same issues, theirs was one not likely to win elections. For this reason, they have increasingly come to fight their campaigns on other grounds, these being (1) the personal qualifications of their candidates, and (2) foreign policy. Because of the former, their candidates, and ultimately the party itself, have come to be identified in the minds of many as the party concerned with probity and integrity. Hence, active churchgoers, both Protestant and Catholic, find the Republicans somewhat more attractive than do their less active coreligionists except in a group such as the Negro Protestant where so very much depends on the stands which governmental officials take on key domestic issues.

The Republican Party also seems to win and hold adherents on the grounds that it is "the party of peace." The fact that the last three wars in which this country has been involved all occurred while the Democrats were in control of the administration in Washington has seemed to some Detroiters to be more than coincidence. The further fact that the Korean War was settled by the Republican successor to a Democratic president has also swayed some. This can be seen in the comments which people gave us in answer to the question of why they were Republicans. A Catholic widow in her fifties who attends Mass regularly told us:

I'm a Republican because under the Republican government we've had peace and prosperity together, and for no other reason.

A Finnish Lutheran die setter justified his support of the Republicans this way:

They can keep us out of war better than the Democrats.

Since active churchgoers may be somewhat more concerned with this type of issue than with domestic economic issues, this would provide a further basis of attraction to the GOP.

The rather surprising affinity of Catholic churchgoers for the Republican Party seems also a by-product of the Americanization process which we discussed in Chapter 2. We found that third- and fourth-generation Catholics (and Protestants as well) tend to be more highly involved in their churches than first- and second-generation immigrants. Our data indicate that third- and fourth-generation Americans may be differentiated from the first and second generations in their political behavior as well. The former show a much greater preference for the Republican Party even when class, socio-religious group, and place of birth are held constant, as shown in *Table 27*. In short, it appears that not only the churches, but the Republican Party as well, have benefited as the population of this country has become more Americanized. To the degree that the *Americanization process* con-

Table 27

PERCENTAGE OF THOSE PERSONS EXPRESSING A PARTY PREFERENCE WHO IDENTIFY AS REPUBLICANS, BY CLASS, SOCIO-RELIGIOUS GROUP, AND IMMIGRANT GENERATION (NON-SOUTHERN-BORN ONLY)

Class: Socio-religious Group: Generation		Per cent Republicans	No. of Cases
Middle Class:			
White Protestants:	third plus	79	48
	1st and 2nd	60	25
White Catholics:	third plus	55	22
	1st and 2nd	41	39
Working Class:			
White Protestants:	third plus	41	22
	1st and 2nd	32	44
White Catholics:	third plus	21	24
	1st and 2nd	10	72

tributes to the relationship between Catholic churchgoing and support for the Republican Party, one cannot say that *associational involvement* causes or stimulates a preference for Republicanism. Rather, it is merely a correlate of Republicanism. However, as our previous discussion of the role of morality and integrity in partisan politics indicates, associational involvement is not merely a correlate of Republicanism. To the degree that Catholic churchgoers support the Republican Party because they perceive it as standing for political morality, the Catholic Church as an organization should be viewed as a cause of Republican Party preference.

Party preference and communal involvement

Among white Protestants no marked relationship was evident between communal involvement and party preference—except among those members of the working class who had little contact with the churches. Here a high level of involvement in the white Protestant subcommunity served as a check on the strong Democratic influences operating on these people. For example, whereas 55 per cent of those who were marginal to *both* the churches *and* the subcommunity (N=62) expressed a preference for the Democratic Party, only 39 per cent of those who were highly involved in the subcommunity (though marginal to the churches) expressed a similar preference (N=18).

Among Catholics, involvement in the subcommunity seemed to have much more influence on party preference. The more involved an individual was in the Catholic subcommunity, the more likely he was to prefer the Democratic Party. For example, 50 per cent of the middle-class Catholics who were highly involved in their subcommunity expressed a preference for the Democratic Party, but only 35 per cent of the marginal members of the group shared this preference. Among working-class Catholics the comparable figures were 78 and 59 per cent.

These figures are of special interest in view of our earlier finding that the more Catholics are involved in their church, the more likely they are to favor the Republican Party. *These two aspects of the Catholic group, the church and the sub-*

*community, seem to exercise contradictory political influences
on its members.*

Such findings invariably pose a special problem for the student of social organization. Why should two aspects of the structure of a single group have such different effects on the behavior of group members? Why should the subcommunity pull Catholics in one direction while the church pulls them in the opposite direction?

The explanation for this seems to be that the Catholic Church and the Catholic subcommunity respond to different aspects of the American political scene. The church tends to be more responsive to the moral aspects of politics, and the subcommunity to issues related to class and status. Thus, while involvement in the church makes individual Catholics sensitive to the moral appeals of the Republicans, involvement in the subcommunity makes them sensitive to the egalitarian appeals of the Democrats (this being a consequence of the historical position of the Catholic subcommunity in the class and status structures of American society).[25] On the whole, however, the pull of the subcommunity seems much stronger than the pull of the church.[26]

[25] One might suppose that this was a spurious relationship arising as a by-product of the Americanization process. This could be true if involvement in the Catholic subcommunity were much more common among first- and second-generation immigrants than among the more Americanized. However, this is not the case. Degree of involvement in the Catholic subcommunity is not related to degree of Americanization.

[26] In a recent, and as yet unpublished, study of the 1960 presidential election, Philip Converse explored the relevance of the distinction between the associational and communal aspects of religious group involvement, using a *national* sample of respondents (op. cit.). His measure of associational involvement was identical with that used in the present study. His measure of communal involvement was based on responses to the following questions:

1. Would you say you feel pretty close to (Catholics) in general or that you don't feel much closer to them than you do to other people?

2. How much interest would you say you have in how (Catholic) people as a whole are getting along in this country? Do you have a good deal of interest in it, some interest, or not much interest at all?

A recognition of the communal aspects of religious groups may help resolve one of the interesting paradoxes of contemporary political sociology. As various observers have noted, the political role which Catholics play varies considerably from one nation to another. In some nations Catholic political influence is strongly conservative; in others, it tends to be liberal.

If one compares those nations in which the Catholic vote tends to be on the conservative side of the political spectrum (e.g., Latin America, Poland, Italy, Hungary, etc.) with those in which it is on the liberal side (e.g., the U.S., England, Australia, etc.), it is immediately evident that the position of the Catholic community is quite different. In the former,

---

In the case of Protestants, the name of their specific denomination was substituted.

While operationally these questions are quite different from those used to measure communal involvement in the present study, it is clear that they refer to the community rather than the church. Furthermore, Converse found that wherever he was able to compare patterns of findings based on his measures, with patterns of findings in the present study, the results consistently paralleled one another. For example, he found Jews reporting the highest level of communalism, with white Protestants and Catholics roughly tied for the second position. Hence he concluded that "there is some degree of functional equivalence between our community identification measure and the results of the Lenski procedure."

Applying these tools to the analysis of the 1960 vote, he found that the shift to Kennedy among Catholic voters (measured by comparisons with their vote in the 1958 congressional elections) was much more strongly correlated with the measure of communal identification than with associational involvement. In short, as some observers have suspected, the enthusiasm for Kennedy among Catholics was more a communal than an associational phenomenon. This was almost inevitable, given his studied efforts to allay non-Catholic fears concerning his views on church-state relations.

Among white Protestants there was a net shift away from Kennedy at both class levels and in both major sections of the country (South and non-South). On the whole this shift seems to have reflected equally the influence of association and community, except among lower-middle- and working-class Southerners where the associational influence was clearly the stronger. These findings provide still further support for the thesis that the distinction between church and community is essential if we are to understand the nature of socio-religious groups and fully appreciate their impact on secular institutions.

Catholics constitute the traditionally dominant community. In the latter, they are a subordinate minority. Thus these differences in political behavior reflect first and foremost a simple, secular (or non-theological) reaction to the position of the group, as a community, in the hierarchy of status groups within the nation. When this is favorable, the community is politically conservative; when it is not, it becomes a liberalizing influence.[27]

This suggests once again that it is both dangerous and misleading to suppose that theology provides the only basis for explaining differences among religious groups. Such differences are often a reflection of the influence of very mundane and materialistic forces—such as the position of the group in the national hierarchy of status groups. Thus neither a materialistic nor an idealistic interpretation can fully explain the differences found among religious groups. Both sets of influences are operative most of the time. This is a subject to which we shall return at greater length in the final chapter.

Voter turnout and associational involvement

Those who attend church regularly are also more likely to vote than those who are less involved in the churches (*Table 28*). This relationship is especially marked among working-class whites, where those who are marginal to the churches are almost twice as likely to be non-voters as active members.

These figures call to mind Herberg's discussion of the "common religion" of Americans, their faith in Democracy, and the increasing permeation of this faith into the life of the churches. In Herberg's opinion, one of the important factors in the recent religious revival has been the willingness of the churches to serve as vehicles for the expression of this civic, or national, faith.

While the figures shown in *Table 28* are consistent with Herberg's analysis, our data on *changes* in church attendance and its relation to voting turnout contradict it. As shown in *Table 29*, we found that those whose church attendance has increased in the last ten or fifteen years do not have an

[27] For a similar interpretation, see S. M. Lipset and Juan Linz, *The Social Bases of Diversity in Western Democracy* (unpublished manuscript, 1956).

Table 28

PERCENTAGE OF PERSONS NOT VOTING IN THE 1956 PRESIDENTIAL ELECTION, BY CLASS, SOCIO-RELIGIOUS GROUP, AND DEGREE OF ASSOCIATIONAL INVOLVEMENT

Class: Socio-religious Group: Associational Involvement		Per cent Not Voting	No. of Cases
Middle Class:			
White Protestants:	high	9	22
	low	16	74
White Catholics:	high	21	72
	low	13	16
Working Class:			
White Protestants:	high	18	33
	low	34	116
White Catholics:	high	26	95
	low	45	31
Negro Protestants:	high	30	33
	low	37	52

especially impressive record of participation in the chief cultic ceremony of American Democracy—voting for a president. These findings are extremely difficult to reconcile with the

Table 29

PERCENTAGE OF DETROITERS VOTING IN THE 1956 PRESIDENTIAL ELECTION, BY CLASS, AND CHANGE IN CHURCH ATTENDANCE DURING LAST TEN OR FIFTEEN YEARS

Class: Change in church attendance	Percentage Voting	N
Middle Class:		
Increased church attendance	82	62
No change in church attendance	87	99
Decreased church attendance	84	74
Working class:		
Increased church attendance	71	87
No change in church attendance	80	127
Decreased church attendance	59	155

hypothesis that the spread of the "common religion" of Americans, this faith in Democracy, is a significant factor contributing to the recent religious revival.

Influence of a Catholic candidate on voting

Earlier we found that the candidacy of a Catholic for high public office influences the voting behavior of both white Protestants and Catholics to some degree. As might be expected, those who are more active in the churches are more affected (*Table 30*). We also found that working-class churchgoers were more affected than those in the middle class. Among active, working-class Catholics, Kelly received 15 per cent of the vote compared with Dewey's 5 per cent. Among active, working-class white Protestants, Kelly received only 14 per cent compared with Dewey's 43 per cent two years earlier.[28] In other words, when a Catholic headed the Republican ticket, the traditional difference between active white Protestants and Catholics was eliminated in the working class.[29]

Table 30

PERCENTAGE OF NON-SOUTHERN-BORN DETROITERS VOTING FOR DEWEY IN THE 1948 PRESIDENTIAL ELECTION AND FOR KELLY IN THE 1950 GUBERNATORIAL ELECTION, BY SOCIO-RELIGIOUS GROUP, AND DEGREE OF ASSOCIATIONAL INVOLVEMENT (1952 SURVEY)

Degree of Associational Involvement Socio-religious Group	1948: Dewey Per cent	N	1950: Kelly Per cent	N
Highly Involved:				
White Protestants	58	45	43	47
White Catholics	20	105	27	95
Marginal Members:				
White Protestants	35	124	33	109
White Catholics	14	43	8	36

[28] Among active, middle-class Catholics the Republican vote increased from 40 to 46 per cent; among white Protestants it dropped from 71 to 65 per cent.

[29] For the best analysis of the influence of Kennedy's religion on the 1960 presidential election, see Converse's paper, op. cit.

Attitudes toward the welfare state

An interesting relationship was noted between respondents' attitudes toward the welfare state and the degree of their involvement in the churches. So long as the question was phrased in general terms, the active churchgoers were usually a bit more favorable toward the idea of increasing the powers of government than were marginal members. However, once we got down to specific cases, the relationship was reversed. Without exception, in fourteen comparisons between active and marginal churchgoers, with class and socio-religious group controlled, those who were marginal members were more favorably disposed toward increasing the powers of government.[30] The mean difference was 11 percentage points and the median 9.5. By contrast, on the ten comparisons based on more general questions, the more active churchgoers took the liberal position more often in six instances. The mean and median differences were two percentage points or less.[31]

This curious pattern of contrasting responses was most pronounced among white Protestants. In the four comparisons between active churchgoers and marginal white Protestants involving *general* questions, the active churchgoers took the more liberal stand in every case, while in the six comparisons involving more *specific* questions the marginal members always took the liberal stand. Negro Protestants proved much more consistent. In all of the comparisons the marginal members of that group took the more liberal stand.

Putting the various facts together it appears that the explanation for this pattern is as follows. More general questions tap a vague and undeveloped humanitarian tendency among active churchgoers which causes them to favor any ill-defined proposal for solving human problems, even through governmental activity. However, when these people are confronted with a more specific proposal for governmental ac-

[30] The questions involved here were the 1952 survey questions concerning National Health Insurance and price controls, and the 1957 survey question concerning socialized medicine.

[31] The questions involved here were the 1952 and 1958 questions concerning the desirability of granting the government broader powers in areas such as housing, unemployment, education, and social security.

tion, like price controls or "socialized medicine," they reject it, because they realize immediately that if it was put into practice, other values to which they are committed might be jeopardized. This is the age-old problem which confronts moral men at every turn: what is to be done in a situation where each alternative course of action involves a denial of one or another of one's cherished values? The solution, of course, is to adopt that alternative which involves the sacrifice of the least important value. In the present instance it appears that white Protestants who are active churchgoers are more strongly committed to the values of individual freedom and enterprise which are embodied in the spirit of capitalism than to the humanitarian values embodied in the parable of the Good Samaritan.

Foreign affairs

A notable indication of the provincialism generated by religious communalism was observed when we analyzed answers to the question concerning the amount of thought which respondents had given to world problems. As a general rule, the greater the degree to which individuals were involved in their subcommunity, the less interest they expressed in world problems. With class, socio-religious group, and associational involvement simultaneously held constant, the mean *net* difference between those whose primary relations were largely confined to their own subcommunity and those with more extended relations was 8 percentage points.

The only segment of the population in which this pattern was not observed was the middle-class segment of the white Protestant group. Their deviation from the general pattern may well be linked with their peculiar position in the structure of the community and the nation. They are the most privileged segment of the nation and its leaders, and are therefore obliged to concern themselves with issues which transcend the bounds of their own subcommunity. Thus, members of this group may find that confinement to their subcommunity does not have the same restrictive consequences which confinement to other subcommunities has. If one excludes the middle-class white Protestants from the analysis, the mean difference in interest in world problems between those who are more involved and those who are less involved in the various subcommunities is over 13 percentage points, a rather substantial figure.

Virtually the same pattern emerged when respondents were questioned about their attitudes toward governmental spending abroad. Those whose primary ties were more narrowly circumscribed tended to favor limiting foreign aid to grants which contributed to American military interests, whereas those whose primary ties were not confined to their own subcommunity were more often willing to grant assistance on grounds other than those of national defense. The mean *net* difference among the four categories of white Protestants and Catholics (with class held constant) was 7 percentage points. Once again, the middle-class white Protestants deviated from the general pattern, and probably for the same reason as before. When we limited the comparison to the other three categories of white Protestants and Catholics, the mean difference was slightly over 10 points.

Rather surprisingly, involvement in the churches seems to have little relationship to the amount of thought given to world problems or to attitudes toward foreign aid. One might suppose that with important moral issues involved, participation in the churches would have some significant effect on people's thinking, but such is evidently not the case. The differences were all so small that even if they were not the result of sampling error, they were too trivial to be important.

There was, however, one difference in this area which seems worthy of note. Among persons who were actively involved in the churches, there was a marked difference between those whose involvement reflected a lifelong, habitual pattern of behavior, and those for whom this high level of involvement represented a change during the last ten or fifteen years. The latter were much more likely than the former to take a liberal view on foreign aid, and not to limit assistance to other countries to that which is required by national defense. The mean difference between the habitual church attenders and the "converts" was 15 percentage points in the three major groups, with the range being from 11 to 18. Evidently those for whom regular church attendance is a lifelong habit are less likely to recognize the broader moral implications of their faith than those for whom active involvement in the church represents a departure from past patterns of action.

Freedom of speech

In the area of civil rights, Catholic involvement in both the church and the subcommunity is linked with a strict (or narrow) interpretation of the principle of freedom of speech. On each of the four questions dealing with criticism of presidential actions, speeches attacking religion, and speeches espousing Fascism or Communism, those Catholics who were more active in their church more often expressed doubt that the Bill of Rights permits these actions than did marginal members of the group. Similarly, those who were more involved in the Catholic subcommunity favored a strict interpretation of the Bill of Rights more often than those who had more extensive primary relations with members of other subcommunities.

Because these two dimensions of group involvement are relatively independent of one another (as noted in Chapter 2), when those individuals who were highly involved in *both* the Catholic association and subcommunity were compared with those who were marginal to both, the differences were almost twice as great as when only a single measure was used. Using this combined measure, differences on the four questions range from 15 to 21 percentage points (see *Table 31*).

Among Protestants, both Negro and white, involvement of the individual in the group tended to strengthen commitment to a liberal interpretation of the Bill of Rights (see *Table 31*). Among white Protestants the differences were not very great, except on the question of the right of non-believers to make speeches attacking religion. Here, somewhat surprisingly, those who were more highly involved in the group more often supported the rights of skeptics than did those less involved in the group. It should be noted that this relationship seems entirely due to the influence of the churches and not at all to the subcommunity. With involvement in the churches held constant, there was no relationship between involvement in

Table 31

PERCENTAGE OF DETROITERS SUPPORTING LIBERAL INTERPRE-
TATION OF THE BILL OF RIGHTS IN AREA OF FREEDOM OF
SPEECH, BY SOCIO-RELIGIOUS GROUP, AND TYPE AND DEGREE
OF GROUP INVOLVEMENT

| | PERCENTAGE TAKING LIBERAL STAND WITH RESPECT TO: | | | | |
S-r. group: Associational inv.: Communal inv.	Criticism of President	Attacks on Religion	Fascist Speeches	Communist Speeches	N
White Catholics:					
High-high	68	34	25	23	62
Low-low	83	50	44	44	34
White Protestants:					
High-high	84	63	47	41	32
Low-low	79	49	42	38	139
Negro Protestants:					
High-high	54	38	38	23	26
Low-low	41	21	28	25	29

the subcommunity and attitudes toward the rights of non-
believers.

Among Negro Protestants there was generally a much
stronger relationship between group involvement and liberalism with respect to free speech than among white Protestants.
The one exception to this occurred where the rights of Communists were involved. Here involvement in the Negro group
seemed unrelated to attitudes toward freedom of speech.

Once again our findings appear to be inconsistent with
certain of Stouffer's findings. He found that churchgoers, both
Catholic and Protestant, were somewhat more likely to be
intolerant in the area of civil rights than were non-churchgoers. On the other hand, Angell's recent report on the 1956
Detroit Area Study is consistent with our findings in 1958.[32]

In large measure these differences seem to reflect methodological differences. Had we combined Negro and white Protestants and counted as churchgoers all those who attended
services at least once a month, and if we had based our con-

[32] Stouffer, op. cit.; Angell, op. cit.

clusions on an index based on the four questions together, we would have gotten results similar to his. Forty-seven per cent of the Protestant churchgoers would have been classed as tolerant, compared with 49 per cent of the non-church-goers. This suggests that Detroit is not so different from the rest of the non-southern population, and that the differences in findings largely reflect differences in methodology. Stouffer's failure to differentiate between Negro and white Protestants together with his reliance on an index combining many diverse aspects of the problem of civil rights seem especially unfortunate. Our findings indicate that white Protestants are much more liberal than Negro, and churchgoers in both groups are much more liberal where the rights of atheists are concerned than where the rights of Communists are involved. The latter difference is not nearly so evident among non-churchgoing Protestants.

Minority group rights

As noted previously, the issue of equal rights for minority groups represents a second important aspect of the subject of civil rights. In this area we found that the degree to which individuals are involved in socio-religious groups is an important factor affecting their attitudes toward racial integration in the schools. However, here again we found that communal involvement and associational involvement have diametrically opposed consequences. The more highly the individual is involved in his church, the more likely he is to favor *integration*. By contrast, the more involved he is in his subcommunity, the more likely he is to favor *segregation*. People who are highly involved in the churches, but marginal to their subcommunity, are the most likely to be integrationists, while those who are highly involved in their subcommunity, but marginal to their church, are the most likely to be segregationists (see *Table 32*). Controls for class, region of birth, and the presence of minor children in the home had no appreciable effect on this relationship, except perhaps among working-class white Protestants, where there was some blurring of the pattern.

One cannot help but compare this pattern of findings with that obtained when respondents were questioned about their

Table 32

PERCENTAGE OF RESPONDENTS FAVORING SEGREGATED SCHOOLS, BY SOCIO-RELIGIOUS GROUP, DEGREE OF ASSOCIATIONAL INVOLVEMENT, AND DEGREE OF COMMUNAL INVOLVEMENT

Associational Involvement: *Communal Involvement*	*White Protestants* Per cent	N	*White Catholics* Per cent	N
High-high	28	32	37	63
High-low	21	43	27	105
Low-high	40	48	59	17
Low-low	36	138	34	35

attitudes toward foreign aid. In both instances a high level of communal involvement seemed to stimulate a "provincial" response—that is, one which indicated a lack of concern with the problems of groups other than one's own. With respect to associational involvement, however, the situation was different. On the issue of school segregation, associational involvement made a difference; on the issue of foreign aid it made no appreciable difference. This seems to indicate that the churches are capable of stimulating a concern for others, but that this potential is frequently not realized. The reasons for this are undoubtedly numerous: lack of time, limited resources, conflicts with other values which are deemed more important, indifference of the leadership, institutional inertia, and many others. However, regardless of the reasons, the failures of the churches in this area leave them highly vulnerable to criticism from those who note the discrepancies between ideals and realities.

Moral norms and social hedonism

As might be expected, the degree to which individuals are involved in the churches greatly affects their attitudes on moral issues which the churches have especially chosen to champion. When the issue involved is one on which the churches disagree, as in the case of gambling, drinking, or birth control, we typically find a neat progression in attitudes from the most involved members of one group to the most

involved members of the other, as shown in *Table 33*. The
most active white Protestants are the most confirmed critics
of gambling and drinking, while the most active Catholics
are close to the opposite extreme. On the issue of birth control,
however, the positions are virtually reversed.

One of the important features here is the behavior of the
marginal members of the two groups. A closer look at the
table will show that the two marginal groups were closer to
the activists supporting *the less demanding moral standard*.
In other words, on the issues of gambling and drinking, the
marginal members of the two groups were closer to the position of the Catholic activists, the less demanding position.

Table 33

PERCENTAGE OF RESPONDENTS STATING THAT FROM THE
MORAL STANDPOINT (a) GAMBLING IS ALWAYS OR USUALLY
WRONG, (b) MODERATE DRINKING IS ALWAYS OR USUALLY
WRONG, AND (c) BIRTH CONTROL IS ALWAYS OR USUALLY
WRONG, BY SOCIO-RELIGIOUS GROUP AND DEGREE OF ASSOCIA-
TIONAL INVOLVEMENT

Socio-religious Group: Associational Involvement*		PERCENTAGE REGARDING SPECIFIED ACTION AS ALWAYS OR USUALLY WRONG:			
		Gambling	Moderate Drinking	Birth Control	N**
White Protestants:	Activists	80	49	18	41
	Regulars	57	26	17	35
	Irregulars	53	23	18	40
	Marginals	44	16	15	150
White Catholics:	Marginals	33	18	18	42
	Irregulars	31	0	46	132
	Regulars	29	12	65	13
	Activists	26	5	81	40

* *Activists* (attend services every week and church-related organizations at least
once a month); *Regulars* (attend services every week, but are not active in
church-related organizations); *Irregulars* (attend services one to three times a
month); *Marginals* (attend services less than once a month, if at all). The term
"marginal" is used here in a more restricted sense than elsewhere in the text
where it is used to include irregulars as well.
** The figures shown in this column refer to the total number of persons in
each category. Since some respondents failed to reply to certain questions, the
number of cases on which percentages are based was slightly smaller.

However, on the issue of birth control the marginal members of the two groups were closer to the Protestant activists. This same pattern can be observed when the position of the irregulars, and even of the regulars, is compared with that of the activists. In each case, the group with the less demanding moral norm seems to exert a greater influence over the members of the other group. These are examples of what might be called *the principle of social hedonism:* when two established and institutionalized religious groups support opposing moral norms, the less demanding norm tends to win the less committed members of *both* groups.

If this principle is valid, one might well wonder how demanding norms come into existence in the first place. The explanation for this is indicated by the qualification in the formulation of the principle. It is suggested that this principle is only valid "when two established and institutionalized religious groups" come into conflict. Rigorous moral norms are usually forged in the fires of sectarianism and crisis. In times of crisis and in newly formed sects rigorous moral norms may be established and the enthusiasms generated by the situation may overcome the "normal" attraction of simple hedonism.[33] In other words, the slow, corrosive influence of social hedonism appears to be counterbalanced by the dramatic, revolutionary influences of crises and sectarianism. Modern Communism, a nontheistic faith, provides an excellent illustration of the moral rigor of new sectarian movements during their rise to power (this facet of Communism is often overlooked because of the great differences between Communist morals and Judaic-Christian morals).

Although the data for Negro Protestants do not appear in *Table 33*, they, too, conform to the general pattern. On the issue of gambling, 86 per cent of the activists in this group (N=21) regarded it as wrong, while only 56 per cent of the marginal members of the group (N=36) shared this view. On the subject of moderate drinking, 29 per cent of the activists and 22 per cent of the marginals viewed it as morally wrong. On the issue of birth control, the pattern was reversed, as

[33] For an interesting discussion of the role of enthusiasm in the development of religious groups, see Ronald Knox, *Enthusiasm* (Oxford: Oxford University Press, 1950).

expected. Fifty per cent of the marginal Negro Protestant church members regarded it as morally wrong, but only 35 per cent of the activists. Among Negroes, as among whites, the relationship of the individual to his church strongly influences his thinking on these controversial moral issues.

On the issues of Sunday business and divorce the churches take a common stand. Both practices are regarded as generally objectionable from the moral standpoint, though almost all the churches make some exceptions on both issues. For example, while noted for its vigorous opposition to divorce generally, the Catholic Church is not opposed to divorce when the marriage of a Catholic to a non-Catholic is involved, and the ceremony was performed by a non-Catholic clergyman. In fact, in these circumstances, divorce may even be encouraged.

Opposition to divorce and Sunday business varies in frequency with the degree of associational involvement in all three of the larger socio-religious groups. As shown in *Table 34*, the differences were greatest, and the opposition most frequent, in the Catholic group, suggesting that this group has been the most vigorous in its attack on these practices.

With respect to the important question of whether the coercive powers of government should be used to enforce con-

Table 34

PERCENTAGE STATING THAT FROM THE MORAL STANDPOINT (a) SUNDAY BUSINESS IS ALWAYS OR USUALLY WRONG, AND (b) DIVORCE IS ALWAYS OR USUALLY WRONG, BY SOCIO-RELIGIOUS GROUP, AND DEGREE OF ASSOCIATIONAL INVOLVEMENT

Socio-religious Group: *Associational Involvement*	PERCENTAGE REGARDING SPECIFIED ACTION AS ALWAYS OR USUALLY WRONG:	
	Sunday Business	Divorce
White Protestants: high	58	52
low	52	28
White Catholics: high	68	72
low	43	40
Negro Protestants: high	61	32
low	54	25

Table 35

PERCENTAGE OF PERSONS BELIEVING A SPECIFIC PRACTICE ALWAYS OR USUALLY WRONG WHO ADVOCATE LEGAL SUPPRESSION OF THE PRACTICE, BY SOCIO-RELIGIOUS GROUP AND DEGREE OF ASSOCIATIONAL INVOLVEMENT

Socio-religious Group: Associational Involvement	Gambling %	Gambling N	Drinking %	Drinking N	Birth Control %	Birth Control N	Sunday Business %	Sunday Business N
White Protestants: high	63	51	46	28	15	13	63	43
low	66	85	52	31	24	25	57	97
White Catholics: high	71	48	50	16	26	110	67	110
low	65	17	(14)	7	15	13	64	22
Negro Protestants: high	82	33	80	10	71	14	87	23
low	67	33	25	12	54	28	62	29

troversial moral standards, the involvement of the individual in his church seems to make a difference. However, the nature of this difference varies with the group concerned (see *Table 35*). The greater the degree to which white Catholics and Negro Protestants are involved in their churches, the greater the frequency with which those who believe a given practice generally wrong think that the powers of government should be used to suppress that practice. By contrast, among white Protestants the active churchgoers are *less* likely to take this position—except on the single issue of Sunday business.[34]

One of the more unexpected findings of this study appeared when the attitudes of Detroiters on these controversial moral issues were related to their involvement in their subcommunities. We expected that involvement in the subcommunities would do little more than reinforce the influence of in-

[34] It should be noted that all of the percentages in *Table 35* are based on the number of persons who believe that the practice involved is always or usually wrong, not on the total number of persons in the category. This is the more meaningful basis on which to calculate the percentages, since obviously people do not favor suppression of practices which they endorse. The real test of whether one favors coercion or free choice in such matters comes only when the moral values to which one is personally committed seem threatened by deviant behavior.

volvement in the churches. Thus, involvement in the white Protestant subcommunity would strengthen opposition to gambling, drinking, Sunday business, and divorce, while involvement in the Catholic subcommunity would strengthen opposition to birth control, Sunday business, and divorce, but weaken opposition to drinking and gambling.

In large measure this proved to be the case, with communal involvement typically having a considerable reinforcing effect. For example, on the issue of birth control, when Catholics who were irregular in their attendance at Mass were divided into two groups based on the degree of their involvement in the Catholic subcommunity, 44 per cent of the more highly involved (N=18) said birth control is always or usually wrong, while only 15 per cent of those who were marginal to the subcommunity as well as to the church (N=35) shared this view.

There were, however, two exceptions to this general rule. Both cases involved the Catholic group. The issues concerned were drinking and gambling. As we have already noted, the greater the degree to which Catholics were involved in their church, the more likely they were to say that generally there is nothing wrong with drinking or gambling from the moral standpoint. Hence, we expected that involvement in the subcommunity would simply reinforce this pattern of behavior. Actually, however, just the opposite occurred. Involvement in the Catholic subcommunity was *positively* correlated with opposition to drinking and gambling, as shown in *Table 36*. In

Table 36

PERCENTAGE OF WHITE CATHOLICS EXPRESSING THE VIEW THAT (1) MODERATE DRINKING AND (2) GAMBLING ARE ALWAYS OR USUALLY WRONG, BY DEGREE OF ASSOCIATIONAL AND COMMUNAL INVOLVEMENT

Associational Involvement: Communal Involvement	Moderate Drinking	Gambling	No. of Cases
High-high	19	35	63
High-low	5	25	107
Low-high	22	56	18
Low-low	9	23	35

short, our data contradict the view sometimes expressed that the Catholic position of tolerance towards drinking and gambling is basically a heritage from the European cultures which Catholic immigrants brought with them and that it is merely perpetuated by the Catholic subcommunity. Our data indicate that the Catholic subcommunity actually contains a tradition of *opposition* to these practices which sets it in opposition to the influence exercised by the church.

Although involvement in the subcommunities was strongly linked with attitudes toward these controversial moral issues, we could find no evidence that it influenced attitudes on the related issue of whether the government should enforce such moral standards. When we studied those persons opposed to drinking, gambling, birth control, or Sunday business, the degree of their involvement in either the white Protestant or Catholic subcommunities seemed unrelated to their stand on the question of whether laws should be established to support their viewpoint.

The clergy and politics

As might be expected, those who were active in the churches were generally more willing to see the clergy take an active role in politics. This was true regardless of the group to which the individual belonged. The one exception occurred when we asked white Protestants whether they thought the clergy should take a stand on the question of governmental aid in the field of medical care. Whereas 36 per cent of the marginal members of the group favored the clergy taking a stand on this matter, only 22 per cent of the more active members shared this view. The explanation for this peculiar pattern seems to be linked with the relationship between involvement in the Protestant churches and commitment to the set of economic values embodied in the spirit of capitalism. It may well be that many white Protestant laymen fear that the humanitarian tendencies of their clergy might outweigh their economic "common sense," so that the clergy would disagree with lay views on this subject. Hence, they prefer that the clergy not speak publicly on such matters. This, however, is necessarily conjecture.

Attitudes toward the political system

The churches appear to play an important role in under-girding the important American political principle of government by law, not by men. This was indicated by answers to the question of whether respondents preferred a president who adheres to the rules or one who ignores them in the interest of efficiency. When we compared members of each of the three major groups who were more active in the churches with those who were less active, we found that the marginal members were roughly half again as likely to prefer the man who ignores the rules.[35] By contrast, there seems to be no significant relationship between degree of communal involvement and regard for the importance of rules.

In the two Protestant groups, involvement in the churches was also linked with a less critical attitude toward public officials, though in the Catholic group it made no difference. Among those white Protestant churchgoers who rejected the view that most people do not care about others, only 9 per cent said they felt that public officials are not interested in the average man. By contrast, the comparable figure for marginal members of the white Protestant group was 23 per cent. Among Negro Protestants, the corresponding figures for churchgoers and non-churchgoers were 32 and 38 per cent respectively.

Various explanations suggest themselves for these patterns. First, one might suppose that involvement in the Protestant churches simply means involvement in an organized segment of a high status group and therefore stimulates a positive attitude toward institutions of the social system which accord that group high status. However, involvement in the Negro Protestant churches has the same effect as involvement in the white Protestant churches, while involvement in the Catholic

---

[35] Among white Protestants, only 13 per cent of those actively involved in the churches preferred the "efficient" president compared with 21 per cent of those less actively involved. Among Catholics the comparable figures were 14 and 20 per cent respectively. Among Negro Protestants they were 10 and 14 per cent. Among persons with no religious preference, fully 30 per cent expressed a preference for the man who does not let rules and regulations stop him (N=20).

churches does not. If these differences in attitude which are linked with involvement in the churches were merely a function of the status of the group in the community, one would expect the biggest differences to occur among white Protestants, the next biggest difference among Catholics, and little or no difference among Negro Protestants, owing to the low status accorded that group. However, this is not the pattern, and therefore the hypothesis seems contradicted by the facts.

Second, one might argue that involvement in the Protestant churches develops or stimulates a belief in the innate goodness of people which then becomes generalized to all types of people, public officials included. This hypothesis does not square with the evidence either. The percentages cited above refer to people who disapprove of public officials but who do *not* hold a negative, or pessimistic, view of people generally. By eliminating from consideration those who feel that people *generally* do not care about others, we should have eliminated any advantage which Protestants might enjoy by virtue of holding a more broadly optimistic view of the nature of man. By comparing only "optimists" it would seem that we have measured discontent generated by the functioning of the political system specifically, rather than a more generalized discontent.

Finally, we might hypothesize that the democratic character of the Protestant churches provides valuable experience in, and stimulates commitment to, democratic procedures—especially for those who are active in the churches. This experience and commitment later become translated into more frequent and effective political action in the secular realm, and ultimately provide the basis for a greater sense of satisfaction with democratic institutions.[36] This is the only explanation which fits well with the evidence. The results of a question in the 1952 survey are of special significance from the standpoint of evaluating this third hypothesis. In that survey respondents were asked whether they had ever spoken or written to a public official concerning any matter of interest

---

[36] J. L. and Barbara Hammond make the same point in their discussion of the influence of Methodism in early nineteenth-century England. See *The Town Labourer: 1760–1832* (London: Guild Books, 1949), Vol. II, Chapter 13, pp. 107–8.

to themselves. Involvement in both the white and Negro Protestant churches was strongly related to this important type of political activity, while involvement in the Catholic Church was not. Twice as many of the active Protestant churchgoers, both white and Negro, reported communication with public officials as compared with marginal members of the groups. Among Catholics there was no relationship between this type of political activity and involvement in the church.

III. RELIGIOUS ORIENTATIONS AND POLITICAL BEHAVIOR

Political philosophy, devotionalism, and orthodoxy

When the interrelations between party preference and religious orientations were examined, we found no consistent relationship between devotionalism and preference for either party. However, there seemed to be good evidence that doctrinal orthodoxy was positively linked with a preference for the Republican Party, at least among middle-class whites. In seven separate subsample comparisons between more and less orthodox members of the *middle* class (with socio-religious group, associational, and communal involvement all held constant), the more orthodox respondents had a larger percentage of Republicans in six instances.[37] The mean *net* difference was 28 percentage points; the median difference was 26 points. Among *working*-class whites also there was some indication of a positive relationship between orthodoxy and support for the Republican Party, especially among Catholics, but the relationship was so small that the possibility of sampling error cannot be ignored.[38]

[37] It was not possible to make the eighth comparison owing to the fact that there were no Catholics who were marginal to both their church and their subcommunity and yet doctrinally orthodox.

[38] In three of the four comparisons among non-southern-born, working-class *Catholics*, with the same controls noted above, the orthodox were more likely to be Republicans than the heterodox. In the fourth case, no difference was observed. However, the mean net difference was only 4 percentage points. Among non-southern-born, white *Protestants* the more orthodox were more likely to be Republicans in one instance, no difference was noted in another, and in the remaining two comparisons the more orthodox were

These findings are generally contrary to what one would expect on the basis of our earlier findings concerning the relations between devotionalism, orthodoxy, and economic values. In Chapter 3 we found that a high level of devotionalism was generally linked with a positive attitude toward the spirit of capitalism and the values embodied in it, while doctrinal orthodoxy was not. On the basis of this one might well expect to find devotionalism associated with support for the Republican Party, and doctrinal orthodoxy playing a more neutral role. Clearly other factors are present which must be taken into account.

Perhaps the most important of these is the *humanitarian* strain which seems to be linked with a high level of devotionalism, but which seems unrelated to doctrinal orthodoxy. This may be seen, for example, in the responses given to our questions on foreign policy. On the important question concerning foreign aid, those who ranked high in terms of devotionalism were uniformly more likely to disagree with the proposition that we should spend money abroad only in the interest of national defense. Among white Protestants 58 per cent of the devotionalistic, but only 47 per cent of the remainder took this position. Among Catholics the comparable figures were 55 and 41 per cent, and among Negro Protestants 42 and 31 per cent.

By contrast, there was no consistent relationship between doctrinal orthodoxy and attitudes toward foreign aid. Among white Protestants there was no appreciable difference. Among Negro Protestants the more orthodox were more inclined toward the view that foreign aid should be used only in the interest of national defense. Only among Catholics was orthodoxy linked with what we have identified as the "humanitarian" point of view.

This same basic pattern was evident also on the question dealing with the problem of school integration or segregation. Among both white Catholics and Protestants support for school integration was positively linked with devotionalism. For example, among those born in the South, both Protes-

more often Democrats. The mean *net* difference was *minus* 1 percentage point, or in other words, on the average the more orthodox were slightly less often Republicans than the heterodox.

tants and Catholics, 50 per cent of the devotionalists (N=16) favored integrated schools, compared with only 38 per cent of the remainder of the population (N=42). Among non-southern-born white Protestants the comparable figures were 74 and 65 per cent (Ns=62 and 144), and among non-southern Catholics 65 and 55 per cent (Ns=102 and 112).

Once again doctrinal orthodoxy stood in a different relationship to the "humanitarian" point of view. Among Protestants, both southern-born and those raised elsewhere, doctrinal orthodoxy was unrelated to attitudes on the issue of school integration. Among Catholics, only 56 per cent of the more orthodox favored school integration whereas 66 per cent of the more heterodox took this humanitarian view.[39]

The implications of this for party preference became even more apparent when we examined the responses given to the question asking whether the government is doing too much or too little about "problems such as housing, unemployment, education, and so on." Despite their pronounced bias in favor of the capitalist spirit and the values incorporated in it, devotionalists usually were more likely than others to say that the government was *not* doing enough.

As an examination of *Table 37* indicates, the differences between devotionalists and others were smaller on this question than on the more purely "humanitarian" questions, and in one instance the relationship was even reversed. This seems to be so because this question introduces an element that is uncongenial to devotionalists: the enlargement of the role of government. We suspect that had this question asked more generally whether Americans were doing enough about these human problems, the difference would have been greater, and this surely would have been the case if the question had asked whether *private* agencies were doing too much or too little in this area. By introducing the *state* as the instrument of action, we undoubtedly influenced the response of some devotionalists who are strongly committed to individ-

[39] Similar findings are reported by M. A. Jeeves in England; see "Contribution on Religion and Prejudice," in *Proceedings of the Fifteenth International Congress of Psychology, Brussels, 1957* (Amsterdam: North Holland Publishing Co., 1959), Theme 20, Symposium: Problems of Religious Psychology, p. 10.

Table 37

PERCENTAGE OF RESPONDENTS STATING THAT THE GOVERN-
MENT SHOULD DO MORE WITH RESPECT TO HOUSING, UNEM-
PLOYMENT, AND EDUCATION, BY CLASS, SOCIO-RELIGIOUS
GROUP, AND DEGREE OF DEVOTIONALISM

Class: Socio-religious Group: Degree of Devotionalism		Per cent saying government should do more	No. of Cases
Middle Class:			
White Protestants:	high	43	37
	low	30	74
White Catholics:	high	43	46
	low	39	41
Working Class:			
White Protestants:	high	43	39
	low	42	108
White Catholics:	high	52	58
	low	53	76
Negro Protestants:	high	64	61
	low	50	26

ualism and voluntarism. However, as we noted earlier, this
question is relatively general in character, and does not divide
respondents as sharply as do more specific questions dealing
with issues such as socialized medicine or price controls.

Apparently, then, devotionalism is conducive to what might
be called *individualistic* or *voluntaristic humanitarianism.*
Hence, when confronted with questions which emphasize humanitarian goals, but de-emphasize the means (at least when
the means are collectivist and coercive), devotionalists give
the "liberal" or "humanitarian" response. However, the more
clearly humanitarian goals are linked with collectivist and
coercive solutions (as are necessarily involved when the instrument of government is employed), the more persons committed to the devotional orientation shy away from the "liberal" position.

Because the Republicans are the proponents of individualistic, or at least non-governmental, means, while the Democrats are generally the proponents of humanitarian goals, it

may well be that these two forces cancel one another out so far as devotionalists are concerned. In other words, because they favor the *means* advocated by the Republicans, and the *ends* advocated by the Democrats, they tend to distribute themselves randomly between the two parties with the result that degree of devotionalism is unrelated to party preference.

If the foregoing analysis is correct, it still leaves unexplained the link between doctrinal orthodoxy and Republicanism. As we have seen, the values embodied in the spirit of capitalism have no special appeal for the orthodox, and neither do humanitarian values. With what values then is this orientation linked, and more specifically, with what values which might account for the preference of the more orthodox for the Republican Party?

One of the important findings which emerged from our search for an answer to this question was the discovery of *the irrelevance of doctrinal orthodoxy for most aspects of secular life*. We had supposed that perhaps the more orthodox might be more concerned than others with the maintenance of social order and that this might be reflected either in a conservative view on the issue of freedom of speech or in a peculiar respect for adherence to rules and regulations. But here again, there was no evidence of any significant relationship. In the end we were driven to the conclusion that the chief appeal which the Republicans have for the orthodox is the same appeal which they have for churchgoers generally: an appeal based on their concern with the personal integrity of their more prominent candidates.

Doctrinal orthodoxy seems to be a very different type of religious orientation from that which we labeled devotionalism. Whereas the latter is linked with many distinctive attitudes toward political and economic issues, the former generally plays a neutral role. One cannot help but conclude that unless our data are seriously misleading in some respect not readily evident, doctrinal orthodoxy fosters a more *compartmentalized* type of religious belief and experience. In other words, devotionalism seems to encourage its adherents to think in terms of "the oneness of life" and to disregard the popular distinctions between that which is religious and that which is secular; but orthodoxy appears to have the opposite effect. Thus, devotionalism may well be capable of effecting changes in secular institutions whereas orthodoxy seems to lack any such inner dynamic.[40] Seen in this light, it may be more than coincidence that the type of religious movement with which Weber was concerned in his attempt to refute the theory of economic determinism was a movement which stressed devotionalism while sacrificing doctrinal orthodoxy.[41] It may be that where devotionalism is dominant, a dynamic potential for social change is present, but that where orthodoxy prevails, this potential for change is lacking, and religion more nearly plays the role attributed to it by the economic determinists.

Drinking, gambling, orthodoxy, and devotionalism

One other finding deserving comment concerns the relationship between religious orientations and attitudes toward drinking and gambling among Catholics. As we have already noted, these are two patterns of action widely condemned by Protestants, but generally condoned by Catholics. However, earlier we found that involvement in the church and involvement in the subcommunity have differing effects on Catholic thinking on these matters. Whereas involvement in the church reduces objection to drinking and gambling, involvement in the subcommunity has the opposite effect.

A similar conflict was found when the influence of devotionalism and orthodoxy were compared. The greater the degree of doctrinal orthodoxy among Catholics, the *less* often they condemned drinking or gambling on moral grounds. However, the greater the degree of devotionalism, the *more* often they condemned them. The differences were not great, but they were strikingly consistent. It seems more than coincidental that disapproval of these practices is linked with

[40] It is interesting to speculate about the theological implications of this distinction. Evidently the cultivation of a personal relationship with God through prayer and meditation is a phenomenon with significant social consequences, while intellectual assent to doctrines seems socially irrelevant.

[41] While in some respects the Puritans and Calvinists were highly orthodox, their movement was most unorthodox, judged by the standards of their day. It represented a radical break with many of the more important elements of medieval Christianity.

what has often been regarded as the "more Protestant" of these two religious orientations, while approval of them is linked with what might be regarded as the "more Catholic" orientation.

IV. A FOOTNOTE ON "LIBERALISM"

Class and liberalism

In the modern literature of political sociology, discussions are often focused on the struggle between "liberals" and "conservatives." Liberals are generally identified with the working classes and the intellectuals, and conservatives with the upper and middle classes. One of the tasks which greatly concerned us in the 1958 survey was that of testing the adequacy of this way of viewing the modern political process. This view of politics is largely a heritage of nineteenth-century Marxian thought. One may well question its applicability to contemporary American society, a society which scholars are increasingly describing as postcapitalist in character.

In our original thinking about this problem we were impressed by the fact that terms like "liberal" and "conservative" are today based on many different criteria. We say that those who favor the modern welfare state are liberals, while those who oppose it are conservatives. However, at other times we distinguish between liberals and conservatives on the basis of the stands people take on freedom of speech. Those who favor the fewest possible restraints are labeled liberals, while those who favor extensive governmental restraints are called conservatives. At still other times we base our distinction on the important issue of the rights of racial minorities. Liberals are those who favor equal rights for all, regardless of race or ethnicity. Conservatives are those who are reluctant to grant such rights, at least at the present time. Finally, many times we utilize the concepts of liberalism and conservatism to refer to the stands men take on international issues. Here we define a liberal as one who favors shouldering international responsibilities, participating in agencies of international co-operation such as the United Nations, and granting foreign aid to other nations. A conservative is one who opposes these things.

When the problem is spelled out in this way, it does not take a great deal of imagination to recognize that liberalism$_1$ is not the same thing as liberalism$_2$ and that liberalism$_2$ also differs from liberalism$_3$ and liberalism$_4$. In short, one may well question the practicality of using the terms liberal and conservative as we do. Such usage seems justified only if it can be demonstrated that the positions men take on these issues are highly interrelated.

The fact of the matter is that they are not. Those who are liberals on the welfare state issue are very often conservatives on other issues, and *vice versa*. As we have seen earlier, and as many other studies have demonstrated, the principles of the welfare state find their strongest support among members of the working classes, and their strongest opposition among members of the upper and upper-middle classes. In this sense then, the familiar conception of the conservatism of the upper classes seems well justified.

If, however, one takes any of the other three conceptions of conservatism, it turns out that the working class is the more conservative. For example, the working class was less willing than the middle class to concede the right to criticize presidential action, attack religion, or speak in favor of Fascism and Communism. Similarly with respect to the issue of school integration, one finds a higher percentage of segregationists among the working class. Finally, on an issue such as foreign aid or support for the United Nations, the greatest opposition appears among members of the working class, and the strongest support among members of the middle class.

These facts raise serious doubts not only about the current usage of terms such as liberalism and conservatism, but also about the accuracy of many popular conceptions concerning the relationships between liberal thought and social structure. Quite clearly the working masses are not the ardent champions of liberal thought that many have made them out to be.[42] Except on the single issue of the welfare state, the evidence indicates that the working masses are more likely to be conservative than is the middle class. The limited lib-

[42] The same point has recently been made by S. M. Lipset in his book, *Political Man*, op. cit., pp. 97–130 and 298–301 and in Bell, op. cit., pp. 197–99.

eralism of the working class appears to be basically an expression of the spirit of self-seeking, a spirit which has always proven profoundly conservative in its ultimate implications. By contrast, the liberalism of the middle classes seems to involve some measure of altruism and idealism, or a readiness to sacrifice some personal advantages in the hope of achieving a more just social order. Clearly the liberalism of the middle classes is a cautious kind of liberalism which moves slowly and is unwilling to gamble much on any single plan or program. It is a liberalism which does not extend far into the area of domestic economic arrangements. Here the middle classes generally act on the basis of self-interest as much as the working classes.

Group membership and the varieties of liberalism

In light of the foregoing discussion, what may be said about the relationship between the various types of political liberalism and socio-religious group membership? Are any of the groups *generally* liberal or conservative, or do the relationships vary, as they do among the classes? Also, what relationship, if any, is there between religious liberalism and the various types of political liberalism?

Only the Jewish group seems to be completely consistent with respect to the stands it takes in these four areas of political controversy. On all four issues, this group leans toward the liberal side when compared with the sample as a whole. Its liberal tendencies are most pronounced on the issue of school segregation.

The Catholic group ranks second in consistency. On three of the four major issues, it falls so close to dead center that it would best be described as moderate in position. The one exception is the issue of racial integration, and here the Catholic group leans in the conservative direction.

The two Protestant groups are the most variable, with each being liberal on two issues and conservative on two. However, the patterns are diametrically opposed. The white Protestants are liberals with respect to the issues of freedom of speech and foreign aid, but conservative on the welfare state and racial integration issues. The Negro Protestants, on the other hand, are liberals with respect to the welfare state and racial integration, but conservatives on civil liberties and foreign aid. In short, neither of these groups can properly be described as liberal or conservative in any general sense. Any attempt to characterize them in such a fashion can only confuse, rather than clarify, the situation.

Religious liberalism and political liberalism

The final point requiring comment concerns the interrelations between religious liberalism and the various types of political liberalism we have identified. As a part of the assumption of the unidimensionality of liberalism it is frequently argued that political liberalism and religious liberalism are mutually reinforcing phenomena. In such discussions "religious liberalism" usually means "doctrinal heterodoxy." Our data indicate that generally doctrinal heterodoxy has little or no relationship to the types of political liberalism we have been discussing.[43] The one exception to this general pattern occurs on the issue of freedom of speech. Here there appears to be a modest relationship between political liberalism and religious liberalism. In the other three areas, however, no relationship is evident, indicating once again the dangers inherent in the assumption that "a liberal is a liberal is a liberal."

[43] For a similar observation based on a very different methodological approach see Samuel Lubell, *The Future of American Politics* (Garden City: Doubleday Anchor Books, 1956), revised edition, p. 122.

Chapter 5

RELIGION AND FAMILY LIFE

34

The kinship system[1] is unique among the major institutional systems of modern societies, since it is organized entirely in terms of relatively small primary groups. It contains none of the massive, large-scale associations which have become such a distinctive feature of urban-industrial societies. In fact, while the trend in the political, economic, religious, and educational systems has been toward larger and ever more inclusive units of organization, the trend in the kinship system has, if anything, been in the opposite direction. This is indicated both by the decline in importance of the extended family system, and the contraction in size of the immediate family.

In analyzing the interrelations between religion and the kinship system in present-day Detroit, we shall organize our materials around three major topics. First, we shall examine the kinship system as a type of institutional system in competition with other institutional systems for the time, energy, and loyalty of individuals. In the modern metropolis men and women are constantly obliged to choose between the competing claims of kin groups and other groups. How do they choose? How does religion affect the choices they make? Religious institutions claim that they strengthen the ties to home and family. Is this true, or do their demands ever compete with those of the family? Do the major religious groups differ in these matters, or do they exert a common influence?

---

[1] The terms "kinship system" and "kin group" are generic terms which include both the "immediate family" (consisting of married couples and their dependent children) and the "extended family" (consisting of a number of immediate families and unattached individuals who are related to one another).

The second area we shall examine is that of *child training*. What values do parents try to instill in their children? Do these differ from group to group? What effect does involvement in the various groups have on the subsequent development of the child's personality?

Finally, we shall examine the subject of *fertility*. How is family size related to religious group membership, degree and type of involvement, or type of religious orientation? In short, what effect, if any, does religion have on the important problem of population growth?

In all of our discussions in this area we shall want to keep in mind our earlier findings concerning mobility differentials. Do the patterns of family life developed within each of the major groups have any effect on upward movement in the class system? What relationship, if any, is there between attitudes toward the family and mobility, between child training and mobility, or between fertility and mobility? Are the differences in economic behavior among the major religious groups in any sense a by-product of differences in family life? These are some of the major questions which we shall seek to answer in this chapter.

I. SOCIO-RELIGIOUS GROUP MEMBERSHIP AND FAMILY LIFE

Strength of loyalty to the kin group

In the great majority of simpler, preliterate societies, life is organized around the kin group. Economic, political, educational, and even religious activities are largely performed within the context of the kin group, which is typically a moderately large organization involving a substantial proportion of the people with whom the average individual comes in contact in the course of daily life.

However, as societies develop and technology advances, more and more functions become separated from the kin group and are taken over by highly specialized institutional systems. Hence, in the modern industrial society the kinship system is only one among a multitude of specialized institutions, and in this setting it is constantly obliged to compete with other institutions for the time, energies, and loyalties of individuals.

In Weber's classic comparison of Confucianism and Puritanism, he develops the thesis that one of the distinctive characteristics of Puritanism which facilitated the rise of capitalism was its substitution of the community of faith for the community of blood.[2] He argues that one of the great achievements of the ascetic Protestant sects was that of shattering "the fetters of the sib," or extended kin group. So long as the basic social relations of men were organized in terms of kinship, the progress of impersonal rationalization in economic relations was blocked. Only as the hold of the kin group was broken could social relations be organized on the basis of functional criteria.

This thesis is an intriguing one, and could throw some light on our earlier finding concerning Protestant-Catholic differences in rates of vertical mobility. If Protestants are less tightly bound to their kin group, this could be a significant economic advantage. In an effort to determine what effect, if any, religion has on the relations of men and women toward the kin group in the modern American metropolis, we examined data from the 1952, 1953, 1955, 1956, and 1957 surveys, as well as those from our 1958 survey.

MIGRATION

One of the best indicators of the importance attached to the family and kin group by modern Americans is their willingness, or unwillingness, to leave their native community and migrate elsewhere. Migration of this type generally involves a physical separation of the individual from those relatives with whom he has the closest ties. He may take some of these relatives with him, but rarely all of them. A man usually migrates in response to the lure of economic or vocational opportunities; hence we may regard migration as an indicator of the importance he attaches to the kin group when its ties compete directly with the prospect of more money or a better job.

Pooling the results of four separate surveys in the Detroit area (1952, 1955, 1956, and 1958), it appears that Catholics

[2] See Max Weber, *The Religion of China*, op. cit., Chapter 8.

are the most likely to be natives, and Negro Protestants the least. The specific figures for the four groups were as follows:

White Catholics	43 per cent	(N=1509)
Jews	31 per cent	(N=153)
White Protestants	26 per cent	(N=1751)
Negro Protestants	7 per cent	(N=607)

While there are obvious difficulties in the interpretation of migration figures from a single community (e.g., national figures would certainly yield a far higher percentage of non-migrants among Negro Protestants when the South was included), there is some reason for believing that these findings reflect certain basic differences. For example, one of the major conclusions of Strodtbeck's interesting and important comparative study of Italian Catholic and Jewish families in New Haven, Connecticut, was that the greater economic success of the Jews was in part a function of their greater willingness to leave kith and kin. Jewish boys were much more likely than Italian to disagree with the statement that "Nothing in life is worth the sacrifice of moving away from your parents."[3] While considerable caution must be exercised in interpreting these findings, since obviously Italian Catholics are not typical of all Catholics, nevertheless the similarity between these two sets of findings suggests the possibility of a more general pattern.

Of special interest in this connection were those persons who had no relatives in Detroit, except their immediate family living in the same dwelling unit. These are generally the people who have most completely severed their ties with the extended kin group. The 1952 survey indicated that 20 per cent of the white Protestants fell in this category, compared with only 10 per cent of the Catholics and Negro Protestants, and 6 per cent of the Jews. This pattern of total separation from the kin group was especially pronounced among middle-class white Protestants. Fully 29 per cent of this group reported no relatives living in the community other than those in the dwelling unit itself. This contrasted with only 9 per cent of the middle-class Catholics, and none of the middle-

[3] Fred L. Strodtbeck, "Family Interaction, Values, and Achievement," in Sklare, op. cit., pp. 147–65.

class Jews. Among members of the working class, 20 per cent of the Jews, 15 per cent of the white Protestants, 10 per cent of the Catholics, and 8 per cent of the Negro Protestants were "alone" in the community.

It is interesting to speculate about the significance of these findings for our earlier findings on vertical mobility. Sociological research on vertical mobility makes it abundantly clear that spatial mobility facilitates or at least normally accompanies vertical mobility.[4] If this is true, then people whose ties with kin bind them to their community of birth are necessarily at a disadvantage in the competition for advancement. This factor may well contribute to the different rates of mobility for Catholics and white Protestants.

RELATIVES VS. NEIGHBORS

In the 1952 survey there were other indications that the attraction of the kin group is stronger for Catholics than for Protestants. For example, respondents were asked how often they visited relatives and neighbors. As shown in *Table 38*, there was an inverse relationship between these two types of activity: the more frequently members of a group visit relatives, the less frequently they visit neighbors. Jews were the

Table 38

PERCENTAGE REPORTING WEEKLY VISITS WITH RELATIVES AND WITH NEIGHBORS, BY SOCIO-RELIGIOUS GROUP

Socio-religious Group	(A) Percentage visiting relatives every week	(B) Percentage visiting neighbors every week	A/B
Jews	75	23	3.3
White Catholics	56	24	2.3
White Protestants	49	34	1.4
Negro Protestants	46	42	1.1

[4] For a good summary of the relevant literature see Bernard Barber, *Social Stratification* (New York: Harcourt, Brace, 1957), pp. 418–21. See also Robert K. Merton, *Social Theory and Social Structure* (Glencoe: The Free Press, 1957), especially pp. 400–1, and Lipset and Bendix, op. cit., pp. 157–64.

most likely to visit relatives every week; Negro Protestants were the least likely. Comparing white Protestants and Catholics, the former were more likely to visit neighbors on a weekly basis, while the latter were more likely to visit relatives.

OTHER INDICES OF FAMILY SOLIDARITY

Another distinctive feature of the white Protestants was the small number who had relatives outside the immediate family (e.g., grandparents) living in the same dwelling unit. This was especially evident in the middle class, where only 5 per cent of the white Protestants reported this pattern, compared with 14 per cent of the Jews and 16 per cent of the Catholics. If we had the data required to eliminate from consideration those married couples who had no parents still alive, the differences between the groups would undoubtedly be even larger.

In the 1958 survey we gave respondents the following list and asked them to indicate which two had had the greatest influence on their religious beliefs:

1. Friends
2. Teachers
3. Husband, wife, children
4. Parents
5. Ministers, priests, or rabbis
6. Books
7. TV or radio

As might be expected, parents and the clergy were cited more often than other categories. However, for the purpose of the present analysis, we were especially interested in the relative influence of friends and family. It was our prediction that the influence of friends (item 1) would be greater among Protestants than among Catholics, and the influence of family (items 3 and 4) greater among Catholics than among Protestants. This prediction was supported by the data. Among those white Protestants citing items 1, 3, or 4, 16 per cent of the citations were of item 1, and 84 per cent of items 3 and 4. For Negro Protestants the comparable figures were 10 and 90 per cent. For Catholics they were 6 and 94 per cent; for Jews 5 and 95 per cent.

Finally, in the 1957 survey, Detroiters were asked whose political opinions had the greatest influence on how they voted: their close friends, family members, religious leaders, union leaders, business leaders, nationality group leaders, or party leaders. Roughly one fifth of the sample cited either close friends or relatives. Of the white Protestants who did so, 30 per cent cited friends, and 70 per cent family members. For both Catholics and Negro Protestants, the comparable figures were 22 and 78 per cent. For Jews the figures were 50 per cent for each category.

By all these criteria it seems clear that Catholics are more highly involved in their kin groups and value them somewhat more than white Protestants. Or, to look at the data the other way around, white Protestants seem more involved in, and favorably disposed toward, groups and social ties where the bond of kinship is absent. In the case of the Jewish and Negro Protestant groups the evidence is less clear, but seems to indicate that the Jews resemble the Catholics in this respect, while the Negro Protestants tend toward the white Protestant pattern.[5]

DIVORCE AND THE IMMEDIATE FAMILY

Not only are ties with the *extended* family weaker among white Protestants than among Catholics, this is also apparently true of ties with the *immediate* family. For example, Protestants, both white and Negro, were much more likely to have been divorced than either Catholics or Jews. The differences were not very great if we compared only persons *currently* divorced, since divorced Catholics are much less likely to remarry than Protestants. Fifty per cent of the Catholics in our sample who had ever been divorced (N=16) had not remarried, compared with 26 per cent of the white Protes-

[5] In a study conducted in New Haven, Connecticut, sharp differences were found in the degree of familialism of Italian Catholics and Jews. Italian Catholics were much more likely than Jews to say that even after marriage a young person's first loyalty is to his parents, and that he should not move away from his parents. See Fred L. Strodtbeck, op. cit.

tants (N=39), and 14 per cent of the Negro Protestants (N=21). However, more important for our present discussion, is the fact that of the 206 Catholics in our 1958 survey who had ever married, only 8 per cent had ever been divorced, compared with 16 per cent of the 247 white Protestants, and 22 per cent of the 94 Negro Protestants. The Jewish families had the lowest divorce rate of all, with only 4 per cent of the 26 Jewish respondents who had ever married reporting a divorce.

Although the interpretation of these figures is complicated somewhat by the differing views of the seriousness of divorce taken by the various religious groups, one point is clear. The immediate family relationship is less durable among Protestants than among Catholics, a fact undoubtedly associated with differing attitudes toward the immediate family. Also of significance is the fact that Catholics remarry after divorce so much less often than Protestants. This means that if Catholics derive any rewards at all from family life they are under greater pressure than Protestants to make their first marriage work. This too must have some effect on the pattern of social relationships within the nuclear family. One would expect Catholics (especially those who are better educated and strongly committed to their faith) to make vigorous efforts to achieve harmonious and rewarding relationships within the family, since the alternatives are so serious and threatening.

FAMILIALISM AND VERTICAL MOBILITY

Before leaving the subject of kin-group loyalty, it is necessary to reconsider the relationship between this type of loyalty and vertical mobility. If weak familial ties facilitate upward mobility, how then may we reconcile the strong familial ties of the Jewish group with their obvious economic success. This is a question which deserves an answer.

Unfortunately, there is no obvious answer to this problem. One might argue that Jews have advanced in the economic realm *despite* their strong family ties, and this may well be correct. However, it is not a very satisfying explanation—it seems too much of an effort to beg the question.

Happily, there is an alternative explanation which is more satisfying and also more intriguing. This explanation is based on the thesis that strong familial ties are only a liability for those who work for firms which the family group does not control. In contrast, such ties may prove an *asset* for those who work for family owned and operated firms. Under these conditions the demands of the work group and the family group are much more nearly co-ordinated and time spent with relatives may greatly advance the individual's economic interests. In view of the high incidence of family owned and operated businesses in the Jewish group (see Chapter 3), the strength of family ties, which may prove an occupational liability for most members of other groups, may prove a definite asset in the case of Jews. Although the present study affords no systematic evidence to support this line of reasoning, the logic of the argument seems sound enough to indicate the need for further study of this question.

Attitudes toward homemaking and child raising

We also expected Catholic women to differ from non-Catholic women in their attitudes toward homemaking and child raising. More specifically, we predicted that Catholic women would find these activities more enjoyable than non-Catholic women. It was our expectation that the Catholic group, with its greater emphasis on family and kin group, would provide greater rewards for women performing family-related activities. By contrast, we expected to find that white Protestant women, especially, would be less enthusiastic about homemaking and child rearing, since their group seems to orient its members, both male and female, to extra-familial activities to a greater degree than other groups.

The best data to test this hypothesis were provided by the 1953 survey conducted by Professors G. E. Swanson and Daniel R. Miller. This survey was specifically concerned with child-rearing practices and was based on a sample made up entirely of married women with children.[6] Each mother was

[6] These data from the 1953 survey were made available for this analysis by Professor Guy E. Swanson, to whom we express our sincere appreciation. These data have been analyzed in a different context by Professors Swanson and Miller and the findings reported in their book, *The Changing American Parent: A Study of the Detroit Area* (New York: John Wiley, 1958).

classified on the basis of (a) whether or not she regarded children as burdensome, and (b) whether or not she had enjoyed rearing the particular child which was discussed at length in the interview.[7] These classifications were based on her answers to a whole series of relevant questions, not on any single question.

Contrary to expectations, no appreciable differences were found among *working*-class mothers in the different groups. However, when *middle*-class Catholic and white Protestant mothers were compared, significant differences emerged, and in the predicted direction. For example, 60 per cent of the white Protestant mothers, but only 47 per cent of the Catholic mothers, felt that children were burdensome to a greater or lesser degree. Furthermore, 68 per cent of these middle-class Catholic mothers regarded the experience of rearing the child with which the interview was chiefly concerned as either "pleasant" or "very pleasant." By contrast, only 51 per cent of the middle-class white Protestant mothers fell in these categories.

Parental values and child rearing

One of the subjects in which we were especially interested was that of the values to which Detroiters subscribe and which they believe should be instilled in children. As a device for exploring this subject, we asked our respondents in the 1958 survey the following question (Q. 33):

> If you had to choose, which thing on this list would you pick as *the most important* for a child to learn to prepare him for life?
> 1. to obey
> 2. to be well liked or popular
> 3. to think for himself
> 4. to work hard
> 5. to help others when they need help

When they had answered this question, they were then

---

[7] Each interview was focused on the experiences of raising *one* of the children in the family. This was done because of time limitations.

asked which item they would rank second, which third, and which last.

Nearly half the Detroiters we interviewed thought that it was most important for a child to learn to think for himself. Obedience came next, with nearly a third ranking it first on their list. Helping others, working hard, and popularity followed in that order. We found that this hierarchy of values remained unchanged when we examined not merely responses to the question of which value Detroiters ranked first, but also their other rankings.

With respect to the three less important values, no major differences were found either between classes or between socio-religious groups. Catholics tended to stress hard work somewhat more than other groups, and helping others somewhat less, but the differences were small. The reverse was true of white Protestants. Jews were somewhat more concerned with popularity than other groups, but not enough to rank it ahead of any of the other four values.

The important differences were all concentrated in the relative ranking of two values: *obedience* and *intellectual autonomy*. There were important differences in the ranking of these two values both along class and socio-religious group lines. For this reason we classified each of our respondents according to whether he ranked obedience above intellectual autonomy, or *vice versa*.

As *Table* 39 indicates, a high valuation of intellectual autonomy is linked with the upper-middle class and with the Jewish and white Protestant groups. Upper-middle-class Detroiters are far more likely than lower-working-class Detroiters to value intellectual autonomy above obedience, and within all of the class levels, Jews and white Protestants are more likely than Catholics to do this. Once again the biggest differences between socio-religious groups occur at the highest status level.

One might suppose that these differences were caused by other uncontrolled factors such as differences in education or class origin. Such was not the case, however, as we proved by controlling *simultaneously* for the class origin of respondents (i.e., the class of their father), their education, and their current class position. The result of using these several con-

Table 39

PERCENTAGE VALUING INTELLECTUAL AUTONOMY ABOVE
OBEDIENCE BY CLASS AND SOCIO-RELIGIOUS GROUP

Class:* Socio-religious Group	Per cent	No. of Cases
Upper-middle Class:		
White Protestants	90	48
Jews	90	10
White Catholics	70	27
Lower-middle Class:		
Jews	(86)	7
Negro Protestants	(78)	9
White Protestants	72	65
White Catholics	63	59
Upper-working Class:		
White Protestants	66	79
White Catholics	51	77
Negro Protestants	41	17
Lower-working Class:		
White Protestants	48	66
Negro Protestants	39	62
White Catholics	38	53

* The middle class is divided on the basis of income, with those earning
$8,000 or more classified as upper-middle class. The same is true of the working
class, with $5,000 per year income for the family head providing the cutting
point.

trols simultaneously was to enlarge rather than diminish the
differences between white Protestants and Catholics. The
mean difference between Catholics and white Protestants in
the four class levels shown in *Table 39* was only 13.5 percentage points, but when these simultaneous controls were
used the mean difference increased to 19 points if one limited
comparisons to those instances in which there were at least
10 members of each group, and to 22 points if all comparisons were used.

These findings seem especially important because of their
implications for vertical mobility. Since commitment to personal autonomy is so widespread in the upper-middle class
(as shown in *Table 39*), people who hope to rise in the system must find the lack of such an orientation a serious lia-

bility. Evidence of this may be seen in *Table 40:* those who have been upwardly mobile are the most likely to have an autonomic orientation while those who have been downwardly mobile are the least likely. The non-mobile occupy intermediate positions.[8] This peculiar pattern of relationships strongly suggests that these orientations are a *cause* of mobility, and not merely a consequence. One might argue that the large number of upwardly mobile persons who display an autonomic orientation is a case of overconformity to

Table 40

PERCENTAGE OF URBAN-BORN DETROITERS VALUING INTEL-
LECTUAL AUTONOMY ABOVE OBEDIENCE, BY CLASS AND
MOBILITY STATUS

Class: Mobility Status	Per cent	No. of Cases
Middle: non-mobile	74	84
Middle: upwardly mobile	77	118
Working: downwardly mobile	48	40
Working: non-mobile	55	227

middle-class norms, but it is difficult to extend this argument to the downwardly mobile. It is hard to believe that they "overconform" to lower-class standards. Furthermore, among persons in the middle class, those who have been upwardly mobile are more concentrated in the lower-middle class while the non-mobile are more often found in the upper-middle class. Because they are more often in the upper-middle class, we would expect the latter to be the more committed to personal autonomy, whereas just the opposite is true.

These findings call to mind the recent findings of others that the Catholic population produces far fewer scientists than one would expect on the basis of its numbers, and even on the basis of the number of college graduates in its ranks.[9]

[8] Unfortunately, it was not possible to carry out this type of analysis with data from the 1953 survey, since information about the class position of the respondents' parents was not obtained in that year.

[9] See, for example, R. H. Knapp and H. B. Goodrich, *Origins of*

Scientific activity, more than any other, demands intellectual autonomy. The college student who constantly looks to others for detailed direction and guidance will probably not choose a career in science in the first place, and if he makes such a choice, will be less likely to achieve his goal of a doctorate, and if he achieves this goal is less likely to make a creative contribution of major importance to his field. At every turn the selective process favors the student who has been trained from childhood to think for himself.

What is true in fields such as science is also true to a lesser degree in other professions and in the ranks of middle and top management. In these fields also, intellectual autonomy is almost a prerequisite for admittance and is clearly a requirement for success.[10] In other words, in virtually all positions of an upper-middle-class character, Catholics operate at some disadvantage in modern society. It seems more than coincidence that in analyses of mobility the greatest differences between Catholics and Protestants are found at the level of the upper-middle class.

An analysis of immigrant generation as related to intellectual orientations revealed that in general intellectual autonomy is gaining at the expense of stress on obedience. This was especially true in the case of *working*-class Catholics: only 36 per cent of the first and second generation thought it more important for the child to learn to think for himself than to obey, compared with 65 per cent of the third generation. However, while these data suggested convergence between the two major groups, data from the *middle* class suggested the reverse. Middle-class Catholics were the only segment of the population in which *fewer* members of the third generation were committed to the principle of intellectual autonomy

---

American Scientists (Chicago: The University of Chicago Press, 1952), which indicates that Catholics produce less than one sixth the number of scientists one would expect from a group of their size. See also Francis Bello, "The Young Scientist," *Fortune Magazine,* June 1954, p. 142 ff., or S. S. Visher, *Scientists Starred, 1903–1943* (Baltimore: Johns Hopkins Press, 1947).

[10] See W. L. Warner and James Abegglen, *Big Business Leaders in America* (New York: Harpers, 1955), p. 89. These authors make this same point on the basis of their study of the recruitment of big business leaders.

than of the first and second generations (59 vs. 66 per cent). Thus, while convergence was occurring in the working class, the middle-class segments of these important groups were diverging.[11]

These findings also have implications for the American political system. In recent years the issue of individual freedom has been increasingly a source of controversy. On the one hand there are those who maintain that liberty has degenerated into license in our society, and that a greater exercise of authority is required if our nation is not to be so weakened that it cannot resist attack from without or crisis within. However, others maintain that, on the contrary, the chief threat to the American way of life comes from unnecessary and undesirable restraints on individual freedom—especially freedom of expression.

If we may judge from the responses of Detroiters to our question concerning the importance of intellectual autonomy, Catholics and Negro Protestants are more likely than either Jews or white Protestants to be responsive to appeals to limit individual freedom and increase authority. The latter are more likely to respond to appeals to limit authority and increase individual freedom.

On the basis of classical, liberal, democratic theory, the intellectual orientation of white Protestants and Jews is more nearly what is required of all citizens if we are to maintain a stable and effective democratic society. More recently, though, some political theorists have come to speculate that democratic systems function best when there is a diversity of political tendencies in the population, providing the majority adopts a moderate position on the issues, and only a small minority adopts extremist views.[12] However, regardless of whether the classical or modern theory is more accurate, the differences in intellectual orientation found among the socioreligious groups are certain to have consequences for the operation of our political system, as well as the economic.

[11] Among first- and second-generation immigrants in the middle class there was a difference of only 12 percentage points between white Protestants and Catholics. Between third-generation Americans there was a difference of 26 points.

[12] See, for example, Berelson, et al., op. cit., Chapter 14.

Use of leisure time

In their 1953 survey of child-rearing practices, Miller and Swanson asked mothers to what uses they would put leisure time if they had a great deal of it. The question was:

> We are interested in what mothers would do if they really had free leisure time. Suppose your housework and children were well taken care of most afternoons, you didn't have to work, and you have some extra money. Imagine this started in the summer. What would you do with the free time?

The range of responses to this question was considerable. Shopping was cited more than any other type of activity. Social service, such as visiting the sick and similar activities, ranked second. Visiting friends ranked third.

For our purposes we divided all of the many responses into two basic categories: (a) forms of self-indulgence; and (b) productive or constructive activities. Under the first heading we included activities such as shopping, visiting friends, relaxing, loafing, attending or participating in athletic events, attending movies or the theater, going on outings or picnics, vacationing, watching television or listening to the radio, attending meetings of social clubs, and going out to eat. Under the second heading we included such things as social service work, sewing, gardening, decorating, art work, reading, taking courses and studying, church work, taking a job, working around the house, and similar activities.

In keeping with Weber's analysis of the Protestant Ethic, we predicted that Protestant women would prefer productive or constructive activities more often than Catholic women, and that the latter would prefer self-indulgent activities more often than Protestant women. In view of our earlier findings we also predicted that Jewish women would resemble white Protestant women more than Catholics. We made no prediction concerning Negro Protestant women.

As *Table 41* indicates, the data supported both of our predictions. White Protestant women at both class levels were more likely than Catholic women to prefer productive or constructive activities, though at the middle-class level, the difference was quite small. Our data indicated that Jewish women were by far the most inclined to favor productive or constructive activities and that Negro Protestant women were somewhat more likely than Catholics to favor self-indulgent forms of activity. These findings pertaining to *women* obtained in the 1953 survey supplement our findings on *men's* attitudes toward work obtained in the 1958 survey. In both instances members of the Jewish group appear to have the most positive attitudes toward work, and Catholics and Negro Protestants the most negative.

One final piece of evidence which should be noted in this connection was obtained in the 1952 survey. In that year considerable information was gathered about the types of organizations to which Detroiters belonged and the frequency with which they attended meetings of these organizations. It was our prediction that Protestants and Jews would be more often active in "serious" organizations, and Catholics in "recreational" organizations. Under the first heading we included charitable and welfare organizations, neighborhood property owners' groups, business or civic clubs, political organizations, PTAs, professional groups, and so forth. Under the latter we included bowling teams, fraternal orders, and similar groups.

We found that of the organizations in which Jewish re-

Table 41

PERCENTAGE OF RESPONSES INDICATIVE OF A PREFERENCE FOR PRODUCTIVE OR CONSTRUCTIVE FORMS OF ACTIVITY, BY CLASS AND SOCIO-RELIGIOUS GROUP (1953 SURVEY)

Class: Socio-religious Group	Per cent	No. of Responses	No. of Respondents
Middle Class:			
Jews	(80)	15	9
White Protestants	54	202	87
White Catholics	51	177	74
Working Class:			
White Protestants	42	301	146
White Catholics	31	306	137
Negro Protestants	27	95	43

spondents were active,[13] 54 per cent were of a "serious" nature. The same was true of 40 per cent of the organizations in which white Protestants were active. However, this was true of only 31 per cent of the organizations in which Catholics were active, and 32 per cent of those in which Negro Protestants were active.[14]

Once again our data indicated that Catholics tend to avoid the more serious and demanding forms of activity in the modern metropolis, and turn instead to activities which provide chiefly personal gratifications. While this may or may not have consequences for vertical mobility when only membership in voluntary associations is involved, it is undoubtedly a serious matter if this same pattern of thought and action carries over into the world of work.

Present vs. future orientation

Turning to the 1953 survey again, there was still another question which afforded insight into the basic social orientations of Detroiters. It was:

Suppose a fourteen-year-old child were interested in some worthwhile activities that gave him (her) little time to spend with other children. The things the other children are doing are just as worthwhile, but they don't interest this particular child. Would you encourage him (her) in going on with his (her) own interests, or would you rather see him (her) change to something he (she) can do with other children?

Having made their choice, mothers were then asked to explain why they answered as they did.

On the major question Negro Protestants were the most likely to favor the child following his own interests, with 73 per cent of the mothers who took a stand taking this one. Among the other three groups no appreciable differences

[13] A person was classified as active in an organization if he reported attendance at at least half of the meetings of that group.

[14] With class controlled, the difference between Catholics and Negro Protestants was increased somewhat. Whereas 28 per cent of the active memberships of working-class Negro Protestants were in "serious" organizations, the same was true of only 24 per cent of the active memberships of working-class Catholics.

were observed. Fifty-eight per cent of the white Protestants and Jews shared this same view, as did 57 per cent of the Catholics.

The important differences came, however, when mothers explained *why* they answered as they did. Many mothers said that following his own interests (*or* doing things with other children) would help a child in his career, or in the development of his personality. Such answers we classified as "future-oriented" or "career-oriented" because whether the mother *chose* one course or the other her *reason* was a forward-looking one. On the other hand, many mothers justified their answers simply on the grounds that this would keep the child out of mischief, or would satisfy his immediate needs, or would make him happier. Such answers we classified as lacking an orientation toward the future.

It was our prediction that white Protestant mothers would be more likely than Catholic mothers to take the long-run view. We made no prediction concerning Negro Protestant mothers.

As may be seen in *Table 42*, our prediction for white Protestant and Catholic mothers was supported by the data, though differences were not large.[15] The fact that differ-

Table 42

PERCENTAGE OF RESPONSES INDICATING AN ORIENTATION TOWARD THE FUTURE IN CHILD REARING, BY CLASS AND SOCIO-RELIGIOUS GROUP (1953 SURVEY)

Class: Socio-religious Group	Per cent	No. of Responses	No. of Respondents
Middle Class:			
White Protestants	44	117	81
White Catholics	37	95	70
Working Class:			
Negro Protestants	48	48	43
White Protestants	41	190	140
White Catholics	35	164	130

[15] Jewish mothers were even more future-oriented than white Protestants, as indicated by the fact that 58 per cent of their re-

ences were not greater is probably due in part to the nature of the data we used. Since the original interviews were not coded with our problem in mind, the code categories employed were often ambiguous from our standpoint. Even so, a statistically significant difference was evident, indicating that to some degree at least Protestant groups develop in their members an orientation which facilitates success in the world of work. To the degree that a child's success depends on his parents' foresight, Catholic children are likely to be at some disadvantage.[16]

---

sponses were classified in this category. However, because only 8 Jewish mothers were involved, this evidence alone cannot be regarded with any great measure of confidence. But the fact that it is consistent with other findings suggests that the finding is due to more than sampling error. See Strodtbeck, op. cit., pp. 151–52, where he reports that in New Haven there was much more emphasis on the future in Jewish families than in Italian Catholic families.

[16] At least two other studies have explored the relationship between religion and planning. In the Strodtbeck studies cited earlier, op. cit., a substantial difference was found between Jewish and Italian Catholic boys in New Haven when they were asked for their reaction to the statement "Planning only makes a person unhappy since your plans hardly ever work out anyhow." Ninety per cent of the Jewish boys disagreed, but only 62 per cent of the Italian.

In another study Orville Brim and Raymond Forer asked a sample of 2700 Connecticut high school students, "How far in advance have you planned your life?" Thirty-nine per cent of the Jews responded with answers of five years or more. This compared with 30 per cent of the Protestants (apparently both white and Negro) and 21 per cent of the Catholics. Without any control for class the latter difference was significant at the .01 level; though correlational measures indicate that over half of this variance remained when class level was controlled, the authors do not say whether the remaining difference was significant at the .05 or .10 level, or whether a one- or two-tailed value of P was employed. They only state that the difference was not significant at the .01 level. In the case of the Jewish group, no tests of significance are reported with class controlled, but the authors state they are confident that there is a real difference. The second sample is much less meaningful, being based on 349 Yale undergraduates in an introductory political science course. Owing to the highly unrepresentative character of the sample, generalizations based on it seem dangerous. Suffice it to say that once again the Jewish group

Methods of discipline

Discipline is one of the most affect-laden aspects of the whole child-rearing process, and hence one of the most important. In the 1953 survey Miller and Swanson examined this subject, asking mothers how they would discipline a ten-year-old child when he or she did something which the mother thought was very wrong.

In every society a wide variety of disciplinary techniques are customarily employed, and American society is no exception. However, for purposes of analysis we divided the responses to this question into two categories: (a) those modes of discipline involving *physical* punishment, particularly spanking; and (b) those involving *symbolic* sanctions, such as scoldings, restriction of privileges, and so forth. Of these two, symbolic sanctions seem far more effective in developing a sense of responsibility and self-control in children, especially older children, such as ten-year-olds.[17] Furthermore (in line with our earlier discussion of intellectual autonomy and obedience), the use of *physical* sanctions where older children are involved reflects an obedience orientation on the part of the parent, and is likely to stimulate such an orientation on the part of the child; on the other hand, *symbolic* sanctions are more consistent with an autonomic orientation. Hence, it was our hypothesis that white Protestants and Jews would favor the use of symbolic sanctions and that Catholics would be more inclined to use physical sanctions.

As predicted, white Protestant mothers relied much more often on symbolic sanctions alone, while Catholic and Negro Protestant mothers were more likely to employ physical sanctions either alone or in conjunction with symbolic sanctions. As *Table 43* indicates, the differences were substantial at both class levels. It is especially interesting to see that the disciplinary practices of *working*-class white Protestants con-

---

had the highest percentage of long-range planners, while no appreciable differences were found between Catholics and Protestants. See "A Note on the Relation of Values and Social Structure to Life Planning," *Sociometry*, 19 (March 1956), pp. 54–60.

[17] See Miller and Swanson, who develop this point more fully. Op. cit., pp. 92–101 and 164–65.

Table 43

PERCENTAGE OF MOTHERS ADVOCATING PHYSICAL PUNISH-
MENTS FOR TEN-YEAR-OLD CHILD, BY CLASS, AND SOCIO-
RELIGIOUS GROUP (1953 SURVEY)

Class: Socio-religious Group.	Per cent	No. of Cases
Middle Class:		
White Protestants	9	55
White Catholics	26	43
Working Class:		
White Protestants	24	70
White Catholics	46	67
Negro Protestants	47	19

form to middle-class standards even more often than those of *middle*-class Catholics.

Miller and Swanson also asked their respondents to imagine that the child has been especially good. They were then asked what they would do on such an occasion. Here again a distinction can be made between the mothers who mentioned some material reward, such as money or a gift, and those who mentioned only symbolic rewards. Once again the latter seem more likely to develop the child's sense of responsibility and intellectual autonomy. Again, a marked difference was observed between the socio-religious groups, though in this instance class differences within each of the groups were negligible. Of the white Protestants, only 27 per cent stated that they would use material rewards to express their pleasure. By contrast, 41 per cent of the Catholics and 56 per cent of Negro Protestants said they would make use of material rewards.

Independence training

We also predicted that Protestant and Jewish children would be expected to assume responsibility at an earlier age than Catholic children. Again our best data on this subject came from the 1953 survey. In that year the sample of mothers was asked at what age they had required (or would require) their child to: (a) put away his own clothes; (b) pick up his own toys; (c) run errands to a nearby store; and (d) dress himself completely.

We divided respondents by socio-religious groups, with class position held constant, and found that on seven of the eight possible comparisons white Protestant mothers expected their children to assume these responsibilities at an earlier age than Catholic mothers. The lone exception was the requirement of picking up toys. Among working-class mothers, Catholics indicated that they required this at a slightly earlier age than white Protestants (2.9 vs. 3.1 years). On the four items as a whole, the median age at which middle-class Catholic mothers expected these responsibilities to be assumed was 5.0 years. For the middle-class white Protestant mothers it was 4.8 years. Among working-class mothers, the corresponding medians were 5.2 and 4.8 years. In other words, the differential was somewhat greater among working-class mothers than among middle-class mothers.

Negro Protestant mothers compared very favorably with Catholic mothers. On two of the items (dressing self and running errands) working-class Negro Protestant mothers expected an earlier assumption of responsibility than working-class Catholics. On the other two items (picking up toys and putting away clothes) Catholic mothers were stricter. The over-all median for the four items was 4.8 years for the Negro mothers and 5.2 for the Catholic mothers.

In the 1958 survey we asked one question which was also relevant to this discussion. People who had children of their own were asked whether they felt that a twelve-year-old child should be allowed to decide for himself whether he would go to church or Sunday school, or whether they felt that his parents should decide this (Q. 137). On this question, as on the questions from the 1953 survey, Catholics were more likely than Protestants to say that the child should wait longer to assume responsibility. Only 7 per cent of the Catholic parents in our sample felt that a twelve-year-old child was old enough to assume this responsibility, compared with 21 per cent of the white Protestants, 23 per cent of the Negro Protestants, and 32 per cent of the Jews. As we shall indicate later in the chapter, these differences cannot be explained simply on the grounds that Catholics are more devout than Protestants or Jews. The biggest differences occurred among those who were the most actively involved in their churches.[18]

Family size

One of the major functions of family life from the standpoint of society as a whole is that of reproduction. Although the American population gains its members to some slight degree through immigration, the vast majority of new members are added through birth, and through births to couples who assume the major responsibility for socializing and training their offspring. Although fertility is a very private matter in some respects, since Malthus' day scholars have recognized that it has broad social implications.

In the last hundred years, fertility rates have declined considerably. Small families of two or three children have become the norm instead of families of four, five, six, or more.

---

[18] The expected pattern of differences failed to appear on only one prediction in this area. In the 1953 survey Miller and Swanson asked the mothers in their sample how long they felt that a mother should supervise her child's activities closely and know what he is doing most of the time. We expected that Protestant mothers would not feel that such supervision was necessary for as long a period as Catholic mothers. This proved to be true among working-class mothers, but not among middle-class mothers.

In retrospect we were inclined to feel that this question may have been a poor one for predictive purposes since it confuses two issues. On the one hand it is related to the issue of how early the child shall assume responsibility for various types of action. On the other hand it is related to the issue of how long the period of parental supervision shall continue. On logical grounds there seems no reason for believing that those who think children should learn to assume responsibilities early should not also believe that the period of parental supervision should continue for an extended period. The longer the period of parental supervision, the greater the opportunity for the child to internalize his parents' values. If the parent is committed to the value of self-reliance and personal responsibility it may well be that these values are best transmitted to the child if the parent retains some measure of supervision over the child's activity for an extended period of time. Obviously this can be overdone. However, it is also possible to put the child on his own too early. In short, with the advantage of hindsight we felt that this particular question was not a good measure of concern for self-reliance and independence training.

During the 1930s many demographers predicted that the industrialized nations of the West were entering a phase of stable, or even declining, populations. Today, we know that they were wrong. In modern urban-industrial societies, fertility rates vary with the business cycle: rising rates follow boom periods and declining rates come quickly on the heels of any major recession. Hence, during the prosperous 1950s American fertility rates have been considerably higher than they were in the depressed 1930s.

In the modern metropolis there are many factors at work which have a leveling effect on fertility, tending to reduce differentials within the population. Religion, however, is not one of these. The influence of the churches has been in quite different directions. The Catholic Church has opposed the use of many of the more efficient means of contraception as immoral and has encouraged the view that large families are pleasing to God. On the other hand, the Protestant churches have increasingly taken the position that there is nothing immoral in the use of modern methods of contraception, and the *failure* to limit family size can be immoral if parents continue to have children when they are unable to provide properly for the spiritual and physical needs of those they already have.

The problem is to determine how far these different viewpoints affect actual practice. In a recent survey of a national sample of white married women between the ages of 18 and 39, Freedman, Whelpton, and Campbell found no significant differences in fertility between Protestants and Catholics.[19] However, they did find evidence which indicated that these Catholic wives would continue having children for a longer period than the Protestants, and that therefore the *completed* fertility of the Catholic wives would ultimately be higher than that of the Protestants.

The second major source of data on this subject is the Current Population Survey of the United States Bureau of the Census, conducted in March 1957. This was the only occasion in American history when the Census Bureau asked a question

[19] Ronald Freedman, Pascal K. Whelpton, and Arthur A. Campbell, *Family Planning, Sterility, and Population Growth* (New York: McGraw-Hill, 1959).

concerning religious preference. This survey obtained data from respondents in a representative sample of 35,000 American households. *Table 44* summarizes the major findings. Non-whites, most of whom were Negro Protestants, had the highest fertility rates in both age groups. Catholics ranked second, white Protestants third, and Jews last.[20]

Table 44

MEAN NUMBER OF CHILDREN BORN TO WOMEN EVER MARRIED, BY AGE AND SOCIO-RELIGIOUS GROUP (DATA OBTAINED IN CURRENT POPULATION SURVEY OF THE BUREAU OF THE CENSUS IN MARCH 1957)

Socio-religious Group	Mean Number of Children:	
	Women aged 15 to 44	Women 45 and over
Non-whites[a]	2.66	3.21
Catholics	2.28	3.06
White Protestants[b]	2.13	2.69
Jews	1.75	2.22

[a] Most non-whites are Negro Protestants.
[b] The figures for white Protestants were calculated by subtracting all non-white births and non-white women from Protestant totals.

Comparing the results of this survey with those of the Freedman survey, one disagreement should be noted, though it is not a major one. The Bureau of the Census survey produced evidence of a small difference in the fertility rates of white Protestant and Catholic women still in the child-bearing years, while Freedman found no difference. There are several possible explanations for this disagreement. First, it may only be due to sampling error in the two surveys. Second it may reflect the fact that the Census survey includes women aged 40 to 44 while the Freedman survey does not (a fact of some importance in light of the Freedman survey's finding that Catholic wives were likely to continue having children longer than white Protestants). Third, the Census survey was conducted two years after the Freedman survey, a fact which could be significant in the light of evidence uncovered by the Freedman survey that Catholic and white Protestant fertility

[20] This table is adapted from Table 40 in *Statistical Abstract of the United States: 1958.*

rates are likely to diverge in the near future.[21] Finally, the Census survey included all women ever married, while the Freedman survey was limited to those women currently living with their husbands. This could account for some of the disagreement in findings, since Protestant women are more often divorced, and divorced women have fewer children on the average than married women.

The findings of the 1958 Detroit survey, like those of the Census Bureau, revealed important differences in fertility among the major socio-religious groups. When Detroiters of all ages were classified by socio-religious group, the mean number of children ever born to members of the various groups was as follows:

Negro Protestants	3.0
White Catholics	2.7
Jews	2.2
White Protestants	1.9

On the whole these figures are similar to the national averages for these groups as determined by the Census Bureau's survey. For the nation as a whole the Negro Protestant figure for women of all ages was 3.0, for Catholics 2.7. For Jews the figure was 2.0, a bit lower than our figure, but sampling error tends to be larger in smaller groups.

The one group which differs sharply from the national average is the white Protestant group. Nationally the mean was 2.4; for white Protestants in our 1958 survey it was only 1.9. In view of the size of this group, sampling error is less likely to be the explanation of this difference. Rather, it seems to reflect the influence of geographical factors. White Protestants are disproportionately concentrated in the southern states and in rural areas generally. Both the South and the farm population have long been noted for their high fertility rates. Hence, in a national survey of fertility, white Protestant rates are likely to be a good bit higher than in a survey in a northern metropolis such as Detroit.

Far more surprising than this, however, was the substantial difference in fertility observed between *younger* white Protes-

21 Freedman, Whelpton, and Campbell, op. cit., p. 275.

tants and Catholics. Both the Freedman study and the Census Bureau's survey suggested that differences between these two groups had almost vanished. The findings of the 1958 Detroit survey indicated that very real differences remain. The 95 white Catholics under 40 years of age who had ever married reported on the average slightly over 2.3 children ever born. The 119 comparable white Protestants reported only 1.9.

The most obvious explanation for this discrepancy between the findings of our study and earlier studies was that of sampling error. Our sample was far smaller than those in either of the previous studies; hence, the difference we obtained might be a spurious one.

However, the three studies were not all conducted in the same year, and this suggested a second hypothesis. The differences in findings may reflect *a trend*—a trend producing increasing divergence between Catholic and Protestant birth rates. The Freedman survey in 1955 showed *no* difference in actual fertility among younger members of the two groups. The Census Bureau's survey in 1957 showed a very *small* difference of 15 children per 100 families. Our survey in 1958 showed a *larger* and more important difference of 43 children per 100 families. While some part of this pattern of increasing divergence might be due to sampling error in one or more studies, or to differences in the composition of the samples, some might also reflect a new trend, a reversal of the long-standing trend toward convergence.

This hypothesis is also suggested by certain findings in the Freedman study. While there were no differences in actual fertility between Catholics and Protestants, the Catholic wives whom Freedman interviewed said they expected eventually to have larger families than did the Protestants. From this Freedman and his associates concluded that by the time the women interviewed reached the end of their child-bearing period, differences between the two groups would develop. They predicted that among women born from 1916 to 1920, Catholics would average 3.1 children compared with 2.8 for Protestants, a difference of only 3 children for every 10 families. By contrast, they predicted that among women born from 1931 to 1937, Catholics would average 3.8 children compared with 2.9 for Protestants, or a difference of 9 children for every 10 families.[22]

To test the hypothesis that the birth rates of the white Protestant and Catholic groups are now diverging, we turned to data gathered by Detroit Area Surveys from 1952 to 1959. In every year except 1953 respondents had been asked how many children they had ever had. As *Table 45* reveals, their responses strongly supported our hypothesis. With the exception of only one year (1955), the difference between the two groups steadily increased throughout this period.

Table 45

MEAN NUMBER OF CHILDREN EVER BORN TO WHITE PROTESTANTS AND CATHOLICS UNDER 40 YEARS OF AGE, BY YEAR REPORTED[a]

| | Catholics: | | Protestants: | | |
Year	Mean	N	Mean	N	Difference
1952	1.72	120	1.57	139	0.15
1953	No data on fertility for this year			*	
1954	1.99	130	1.67	140	0.32
1955	1.84	87	2.13	86	-0.29
1956	2.00	119	1.65	137	0.35
1957	2.45	135	2.09	175	0.36
1958	2.33	95	1.90	119	0.43
1959	2.38	111	1.84	97	0.54

[a] The 1955 sample was limited to married women living with their spouse (i.e., not divorced, widowed, or separated). All other years for which data are shown include responses of male as well as female respondents, and all persons ever married and not merely those currently living with their spouse.

Our evidence indicates that younger couples in both groups are having more children, but the increase has been much more rapid in the Catholic group. Further analysis revealed that this same basic pattern occurs in both the middle and working classes, though it is more pronounced in the latter. It also occurs both among Detroiters raised in the northern part of the United States, and those born elsewhere (i.e., either in the South or abroad). In short, all our evidence indicates that the older trend toward convergence in this area has

22 Freedman, Whelpton, and Campbell, op. cit., p. 275.

come to an end, and has been replaced by a trend toward increasing divergence.

Especially noteworthy in this connection is the rapid growth of the large family among Detroit Catholics during the fifties. In the 1952, 1954, and 1955 surveys combined, only 10 per cent of the Catholic respondents under 40 reported having had four or more children. In the 1957, 1958, and 1959 surveys, by contrast, 22 per cent reported four or more children. Among white Protestants there was no change: in both periods 9 per cent reported four or more children.

The birth rate also seems to be increasing among young Negro Protestants, but here, as in the case of the white Protestants, the increase has been slower than in the Catholic group. In fact, as *Table 46* indicates, the rise in the Negro Protestant rate has been smaller than that in any of the other three major groups. In recent years the traditional differential between the Catholic and Negro Protestant groups seems to have been completely eliminated. It seems likely that the Negro Protestant rate will increasingly gravitate toward the white Protestant rate, leaving the Catholics the lone high-fertility group in the modern American metropolis.

In the Jewish group, our data seemed to indicate a rather rapid increase in the birth rate. However, owing to the limited

Table 46

MEAN NUMBER OF CHILDREN EVER HAD BY PERSONS EVER MARRIED AND UNDER 40 YEARS OF AGE, BY SOCIO-RELIGIOUS GROUP AND BY YEAR

Years*	Catholics		Wh. Prots.		N. Prots.		Jews	
	Mean	N	Mean	N	Mean	N	Mean	N
1952, 1954, and 1956 combined	1.91	369	1.63	416	2.18	158	1.59	27
1957, 1958, and 1959 combined	2.40	341	1.97	391	2.38	136	2.13	38

* 1955 was omitted from this table owing to some doubt as to the reliability of the data from that year (see *Table 45*). If 1955 had been used instead of 1956, it would have made the rise in the Catholic birth rate seem greater and that in the two Protestant groups less.

number of cases on which this conclusion is based some caution must be exercised in its interpretation.

In addition to asking how many children people had had, in the 1958 survey we also asked how many children they expected and wanted to have (Q. 135, 135c, and 135d). The most striking finding here was that younger Catholics (under 35) were much more likely than non-Catholics to desire a substantial enlargement in their family. Young Catholics expressed a desire for 2.0 more children than they already had. By contrast, young white Protestants wanted only 1.2 more children on the average, and Negro Protestants only 0.5.

The sharp contrast between the white Catholics and the Negro Protestants suggests that the high fertility rates of these two groups rest on very different foundations. In the latter group a desire for large families seems generally absent. Hence, it is likely that as knowledge of contraceptive methods becomes more widespread in the Negro group, birth rates will decline, or at best stabilize at their present level. In the case of the Catholic group, a further rise is very possible.

FERTILITY AND VERTICAL MOBILITY

These findings almost certainly have implications for our earlier findings concerning differences in the rates of mobility among the various socio-religious groups. The high rates of fertility in the Catholic and Negro Protestant groups have undoubtedly contributed to the low rates of upward mobility in these groups. Higher education has always been an asset in the job world; today it is a prerequisite to entry into most of the better positions. But higher education is expensive, and especially so at the better colleges and universities which provide entree to the best positions. Hence, children from larger families are bound to be at some disadvantage in the competition for good jobs, even when their fathers have incomes as large as those of fathers of smaller families.

What is often overlooked is the fact that the addition of one more child to a family reduces the probabilities of the family being able to afford higher education for its children by *far* more than it would at first appear. Funds for higher education come out of the residue which is left after parents feed, clothe, and house themselves and their children. Adding children to a family inevitably results in the transfer of some of this "uncommitted" residue to the basic necessities, unless the income of the family increases in proportion to the number of children (which is not common). In families with limited and relatively stable incomes, the addition of a third or fourth child may reduce the chances of sending *any of the children* to college by a third, a half, or more.

The large-family pattern of the past undoubtedly hindered the economic advancement of many Catholic families, and its return is likely to have the same effect. While it is true that the rise of junior colleges and state-supported universities has done much to reduce the costs of higher education, the costs are still considerable, and especially at the better institutions. Thus it would be a mistake to suppose that the recent divergence in white Catholic-Protestant fertility rates will have no effect on rates of vertical mobility.

It is especially significant to note that Catholic-Protestant differences in fertility rates have been greater in the middle class than in the working class. This could well be a factor contributing to our earlier finding that differences in rates of mobility are greater in the middle class than in the working class.

II. GROUP INVOLVEMENT
AND FAMILY LIFE

In the first section of this chapter we found that kinship ties are valued differently in the several socio-religious groups. White Protestants are inclined to place a lower value on them than members of other groups. Catholics in particular seemed to value them highly. One question these findings obviously raise is, what role, if any, the churches and the subcommunities play in creating these differences.

The white Protestant churches and the family

Surprising as it may seem, the evidence suggests that the white Protestant churches *weaken* kinship ties, or at least ties with the extended family. For example, in the 1952 survey it was found that 51 per cent of the *marginal* members of the white Protestant churches, but only 43 per cent of the *active* churchgoers, reported visiting their relatives at least once a week. Middle-class Protestants visited their relatives less often than working-class Protestants, but the difference between active churchgoers and marginal members was equal at the two class levels. Also, marginal churchgoers were more likely to report that they visited their relatives more often, or as often, as they visited any other category of persons. Sixty-three per cent of the marginal white Protestants reported this, compared with only 52 per cent of the active churchgoers. This again suggests that activity in the white Protestant churches is linked with *an extrafamilial orientation*.

Again, in the 1958 survey we asked respondents which meant more to them: their ties with relatives, or their ties with friends (Q. 117). While this question did not discriminate to any great degree among the larger socio-religious groups,[23] it did discriminate *within* the two larger groups. Among white Protestants, 67 per cent of the marginal members valued their ties with relatives more than their ties with friends. By contrast, only 56 per cent of the active churchgoers shared this view.

While churchgoing white Protestants were *less* likely than marginal Protestants to be highly involved in the kin group, they were much *more* likely to be involved in voluntary associations. In the 1952 survey, active churchgoing Protestants reported 60 memberships in voluntary associations (other than churches or unions) per 100 adults whereas marginal Protestants reported only 28 per 100 adults. In both middle and working classes there were approximately twice as many organizationally active persons among churchgoing Protestants as among marginal Protestants.[24]

As these data made clear, involvement in the white Protestant churches is negatively correlated with involvement in the kin group, but positively correlated with involvement in volun-

[23] Sixty-five per cent of the Catholics as compared with 63 per cent of the white Protestants reported that their ties with relatives meant more to them than their ties with friends.

[24] In part this difference reflects the participation of the churchgoers in church-related organizations, but this is by no means the only source of the difference. The active churchgoers reported 41 memberships per 100 adults in *secular* associations compared with only 26 per 100 adults for marginal Protestants.

tary associations and relationships with individuals outside the kin group. But do these correlations indicate a *causal* relationship, with involvement in the white Protestant churches being the moving force? Is it not possible that among mobile people who are cut off from their relatives involvement in the churches becomes a substitute for the extended family? Is it not possible that involvement in the white Protestant churches is the *consequence* of geographical mobility and the resultant weakening of kinship ties, rather than the *cause* of these things?

Such may be the case in some instances, but the data indicate that more often than not the causal influences flow in the other direction. For example, we found that church attendance rates are higher among native-born Detroit Protestants than among those who have migrated to the community from elsewhere. This is not what we would expect if involvement in the churches is a by-product of mobility. Furthermore, if involvement in the churches is a *consequence* of migration, why should this not be true of involvement in the Catholic Church? As we shall indicate shortly, involvement in the Catholic Church is positively correlated with involvement in, and valuation of, the extended kin group.

In recent months a small but growing number of voices have been raised in Protestant circles questioning the tendency of clergy and laity alike to equate the Kingdom of God with church-related organizations. These critics have also pointed out some of the disruptive effects which this tendency can have on family life.[25] During the fall of 1959 a number of letters appeared in one of the popular Detroit newspaper columns from people complaining about the disruption of family life caused by the excessive involvement of one or the other of the parents in church-related activities. In most instances the writers seemed to be referring to Protestant organizations.

The 1958 survey shows clearly that church-related organizations play a much more prominent role in Detroit Protestantism than in Detroit Catholicism. Fifty-four per cent of

[25] Articles and letters expressing this view have appeared in various religious journals such as *The Christian Century*.

the active, churchgoing, white Protestants are currently active in some such organization compared with only 24 per cent of the active, churchgoing Catholics.

In this respect modern Protestantism seems to exemplify the sectarian approach to Christianity—in the sense that this term was used first by Max Weber and later amplified and systematized by Ernst Troeltsch.[26] Sect-type religious groups, as contrasted with what Weber labeled the church-type group, have always been distinguished by their familiar call, "Come ye apart." From its very earliest days Christianity has contained a radical element which stresses the importance of the individual breaking completely with the world and with secular social relationships, even those of the family. This tradition is rooted in the statement of Jesus that He did not come to bring peace on earth, but a sword:

> For I have come to set a man against his father, and a daughter against her mother, and a daughter-in-law against her mother-in-law; and a man's foes will be those of his own household. He who loves father or mother more than me is not worthy of me; and he who loves son or daughter more than me is not worthy of me.
> (Matthew 10:35–37)

This has long been a key element in the sectarian tradition.

Obviously present-day Detroit Protestantism is not a good example of sectarian Christianity. It has gone too far down the road of compromise with the powers that be and with the secular institutions of society. Nevertheless, in the beginning Protestantism was to a considerable degree a sectarian-type revolt against the politically supported, socially respectable, worldly-wise, church-type organization. Though it has largely reverted to the parental type, in some ways Protestantism still retains lingering traces of its more radical past. One of these traces may be found in its attempts to create through

[26] Max Weber, *From Max Weber: Essays in Sociology*, op. cit.; see especially the essays entitled "The Social Psychology of the World Religions" and "The Protestant Sects and the Spirit of Capitalism." Weber defines the two key terms, "church" and "sect," on pages 288 and 306. Ernst Troeltsch has expanded on Weber's concepts in *The Social Teaching of the Christian Churches*, op. cit., Vol. I, pp. 331–49.

church-related organizations a substitute for secular social relationships, especially those of the extended family.

To the degree that they succeed in this attempt, the Protestant churches weaken the hold of the family on the individual and orient him to associational-type relationships in which the bond of kinship is replaced by the bond of common faith—as Weber noted more than a generation ago. One can hardly take a broad comparative view without seeing the Protestant churches as a training ground for participation in voluntary associations. Visitors to America from countries with a strong Catholic tradition are often amazed at the number and variety of voluntary associations in American communities, and in the degree of involvement of Americans in these organizations.[27] In brief, a great body of evidence both from this study and elsewhere points to the conclusion that the Protestant churches have long been, and continue to be, a force in society weakening the bonds of the extended family (and perhaps of the immediate family as well) and simultaneously stimulating the formation of, and participation in, voluntary associations. The relatively high divorce rate among Protestants may well be linked with this peculiar feature of the group. This is not to suggest that the Protestant churches ever encourage divorce, but only that by their tendency to turn the interests of individuals beyond the limits of family and kin, they set in motion a chain reaction which ultimately has this effect.

The Catholic Church and the family

The relationship of the Catholic Church to the kin group seems to be quite different from that of the Protestant churches. Whereas the Protestant churches appear to stand in a competitive relationship with the kin group to some degree, the Catholic Church stands in what is more nearly a

[27] See, for example, Alexis de Tocqueville, *Democracy in America* (New York: Vintage Books, 1954), Vol. II, especially p. 114 ff. This point was brought home to the author once again not long ago by a graduate student from Poland who spent a year and a half in this country, traveling extensively, and participating in American life to a degree few visitors from abroad are willing or able to do. In his opinion this was one of the most distinctive and impressive features of American life.

complementary relationship. The church and the kin group seem more often to be mutually reinforcing organizations in the lives of devout Catholics.

This can be seen quite clearly in the responses of Catholics in the 1952 survey. A high degree of involvement in the Catholic Church was *positively* correlated with a high degree of involvement in the kin group. Whereas 60 per cent of those who reported weekly attendance at Mass reported that they visited with their relatives at least once a week, the same was true of only 45 per cent of those who reported irregular attendance at Mass. This was just the reverse of the white Protestant pattern. The difference between *active* white Protestants and Catholics in this respect was considerable. Sixty per cent of the active Catholics, but only 43 per cent of the active white Protestants, visited relatives weekly.

Involvement in the Catholic Church was not linked to informal relationships with coworkers as was involvement in the white Protestant churches. On the contrary, the more active a Catholic was in his church, the less informal interaction he had with coworkers off the job. Only 9 per cent of the regular attenders at Mass reported weekly visits off the job with coworkers, compared with 21 per cent of the marginal Catholics. Again the pattern was just the opposite of the white Protestant pattern (for white Protestants the comparable figures were 16 and 12 per cent).

This same reversal was indicated by the 1958 question about the relative value attached to ties of friendship and kinship. A high valuation of kinship ties was *negatively* correlated with frequency of church attendance among white Protestants, whereas it was *positively* correlated with church attendance among Catholics. Sixty-six per cent of the active Catholics valued their ties with relatives more than their ties with friends, compared with 60 per cent of the marginal Catholics. While this difference is not great, it is the contrast with the white Protestant pattern which is important.

Finally, involvement in the Catholic Church was positively linked with having relatives outside the immediate family living in the household. Sixteen per cent of the active Catholics reported such an arrangement, compared with 12 per cent of the marginal Catholics. Again, this was the reverse of the white Protestant pattern.

On the basis of such evidence it seems clear that church and kin group stand in one relationship to each other among Catholics and another among white Protestants. The Catholic pattern is one which is highly appropriate in a "church-type" religious organization. As defined by Weber and Troeltsch, a church-type organization seeks to transform the world gradually through an evolutionary process. To achieve its ends it seeks to use, rather than destroy, existing institutions, whether these be the state or the family.

Of all the many institutional systems in society none has been more amenable to religious influence than the kin group. Unlike most institutional systems it involves no large number of people. Usually it possesses no intellectual leaders. Hence, conditions are highly favorable for religious organizations to influence the normative structure of kin groups. Such influence is exercised much more easily and effectively than in the case of larger organizations, such as nations, which frequently possess an intellectual leadership of their own and are therefore better able to resist the efforts of church-type groups to influence policy decisions. The important point is simply that *church-type religious organizations normally see the kin group as an ally deserving support, whereas sect-type organizations tend to see it as something of a competitor.*

Having stated this principle baldly, it is necessary to add that at the present time sectarian and churchly tendencies are considerably intermingled in both Protestantism and Catholicism. Neither is a good example of either of the ideal types. Protestantism has gone a long way down the road of compromise with existing institutions, so much so that leaders of major secular institutions find it easy, even convenient, to hold membership in one or another of the Protestant churches. On the other hand, American Catholicism shows certain distinct sectarian tendencies. The ancient sectarian call, "Be ye separate," has a strong appeal for contemporary American Catholic leaders, as evidenced by their encouragement of parochial schools and a host of separatist organizations such as the Catholic Youth Organization, the Knights of Columbus, and so forth. Similarly, the intransigence of Catholic leaders on the subject of birth control has more in common with the unyielding spirit of sectarianism than with the compromising spirit of the church-type organization. As a consequence of this blurring of the lines, distinctions between Protestants and Catholics are not as marked as they might be were Detroit Protestantism closer to the sect-type pattern and Detroit Catholicism closer to the church-type.

On first inspection the data on the organizational memberships of Catholics seem to contradict much of the foregoing analysis. Catholic churchgoers are much more likely than non-churchgoers to be active in voluntary associations. Among all Catholics, regardless of class, 34 per cent of the active churchgoers were also active in voluntary associations other than church or union, compared with 18 per cent of the non-churchgoers. This difference seems at least partly due to the Americanization process. Catholics who are inactive both in church and voluntary associations are disproportionately first- and second-generation immigrants. Among the more Americanized, involvement in the Catholic Church is only *mildly* linked with increased involvement in voluntary associations, while involvement in the white Protestant churches is *strongly* linked with increased involvement in voluntary associations. Thus, even here there seems to be a difference between the two groups.

The Negro Protestant churches and the family

We predicted that involvement in the Negro Protestant churches would have consequences similar to those of involvement in the white Protestant churches, and that the consequences might be even more pronounced, owing to the greater strength of sectarian tendencies in the Negro group. Our predictions proved correct so far as organizational involvement was concerned. Active churchgoers among the Negro Protestants were much more active in voluntary associations than marginal members of the group (53 vs. 25 active memberships per 100 adults). With class controlled, the figures for white and Negro Protestants, both active and inactive, were almost identical.[28]

[28] Among working-class white Protestants there were 51 active memberships per 100 adults active in the churches compared with

However, the data on involvement in the kin group ran contrary to expectations. On the question of whether they valued their ties with relatives more than those with friends, no relationship with church attendance was observed among Negro Protestants. On a second measure based on frequency of contact with relatives, active churchgoers in the 1952 survey reported weekly contacts with relatives *more* often than marginal members, though the difference was only half as great as in the case of the Catholic group. Finally, active Negro Protestants were *more* likely than marginal members of the group to have relatives outside the immediate family living in the household. The difference here was about the same as in the Catholic group.

Putting all of the various bits of evidence together, it appears that the Negro Protestant churches occupy a position intermediate between that of the white Protestant and Catholic churches in these matters. Why this should be so is not clear.

The subcommunities and the family

By contrast with involvement in the churches, which produces differing attitudes toward the kin group depending upon the church involved, involvement in the subcommunities has a more uniform effect. Our evidence on this subject is quite limited, since data on involvement in the subcommunities were not obtained in any year other than 1958. Hence, we are obliged to rely entirely on the question concerning the relative importance of ties with relatives and friends. Here we found that a high valuation of kinship ties was encountered more often among those who were highly involved in the subcommunities, both Protestant and Catholic. However, the differences were not great in either case. Among white Protestants who were highly involved in their subcommunity, 69 per cent valued ties with relatives more than ties with friends. This compared with 61 per cent of the less involved members

---

48 for active Negro Protestants. Among marginal white Protestants in the working class there were 23 active memberships per 100 adults compared with 25 per 100 for marginal Negro Protestants. For working-class Catholics the comparable figures were 29 and 11 per 100 respectively.

of the group. Among Catholics the comparable figures were 68 and 63 per cent.

Personal values

Turning to the subject of the values which Detroiters sought to instill in their children, we found that involvement in the *churches* had little or no relationship to commitment to the principle of intellectual autonomy.[29] However, the relationship of individuals to their *subcommunity* seemed to be a matter of some importance. Those who were highly involved in their subcommunity valued obedience more highly than those who were marginal. Among white Protestants 39 per cent of the highly involved ranked obedience above autonomous thought compared with 29 per cent of the marginal members of the group. Among Catholics the comparable figures were 53 and 44 per cent respectively.

With respect to the values of hard work and helping others the situation was exactly reversed. The relationship of the individual to the *subcommunity* had little or no effect on his preference between them, but his relationship to the *churches* did. Involvement in the white Protestant churches seemed to stimulate a preference for the more humanitarian value of helping others, while involvement in the Catholic and Negro Protestant churches seemed to stimulate a preference for the more achievement-oriented value of hard work, with this latter pattern being more pronounced in the Catholic than in the Negro Protestant group.

As we expected, the greater the involvement of white Protestant mothers (in the 1953 survey) in their churches, the greater was their preference for constructive use of leisure time (as contrasted with self-indulgent uses), and for "serious" organizations (as contrasted with purely social organizations). Also, involvement in these churches was positively correlated with an orientation toward the future rather than a concern with the present. However, contrary to expectations,

[29] Among white Protestants 69 per cent of the actively involved expressed a commitment to this principle compared with 67 per cent of the marginal members of the group. For Negro Protestants the comparable figures were 45 and 44 per cent respectively. For Catholics they were 53 and 53 per cent.

this same pattern was observed in all three of the major socio-religious groups, and what was most startling of all, it was most pronounced in the Catholic group. In the Catholic group the differences between those actively involved in the church and those who were marginal tended to be substantial, ranging from a 16-percentage-point difference on the use of leisure time to a 29-point difference on the preference for "serious" organizations. Among white Protestants the differences were quite modest, ranging from a 3-point difference on the preference for "serious" organizations to an 8-point difference on the use of leisure time.

These facts make it clear that insofar as Catholics fail to rise in the secular world with the same frequency as non-Catholics, and insofar as this relative failure is a function of the values and orientations they have internalized in these areas, the church cannot be held accountable. One can only wish that data were available to determine what influence, if any, the Catholic *subcommunity* has on these relationships.

Discipline and independence training

Degree of involvement in the white Protestant churches seemed strongly linked with reliance on *symbolic* means of discipline. Among mothers who were actively involved in the white Protestant churches only 26 per cent reported that they would use physical means of punishing a ten-year-old child who had done something seriously wrong. By contrast, 45 per cent of the marginal mothers indicated that they would administer a spanking or some other physical punishment. Among Catholics, by contrast, there was a slight positive relationship between involvement in the church and the use of *physical* punishments. Whereas 39 per cent of the active Catholic mothers reported they would favor physical punishment for a ten-year-old only 35 per cent of the marginal mothers took the same stand.

In the area of independence training there seemed to be no relationship at all between involvement in the churches and the age at which children were expected to assume responsibility for various types of actions. The limited relationships observed all seemed well within the range of sampling error. Because the data on this subject were gathered in the 1953 survey, it was not possible to determine whether communal involvement had any effect on this relationship.

Family size

In all three of the larger socio-religious groups, those who attend church regularly tend to have larger families than those who do not. This relationship is most marked in the Catholic group where, on the basis of the 1952, 1954, and 1956–59 surveys it was found that those of the younger adults who attended Mass every week had had 2.22 children on the average (N=530), while those who were less regular had had 1.88 (N=178). Among white Protestants the comparable figures were 1.90 (N=239) and 1.75 (N=568). Among Negro Protestants they were 2.32 (N=106) and 2.25 (N=188).

By comparing results from the earlier years (1952, 1954, and 1956) with those of the later years (1957, 1958, and 1959), some insight into trends can be obtained. In the white groups, the largest gains in family size were found among the active, churchgoing Catholics, where, comparing the earlier period with the later, an increase of five children for every ten families was indicated. Among marginal Catholics, and active and marginal white Protestants, the increase averaged about three children for every ten families. In other words, though the recent rise in the birth rate has affected all segments of the white population, it seems to have been most marked among Catholics who are active in their church.

Among Negro Protestants, trend data yielded a rather surprising pattern. Among active churchgoers there was a *decline* of three children for every ten families, while among marginal members of the group there was an increase of five. This pattern is consistent with our earlier findings which indicate that the Negro Protestant churches tend to be a force undermining traditionalistic values in the Negro minority.

Although involvement in the churches was linked with *larger* family size, involvement in the socio-religious subcommunities was linked with *smaller* size. In the white Protestant subcommunity there was a difference of approximately two children for every ten families, with the children of marginal families being larger. Among Catholics there was a difference of one child for every ten families.

Why there is this difference between the influence of the churches and of the subcommunities is not at all clear. But one thing is certain: these two aspects of group involvement are not mutually reinforcing, nor are they what Lazarsfeld has labeled "interchangeable indices."[30] Each seems a unique phenomenon in its own right, with its own peculiar pattern of relationships with other variables.

III. ORTHODOXY, DEVOTIONALISM, AND FAMILY LIFE

Doctrinal orthodoxy and intellectual autonomy

Probably the most important finding in this area concerned the relationship between doctrinal orthodoxy and intellectual autonomy. As predicted, autonomy was negatively correlated with orthodoxy, at least among Protestants, both Negro and white. In each case the relationship was rather marked. For example, among heterodox white Protestants, three quarters felt that in a child's preparation for life it is more important for him to learn to think for himself than to learn to obey. By contrast, only half of the orthodox shared this view. Among Negro Protestants the comparable figures were one half and one third respectively.

These figures call to mind the frequent assertion that the Protestant Reformation was influential in ushering in the modern era chiefly because it weakened the hold of religion on the minds of men and with it the hold of dogma and superstition. Our data indicate, however, that the problem is much more complex than this popular positivist view would have it.

To begin with, among Catholics heterodoxy is *not* linked with a commitment to intellectual autonomy. On the contrary, *unorthodox* Catholics tend to value training in obedience ahead of autonomy somewhat more often than *orthodox* Catholics (52 vs. 45 per cent), though this difference is partly due to the slight educational advantage enjoyed by the orthodox.

A second finding which fits poorly with the popular posi-

[30] See the essay by Paul Lazarsfeld on methodology in Robert K. Merton, Leonard Broom, and Leonard Cottrell, Jr., eds., *Sociology Today* (New York: Basic Books, 1959).

tivist view is the fact that among *unorthodox* Protestants, those who attended church regularly were more likely to value intellectual autonomy than those who were irregular in their attendance or never attended. This pattern recurred in all three subdivisions of the Negro and white Protestant groups where comparisons were possible. Among heterodox, middle-class white Protestants, 90 per cent of the regular churchgoers (N=21) valued intellectual autonomy compared with 79 per cent of the heterodox who did not attend regularly (N=63). Among working-class white Protestants the comparable figures were 75 per cent (N=16) and 67 per cent (N=84). Among working-class Negro Protestants the figures were 67 per cent (N=15) and 38 per cent (N=32). In short, *the locus of the autonomous orientation among Detroiters was found among unorthodox Protestants (both white and Negro) who attend church regularly.* Among these persons (N=52), 79 per cent expressed a commitment to intellectual autonomy. Ranking second in this respect were those unorthodox Protestants who were not active in the churches (66 per cent, N=179). For the remainder of the membership of the three major socio-religious groups only 51 per cent (N=252) shared this orientation. This clearly is not the pattern popular positivism would lead one to expect.

Instead, this pattern suggests that the movement within Protestantism aimed at freeing the churches from the more dogmatic doctrinal formulations of the past has been one of the important sources of intellectual autonomy. The greater the exposure of individuals to this movement, the greater the probability of their commitment to the autonomic orientation. This hypothesis permits one to explain why unorthodox Protestants who are *not* greatly involved in the churches express commitment to this principle less frequently than those who *are* highly involved, and why unorthodox Protestants express such a commitment so much more often than unorthodox Catholics.

We do not mean to suggest here that the liberal Protestant movement is the only force, or even the most important force, promoting intellectual autonomy in contemporary American society. Clearly other forces are at work, as indicated by the very strong commitment of the Jewish members of our sample to this principle. The modern scientific movement has also had a very great influence.

Catholic orthodoxy and valuation of the kin group

As we observed earlier, involvement in the Catholic Church and subcommunity were both correlated with a preference for relatives over friends. However, even when one controls for the influence of both of these types of group involvement, there is a strong positive relationship between doctrinal orthodoxy and a preference for relatives over friends. In four separate subsamples in which associational and communal involvement were varied (associational involvement high, communal involvement high; associational involvement high, communal involvement low, etc.), the more orthodox members of the subsamples expressed a preference for their ties with relatives more often than the heterodox. The mean difference was 15 percentage points, indicating that doctrinal orthodoxy is a strong factor contributing to the general Catholic pattern of concern for the kin group.

When migration was used as a measure of the value placed on ties of kinship, again the data indicate that among Catholics the orthodox orientation is linked with a concern for the kin group. Whereas 49 per cent of the orthodox were lifelong residents of Detroit, this was true of only 37 per cent of the heterodox. Given this relationship one might, of course, contend that migration weakens orthodox beliefs and that orthodoxy is the dependent variable in the relationship. We would not deny that this pattern occurs in some instances, but it seems significant that orthodoxy was not related to migratory status in either of the Protestant groups. While it could be argued that migration weakens only Catholic orthodoxy, it is more reasonable to believe that Catholic orthodoxy inhibits migration by virtue of the importance which Catholic orthodoxy places on the family bond and ties of kinship.

Fertility

Finally, it seems appropriate to note that in all three of the larger socio-religious groups, both devotionalism and doctrinal orthodoxy were positively linked with fertility and at both class levels. Those who ranked high in terms of either of these two religious orientations were more likely to desire, and to have had, larger families than those who ranked lower.

IV. A CONCLUDING NOTE ON FAMILY LIFE AND VERTICAL MOBILITY

The data analyzed in this chapter underline the crucial importance of the family as a source of those traits of personality which are so crucial for success in the job world. In much of the recent literature on the interrelations of personality and mobility, attention has centered chiefly on one such trait: ambition, or the desire to get ahead. Our data indicate, however, that motivation is *only one of many* personality traits that influence the rise and fall of individuals and families. Furthermore, its importance may be greatly overrated, at least from the standpoint of explaining why some socio-religious groups are more successful than others. Our findings suggest that other personality characteristics such as *values, beliefs,* and *abilities* are of greater importance. Success may depend as much (or more) on the devaluation of kinship, the belief in the existence of opportunity, or the ability to think for one's self, as on sheer ambition. In fact, those with only limited ambition may fare quite well in our society provided they possess these other important personality traits.[31] A recognition of this fact is likely to increase our awareness

---

[31] In a recent study of school administrators, Melvin Seeman reported only a modest relationship between success and ambition. On the basis of his study he concluded that it is necessary to think in terms of four types of individuals: (1) the successful striver, (2) the unsuccessful striver, (3) the successful non-striver, and (4) the unsuccessful non-striver. See Seeman, "Social Mobility and Administrative Behavior," *American Sociological Review,* 23 (December 1958), pp. 633–42. A recognition of the importance of values, beliefs, and abilities as major factors influencing chances for success in the job world should do much to increase our understanding of the otherwise baffling second and third categories of Seeman. Of all the recent work on the social psychological sources of individual mobility, Strodtbeck's work is probably the most sophisticated from the standpoint of the range of personality characteristics considered (op. cit.).

of the influence of socio-religious groups on the mobility process, since, although their influence on ambition is negligible, their influence on other traits of personality is more substantial.)

Chapter 6

RELIGION, EDUCATION, AND SCIENCE

all

In modern industrial societies educational institutions play an increasingly important role in the socialization of the individual. This trend has been inevitable. When occupational specialization is carried to extremes, and when the place of work is separated from the place of residence, it is impossible for most children to learn many of the necessary skills required by the world of work within the context of home and family. This is not to say that the family is no longer important in the preparation of the child for future employment. Far from it. The family is still the source of basic personal skills, values, and ideological commitments which are so vitally essential for success. However, for many crucial technical skills the child is obliged to turn to the schools.

One of the distinctive features of the modern world of work is the growth of large-scale enterprises directed by complex bureaucracies. In these enterprises, which employ an ever increasing percentage of the American labor force, something resembling a caste system has developed in the last twenty-five to fifty years. Employees of the modern corporation are typically divided into two discrete categories, the salaried employees and the wageworkers, and there is little opportunity for the hourly rated wageworkers to rise to the ranks of salaried employees. With the increasing bureaucratization of these organizations, educational prerequisites for salaried positions have been established, so that those with limited education who enter the firm as wageworkers have very little chance of advancing.

The system closely resembles the traditional military model, with its basic distinction between officers and enlisted men. With rare exceptions, officers were, and are, recruited from outside the military organization, and moved into the system in an advanced position. Similarly, the salaried employees of modern corporations, especially those in managerial positions, are generally recruited from outside the organization, and brought in over the heads of the hourly workers. Even to be considered for such a position a man must usually have had a specified amount of formal education. In short, in many respects the educational system of modern American society serves as a screening and evaluative mechanism for the economic institutions.[1]

In this chapter our primary concern will be to discover what effect religion has on the educational institutions of contemporary American society and on the experiences of individuals in these institutions. In this chapter we shall be especially concerned with the influence exercised by the massive educational system established by the Catholic Church which parallels the public school system. How does training in the Catholic school system influence the careers, behavior, and values of its students? Does it increase or decrease their chances for advancement in the job world? How does it influence the thoughts and actions of its graduates in the realms of politics and economics? What effect does it have on family life, and on child rearing? Does it strengthen loyalty to the Catholic Church and its normative standards? These are only a few of the questions to which we shall seek answers in this chapter.

In the latter part of this chapter we shall also examine briefly the views of Detroiters on the interrelations between religion and science. Do they think the teachings of science conflict with the teachings of their own church? How serious do they feel these conflicts are? What effect do such views have on career choices? These, too, are questions to which we shall seek answers.

[1] See Pitirim Sorokin, *Social Mobility* (New York: Harper, 1927), pp. 187–93.

I. EDUCATIONAL ATTAINMENTS
IN THE FOUR GROUPS

Somewhat to our surprise, differences in the educational attainments of the three white groups were not large (see *Table 47*). Jews were the most likely to have received some college education, and Catholics were the most likely to have received only a grammar school education. However, Catholics were as likely as Protestants to have received some college education, and Jews were more likely than Protestants to have received only a grammar school education.

Table 47

PERCENTAGE OF RESPONDENTS RECEIVING SPECIFIED AMOUNTS OF FORMAL EDUCATION, BY SOCIO-RELIGIOUS GROUP

Amount of Education*	White Protestants	White Catholics	Jews	Negro Protestants
College	20	20	26	12
High school	62	55	51	50
Grammar school	18	24	22	36
None	0	1	0	2
TOTAL	100	100	99	100

* Classification in these categories indicates that the individual did at least some work at this level; it does not mean completion.

The group which differed most from the others was the Negro Protestant, but even here differences were not as great as had been expected. Differences in education were not nearly as marked as differences in class. This suggests that either the class position of Negroes in Detroit is affected by occupational discrimination, or that the education which they received was inferior to that received by whites, *or both*. This last possibility seems quite likely in view of the fact that the majority of Negroes in our sample attended segregated schools in the South.

Dropouts

(Although differences among the three white groups were relatively small when judged by the general level of education, there were much larger differences in the frequency with which individuals dropped out of school before completing the unit of education on which they had embarked.) Jewish respondents were the most likely to have completed a given unit, regardless of whether this unit was grammar school, high school, or college. Seventy-one per cent of the Jewish respondents carried their education to the point where they completed the last unit they entered, and only 29 per cent dropped out part way through. White Protestants ranked second, with 61 per cent completing their last unit of education. Among Catholics and Negro Protestants, by contrast, only 48 and 33 per cent were able to do this.[2]

One might suppose that these differences merely depended on the class origins of the members of the different groups, with those of middle-class background being more likely to complete their education than those of working-class or farm background. While there is some reason for believing that this interpretation may largely account for the very high rate of completion among Jewish respondents and the very low rate of completion among Negro Protestants, it does not provide any explanation for the difference between white Protestants and Catholics. In our sample, the latter were actually raised in middle-class families more often than the former. Whereas 24 per cent of the Catholics were the children of urban, middle-class parents, only 20 per cent of the white Protestants were in this same category.[3] Despite the fact that dropouts occurred among children of middle-class parents much less often than among children of working-class parents (38 vs. 54 per cent), Catholics were much more likely than Protestants to have dropped out of school without com-

[2] Weller obtained similar results. He found 51 per cent of the white Protestants in his six-year sample completed their last unit of education compared with only 38 per cent of the Catholics. See *Dissertation*, Chapter 4.

[3] If one includes only those of *urban* origin, 28 per cent of the Catholics, compared with 24 per cent of the white Protestants, were of middle-class origin.

pleting the unit of education they had begun (52 vs. 39 per cent). (In short, class origins had nothing to do with the substantial difference between white Protestants and Catholics.)

The implications of this pattern for subsequent career history can hardly be exaggerated. Those who fail to complete a given unit of education are much less likely to get ahead in the world of work than those who carry their education through to completion. For example, of those in our sample who attended college, but did not graduate, only 64 per cent achieved middle-class status, compared with 96 per cent of those who graduated. Among those who attended high school but did not graduate, only 28 per cent achieved middle-class status, compared with 43 per cent of the graduates. Among those who attended grammar school but did not graduate only 8 per cent attained middle-class status, compared with 18 per cent of the graduates. In other words, the dropouts in each unit had one third to one half fewer chances of attaining middle-class status than those who went on to complete the unit.[4] For this reason it appears that the high dropout rate of Catholics is a *major* factor contributing to their relatively low rate of upward mobility and high rate of downward mobility.

While the failure of Catholics to complete given units of education may be an *immediate* cause of their failure to advance in the occupational system to the same degree as white Protestants and Jews, clearly it is not the *ultimate* cause. This high dropout rate itself requires some explanation. Having found that this cannot be accounted for by the class origins of our respondents, we are led to speculate about the role of religion in the process. In view of our earlier findings concerning the spirit of capitalism, it seems reasonable to suppose that Protestantism and Catholicism generate differing views of education and its value, or perhaps differing attitudes toward particular behavior patterns which are essential for success in the educational system.

Students who drop out of school before attaining their

[4] These same relationships may also be observed in census data. See, for example, U. S. Bureau of the Census, *Current Population Reports, Labor Force*, Series P-50, No. 14 (May 23, 1949).

immediate goals often seem attracted by extraeducational goals such as marriage and economic independence, and sometimes by dislike for the educational system itself which denies them rewards which they seek, most notably (in the case of slower students) self-respect. We cannot be certain whether the high frequency of Catholic dropouts is a function of "push" or "pull," or both. However, our data do provide some insights into the problem.

(A great variety of studies have demonstrated conclusively that those who quit school without graduating are largely weak students.) Research has also demonstrated that performance in school is positively correlated with I.Q., that I.Q. is negatively correlated with family size, and finally (as our own and other studies have shown) that Catholics have larger families than white Protestants.[6]

(In view of these relationships we would predict that Catholics would perform less well in school than white Protestants, and hence drop out of school more often. We might further predict that this difference would be more marked in schools in which Catholics were obliged to compete with non-Catholics. A test of this latter hypothesis proved that this was, in fact, the case. Among Catholics who had most or all of their education in parochial schools, only 45 per cent had dropped out of school without completing the unit which they had begun. By contrast, among Catholics who had all or most of their education in public schools, 55 per cent were dropouts. This difference was especially pronounced when we omitted grammar school students from the comparison. Among Catholics who attended either high school or college, 54 per cent of those who received all or most of their education in the public schools were dropouts, compared with only 37 per cent of those who received all or most of their education in Catholic schools. In other words, the further Catholics go educationally, the greater is the differential between those who attend Catholic and public schools.

[5] See, for example, A. B. Hollingshead, op. cit., Chapter 13.

[6] For an excellent summary of the literature on the crucial link in this chain, the relationship between I.Q. and family size, see Lipset and Bendix, op. cit., pp. 238–43.

While this does not prove the hypothesis that the high drop-out rate of Catholics is partly a result of competition encountered in the public schools, it is at least consistent with it.[7]

There may also be an element of "pull" involved. Much has been written on the subject of "deferred gratification," or the ability to postpone the enjoyment of rewards, and it may be that Catholics are less willing than Protestants to postpone rewards like a steady income or marriage. This idea is consistent with our finding that Catholic mothers preferred self-indulgent forms of activity more than Protestant mothers. On the other hand, we cannot ignore the findings of recent research which indicate that Catholic girls marry approximately eighteen months later on the average than white Protestants.[8]

To summarize the evidence thus far, we may say that:

(a) Catholics are more likely than Protestants or Jews to drop out of school without completing the unit of education they have begun;

(b) dropouts do not fare as well subsequently as those who complete an educational unit;

(c) there is some evidence that the Catholic pattern of dropouts is a response to competitive difficulties encountered in the public schools;

(d) possibly the Catholic dropout pattern is a result of the positive attraction of earning one's own income and an unwillingness, or inability, to defer gratifications.

This last point, however, is the most questionable of the four.

[7] Recent research by Harold Organic suggests that the ethnic factor may be important here and the high dropout rate of public school Catholics may reflect the large number from South and East Europe (op. cit.).

[8] John Beresford, unpublished doctoral dissertation, The University of Michigan, forthcoming.

II. THE CONSEQUENCES
OF ATTENDING CATHOLIC SCHOOLS

Which Catholics attend Catholic schools?

Before turning to the interesting and important question of the *effects* of Catholic vs. public education, it may be well to see how Catholics educated in Catholic schools differ in *background* from those educated in public schools. For this purpose we divided the Catholic respondents in our 1958 survey into two categories: (a) those who received more than half of their education in Catholic schools, whom we shall refer to as those with a *Catholic education,* and (b) those who received half or less in Catholic schools, whom we shall refer to as those with a *public education.* Thirty-five per cent of our sample were in the former category, 65 per cent in the latter.

From the standpoint of class, Catholics from a middle-class home were a bit more likely to have received a Catholic education than those from working-class or farm families. Thirty-eight per cent of the former received a parochial education compared with 34 per cent of those from working-class families and 31 per cent of those from farm families. These differences are not very great, and neither are differences great if we classify respondents on the basis of their present class position. Thirty-nine per cent of the middle-class Catholics had received a Catholic education compared with 33 per cent of the working-class Catholics. If the income of the family head is substituted as the criterion, the differences remain about the same. Thirty-nine per cent of those Catholics in families in which the head reported an annual income of $8000 or more, received a Catholic education compared with 30 per cent of the Catholics in families in which the head earned under $5000 per year. Those in families with an income of $5000–$7999 per year were quite similar to those with higher incomes, with 38 per cent reporting a Catholic education.

In one respect the probabilities of obtaining a Catholic education were negatively correlated with a socio-economic variable. Among those Catholics who had received at least some college education, only 32 per cent reported a Catholic education, compared with 36 per cent of those who had not reached the college level. (This difference is probably due to the fact that there are a far greater number of Catholic schools at the elementary level than at the higher levels, so that the farther a Catholic goes in the educational system the fewer are his opportunities to attend a Catholic institution)

From the standpoint of sex a slight difference was observed. (Catholic women were a bit more likely to have had a Catholic education than Catholic men.) Thirty-eight per cent of the women, compared with 32 per cent of the men, reported a Catholic education. Again the difference was not very great.

When Catholics were classified by age, a curious curvilinear relationship was observed. The youngest and oldest adults were the most likely to have obtained a Catholic education, and those from 35 to 49 years of age the least likely. Whereas 39 per cent of the young Catholics and 37 per cent of the older Catholics reported a Catholic education, only 29 per cent of those in the middle years reported this. This probably reflects the influence of the depression of the 1930s on this generation.

The one really substantial difference associated with the type of education Catholics received appeared when we considered nationality background. Although 46 per cent of the Catholics of northwest European background (N=95) reported a Catholic education, only 28 per cent of the Catholics with a south or east European background (N=122) reported this. (The fact that there was so little relationship between class or income and education suggests that more than financial factors are involved here) Evidently it is not simply that south and east European Catholics are not able to afford parochial schools for their children. Rather it appears that something of the Latin anti-clerical tradition may still survive.

Two confounding factors

In any comparison of the consequences of Catholic and public education there are at least two confounding factors which are not easily controlled and which must be considered. Fortunately, however, these factors have opposing consequences, so we may hope that they partially cancel out each other.

(On the one hand, there has probably always been a selective process operating determining which Catholic young people receive a Catholic education.) For example, in our present sample we found that 79 per cent of the respondents who attended Mass every Sunday had at least some of their children enrolled in Catholic schools, compared with 31 per cent of the respondents who were irregular in their attendance at Mass. This is important because it means that if one compares the behavior of those Catholics who have attended parochial schools with that of those who received a public education, the differences which one observes may be partly a function of differences in *parental* influence. If those who attended Catholic schools are more regular in attendance at Mass or otherwise seem "more Catholic" in their behavior, this difference cannot be credited entirely to the influence of Catholic schools.)

(On the other hand, among adult Catholics there is a great deal of interaction between those who received a Catholic education and those who did not. For instance, Catholics who received a Catholic education frequently marry Catholics who did not. Through such interaction those Catholics who did not receive a Catholic education come to think and act more like those who did, while those who did receive a Catholic education come to think and act more like those who did not. (As a result, the influence of Catholic education comes to be diffused throughout the Catholic population generally, and differences between the two categories of Catholics are reduced.)

Because these two factors have opposing consequences, in the first instance exaggerating the influence of a Catholic education and in the second instance minimizing it, we are hopeful that a simple comparison of Catholics who have and have not received a Catholic education will yield a reasonable approximation of the influence of the Catholic schools themselves. Despite the limitations of this mode of analysis, we feel that in the absence of any comparable body of data on many of the topics with which we shall be concerned, and in view of the growing importance of the Catholic system of education, our findings will be of interest and importance.

Loyalty to the Catholic Church and its norms

(The primary justification which the Catholic Church gives for building and maintaining a separate school system in America is the need for indoctrinating the young in the principles of the Catholic faith.[9]) This is a task which the public schools are constitutionally unable to perform and which Catholic leaders feel must be performed. But how successful are Catholic schools in their appointed task? Does a Catholic education make a difference, or are Catholics with a Catholic education indistinguishable from those with a public education?

(If we use attendance at Mass as a measure of the religious influence of Catholic education, it is clear that the schools do make a difference, though the degree of influence may be less than many might imagine.) Among Detroiters who had received a Catholic education (N=81), 86 per cent attended Mass at least once a week. By comparison, only 71 per cent of those with a public education (N=149) reported weekly attendance at Mass. If one divides the latter category into (a) those who received part of their education in Catholic schools, and (b) those who received none, the difference becomes a bit larger. Whereas 78 per cent of the former reported weekly attendance at Mass, only 67 per cent of the latter did so. Our findings here confirm earlier research in this area.[10]

(Not only are Catholics with a Catholic education more regular in attendance at Mass, they also tend to be doctrinally orthodox with somewhat greater frequency than those with a public education.) We found that 68 per cent of those who had received a Catholic education were classified as

[9] See, for example, Joseph H. Fichter, S.J., *Parochial School: A Sociological Study* (Notre Dame, Ind.: University of Notre Dame Press, 1958), p. 77.

[10] See, for example, George A. Kelly, *Catholics and the Practice of the Faith* (Washington: Catholic University Press, 1946), pp. 122–33.

doctrinally orthodox compared with 56 per cent of those with a public education.

A Catholic education also appears to increase somewhat the probabilities that Catholics will adopt a devotional orientation. Fifty-two per cent of those who had received a Catholic education ranked high by our measure of devotionalism, compared with 44 per cent of those who had received a public education.

It seems noteworthy in this connection that the larger differentials were linked with ritual and doctrine, and the smaller differentials with matters of personal devotion. It looks as if Catholic schools are more successful in cultivating the former than the latter—though this is not too surprising, given the secondary character of social relationships in a school setting and also the character of the Catholic Church itself.

One of the largest differences of all appeared when we asked our respondents whether they believed that the Catholic Church is the only true church established by God and that other churches were only established by men. Whereas 78 per cent of those with a Catholic education agreed with this central Catholic doctrine, only 61 per cent of the remainder shared this belief. Since so many aspects of Catholic faith and practice derive from this doctrine, it would seem that from the Catholic standpoint, the successful inculcation of this one doctrine alone might be sufficient justification for maintaining the Catholic educational system.

Loyalty to the Catholic subcommunity

Not only does a Catholic education strengthen the bonds that unite the individual to the church, it also seems to strengthen his ties with the Catholic subcommunity. Catholics who had received a Catholic education were one third more likely to be highly involved in the Catholic subcommunity than those who had not. Forty-four per cent of the former, but only 32 per cent of the latter, were highly involved in the subcommunity.

This same tendency was also observed in the responses of Catholics to the questions concerning the wisdom of marrying and associating with those of one's own faith. In both in-

stances those who had received a Catholic education were
more inclined to think that Catholics should marry and limit
their close friends to other Catholics. The difference between
those with a Catholic education and those with a public education was greater in the latter instance, partly because the
great majority of Catholics (regardless of the type of education they had received) favored endogamy, while this was
not true with respect to selection of friends. Eighty-four per
cent of those with a Catholic education favored endogamy,
compared with 79 per cent of other Catholics. Thirty-eight
per cent of those with a Catholic education favored limiting
one's close friends to other members of the group compared
with 27 per cent of the others.

Catholic images of other groups

One might suppose that as a corollary of the foregoing,
Catholics who received all or most of their education in
Catholic schools, and therefore had less contact with non-
Catholics, would have more unfavorable images of Protestants and Jews than those with a public education. "Prejudice," or unfavorable intergroup imagery, is commonly
believed to flourish where contacts with the out-group are
limited, and where the individual has limited opportunities
to check his beliefs against reality.

However, our data do not support this very plausible line
of reasoning—at least as applied to those who have received
all or most of their education in Catholic schools. Catholic
images of Protestants and Jews are virtually unaffected by
the type of school they attended. Those with a Catholic
education were a bit more likely to feel that Protestants have
too much power in this country (16 vs. 12 per cent). On the
other hand, however, they were somewhat less likely to feel
that Protestants are less tolerant than Catholics in religious
matters (14 vs. 19 per cent). On all the other four items in
this area the differences between the two categories of Catholics ranged from 0 to 2 percentage points, with no consistent
directional pattern.

One might argue that our failure to uncover differences
reflects subsequent experiences during the adult years and
that during the period of formal education, and in the ado-

lescent years, important differences did exist. Our data do not permit us to test this hypothesis, but Father Joseph Fichter's recent study indicates that even here, no differences exist.[11] In a comparison of Catholic children from a single parish in Indiana, there were virtually no differences in attitudes toward Protestants and Jews between those children attending the parochial school and those attending the public school.

We could also find no evidence that attendance at Catholic schools had any influence on Catholic attitudes toward Negroes. Those who had received a Catholic education, and those who had not, were equally likely to favor integrated schools, not to be disturbed if a Negro moved into their block, and to show little hostility. Here our findings diverge somewhat from those of Fichter, who reports that the Catholic children attending public school had somewhat less favorable attitudes toward Negroes than those attending parochial school, but he does not specify how great the difference was.[12]

Moral norms

Another area in which we expected differences was that involving controversial moral issues such as birth control, divorce, drinking, gambling, and Sunday business openings. On many of these matters the Catholic Church has taken a definite stand, and we expected this to be communicated with greater effectiveness to those who had attended Catholic schools. There church authorities have an excellent opportunity not only to present their church's teachings on these matters, but also to develop the underlying rationale.

In two of the five areas of moral conflict which we explored, Catholic schools apparently had a definite impact on the values of Catholic laymen. In a third area they seem to have had some minor influence. In the two remaining areas they had no appreciable influence.

The two areas in which Catholic schools had the greatest influence concerned family life. Sixty-eight per cent of those Catholics who had received a Catholic education said that it is always or usually wrong from the moral standpoint for

11 Op. cit., pp. 120–24.
12 Ibid., p. 119.

married couples to practice birth control, while only 54 per cent of the remainder shared this view. With respect to divorce, 73 per cent of those with a Catholic education believed that divorce is always or usually wrong, compared with only 60 per cent of those with a public education.

On the subject of gambling, those with a Catholic education were less likely than the others to take the position that this is always or usually wrong. However, the difference between the two categories was not great. Twenty-six per cent of those with a Catholic education condemned the practice, compared with 32 per cent of those with a public education. Here again the Catholic schools seem to strengthen the commitment of individuals to Catholic teaching.

On the two remaining issues of drinking and Sunday business no differences were observed between the two categories of Catholics. The first of these findings was not so surprising, but on first inspection it did seem somewhat strange that no difference was found with respect to Sunday business. For some years Catholic leaders in Detroit have been waging a vigorous battle against Sunday business openings. Apparently this is a subject which is not, or was not, dealt with to any great degree in Catholic schools. One might have expected, however, that those who had attended Catholic schools would prove more responsive to programs now being initiated by Catholic leaders. But even this hypothesis is not supported by the data.

Economic behavior

One of the largest differences of all appeared when we compared the attitudes toward work held by *middle-class Catholic men.* Those who had received a Catholic education rarely held a positive attitude toward work. Either they disliked work, or they regarded it as the lesser evil when compared with idleness, or they valued it for the extrinsic rewards it provides such as pay and contacts with others.

Only 6 per cent of the middle-class Catholic males in our sample with a Catholic education (N=17) had a positive attitude toward work. By contrast, 28 per cent of the middle-class Catholic males with a public education (N=29) had a positive attitude. At the opposite extreme, 35 per cent of the men with a Catholic education had a negative attitude toward work, but only 17 per cent of those with a public education shared this view. In short, among middle-class Catholic males with a Catholic education, substantially more have a negative attitude toward work than have a positive attitude, but among those with a public education, more have a positive attitude than have a negative attitude.

Among *working-class* Catholic men, the type of education received had much less effect on attitudes toward work. Of those who received a Catholic education (N=18), as many reported a positive attitude toward work as reported a negative attitude (22 per cent). Of those who received a public education (N=42), 26 per cent reported a positive attitude toward work and 17 per cent reported a negative attitude. These findings pinpoint one of the possible sources of the difference between Catholics and non-Catholics in vertical mobility. Evidently Catholic schools do not generally develop in boys those attitudes, values, beliefs, and intellectual orientations which make it possible for a man to enjoy the more demanding jobs in the modern metropolis. It seems significant that the only middle-class Catholic male in our sample who had received a Catholic education and who *also* had a positive attitude toward work no longer attended Mass regularly. Of the fifteen middle-class Catholic males who both had a Catholic education and attended Mass regularly, *not one* reported a real liking for work, and fully one third said they would quit tomorrow if their financial situation permitted.

Our findings here clearly complement the earlier findings of Knapp and Goodrich, which indicate that Catholic colleges and universities produce far less than their proportionate number of scientists.[13] Their study dealt only with the contributions of institutions of higher education to a single kind of occupation. Our study, by contrast, is concerned with the influence of educational institutions at all levels for all types of middle-class, male occupational roles. Both studies, however, point to the same basic conclusion.

On most of the other economic variables discussed in Chapter 3 differences between Catholics with and without a Catholic education were too small to deserve attention. The one

[13] Knapp and Goodrich, op. cit.

possible exception involved installment buying. Here we found that criticism of installment buying was greater among those with a public education (42 per cent) than among those with a Catholic education (35 per cent).

Political behavior

In the area of politics, differences were somewhat more numerous. To begin with, we found that a Catholic education *increased* the probability of Catholics being Republicans. This is, of course, consistent with our earlier finding that involvement in the church, as measured by attendance at Mass and participation in church-related organizations, increases the probability of Catholics being Republicans. Among those Catholics who received a Catholic education and who expressed a party preference, 27 per cent reported themselves to be Republicans, compared with 24 per cent of those who had received a public education.

One might suppose that this modest difference was simply a reflection of differences in parental preferences. Partisan preferences in America are normally inherited by children from their parents, especially their fathers. In the present instance, however, this cannot be the explanation for the difference between the two categories, since those who received a public education came from Republican families more often than those who received a Catholic education. Twenty-four per cent of the fathers of Catholics who had received a public education were Republicans, compared with only 11 per cent of the fathers of Catholics who had received a Catholic education. In other words, the simple comparison with which we began grossly underestimates the political influence of parochial schools. *Among Catholics with a Catholic education there was a shift of 16 percentage points toward the Republican camp, whereas among Catholics with a public education there was no shift either way.*

From this it appears that the public schools have no effect on political preference but that the Catholic schools are an active force. We do not mean to suggest that students in Catholic schools are exposed to Republican proselytizing. It appears, however, that in some way attending parochial school predisposes Catholic students to reconsider their inherited political loyalties, with a substantial minority eventually shifting from the Democratic to the Republican camp. It seems likely that this shift occurs in response to the appeals to traditional morality of Republican candidates, and reflects an enhanced sensitivity to such appeals acquired through years of exposure to the Catholic system of education.

Judging from the voting behavior of Detroit Catholics in the 1956 elections, a Catholic education greatly weakens traditional party loyalties and increases voter independence. Those who had received a Catholic education were much more likely to vote for the combination of Eisenhower for president and Williams for governor than Catholics who had received a public education. Eisenhower ran only 16 percentage points ahead of his Republican running mate for governor among Catholics with a public education, but among those with a Catholic education this margin jumped to 37 points.

Catholic schools also seem to increase voter turnout to some extent. Among those with a Catholic education, 81 per cent claimed to have voted in the 1956 elections, compared with 70 per cent of the Catholics who had received a public education.

In the area of foreign relations, a Catholic education was linked with a disinclination to think about world problems, but with humanitarian tendencies in the area of foreign aid. Of those Catholics who had received a Catholic education, only 16 per cent had given much thought to world problems, compared with 27 per cent of those with a public education. However, 52 per cent of those with a public education took the position that not a penny should be spent abroad except in the interest of national defense, compared with but 37 per cent of those with a Catholic education.

In the area of freedom of speech there were no appreciable differences on the four questions pertaining to the Bill of Rights. However, a difference appeared when Catholics were asked whether ministers of other faiths should be permitted to preach publicly things which are contrary to Catholic teaching (Q. 95). Forty-six per cent of the Catholics who had received a public education were willing to allow ministers of other faiths to do this, but only 35 per cent of those who had received a Catholic education. Especially disturbing from the perspective of traditional American beliefs in this area was the fact that the differences were more pronounced among middle-class Catholics; furthermore, middle-class Catholics with a Catholic education were less willing than working-class Catholics with a Catholic education to concede this liberty to non-Catholic leaders. Whereas 55 per cent of the middle-class Catholics with a public education (N=56) and 38 per cent of the working-class Catholics with a Catholic education (N=45) were prepared to grant this right to non-Catholics, only 31 per cent of the middle-class Catholics with a Catholic education (N=36) shared this view. This seems to indicate that in this one important respect, the further Catholics advance in their educational system the further they depart from the traditional American norm. With advancing education and with the expansion of the Catholic educational system, acute tensions could develop in the future because of the conflict between Catholic and non-Catholic viewpoints on this matter. If America is to maintain a pluralistic society containing something more than a series of watertight socio-religious groups which merely tolerate the existence of one another, it seems likely that there must be some modification in the teachings of Catholic schools and colleges at this point. This teaching can only generate conflict of a type which promises ill for any religiously divided society.

Finally, on a somewhat more optimistic note, we may note that the Catholic system of education seems to increase respect for constitutional government. When asked what type of candidate they would prefer in the 1960 elections, those Catholics who had received a Catholic education were overwhelmingly in favor of the man who followed the rules rather than one who got things done by never letting rules stand in his way. Ninety-one per cent of the Catholics who had received a Catholic education took this stand, compared with 81 per cent of those who had received a public education.

Family life

Our evidence indicated that attendance at Catholic schools generally strengthens the bonds of kinship. To begin with, we found that Catholics who had received a public education were much more likely to be migrants to the community than were those who had received a Catholic education. Sixty-one per cent of those receiving a public education, but only 43 per cent of those with a Catholic education were migrants.

It seems likely that this difference somewhat exaggerates the relationship between Catholic education and unwillingness to migrate. In some small towns the Catholic population is not large enough to maintain separate schools, and hence Catholics who live there are obliged to attend public schools. In a large city like Detroit this is less likely to happen, though even there some parishes do not yet have their own schools. However, the probabilities of native Detroit Catholics obtaining a Catholic education seem greater than for migrants. This means that to some extent the relationship between being a native Detroiter and having received a Catholic education exists independently of any peculiar affinity for family ties and simply reflects differential opportunity to obtain this type of education.

Our data indicate, however, that there is more to this relationship than mere opportunity to attend Catholic schools. Those who had received a Catholic education were likelier to value ties with relatives more than ties with friends than were those who had received a public education. The differences were not great, but pointed in the expected direction. Sixty-eight per cent of those with a Catholic education and 63 per cent of those with a public education expressed a preference for relatives over friends.[14]

We also found that attendance at Catholic schools was correlated with a belief that it is more important for children to learn to obey than to think for themselves. The difference was not as large as expected, but as expected, it was larger among middle- than working-class Catholics. Among middle-class Catholics, 41 per cent of those with a Catholic education ranked obedience ahead of intellectual autonomy, compared with 33 per cent of those with a public education.[15] Among

[14] Unfortunately, it was not possible to test this relationship using the data concerning frequency of visits with relatives, since these data were not obtained in the 1958 survey.

[15] For an extended discussion of this subject, see Thomas F. O'Dea, *American Catholic Dilemma: An Inquiry into the Intellectual Life* (New York: Sheed & Ward, 1958).

working-class Catholics there was almost no difference (58 vs. 55 per cent).

We also expected to find that those with a Catholic education would have larger families than those with a public education. This was clearly the case among older Catholics. Among persons past the child-bearing years, those with a Catholic education (N=26) reported 3.5 children on the average, while those with a public education (N=38) reported only 2.6. Among younger Catholics we were surprised to find that those with a public education (N=75) reported larger families (2.6) than those with a Catholic education (N=38, average 2.1). In view of our other evidence concerning the commitment of the latter to normative standards of their church, it seems hard to believe that in this area of behavior, to which their church attaches such great importance, they should deviate from its standards more than those with a public education. Rather, we suspect that those with Catholic educations postpone marriage longer than others, because of fear of overly large families, and hence on the average have fewer years of married life. However, by the time they reach the end of the child-bearing period, we predict that they will have larger families than those with a public education.

III. RELIGION AND SCIENCE

At various points in this and earlier chapters we have mentioned the interrelations between religion and science. In these earlier discussions, however, we were concerned chiefly with scientific jobs as one type of high-status position in modern society, and with the demands that such jobs generally make on those who hold them or those who aspire to them. As we observed, there are important differences among the religious groups in the degree to which they equip their youth to fill this type of role.

While scientific roles have much in common with other responsible positions, in some respects they are unique. If for no other reason, they are unique because they are imbedded in a distinctive institutional system. Someone has aptly described the modern scientific movement as "the institutionalization of the spirit of doubt and skepticism." It is certainly

the institutionalization of the intellectual outlook which is prepared to re-examine critically any proposition about the ob-
servable elements of the world in which we live. As a result,
modern science has frequently encountered the organized
opposition of religious groups—which might well be described
as "the institutionalization of the spirit of faith." Although it
is clear that both faith and doubt are necessary elements in
any stable or progressive social system, it does not follow that
the institutions which embody these two contrasting orientations should necessarily appear mutually compatible to the
members of society. On the contrary, as the events associated
with the development of both Copernican and Darwinian
theory make clear, religious and scientific institutions may
frequently be at swords' points.

Because of this it seemed particularly important to explore
the images which each of the groups had of modern science,
and more especially to see whether they saw the modern
scientific movement as engaged in conflict with organized
religion. We therefore asked all the respondents in the 1958
survey who expressed some religious preference the following
question:

> Do you feel that there are any disagreements between
> what science teaches and what your religious group
> teaches? (Q. 66)

If the respondent felt there were such disagreements, we then
asked:

> Would you say that these disagreements are very serious,
> somewhat serious, or not very serious? (Q. 66a)

Jewish respondents were the least likely to feel that there is
any conflict between the teachings of science and those of
their religious group, with 74 per cent expressing this view.
Differences among the other three groups were not large, with
57 per cent of the Negro Protestants seeing no conflict, and
the same being true of 54 per cent of the Catholics and 51 per
cent of the white Protestants. Catholics were the most likely
to perceive the conflict as "very serious" or "somewhat serious," with 28 per cent of all Catholics taking this position.
For white Protestants the comparable figure was 23 per cent,

for Negro Protestants 20 per cent, and for Jews 15 per cent.

In all except the Jewish group, *young* adults were much more likely to take the position that a serious conflict exists (i.e., they saw it as either "very serious" or "somewhat serious"). This is probably a reflection, not of any trend, but only of the more recent exposure of young people to the school system. Older people are likely to have moved on to other problems and to have set aside any earlier difficulties which may have troubled them in this area.

One of the biggest differences between white Protestants and Catholics occurred among those who had received some college education. Only 17 per cent of the white Protestants in this category saw a serious conflict between the teachings of science and their church, while 32 per cent, or nearly twice as many, of the college-trained Catholics expressed this view. Among people with less than a college education, 24 per cent of the white Protestants said there are serious disagreements between the teachings of science and their church, compared with 27 per cent of the white Catholics. In short, higher education seems to *increase* the sense of conflict between science and religion for Catholics, but to *reduce* it for white Protestants. This is undoubtedly an added factor contributing to the small number of Catholics choosing scientific careers, since today scientists are recruited almost exclusively from among college graduates.

As might be expected, the sense of conflict is more pronounced among those persons who are doctrinally orthodox. In both the white Protestant and Catholic groups 19 per cent of the heterodox thought that a serious conflict exists. This view was expressed by 31 per cent of the orthodox white Protestants and 34 per cent of the orthodox Catholics.

There was very little relationship between devotionalism and views on the relationship between religion and science. This suggests that when religiously active persons enter scientific careers they are more likely to be recruited from the ranks of those with a devotional orientation than from those with an orthodox orientation.[16]

On the basis of the findings of this study it appears that

[16] For Catholics, it also made little difference whether they had received a Catholic education or not.

overt conflict between the churches and the modern scientific movement (itself a highly organized social movement), is only one of the factors accounting for the disinclination of Catholics to enter scientific careers. In our opinion, other, less visible, factors are equally important; perhaps far more important. Especially influential is the basic intellectual orientation which Catholicism develops: an orientation which values obedience above intellectual autonomy.[17] Also influential is the Catholic

[17] In a recently completed doctoral dissertation, Father Andrew M. Greeley has analyzed data from a very large sample of 1961 college graduates on the basis of which he concludes that Catholics are as intellectually and scientifically oriented as Protestants. These data indicate that in the class of 1961, Catholics were more likely than Protestants to plan to continue their education in graduate or professional school. Furthermore, they were nearly as likely to plan careers in science and to find college science courses interesting. Though they were a bit less interested in ideas, and a shade less interested in research, they valued a chance to be creative as much as the Protestants, and they were even more interested in making a lot of money. On the basis of these and many other findings, Father Greeley concludes that there is no longer (if indeed there ever was) any basis for charges of "Catholic anti-intellectualism" or "Catholic anti-scientism" which he imputes to me and to others. (See Andrew M. Greeley, *The Influence of Religion on the Career Plans and Occupational Values of June 1961 College Graduates*, unpublished doctoral dissertation, University of Chicago, 1962).

The data on which this dissertation is based clearly represent an invaluable source of information on the interrelations between religion on the one hand, and education, science, and career plans on the other. Greeley's analysis of these data represents a good beginning, but the critical reader is left with many unanswered questions, and, indeed, some reservations about the relationship between his findings and his sweeping conclusions. Personally, I was much disturbed by his frequent references to my thesis of "Catholic anti-intellectualism." I had supposed that I had made my position clear. On the basis of the findings of this study, and others, it appears to me that Catholics are not anti-intellectual. Rather, they have adopted a variant form of intellectualism—one which lays unusually heavy emphasis on revealed truth and the importance of individual assent to this truth. The nature of this difference has probably never been stated better than in Thomas F. O'Dea's challenging book, *American Catholic Dilemma: An Inquiry into the Intellectual Life,* op. cit. This same thesis is also stated by many of the other Catholic writers whose works are included in the excellent compilation of writings on this subject

tendency to value family and the kin group above other relationships. In brief, at both the conscious and subconscious levels of thought and action, membership in the Catholic group is more likely to inhibit the development of scientific careers than is membership in either the Protestant or Jewish groups. The implications of this for the future of American society are not difficult to discover.

edited by Frank L. Christ and Gerard Sherry, *American Catholicism and the Intellectual Ideal* (New York: Appleton-Century-Crofts, 1961).

Perhaps the key to the explanation of Father Greeley's unique and intriguing findings is to be found in the fact that they deal with the intentions and aspirations of young people on the verge of graduate school whereas the other studies which have so troubled Catholic educators and intellectuals deal with established men of science. The findings of our study suggest that in general the aspirations of Catholics are as high as those of non-Catholics. Contrary to the popular understanding of the Protestant Ethic, Catholics are ambitious and hard working. If they fail to get ahead in certain areas, it seems to be due more to the influence of other factors whose importance is easily overlooked as I stressed at the end of Chapter 5. Whatever the ultimate outcome of this controversy, Father Greeley has certainly performed the useful function of adding fuel to the flames, which, while dangerous in some spheres, is essential to the advance of knowledge.

Chapter 7

THE CLERGY

14

In socio-religious groups the clergy naturally play an especially important role. By virtue of their office they are the acknowledged leaders in the religious associations. This does not mean that they are also automatically leaders of the religious subcommunities; nevertheless, because of the interdependence of church and subcommunity, and the limited development of formal organization in most subcommunities, the clergy normally exercise considerable influence there as well.

The power of the clergy stems from two main sources. In the first place, it derives from the attitude of the laity, and their respect for the office. Laymen in general, and more devout laymen in particular, *expect* the clergy to be leaders, and are prepared to take their ideas and proposals seriously. Robert Merton quotes one Protestant minister as saying:

> The advantage of being a minister is that you don't have to prove yourself. You are immediately accepted and received in all homes, including the best ones.[1]

While obviously there are limits to the areas in which the laity are prepared to follow the leadership of the clergy, their position as leaders of *religious* organizations affords greater scope than leadership roles in most other types of organizations. For example, as some have observed, the phrase "faith and morals," which Catholics employ to define the proper sphere of action for religious leaders, is extremely broad and inclusive.

A second source from which the power of the clergy flows

[1] Robert K. Merton, "Patterns of Influence: Local and Cosmopolitan Influentials," in *Social Theory and Social Structure*, rev. edit. (Glencoe: The Free Press, 1957), p. 400.

may be identified if one examines their place in the communications network of socio-religious groups. Both preaching and pastoral functions bring priests and ministers, far more than other people, into "group-relevant" contacts with other members of their group. By this we mean that while some other person within a group, for example a newspaper editor, may have access to an even larger number of group members than does any single clergyman, his relationship is not distinctly relevant to the group, and cannot be made so. The Catholic editor of a large city newspaper cannot address himself specifically to fellow-Catholics through the medium of his paper without getting himself and his paper into serious difficulties. To the degree that he speaks as a Catholic, rather than as an editor, he is almost certain to alienate non-Catholic subscribers and advertisers. The situation of the clergy, however, is quite different. They are able to speak as a member of their particular group, since they are not directly dependent upon anyone outside it.[2] Hence, the views, opinions, beliefs, and actions of the clergy are of special interest and importance in any study of the influence of religious institutions on secular institutions.

The clergy are also of special importance to us in this study since they, more than other members of the groups to which they belong, have been exposed to, and indoctrinated in, the distinctive teachings of their churches. Also, by virtue of their office they have been more confined to their own subcommunity than most of the laity, and thus more exposed to its influences. In short, if socio-religious groups are forces giving rise to peculiar and distinctive patterns of thought and

[2] Kenneth Underwood's study of Holyoke, Massachusetts, makes it clear that there are even limits to the independence of the clergy. The clergy are dependent on the laity, and many of the laity, especially the retail businessmen, are economically dependent on those outside their own socio-religious group. Thus, if the clergy of one group take action which sufficiently arouses the members of another group, especially a large or financially powerful group, the latter can retaliate by taking action against the laity of the former group. As Underwood points out, these tactics were used by the Catholics of Holyoke to prevent Margaret Sanger from speaking on the subject of birth control in a Protestant church in that community. See Underwood, *Protestant and Catholic* (Boston: Beacon Press, 1957), Chapter 1.

action in the modern metropolis, we would expect to find group differences more marked among the clergy than among the laity. The clergy thus provide us with an added check on our previous conclusions about the influence of religion on modern society.[3]

As indicated in Chapter 1, our data on the clergy were obtained in a special follow-up survey conducted during the summer of 1958. After the interviews with the cross-section of Detroiters had been completed and coded, a list was prepared of the churches which members of the sample attended. From this list every third church was chosen at random and the head pastor interviewed. Jewish rabbis and Eastern Orthodox priests were not included owing to the small number of respondents in these groups. We felt that no valid generalizations could be made based on interviews with five or six Jewish rabbis and one or two Eastern Orthodox priests. Altogether 146 Protestant and Catholic clergymen were on our list, and interviews were completed with 127, giving a response rate of 87 per cent.

I. SOCIAL ORIGINS OF THE CLERGY

Before examining the views of the clergy it may be well to see what manner of men they are, and how they compare with the laity on various important social characteristics. Are the clergy recruited from a cross-section of the population, or are they recruited selectively? Also, how does the economic position of the clergy compare with the laity? Are the clergy a disadvantaged segment of the population, as is often asserted, or are they one of the more prosperous segments?

The Catholic clergy

Two facts stand out prominently when the social origins of the Catholic clergy are compared with those of the Catholic laity. In class background the Catholic clergy (N=49) seem highly representative of the Catholic population as a whole. However, in ethnic background they are highly atypical.

[3] We say that the data pertaining to the clergy provide an "added" basis for forming such judgments since these can also be made on the basis of statistical tests of significance.

Of the 48 Catholic pastors who reported their father's usual occupation, 27 per cent reported some middle-class occupation. An additional 53 per cent reported a working-class occupation, and 20 per cent said their fathers were farmers. Among Catholic laymen (and women) in our 1958 sample, the comparable figures were 24, 61, and 15 per cent. In other words, the clergy are somewhat underrepresented among the sons of workingmen and somewhat overrepresented among the sons of middle-class and farm families. However, the differences are small.

When we examined ethnic background we found that the Irish are greatly overrepresented in the ranks of the clergy, while most of the other ethnic groups are underrepresented to a greater or lesser degree. Although the Irish constitute only 14 per cent of the Catholic laity in Detroit, they contributed 47 per cent of the Catholic pastors in our sample. By contrast, the Poles, who constitute 27 per cent of the Catholic population, account for only 22 per cent of the priests. For the Germans, the comparable figures are 9 and 10 per cent. For the Italians they are 10 and 6 per cent, for the French 7 and 0 per cent.

In part this heavy Irish concentration in the Catholic clergy may be a reflection of the way we selected the clergy to be interviewed. Where there were two or more priests or ministers, we interviewed only the head pastor. Since promotions to pastorates are made largely on the grounds of seniority and experience, the priests we interviewed were above average in age. Some of the ethnic groups which make up a goodly portion of the Catholic population of Detroit are relatively recent immigrants (e.g., the Poles and Italians), and they may have had less opportunity to enter the clergy a generation or more ago when the pastors we interviewed were being recruited. However, this is no more than a part of the explanation; the Germans and the French, who have been in Detroit as long as the Irish, or even longer, are not found nearly so often in the ranks of the clergy. Together these two groups constitute 16 per cent of the Catholic population of Detroit but only 10 per cent of the clergy, compared with the Irish, who constitute 14 per cent of the Catholic population but 47 per cent of the clergy.

(One final characteristic of the Catholic clergy deserves comment, and this is their place of birth. As we have already observed, Catholics are especially likely to be natives of Detroit,) with 48 per cent of the 1958 sample falling in this category. The same is not so true of the clergy. Only a third are natives. (However, although the Catholic clergy were not born in Detroit as often as the laity, they are more often natives of other Michigan communities) Whereas 10 per cent of the laity were born in such communities, 24 per cent of the clergy were.[4]

The white Protestant clergy

If the Catholic clergy are atypical with respect to ethnicity, but representative in class origin, just the reverse is true of the white Protestant clergy. Roughly one third of the white Protestants in Detroit are of English, Scotch, or Welsh background, or some combination of these three, and the same is true of the white Protestant clergy (N=57). Approximately one fifth of the laity are of German descent, and about one fourth of the clergy. The Scandinavians, who constitute 6 per cent of the white Protestant laity, supply the same percentage of the clergy.

(While the Protestant clergy are highly representative of the various ethnic strains found in the Protestant population of the community, the same cannot be said of their class origins) If our sample was at all representative, the white Protestant ministers of Detroit are disproportionately recruited from middle-class homes. Sixty-six per cent of them were raised in middle-class families, compared with 20 per cent of the white Protestant laity. Only 22 per cent of the clergy, but 63 per cent of the laity, were raised in working-class homes. Thirteen per cent of the clergy and 18 per cent of the laity were raised in farm families.

To some extent this difference is a reflection of the nature of our sample. The clergymen interviewed were not a random

[4] It may also be noted that the Archdiocese of Detroit seems now staffed overwhelmingly with native American priests. Among the Catholic pastors in our sample, only 12 per cent were foreign-born. With a single exception, all of the foreign-born pastors were Polish.

cross-section of all the clergy in Detroit, but rather a sample of the head pastors in the churches attended by respondents in our community-wide survey. This means that the sample included a disproportionate number of Protestant ministers from the larger churches and was underrepresentative of the ministers in the smaller churches. Furthermore, our data indicate that there is a relationship between the size of the church a minister serves and his class origin. For example, 41 per cent of the white Protestant ministers raised in middle-class families serve congregations of a thousand or more members, compared with 26 per cent of the ministers raised in working-class or farm families. Or, taking 500 members as the criterion, 69 per cent of the ministers from middle-class families serve congregations of at least this size, compared with 63 per cent of the ministers raised in working-class or farm families.

These facts suggest that if we had a sample of *all* the white Protestant ministers in Detroit the imbalance in class origins would not be as large. However, these figures also make it clear that the imbalance would not disappear. The white Protestant clergy of Detroit are disproportionately of middle-class origin.

They also seem to be disproportionately concentrated in the middle and upper-middle income brackets at the present time. If the free use of a parsonage is the equivalent of $1000 a year in added income,[5] and if one adds this sum to the reported incomes of those ministers receiving the use of a parsonage, then it appears that only 4 per cent of the white Protestant ministers in our sample had an annual income of less than $5000.[6] By contrast, 35 per cent of the white Protestant laity reported that their family head earned less than $5000 a year. Fifty-four per cent of the white Protestant clergy and 41 per cent of the laity reported incomes between $5000 and $7999 per year; and 43 per cent of the clergy,

[5] If anything, this figure is too low since in the first place this is income on which the minister has to pay no tax, and in the second place few parsonages could be rented for $80 a month with utilities provided, as is the usual arrangement. A more accurate estimate would probably be in the area of $1500.

[6] We are not including the income of wives or other members of the family who may be employed.

compared with 24 per cent of the laity, reported incomes of $8000 or more per year.

These facts are especially important because of the peculiar position of the clergy in the organizational structure of socio-religious groups. Members of the clergy are in a unique position to exercise influence. The question is: What is the nature of their influence?

By virtue of their training and personal commitment, we would expect the clergy to exercise a Christian influence, and more especially a Protestant influence. But what is equally important, by virtue of their social origin and their current position in the class structure of the community, we would expect them to exercise a middle-class influence as well. In short, the key leadership roles in the white Protestant group are filled by men disproportionately recruited from the middle class, and even more disproportionately identified with the middle class through their current economic position. This must surely have consequences for the group as a whole, just as the disproportionate concentration of the Irish in the Catholic clergy is almost certain to have an effect on that group.

The Protestant ministers in our sample were not unaware of their economic advantages. When asked whether they felt that from the economic standpoint their family was more prosperous than the average, about average, or less prosperous than average when compared with other families in the country, 44 per cent classified their family as more prosperous than average, and only 7 per cent as less prosperous than average. A conscious awareness of their privileged position in the community may to some degree influence the economic and political viewpoints of the clergy, partly freeing them from normal class bias. However, one should beware of exaggerating the extent to which this is true.

In any appraisal of the white Protestant clergy of Detroit it is necessary to take into account their relationship to the community. Earlier we observed that a third of the Catholic clergy are natives of the community, and nearly three fifths natives of the state. By contrast, only 14 per cent of the white Protestant clergy are natives of Detroit, and only 35 per cent natives of Michigan. They are even more mobile than their laity, 31 per cent of whom are natives of Detroit, and 46 per cent natives of Michigan.[7] By and large the Protestant clergy of Detroit are migrants to the community and to the state, and have deep roots in neither. Hence they are likely to be a force promoting a cosmopolitan view of life which looks beyond the bounds of family, kin group, neighborhood, community, and state.

The Negro Protestant clergy

Turning to the Negro Protestant clergy (N=21) one is impressed first and foremost by their striking homogeneity. All but two said their fathers were either farmers or clergymen. Over 80 per cent had spent some part of their lives on farms, and over 60 per cent listed farming as their father's chief occupation. Furthermore, over 80 per cent were born in the South. Only one was born in Detroit, and two in Michigan.

In several respects the Negro clergy seem fairly representative of the group as a whole. Slightly over 80 per cent of the laity were also born in the South. Very few were from middle-class families. However, unlike the clergy, many of the laity were raised in urban working-class families and were the sons and daughters of manual workers. This was true of 40 per cent of the laity, but *none* of the clergy in our sample.

The sharpest discrepancy between the Negro clergy and laity was in current economic status. As in the case of the white Protestants, the Negro clergy appeared to be a relatively favored group. Ten per cent had an annual income of $8000 or more (if an allowance of $1000 is made for the value of a parsonage), compared with only 2 per cent of the laity. Eighty-one per cent of the clergy had an annual income of $5000 or more, compared with 23 per cent of the laity. It seems likely that the higher incomes of the Negro Protestant clergy have some effect on their thoughts and actions, though the fact that they were raised in families whose economic cir-

[7] One might suppose that the Protestant clergy are simply typical of professional men generally, who are also highly mobile. However, our data indicate that the white Protestant clergy are migrants far more often than other professionals. Of the 572 white professional men on whom data have been gathered in Detroit Area Study surveys since 1952, 38 per cent were native Detroiters compared with 14 per cent of the white Protestant clergy.

cumstances were similar to those of the laity should serve as a unifying bond of a type not so common among white Protestants.

II. THEOLOGICAL COMMITMENTS OF THE CLERGY

While our interviews with the clergy were primarily concerned with their views on secular matters, a portion of them dealt with matters specifically religious in character. Their responses to these questions are not of central concern in this study, but are reported here since they provide an additional perspective on these men.

One of the first questions asked of all the Protestant ministers was worded as follows:

> On the whole, do you think of yourself more as a liberal or as a conservative from the theological standpoint?

Among the 57 white Protestants, 14 identified themselves as liberals, and 34 as conservatives. The remainder described themselves as neither, but rather as "middle of the roaders." Among the 21 Negro Protestants, 9 identified themselves as liberals, 9 as conservatives, and 3 as middle of the roaders.

The differences among the white Protestants were strongly linked with denominational affiliation. Among the larger denominations, the Methodists were the only group in which a majority classified themselves as liberals. Four of the 6 Methodist ministers put themselves in this category, with the other 2 describing themselves as middle of the roaders. Presbyterians were evenly balanced, with 3 of the 8 describing themselves as liberals, and 3 more calling themselves conservatives. Lutherans and Baptists, on the other hand, generally said they were conservatives. Fifteen of the 19 Lutheran pastors described themselves in this way, as did 7 of the 11 Baptists. Two in each of these groups labeled themselves liberals.

We also asked each of the Protestant ministers whether they had become more liberal or more conservative theologically during the last ten years. Eighteen of the white Protestants said they had become more liberal, while only 10 said they had become more conservative. The majority believed they had not changed appreciably in that time. Among Negro Protestant ministers, 8 thought they had become more liberal, five more conservative, and 8 thought there had been no change. In most of the white denominations the shifts toward the liberal position just about equaled in frequency the shifts in a conservative direction. The one exception to this pattern occurred in the case of the Lutheran group. Six of the Lutheran pastors described themselves as more liberal than in the past, while only one thought he was more conservative. This is yet another indication of the general trend toward convergence within Protestant circles.

We also asked Protestant ministers to summarize briefly their beliefs about God. Here we were especially interested to see how far they conformed to the traditional Trinitarian doctrine. Of the 57 white Protestants, all but 5 seemed to conform; among the 21 Negro Protestants, only 1 could not be classified as a Trinitarian. Three of the 6 non-Trinitarians were Methodists, 2 were Congregationalists, and 1 a Baptist.

All of the Protestant ministers, without exception, both Negro and white, expressed belief in a life after death. However, 11 of the whites and 1 of the Negroes did not believe that in the next life some will be punished and others rewarded. Four of the whites and 1 additional Negro expressed uncertainty about this traditional Christian doctrine of judgment.

Both Catholics and Protestants were asked about their views concerning the Bible. Each priest or minister was asked to indicate which of the following views concerning the Bible came closest to his own views:

(a) The Bible is God's Word and all it says is true;

(b) The Bible was written by men inspired by God, and its basic moral and religious teachings are true, but because the writers were men, it contains some human errors;

(c) The Bible is a valuable book because it was written by wise and good men, but God had nothing to do with it;

(d) The Bible was written by men who lived so long ago that it is of little value today.

None of the clergy chose either the third or fourth alternative. Of the white Protestants, 28 chose the first alternative, 29 the second. For Negro Protestants, the comparable figures were 4 and 17, which was quite surprising. For Catholics the figures were 21 and 27, with one priest stating that none of the categories came close to his view. The Lutherans were by far the most strongly committed to literal inspiration, with 15 of the 19 pastors expressing this view.

At one point a very striking difference was observed between the white Protestant and Catholic clergy. Each of the priests and ministers in our sample was asked whether he had ever doubted God's existence. No less than 39 per cent of the white Protestant clergy admitted that they had, at some time, doubted God's existence. Not one of the Catholics indicated that he had ever had this experience. In this respect the Negro Protestants more closely resembled the Catholic clergy, since only 1 out of the 21 Negro ministers said he had ever had doubts of this nature.

III. THE CLERGY
AND THE SUBCOMMUNITIES

As might be expected, the clergy are much more often highly involved in the socio-religious subcommunities than are the laity. The clergy were much more likely to report that all or nearly all of their close friends and relatives were members of the same group as themselves. For example, only a third of the white Protestant laity said all or nearly all of their close friends were Protestants, but two thirds of the clergy reported this. Or, whereas three quarters of the white Protestant laity reported that all or nearly all of their close relatives were also Protestants, 96 per cent of the clergy reported this. Among the Catholic laity, 44 per cent reported that all or nearly all of their close friends were Catholics and 79 per cent reported that this was true of all or nearly all of their close relatives. Among the Catholic clergy the corresponding figures were 84 and 98 per cent. Among Negro Protestant laymen, 61 per cent said all or nearly all of their close friends were Protestants, and 85 per cent reported the same for close relatives. For the Negro Protestant clergy the comparable figures were 95 and 100 per cent.

Interfaith contacts among the clergy

We were especially interested to see how often Detroit clergymen have contact with clergymen of other socio-religious groups. As expected, these contacts were exceedingly infrequent. Only 19 per cent of the white Protestant clergy and 5 per cent of the Negro Protestant clergy said they had spoken with any member of the Catholic clergy during the preceding month. Only 16 per cent of the Catholic clergy reported conversations with a Protestant minister. Slightly over half of those who had had any conversations of this nature reported only a single conversation. The remainder reported no more than two or three such conversations. None indicated any personal friendships with clergy of the other group.

Contacts with Jewish rabbis were even less frequent, at least in the case of Catholics. Not one of the Catholic priests in our sample reported any contacts with Jewish rabbis during the preceding month. Only 14 per cent of the white Protestant ministers and 5 per cent of the Negro Protestants reported conversations with rabbis. In only one instance was there any indication of frequent contacts. One white Protestant minister reported contacts with a Jewish rabbi two or more times a week.

Contacts between Negro and white Protestant ministers were much more frequent occurrences. Approximately half of both sets of ministers reported at least one conversation with a minister in the other racial group. Roughly 15 per cent reported at least weekly contacts with ministers across the racial line, and 4 per cent had such contacts several times a week or more. In two instances white Protestants regarded one of the Negro ministers with whom they had contact as a close personal friend.

On the whole, however, one cannot escape the conclusion that the clergy have far fewer contacts with members of other socio-religious groups than do the laity, and furthermore, contacts between the leaders of the various churches are exceedingly rare. This situation is probably inevitable given the nature of the work of the clergy, and the views which the groups hold of each other. Nevertheless, it is a situation which has many far-reaching consequences not only for the churches but for the whole community.

For one thing, this situation makes for the continuation, and perhaps even the extension, of socio-religious communalism. Clergymen are much more likely than laymen to feel that it is unwise for people to marry outside their own group, or even find close friends outside it. For example, only 16 per cent of the white Protestant laity thought that Protestants should only choose other Protestants for their close friends, but 54 per cent of the white Protestant clergy held this view. Or, 75 per cent of the laity, but 93 per cent of the clergy favored endogamous marriage. Among Catholics, 31 per cent of the laity and 53 per cent of the clergy favored restrictions on close friendships,[8] and 81 per cent of the laity and 100 per cent of the clergy favored endogamous marriages. Among Negro Protestants, the clergy were a bit less restrictive than the laity in their views on friendship. Whereas 26 per cent of the laity favored restrictive friendships, only 19 per cent of the clergy shared this view. However, on the matter of marriage the familiar pattern reappeared. Forty-four per cent of the laity and 79 per cent of the clergy came out in favor of endogamous marriages.

These relationships are largely what we should expect on the basis of sociological theory. As Simmel put it years ago, "All leaders are also led [by their followers]."[9] He cites a famous nineteenth century German party leader who said: "I am their leader, therefore I must follow them." In many ways this seems to apply to the clergy. As leaders they are obliged to conform to the group's standards even more faithfully than the rank and file. The important point here is that *the behavior and attitudes of the clergy in these matters represent more than personal likes and dislikes; they express the values and norms of the groups they lead.* Because of this the attitudes

[8] For one priest's views on the subject, see *Time*, July 4, 1960, p. 38. Msgr. DeBlanc, Director of the National Catholic Family Life Bureau, is quoted as saying that Catholics should not have close associates who are not also Catholics.

[9] Georg Simmel, "Superordination and Subordination," in *The Sociology of Georg Simmel,* translated and edited by Kurt H. Wolff (Glencoe: The Free Press, 1950), p. 185.

and actions of the clergy are of special importance to everyone concerned with the American metropolis and with the socio-religious groups which are such an important element in it.

Images of other groups

In view of Simmel's theory of the constraints which groups exert on their leaders, and in view also of the limited contacts which the clergy have outside their own group, we might expect them to have less favorable images of other groups than do the laity. However, if the evidence in *Table 48* is at all

Table 48

PERCENTAGE OF CLERGY AND LAITY EXPRESSING UNFAVORABLE OR NONCOMMITTAL VIEWS OF OTHER GROUPS' TOLERANCE, FAIRNESS, AND POWER

| Judges and Subjects | PERCENTAGE EXPRESSING UNFAVORABLE OR NONCOMMITTAL VIEWS OF OUT-GROUP: | |
	Clergy	Laity
White Protestant judgments of:		
Catholic tolerance	91	70
Catholic fairness	25	29
Catholic power	93	51
Jewish tolerance	20	51
Jewish fairness	27	53
Jewish power	30	44
Catholic judgments of:		
Protestant tolerance	53	40
Protestant fairness	18	22
Protestant power	35	31
Jewish tolerance	42	46
Jewish fairness	40	54
Jewish power	61	42
Negro Protestant judgments of:		
Catholic tolerance	81	55
Catholic fairness	33	36
Catholic power	90	37
Jewish tolerance	33	50
Jewish fairness	45	60
Jewish power	43	56

reliable, the problem is more complex than this.[10] Of the 18 comparisons between clergy and laity shown in this table, the laity expressed unfavorable images of the outgroup[11] more often than the clergy in 11 instances. Clearly more is involved here than the constraint of the leaders by the followers, or the isolation of leaders from other groups.

Some of the most surprising findings involve Protestant images of the Jewish group. Among both Negro and white Protestants, the clergy were much less likely than the laity to express an unfavorable view of the Jewish group. At the same time, however, the Protestant clergy were much *more* critical of the Catholics.

This difference probably reflects important changes in intergroup relations during the last generation. In recent years there has been increasing co-operation between Protestant and Jewish leaders in a variety of forms. Both take an active part in interfaith organizations such as the National Conference of Christians and Jews. Even more important, the two groups frequently find themselves on the same side of the fence in controversies involving the explosive issue of church-state relations.

By contrast, the Catholic clergy do not participate in interfaith activities as often as Protestants and Jews, and on church-state issues they frequently form the opposition party.

Because these developments have involved the clergy far, far more than the laity, the views of the clergy have been affected to a much greater degree. Because of their increasingly cordial relations with Jewish leaders, Protestant clergymen have apparently developed a much more favorable image of the Jewish group than have their parishioners. However, their relations with the Catholic clergy have not im-

[10] The questions dealt with in *Table 48* were identical for clergy and laity. See the discussion of intergroup images in Chapter 2.

[11] *Table 48* combines both the expression of unfavorable images and noncommittal responses. The reasons for this are set forth in Chapter 2. If we exclude the noncommittal responses, which are somewhat more common among the laity, the pattern is altered only slightly. The laity still express unfavorable images more often than the clergy in seven instances.

proved appreciably, so as one would expect, their views tend to be even more critical than those of their parishioners.

A second factor in the unexpected reversals in *Table 48* is probably the influence of the vigorous campaign for racial and religious tolerance which has been a prominent feature of American life in the last generation. By virtue of their education and position the clergy are more exposed to this campaign than are the laity, and they are therefore more likely to abandon unfavorable images on secondary matters, and on matters with which they have limited personal experience. In our opinion this is why the clergy were consistently less critical of outgroups on the issue of fairness in business dealings. From the standpoint of the church and its interests, this is a secondary matter. Furthermore, the clergy have only limited experience in this area. Hence they are willing to accept what "the authorities" say. However, where the interests of the church are involved (e.g., on the issue of power), or where personal experience provides a basis for judgment (e.g., the issue of religious tolerance), they are less willing to accept the views of "the authorities."

IV. SOCIAL VALUES OF THE CLERGY

Intellectual autonomy

Of all the differences between the Protestant and Catholic clergy, few were more pronounced than those involving the question of what a child must learn to prepare him for life. On this important question the Catholic clergy overwhelmingly stressed the importance of obedience and ranked it well ahead of intellectual autonomy. Eighty-one per cent of the Catholic clergy took this position, compared with only 43 per cent of the Negro Protestant and 40 per cent of the white Protestant clergy.

The uniqueness of the views of the Catholic clergy become evident when they are compared with those of the laity. Of all the subsegments of the Detroit population, lower-working-class Catholics were the most likely to rank obedience ahead of intellectual autonomy. Yet even in this group only 62 per cent took this position, compared with 81 per cent of the

Catholic clergy. Among Catholics of *all* class levels only 48 per cent valued obedience above autonomy (though even this was well above the white Protestant figure of 32 per cent). These figures clearly indicate that the Catholic clergy are a major force promoting respect for authority in Detroit today. If Catholics are less often committed to intellectual autonomy than Protestants, this is not so much due to the influence of class as of the church.[12]

The strong concern for authority of the Catholic clergy manifested itself at numerous points in our interviews with them. In response to questions, priests often replied, "The Catholic Church teaches . . . ," or, "The Catholic Church's position is . . . ," even when the questions dealt with matters where Catholic teaching permits some latitude for individual differences of opinion—for example, on the morality of drinking. Catholic teaching on this subject is not a matter of dogma requiring the unconditional assent of the individual. For instance, one may believe that while it is possible to drink without committing any moral offense, owing to the nature of the circumstances usually involved, or the consequences resulting, drinking is usually wrong from the moral standpoint. In fact, several priests expressed this opinion. However, many more did not seem to have given the matter any personal thought, and instead simply fell back on the formula, "The Catholic Church teaches . . ."

The Catholic clergy's concern for authority apparently is a consequence of two things: (*a*) the monarchical constitution of the church, which vests ultimate human sovereignty in one man; and (*b*) the highly elaborated system of rules, regulations, and doctrines which have their roots to a considerable degree in the Gregorian reform movement of the eleventh century and which have been amplified and extended so greatly by the popes since Leo XIII.

By contrast, the Protestant system offers much less encouragement to those who value authority more than intellectual autonomy. It has neither infallible clerical authorities to whom the individual pastor may turn for guidance, nor an extensive

[12] In this connection it is important to note that Catholic clergy of middle-class background were no more likely to favor autonomy than those of a working-class background.

system of rules, regulations, and doctrines. Such legislation as the Protestant churches have devised deal chiefly with such necessary, but limited, matters as church government and liturgical forms. On the crucial matters of daily life the Protestant churches offer their clergy and members a limited number of general principles of action, but a minimum of detailed prescriptions. In recent years, partly in response to pressures generated by contacts with Catholicism, Protestant church bodies have issued a series of statements on various issues ranging from birth control to labor conditions. However, these have never been in any sense binding on the individual, but typically have been issued either for his guidance, or to express the prevailing view of the leaders of the group on a particular subject. Hence, there are relatively few matters on which a Protestant minister could honestly say, "My church teaches . . ." This again is part of the sectarian heritage of Protestantism, a heritage which, while partly abandoned, is still far from dead.

Of crucial importance here is the whole Protestant and sectarian tradition that the conscience of the individual cannot be bound by ecclesiastical bodies, but only by the Word of God. Luther contrasted his own view with that of the Catholic Church in this way:

> The Romanists say, "How can we know this or that to be true and God's Word? We must learn it from the Pope and the councils." Very well, let them decree and say what they will, still say I, thou canst not rest thy confidence thereon, not satisfy thy conscience. *Thou must thyself decide. Thy life is at stake. Therefore must God say unto thee in thy heart, "This is God's Word," else it is still undecided.*[13]

While some of the Protestant churches have compromised on this principle to a greater or lesser degree, retreating to the church-type position of Catholicism and Eastern Orthodoxy, the great majority of Protestant ministers have not. This was clearly indicated in our interviews when we asked whether

---

[13] Quoted by G. Ernest Wright, *The Challenge of Israel's Faith* (Chicago: The University of Chicago Press, 1944) pp. 11–12. Emphasis added. Copyright The University of Chicago Press.

or not they believed they had the right to question the teachings of their church. Ninety per cent of the Negro Protestants and 89 per cent of the white were convinced they did. By contrast, only 20 per cent of the Catholic clergy believed they had this right.

When the views of the clergy are compared with those of the laity, it becomes clear that the Protestant churches are a force generating an autonomic orientation in our society. Listed below are the percentages of various categories of Detroiters believing they have the right to question what their church teaches:

White Protestant clergy	89 per cent
Active white Protestant laymen	83 per cent
Marginal white Protestants	74 per cent
Marginal white Catholics	67 per cent
Active white Catholic laymen	47 per cent
White Catholic clergy	20 per cent[14]

One might easily imagine that those who are marginal to the churches would be the strongest adherents to the principle of the individual's right to question church teachings, but this is clearly not the case with Protestants. Rather, the locus of intellectual autonomy on this important question is in the ranks of those *most* committed to Protestantism.

Economic values

The greatest difference observed in the area of economic values occurred in the ranking of *job security*. Members of the Catholic clergy valued it much more than did Protestant ministers, either white or Negro. Twenty per cent of the priests in our sample ranked job security first or second among the five items with which we confronted them (see Chapter 3). This compared with a figure of 10 per cent for Negro Protestant ministers, and 3 per cent for white Protestant. Seventy per cent of the Catholic clergy ranked security among the top three job attributes, compared with 40 per cent of the white Protestants.

On the other hand, Protestant ministers were more likely

[14] For Negro Protestants the figures were 90, 88, and 79 per cent respectively, from clergy to marginal members.

to rank *chances for advancement* high. Ninety-eight per cent of the white Protestants ranked it first or second, compared with 86 per cent of the Negro Protestants, and 82 per cent of the Catholics. In this area the clergy conformed to the expected pattern much more closely than the laity.

On the question of savings, Protestant members of the clergy were more likely than Catholic to say that people should save a part of their income every month even if it meant doing without some things that the family could really use. Sixty-four per cent of the white Protestant ministers, 61 per cent of the Negro Protestants, but only 47 per cent of the Catholic priests took this position.

On the question of whether God prefers to see men strive to get ahead or to be satisfied with what they have, differences among the clergy were generally small, though Protestants were more likely than Catholics to believe that God endorses striving. Seventy-four per cent of the Negro Protestant ministers, 73 per cent of the white Protestants, and 67 per cent of the Catholic priests expressed this view. It was interesting to observe that in each instance the clergy were more likely than the laity to hold this view. This difference was especially pronounced among the Negro Protestants: while only 34 per cent of the laity felt that God prefers to see men strive to get ahead, 74 per cent of the clergy held this view.

In the area of economic attitudes and behavior, the one reversal in form occurred on the question concerning installment buying. Forty-three per cent of the Catholic clergy condemned installment buying as unwise or wrong, compared with 30 per cent of the white Protestant clergy, and only 14 per cent of the Negro Protestants. On this matter the thinking of the Catholic clergy corresponded rather closely with that of their more active laity, 37 per cent of whom also condemned installment buying. The same cannot be said of the Protestant clergy. Forty-seven per cent of the active churchgoing white Protestants and 30 per cent of the active Negro Protestant laymen were opposed to the practice, so that opposition was far more frequent among the laity than among the clergy in both instances.

Political values and behavior

(Compared with other Detroiters, the clergy were much more likely to say they had no preference between the Republican and Democratic parties.) Over half denied having a partisan preference, compared with slightly less than a quarter of the population as a whole. Apparently many clergymen feel that they can serve their politically divided congregations and parishes better if they have no visible political identification.

Among those members of the clergy who were willing to express a party preference, (the Republicans found considerable support—far more than in the population as a whole.) Three quarters of the white Protestant ministers with a party preference (N=28) declared themselves to be Republicans as did almost half of the white Catholics (N=22) and Negro Protestants (N=11).

Although clergymen were less likely than the rest of the population to have (or express) a party preference, they were more likely to vote, and they were also willing to say how they voted. Depending on the group involved, from 91 to 95 per cent of the clergy said they voted in the 1956 elections, compared with only 71 to 77 per cent of the laity.

Because ministers and priests were willing to discuss their voting behavior, and because of their high turnout rate, it was possible to get some insight into the partisan tendencies of even those who professed to be independents. (The striking fact which emerged from our analysis of their voting record was the strength of their Republican bias.) Among the three major groups, 72 per cent of the clergy who voted in 1956 (N=116) reported voting for Eisenhower, and 49 per cent for Cobo (the Republican candidate for governor). By contrast, only 49 per cent of the laity in the 1958 survey who went to the polls voted for Eisenhower, and only 30 per cent for Cobo.

The meaning of these figures becomes much more apparent when we compare the votes of the clergy with those of their middle-class parishioners, and omit the entire working class. Of the middle-class members of the three groups, 70 per cent voted for Eisenhower and 50 per cent for Cobo. In short, the voting behavior of the clergy was indistinguishable from that of the middle-class portion of the laity. In the Catholic group the clergy inclined even more to the Republican candidates than did their middle-class parishioners. For example, 75 per cent of the priests reported voting for Eisenhower, but only 65 per cent of the middle-class laity. In the case of Cobo the comparable figures were 45 and 37 per cent. This pattern was not nearly so evident among the Protestants.[15]

As noted previously, the economic position of the Protestant clergy is such that the majority of both Negro and white ministers can only be described as members of the middle class. While the actual cash income of the Catholic clergy is low, their economic situation has far more in common with that of the middle class than the working class. They enjoy a high measure of economic security and their level of living is also comparable to that of the middle class. Furthermore, the work of the modern city pastor—Protestant or Catholic—involves a great many administrative and financial responsibilities, so that without exaggeration he can be described as at least half businessman and executive.[16] Finally, there seems good reason for believing that members of the urban clergy interact with members of the middle class far more often, and on a far more intimate basis, than with members of the working class. Hence, the social situation of most clergymen strongly predisposes them to adopt middle-class political norms.

However, not all clergymen in any of the three groups can be considered members of the middle class. Hence, if class were the only factor influencing voting behavior we would expect the percentage of Republicans among the clergy to be *lower* than among middle-class laymen. The fact that the clergy support the Republicans at least as strongly as their middle-class parishioners suggests that some other factor is at work. Our analysis suggests that this factor is the wide-spread

---

15 Among Negro Protestants, 40 per cent of the clergy and 42 per cent of the middle-class laity supported Eisenhower, and 20 per cent of the clergy but none of the laity supported Cobo. Among white Protestants the comparable figures were 81 and 77 per cent, and 62 and 66 per cent.

16 For a discussion of this subject see Joseph H. Fichter, S.J., *Social Relations in the Urban Parish* (Chicago: The University of Chicago Press, 1954), Chapter 10 and especially pp. 129–31.

identification of the Republican Party as the party of personal morality and integrity noted previously.)

On the question of whether the government is doing too much or too little in areas such as housing, unemployment, and education, the white clergy were again a good bit more conservative than their parishioners. The Catholic clergy were even more conservative than their middle-class parishioners. None of the white clergy came out in favor of the nationalization of basic industries, though three white Protestant ministers expressed uncertainty on the matter.

The white clergy were more conservative in this respect than their parishioners, but the same could not be said of the Negro Protestant clergy, despite their Republican leanings. Seventy-nine per cent thought that the government was doing too little, compared with only 63 per cent of the laity. However, whereas 38 per cent of the Negro Protestant laymen either favored nationalization of basic industries, or at least expressed uncertainty on the matter, only 10 per cent of the clergy took similar positions. In brief, while the Negro Protestant clergy may be politically liberal, it is certainly not radical.

CIVIL RIGHTS

(Some of the most striking differences among the clergy occurred in the area of civil rights, especially on the subject of free speech.) As we observed earlier, the differences between Catholic and white Protestant laymen were generally small in this area, especially if one included the marginal members of these groups. However, when comparisons were limited to the more active members of the two groups, the disagreement became more pronounced, with an average difference of 14 percentage points on the questions involving the rights of atheists, Fascists, and Communists.

In the case of the ordained members of these two groups the differences were extreme on all of the questions involving freedom of speech, with one exception: (that dealing with the right of Americans to criticize presidential actions. On this question there was no appreciable difference between white Protestant ministers and Catholic priests.) On the other three items, however, the difference between the two groups ranged from 50 to 59 percentage points, with the mean being 54.

On the question of whether the Bill of Rights should be interpreted as permitting someone to make speeches attacking
religion, 94 per cent of the white Protestant ministers, but
only 41 per cent of the Catholic priests, expressed the view
that such a right exists. Seventy-nine per cent of the Protestants, but only 29 per cent of the Catholics, felt that the
American Constitution guarantees the rights of Fascists to
speak in favor of their beliefs. On the rights of Communists the
comparable figures were 75 and 16 per cent.

In general the differences between the clergy are larger
than those between the laity because of the strong commitment of the Protestant clergy to a liberal interpretation of the
Bill of Rights. As shown in *Table 49*, the white Protestant
clergy were much more likely than the laity to favor a liberal
interpretation of the historic right of freedom of speech, while
in the case of Catholics the reverse proved true. In general,
however, the Catholic clergy are closer to the laity in their
point of view, though on the issue of freedom for Communists, a fairly significant difference is evident in Catholic
ranks.

Table 49

PERCENTAGE OF DETROITERS EXPRESSING BELIEF THAT THE
AMERICAN CONSTITUTION PROVIDES FOR FREEDOM OF SPEECH
TO THOSE ATTACKING RELIGION, SPEAKING IN FAVOR OF
FASCISM, OR SPEAKING IN FAVOR OF COMMUNISM, BY SOCIO-
RELIGIOUS GROUP, FOR CLERGY AND LAITY

Issue	White Protestant Clergy	White Protestant Laity	Catholic Laity	Catholic Clergy
Right to attack religion	94	51	44	41
Right to advocate Fascism	79	43	36	29
Right to advocate Communism	75	39	32	16

These figures provide further support for our earlier conclusion that the Catholic Church and the Protestant churches,
as organized associations, tend to pull the American population in opposite directions on the issue of freedom of speech.
This is not to say that the Catholic Church is opposed to free-

dom of speech, or that the Protestant churches favor un-limited freedom. However, compared with the Protestant churches the Catholic Church certainly seems to promote a much stricter interpretation of this central Constitutional principle.

A sharp difference was also found when we compared the responses of the Protestant and Catholic clergy to the question of whether an atheist could be a good American (Q. 54). Whereas 81 per cent of the white Protestant clergy thought this was possible, their view was shared by only 46 per cent of the Catholic clergy, and 52 per cent of the Negro Protes-tant clergy. In the case of the two Protestant groups, 30 to 100 per cent *more* of the clergy than of the laity held this view.[17] By contrast, 25 per cent *less* of the Catholic clergy held this view. Such views have rather obvious implications for civil rights legislation. When one segment of the popula-tion doubts the capacity of another segment to perform as good citizens, the probabilities are increased that the first group will try to take legislative action against the second, since this is a very serious matter. Bitter controversy can be expected to ensue.

Returning to the questions dealing more directly with the subject of freedom of speech, the Negro Protestant group proved especially interesting. Earlier we found that the Negro Protestant laity were more conservative in this area than any of the other major socio-religious groups. The same cannot be said of the Negro Protestant clergy. On the three important issues of freedom of speech for those attacking religion, and for those promoting Fascism or Communism, Negro Protes-tant ministers occupied a position intermediate between that of the white Protestant and Catholic clergy. On the important question of whether the Constitution provides for the right to attack religion, 67 per cent of the Negro Protestant clergy thought that it does. On the rights of Fascists and Commu-nists, 38 per cent took the liberal position. The Negro Prot-estant clergy was closest to the white Protestant clergy on the historic issue of religious freedom, and closest to the Catholic

---

[17] Sixty-one per cent of the white Protestant laity, 63 per cent of the Catholic, 27 per cent of the Negro Protestant, and 77 per cent of the Jews believed that an atheist can be a good American.

clergy on the modern issue of political freedom, especially as it involves the rights of Fascists.

MORAL NORMS AND GOVERNMENTAL RESTRAINT

The clergy were also sharply divided on the various controversial issues concerning personal morality. In pretest interviews we found that it was impractical to even question the Catholic clergy on birth control and divorce, since most regarded questions on these topics as either a personal affront implying some lack of orthodoxy on their part, or as evidence of abysmal ignorance on our part. Hence, we omitted these questions from the main body of interviews with the Catholic clergy, though pretest experiences indicated that the use of these questions would have produced unanimous agreement that the practices were always wrong morally.

Perhaps the most striking finding in this area was the near-unanimity of the Catholic clergy on the issues of gambling, drinking, and Sunday business. On the question of Sunday business, 98 per cent agreed that it is always or usually wrong from the moral standpoint. On the issue of gambling 85 per cent agreed that it is seldom or never wrong. On the issue of moderate drinking, 88 per cent expressed the view that from the moral standpoint it is usually not wrong to drink in moderation. The relevance of these findings for our earlier discussion of intellectual autonomy is not difficult to find. In all of these areas, those well trained in the Catholic faith recognize that the basic solutions to problems have already been devised. The most that is required of the individual is a certain measure of diligence in the application of the solutions to his own specific problems. Hence, it appears that the greater the number of clearly defined solutions which a group provides for its members, the less is the likelihood that they will develop an autonomous orientation, and the greater the likelihood that they will stress the importance of obedience.

The contrast between the Protestant and Catholic clergy was striking not only because they frequently took diametrically opposed positions on these moral issues, but also because of the relative lack of unanimity among the Protestants. The only issue on which they came close to complete agreement was that of gambling. Ninety-six per cent of the white Protestant clergy and 95 per cent of the Negro Protestants condemned this practice as generally wrong on moral grounds. On the issue of birth control, 93 per cent of the white Protestants, but only 75 per cent of the Negro Protestants agreed that this practice is seldom if ever wrong on moral grounds. Only 70 per cent of the white Protestants and 62 per cent of the Negro Protestants were prepared to say that divorce is always or usually wrong. On the issue of Sunday business, 61 per cent of the white Protestants and 57 per cent of the Negro Protestants condemned the practice. Finally, only 42 per cent of the white Protestants and 67 per cent of the Negro Protestants expressed the belief that moderate drinking is always or usually wrong.

As a general rule, the clergy conformed to group norms more faithfully than the laity. Thus the Protestant clergy, both Negro and white, were much more often opposed to gambling, moderate drinking, and divorce than were the laity. Similarly, the Catholic clergy were much more often opposed to Sunday business, and presumably also birth control and divorce, than were the laity. Also, as might be expected from the theory that leaders must conform to group norms more closely than followers, the Protestant clergy were less critical of birth control than the laity, and the Catholic clergy were less critical of gambling than the laity. The only instances in which this general hypothesis did not fit involved the Negro Protestants on the issue of Sunday business and the Catholics on the issue of drinking. On these two issues no differences were observed between the laity as a whole and the clergy.

Only one of the five areas provided a good opportunity to compare the clergy of the three major groups with respect to their readiness to invoke legislative support for their moral standards. This was the area of Sunday business openings, which may or may not be typical. Here the Protestant clergy who condemned Sunday business as always or usually wrong were much more likely than the Catholic clergy to favor legislative action. Two thirds of the Negro Protestant clergy and half of the white Protestants favored legislative restraints, compared with only one sixth of the Catholic clergy. On the two other questions (gambling and drinking) where the issue of legal restraints was raised, so few Catholic priests condemned these practices that comparisons were not possible. However, comparing the two groups of Protestant clergy we found that in both groups roughly two thirds of those who condemned gambling favored laws against gambling. In the case of drinking the situation was quite different. Here about two thirds of the white Protestant clergy who condemned the practice favored governmental controls, but this view was shared by only a third of the Negro Protestants.

As a general rule the clergy were *less* favorably disposed toward governmental restraints than were the laity. The only two exceptions to this generalization occurred in the white Protestant group. On the issue of gambling there was no appreciable difference between laity and clergy, and on the issue of drinking the white Protestant clergy were much *more* favorably disposed toward legislation than the laity. Two thirds of the clergy, but only half of the laity, who condemned drinking favored legislative restraints.

FOREIGN AFFAIRS

The white Protestant clergy were much more likely than either the Negro Protestant or Catholic clergy to report having given much thought to world problems. Slightly over two thirds of the white Protestant ministers reported this compared with slightly less than half of the clergy of the other two groups. Protestants, both Negro and white, were more likely than Catholics to disagree with the proposition that we should not spend a penny abroad except in the interests of national defense. Seventy-nine per cent of the white Protestant ministers and 71 per cent of the Negro Protestants took this stand, compared with 63 per cent of the Catholic clergy.

Protestants were also more likely to say they would like to see the United States become a part of a single world government if a practical plan for this could be devised. Seventy per cent of the white Protestant clergy and 67 per cent of the Negro Protestants expressed this view compared with 58 per cent of the Catholic clergy. Catholics were much more likely to oppose such a development wholly or primarily on the grounds of what Americans would lose by such an arrangement. Fourteen per cent of the Catholics opposed American participation in a practical plan of world government on what might be described as basically nationalistic grounds, compared with 5 per cent of the white and Negro Protestant ministers.

Compared with the laity, the clergy appeared much more often interested in world affairs. This was especially true of the white Protestant and Catholic clergy. Although only 25 per cent of the white Protestant laity expressed much interest in world problems, 68 per cent of the white Protestant clergy did so. Among Catholics the comparable figures were 23 and 49 per cent. Among Negro Protestants they were 34 and 48 per cent.

One might suppose that these differences between clergy and laity merely reflected differences in education since higher education increases people's concern with problems of larger and more inclusive social systems, and the clergy generally have college training while the laity do not. However, our data indicate that the high level of interest in world affairs expressed by the clergy was due to something more than mere exposure to higher education. For example, among white Protestant laymen who had attended college, only 31 per cent expressed much interest in world problems. By contrast, among the white Protestant clergy 68 per cent expressed such interest. Among Catholics the differential was not nearly so great, but even here some difference was evident. Whereas 39 per cent of the Catholic laity with some exposure to higher education expressed much interest in world problems, 49 per cent of the clergy expressed such interest. These figures indicate that over and above the liberating influence of higher education, intense involvement in the churches also has a liberating influence, freeing the individual from the "natural" preoccupations with self, family, and the local community. Judging from our evidence, this liberating influence is greater in Protestantism than in Catholicism.

The differences between clergy and laity, and between Catholic and Protestant clergy, probably also reflect differences in their social roles. Clergymen in general are expected to provide intellectual leadership in their congregations and parishes, and hence are under some pressure to keep up with the news, including news of events abroad. Such an expectation is likely to be especially strong in the case of Protestants in view of the great importance attached to the preaching function in Protestant churches. (Hence social pressures compel the clergy, especially in the Protestant churches, to keep informed on events at the international level.)

(Compared with the laity, the clergy also appeared to support a more liberal and humanitarian foreign policy.) The clergy were much more likely to disagree with the proposal that foreign aid should be granted only when it served the interests of national defense. Seventy-nine per cent of the white Protestant clergy, but only 6o per cent of the middle-class members of the laity, disagreed with this proposal. Among Negro Protestants the comparable figures were 71 and 62 per cent, and among Catholics 63 and 51 per cent. The clergy were also more likely than the laity to favor American participation in any united world government, with the differences again being more pronounced among the Protestants. Seventy per cent of the white Protestant clergy, but only 51 per cent of the middle-class members of the laity, favored such a proposal. Among Negro Protestants the comparable figures were 67 and 54 per cent, and among Catholics 58 and 54 per cent.

The humanitarian orientation of the clergy was also evident in the area of race relations. Seventy-nine per cent of the white clergy, compared with 70 per cent of the middle-class laity, expressed a preference for integrated schools. Differences between the Protestant and Catholic laity and clergy were negligible at this point, though in both categories the Protestants were slightly more inclined to the integrationist viewpoint despite the larger number of men of southern extraction among them. Members of the white Protestant clergy were also asked how they would feel if a Negro of comparable income and education moved into the block where they lived.[18] Whereas 56 per cent of the middle-class members of the white Protestant laity said they would be disturbed or unhappy if this happened, this feeling was shared by only 18 per cent of the clergy. Also, in explaining why they would be

[18] This question was not asked of the Catholic clergy since we felt comparability would not be possible, owing to the fact that members of the Catholic clergy, except in certain Eastern rites, are unmarried.

disturbed or unhappy, 37 per cent of the laity indicated that they had an unfavorable image of the Negro group, but only 7 per cent of the clergy indicated a similar image.

THE POLITICAL ROLE OF THE CLERGY

Members of the clergy also differed from the laity in their conceptions of the political responsibilities of the clergy. In all eight of the comparisons between clergy and laity, the clergy were more likely to believe that they *should* take a public stand on controversial political matters. In some instances the differences were rather substantial. This was especially true in connection with the controversies relating to racial integration. For example, 74 per cent of the white Protestant ministers said that the clergy should take a public stand in this area, but only 42 per cent of the laity shared this view. Among Negro Protestants the comparable figures were 95 and 76 per cent. Among Catholics they were 65 and 46 per cent.

Differences were also substantial with respect to the responsibilities of the clergy in supporting and opposing individual candidates for public office. Although only 11 per cent of the white Protestant laymen felt that the clergy should take public stands, 46 per cent of the clergy felt that this should be done. Among Negro Protestants the comparable figures were 42 and 86 per cent. This question was not directed to members of the Catholic clergy since in the pretest interviews we found that the Archdiocese of Detroit has a regulation which specifically forbids individual priests to take such actions.

Differences between the laity and clergy were not so great in their conceptions of the responsibilities of the clergy on such issues as government aid in the medical field. Among both Catholics and white Protestants 32 per cent of the laity and 37 per cent of the clergy felt that the clergy should take a public stand on such matters. Among Negro Protestants the comparable figures were 71 and 86 per cent.

As the preceding figures indicate, Negro Protestants, both clergy and laity alike, most often believed that the clergy should take an active part in politics. There was little difference between white Protestants and Catholics on this subject.

Hard work and helping others

Earlier we noted that the Catholic and Protestant clergy differ sharply in the relative value they attach to obedience and autonomous thought. They also differ considerably in the relative importance which they attach to the humanitarian value of helping others and the acquisitive value of working hard. Sixty-six per cent of the white Protestant ministers in our sample believed that it is more important for a child to learn to help others than it is for him to learn to work hard. This view was shared by only 52 per cent of the Negro Protestants and 46 per cent of the Catholic clergy.

It is especially interesting that both the Catholic and Negro Protestant clergy value hard work ahead of helping others even more often than the laymen in their groups. Considering the clear and unequivocal teachings of Jesus on the importance of loving one's neighbor,[19] it seems ironic that the clergy should so often rank hard work ahead of helping others. While the white Protestant clergy were a bit more likely than the laity to rank helping others ahead of working hard, the difference between the two groups was so small (66 vs. 62 per cent) that it can hardly be a source of satisfaction. Perhaps even more startling is the fact that only 11 per cent of the clergy of the three groups ranked helping others as the most important thing for a child to learn to prepare him for life. The comparable figure for the cross-sectional sample of non-clergy of all faiths and no faith was 13 per cent. In this area at least no one can accuse the clergy of exaggerated idealism or unrealistic commitment to the ethical teachings of the Founder of their faith.

It is interesting to speculate why the clergy should emerge as the proponents of a humanitarian outlook in foreign affairs and race relations, and not on child training. Obviously, few people are completely consistent in all their many patterns of action, and the clergy seem no exception. So far as we can judge, the explanation for this curious phenomenon is that the clergy here are merely following a middle- or upper-

[19] See, for example, Jesus' response to the question of which is the most important of the commandments of God, the parable of the Good Samaritan, and the parable of the Last Judgment.

middle-class pattern of thought and action. On the basis of our cross-sectional sample it can be said that *the higher the status of an individual, the greater the probability that he will take a humanitarian stand on impersonal political issues, but the less the probability that he will take a humanitarian stand so far as personal relationships are concerned.* Thus, the middle and upper-middle classes are more likely than the working class to take a humanitarian stand on political issues such as racial integration and foreign aid, but are less likely than the working class to believe that it is important for children to learn to help others. A critical examination of the moral implications of this finding can be deeply disturbing.

Religion and science

We found significant differences between Protestant and Catholic clergy in the frequency with which they saw disagreements between the teachings of science and the teachings of their church. The Catholic clergy were much more likely than the Protestants to indicate an awareness of conflicts, though the majority of Catholic priests who expressed such an awareness said the conflicts were between their church and *certain* scientists. As one of them expressed it in an interview with the writer:

> There is no conflict between true science and Catholic teaching, since God is the author of both. However, there are, of course, many conflicts between the teachings of individual scientists and the teachings of the Church.

Since our concern was with the relationships between these two institutional systems as they exist in the world today, rather than in their ideal or perfected forms, we classified such responses as indicating a belief in the existence of conflict and disagreement. On this basis, 65 per cent of the Catholic clergy were classified as feeling that such a conflict exists, compared with 48 per cent of the Negro Protestant ministers and 45 per cent of the white Protestants. It may be recalled that among the laity no substantial differences were observed in these three groups, with 43 to 47 per cent in each group believing that conflict exists. However, among the laity there were some modest differences in the frequency with which members of the several groups believed that really *serious* conflicts exist. Twenty-eight per cent of the Catholic laity, 23 per cent of the white Protestant, and 20 per cent of the Negro Protestant held this view. These differences were roughly paralleled by differences among the clergy. The Catholic clergy were the most likely to believe that the disagreements between science and religion were a serious matter, with 42 per cent expressing this view. Thirty-three per cent of the Negro Protestant clergy, and 31 per cent of the white Protestant clergy shared this view.

V. THE SIGNIFICANCE OF THESE DATA

Our findings on the clergy are especially important from the standpoint of the study as a whole since, as we have already noted, they provide an independent check on the influence of socio-religious groups on their members' actions. More than this, comparisons of the attitudes and actions of clergy and laity (and especially the middle-class members of the laity) provide a valuable supplement to our earlier comparisons of members of the laity based on degree of involvement in the churches. In other words, they provide an additional test of the proposition that the churches are active forces shaping and molding men's relationships to secular institutions, and that such influence varies with the degree of the individual's involvement.

The bulk of the evidence obtained from interviews with the clergy strongly supported our earlier conclusions based on the cross-sectional surveys. In particular they supported our earlier conclusion that the Protestant churches tend to develop in their adherents beliefs, values, and behavior patterns which facilitate upward mobility. Especially noteworthy were the data on intellectual autonomy and migration. Data from clerical interviews also provided substantial support for the thesis that the Catholic and Protestant churches pull their adherents in opposite directions on the question of freedom of speech, an issue of fundamental importance in any pluralistic society.

Chapter 8

CONCLUSIONS

all

What does it all mean? What do the findings presented in this book mean for students of human society and what do they mean for practical men of affairs? In this final chapter we shall attempt to look at the data in theoretical perspective, so that we may see the woods as a whole, and not merely the trees. First, however, it may be well to recall the more important conclusions which have emerged from our investigation.

I. SUMMARY OF FINDINGS

To begin with, it seems clear that, contrary to the expectations of the nineteenth-century positivists, religious organizations remain vigorous and influential in contemporary American society. Only in the case of the Jewish group is there any evidence of serious organizational weakness, and this is limited entirely to the religious associations. In fact, the vigor of Jewish communalism more than compensates for the weakness of the religious associations. In the case of the two largest groups, the white Protestants and Catholics, the evidence indicates considerable associational and communal vitality at present, especially among the Catholics.

Second, and more important, are our findings relevant to probable future trends. As reported in Chapter 2, most signs point to *gains* in associational vigor and vitality in the foreseeable future. Most of the changes now occurring in the structure of American society are weakening and reducing in relative size those elements in the population least involved in the churches (e.g., first-generation immigrants and members of the working class), and strengthening and enlarging those elements most involved in the churches (e.g., third-generation Americans and members of the middle classes). There are indications that the next twenty or thirty years will see a weakening of the Negro Protestant churches, but since most members of the other major groups are unwilling to establish primary relations with Negroes, it seems unlikely that this development will seriously weaken the internal solidarity of the group.

Third, (and this is the central finding of our study) from our evidence it is clear that religion in various ways is constantly influencing the daily lives of the masses of men and women in the modern American metropolis. More than that: through its impact on individuals, religion makes an impact on all the other institutional systems of the community these individuals staff. Hence the influence of religion operates at the social level as well as at the personal level.

Depending on the socio-religious group to which a person belongs, the probabilities are increased or decreased that he will enjoy his occupation, indulge in installment buying, save to achieve objectives far in the future, believe in the American Dream, vote Republican, favor the welfare state, take a liberal view on the issue of freedom of speech, oppose racial integration in the schools, migrate to another community, maintain close ties with his family, develop a commitment to the principle of intellectual autonomy, have a large family, complete a given unit of education, or rise in the class system. These are only a few of the consequences which we have observed to be associated with differences in socio-religious group membership, and the position of individuals in these groups.

In analyzing these relationships we constantly sought to determine whether religion is a *causal* factor, itself increasing or decreasing the probabilities of various patterns of action, or whether it is merely a factor *correlated* with them but having no influence on them. As a first step in this direction we repeatedly applied controls of various types to our data to make sure that a given relationship was not merely a by-product of other factors such as class, region of birth, or immigrant generation. In the majority of instances such controls did not appreciably affect the relationship in question, and when they did have a more substantial effect, they were almost as likely to strengthen the relationship as to weaken it.

As a second step in our effort to test the causal hypothesis we tried to establish the existence of a temporal sequence in which religious differences existed *before* differences in secular behavior appeared. For example, in examining the relationship between religion and vertical mobility we found that individuals raised in devout white Protestant families are more likely to become upwardly mobile in their adult years than are individuals raised in less devout white Protestant families or in Catholic families. Similarly, we were able to demonstrate that individuals raised in white Protestant families are more likely to shift their political affiliation to the Republican Party in later years than are individuals raised in Catholic families. Although our evidence in connection with this problem is hardly definitive, it tends to support the hypothesis of causality and contradict the hypothesis of mere correlation or association.

Third, and finally, we checked the causal hypothesis by making intragroup comparisons to see if those who are more highly involved in the religious groups display patterns of action peculiar to their groups more often than those who are less involved. This required comparisons among laymen and also between the laity and the clergy. As a general rule we found that when there are differences of any magnitude *between* two socio-religious groups, *internal* differences are also present, suggesting that the differences between groups reflect the influence of the groups, and are not merely a statistical correlation.

On many of the variables analyzed, the four major socio-religious groups split into two divisions: white Protestants and Jews on the one hand; Negro Protestants and Catholics on the other. This pattern is most evident in economic behavior. White Protestants and Jews have a positive attitude toward work more often than Negro Protestants or Catholics, especially in upper-middle-class jobs. They are likelier to believe that ability is more important than family connections; to be self-employed; to believe in intellectual autonomy; and to have small families. However, in some respects members of the Jewish group resemble Catholics more nearly than white

Protestants. This is especially true of party preference and of attitudes toward the kin group.

The Negro Protestant group was especially interesting. With no controls for socio-economic factors, it resembles the Catholic group far more closely than the white Protestant group. However, we usually found that the more carefully one controls for these socio-economic factors, the more nearly Negro Protestants resemble white Protestants. In short, our findings suggest that the similarities between the Negro Protestant and Catholic groups are largely induced by the *uniquely* unfavorable social and economic situation in which the great majority of Negro Protestants find themselves.

In our examination of these differences among the major socio-religious groups, we repeatedly sought to determine whether they are declining in importance, holding their own, or gaining in strength. The classical theory of urbanism stresses the importance of those forces which increase contact and communication among people and thus have a homogenizing effect. On the basis of this theory one would expect the differences between groups to decline. While it is difficult to ascertain social trends on the basis of data gathered in a single survey at any one point in time, we were able nevertheless to make some estimates of trends. We based these estimates on comparisons between third-generation Americans and more recent immigrants, middle-class Detroiters and working-class Detroiters, Detroiters of urban origin and those of rural origin. These comparisons were based on the assumption that the third generation, the middle class, and people of urban origin represent the "wave of the future," or those segments of the population destined to expand, while the first and second generations, the working class, and the rural element represent those segments of the population destined to decline in relative numbers. On the basis of such comparisons we can only conclude that differences among the socio-religious groups are *not* declining and are not likely to decline in the foreseeable future. They are, at the very least, as sharply drawn as ever, and there are numerous indications that they may become more pronounced in the future. This possibility is especially suggested by data based on interclass comparisons, which generally reveal that socio-religious differences are greater among members of the middle class than among members of the working class.

Not only is the behavior of men influenced by the socio-religious groups to which they belong; our evidence also indicates it is influenced by their *religious orientations*. Repeatedly throughout this study we found that the orthodox and the devotional orientations are linked with differing and even opposed behavior patterns. In general, the orthodox orientation is associated with a compartmentalized outlook which separates and segregates religion from daily life. By contrast, the devotional orientation is linked with a unified *Weltanschauung*, or view of life, with religious beliefs and practices being integrated with other major aspects of daily life. In particular, the devotional orientation is linked with a humanitarian orientation.

In a review such as this it would be a mistake to overlook the fact that on some of the variables examined no appreciable differences were observed within or between groups. For example, this was evident in the case of most of the questions concerning foreign policy (though even here devotionalism seemed to influence attitudes appreciably). Clearly there are some matters on which socio-religious group membership has little influence, or at least little *differentiating* influence.

In those instances where religion did appear to be an active factor, the *magnitude* of its influence on patterns of thought and action was highly variable. Sometimes the differences between groups ranged up to 40 or 50 percentage points; sometimes they were so small that it was difficult to decide whether or not the difference was due merely to sampling error. In any sociological analysis, one of the problems which inevitably arises is that which is sometimes called the "fully-only" problem. A difference of 15 percentage points between two groups may be described as "fully 15 percentage points," or "only 15 percentage points." Obviously the qualifying word a writer uses depends to a great extent upon his previous expectations.

To avoid such subjective criteria, some kind of objective criterion has to be substituted. One which has been suggested many times is the "criterion of perfection." In other words, if one is comparing two groups with respect to a certain characteristic, such as party preference, and all the members of one group are Republicans while all the members of the other group are Democrats, one is justified in using the qualifying word "fully," but if the difference departs far from this standard of perfection, one should use the word "only."

For those familiar with the findings of modern sociological research, it is clear that the criterion of perfection is most unrealistic. Almost every human action reflects the influence of countless forces, so that the degree of influence exercised by any single factor normally falls far short of that which would be determinative. Hence, a much more realistic measure of the influence of any single factor is a comparison with the

Table 50

COMPARISON OF THE RELATIVE DISCRIMINATING POWER OF CLASS AND SOCIO-RELIGIOUS GROUP MEMBERSHIP FOR A SAMPLE OF DEPENDENT VARIABLES (WHITE PROTESTANTS AND CATHOLICS ONLY)

Dependent Variable	Mean Percentage difference between classes [a]	Mean percentage difference between socio-religious groups [b]
1. Happy working (males only)	0.5	8.5
2. Installment buying wrong or unwise	3	4
3. Multiple reasons for saving	6	11
4. Chances for upward mobility good (1952)	11	11
5. Ability more important than family (1952)	4	15
6. Republican preference (1957 and 1958)	37.5	22.5
7. Non-voter in 1956 elections	14.5	3.5
8. Constitution allows attacks on religion	18.5	6.5
9. Constitution allows Communist speeches	7.5	6.5
10. Much thought given world problems	2	3
11. Spend abroad only for national defense	11.5	4.5
12. Prefer segregated schools	12.5	0.5
13. Disturbed if Negro moved in block	9	7

Dependent Variable	Mean percentage difference between classes [a]	Mean percentage difference between socio-religious groups [b]
14. Public officials not interested in average man	8.5	8.5
15 Government should do more	15	13
16. Government should run big industries	8	10
17. Favor national health insurance (1952)	14.5	15.5
18. Favor stronger price controls (1952)	17	13
19. Expects CIO members to agree with him re controversial issues (1952)	37	17
20. Expects businessmen to agree with him re controversial issues (1952)	18	12
21. Relatives in Detroit (1952)	6.5	12.5
22. Visit relatives once a week (1952)	6.5	6.5
23. Native Detroiter	10.5	16.5
24. Future oriented in child rearing (1953)	11	7
25. Use physical punishment on 10-year-old (1953)	17.5	19.5
26. Indulgence oriented re leisure time (1953)	25	22
27. Value autonomous thought over obedience	19	15
28. Four or more children	6	17
29. Gambling wrong	13.5	24.5
30. Birth control wrong	3.5	44.5
31. Moderate drinking wrong	3	12
32. Sunday business wrong	4	8
33. Divorce wrong	1	30
34. Jews less fair in business dealings	6	3
35. Jews trying to get too much power	5.5	1.5
Mean difference	11.3	12.3
Median difference	9.0	11.0

[a] With socio-religious group held constant.
[b] With class held constant.

influence of some other single factor generally recognized to be of major importance.

In this study we have repeatedly compared the differences associated with socio-religious variables with the differences associated with class position. Among the many variables which sociologists customarily employ to account for behavioral differences, there is probably none which is generally regarded to be of as great importance with respect to as wide a range of variables as class position. Hence it provides a realistic and meaningful standard for judging the magnitude and importance of the differences uncovered in this study.

Using such a standard, it seems clear that the differences associated with religion are substantial. In general they are of a magnitude comparable to the differences associated with class on the same questions. What is even more important, the *range* of variables affected by religion seems to be fully as great as that affected by class. As an illustration, a sample of the findings associated with a wide range of dependent variables is summarized in *Table 50*. Here are presented in parallel columns (*a*) the mean differences between the middle and working classes among white Protestants and Catholics, with socio-religious group membership held constant, and (*b*) the mean differences between these two socio-religious groups, with class held constant. The dependent variables selected for inclusion in this table were not chosen selectively to prove the point; on the contrary they were chosen to represent the widest possible range. For the whole set of 35 variables, socio-religious group is slightly more powerful than class.[1] With a different set of dependent variables (of comparable diversity) one might get a somewhat different result, but the main point seems clear: *socio-religious group membership is a variable comparable in importance to class, both with respect to its potency and with respect to the range, or extent, of its influence.*[2]

[1] Charles Westoff reports a similar finding in his study of seven of the eight largest metropolitan communities in the U.S. (op. cit.).
[2] When we use more refined measures of both class and religion, larger differences are obtained for both. Thus, if we compare those in the upper-middle class with those in the lower-working class, the differences in behavior are normally greater than if we compare

This is not to say that religion is such a powerful factor in the modern metropolis that knowledge of a man's socio-religious group and his position in the group is sufficient to predict accurately how he will vote, whether he will be upwardly mobile, whether he will migrate from his native community, how often he will visit with relatives, and so forth. This is simply not the case; but it is well to remember that no single variable exists which permits predictions of this type for any significant range of phenomena. Despite the fond hopes of the economic determinists, there is no "magic key" that opens all doors. Human beings and the social organizations which they create are far more complex phenomena than the determinists credit them with being.

A fourth major finding of this study concerns the utility of our conceptual distinction between the communal and the associational aspects of socio-religious groups. The evidence uncovered in this study makes it clear that this is not only a useful, but also a necessary, distinction if one is to understand the role which religious groups play in modern society, and the means by which they play it.

In Chapter 2 we found that contrary to common sense, there is only a very limited relationship between the degree to which individuals are involved in a formal religious association and the degree to which they are involved in the corresponding subcommunity. Hence, the subcommunity is a vehicle by means of which large numbers of persons are effectively indoctrinated with the norms of the group. This is especially important in the case of groups such as the Jewish and white Protestant where associational ties are often quite weak. Thus the subcommunity becomes an important instrument for extending the influence of religious groups in the life of the community.

However, as we noted on numerous occasions in the discus-

---

all persons in the middle class with all in the working class. Similarly, comparisons of active Protestants with active Catholics normally yield larger differences than comparisons between all Protestants and all Catholics. Our evidence indicates that refinement of the class measure has a somewhat greater effect than a refinement of the religious group measure, but the difference should not be exaggerated.

sions of economics, politics, and family life, the subcommunity is something more than an instrument for reinforcing the influence of the association. It is a distinct social system in its own right, and only imperfectly co-ordinated with the religious association. At times, in fact, it exercises an influence which brings it into conflict with the formal association.

By and large, our evidence leads us to the conclusion that religious subcommunities *foster and encourage a provincial and authoritarian view of the world.* In Chapter 2 we noted that unfavorable images of other groups are consistently linked with a high level of communal involvement, but not with a high level of associational involvement. In fact, there was some evidence that a high level of associational involvement, among Protestants at least, had the opposite effect. A high level of communal involvement was also linked with a high valuation of the kin group, of obedience, and low rates of vertical mobility (both up and down). In short, involvement in socio-religious subcommunities seems to promote many of the virtues and vices which Tönnies and others have identified with the *Gemeinschaft,* the folk community, or the little community as it has been variously designated. However, what is startling about our present study is the finding that communalism survives, and even thrives, in the heart of the modern metropolis, though admittedly in a guise which makes its recognition difficult for those accustomed to associating communalism with geographically isolated and numerically small populations.

The discovery of socio-religious subcommunities is also significant from one other standpoint. Many of the critics of the churches have often charged them with promoting intolerance, narrow-mindedness, and similar characteristics. Our findings suggest that these critics have been a bit wide of their mark, since it is the subcommunities rather than the churches which seem to foster these traits. This is a subtle, but important, distinction. Obviously, if there were no churches, there would be no subcommunities, and hence this particular source of intolerance would disappear. However, there seems good reason for believing that the development of subcommunities is a phenomenon which may not be dependent solely on the existence of churches in the strict sense of this latter term. For example, there is some reason for believing that there is a secularist subcommunity in America today which fosters its own distinctive brand of intolerance and narrow-mindedness. While this is a highly speculative judgment, we feel safe in asserting that our findings demonstrate that the concept of communalism is one which is essential to an adequate understanding of intergroup hostility and tension.

Fifth, and finally, our findings provide ample justification for the further investigation of the consequences of those religious orientations, such as doctrinal orthodoxy and devotionalism, which transcend socio-religious group boundaries. The two which we selected for preliminary investigation in this study have clearly emerged as linked with distinctive patterns of action in the secular world. On the whole, doctrinal orthodoxy appears to be a type of religious orientation which is linked with (and we suspect fosters) *a compartmentalized view of life*. It seems to foster the view that one's religious commitments are irrelevant to one's political and economic actions and other aspects of secular life—except, of course, that in interpersonal relations one should be honest and fair. Devotionalism, by contrast, seems linked both with the spirit of capitalism and with a humanitarian outlook when confronted with problems of social injustice. This interesting combination of attributes seems to create a dilemma for persons committed to this orientation when faced with proposals for humanitarian activity by agencies of government. Our evidence indicates that such persons prefer humanitarian action by private individuals and agencies, distrusting, as they appear to, the welfare state.

Our evidence concerning these orientations is far from satisfactory. We have no information concerning the important question of when and how such orientations are acquired by the individual. Hence, it proved impossible to deal effectively with the difficult problem of causality. Furthermore, orthodoxy and devotionalism are but two among a much larger number of religious orientations which deserve to be explored. Although we gathered data on certain other important orientations, our resources were too limited to analyze these data at this time. Hence, our major conclusion on this point must be that the limited investigation undertaken up to this point fully justifies further work in this area.

II. THE FINDINGS IN THEORETICAL PERSPECTIVE

These, then, are our findings. But what do they mean? How do they affect our understanding of contemporary American society and of modern industrial societies generally? How do they affect our understanding of the processes of social change and our predictions concerning future patterns of development? In the following pages we shall try to pull together, expand, and systematize our interpretation of these findings. Our goal is to formulate a theory designed to clarify and explain the place of religious institutions in contemporary society and their influence on the functioning of other social institutions. In so doing, we shall often be obliged to go beyond the bounds of what has yet been clearly demonstrated in sociological research.[3]

The nature of religion

As a starting point we should state clearly what we mean by the highly ambiguous term "religion," which means so many different things to different people. Some limit the term so that theism is an integral element in the definition, while others define it more broadly so as to include non-theistic faiths.

From the sociological standpoint much can be gained by a moderately inclusive definition of religion. The use of a more inclusive definition directs attention to important similarities between apparently diverse phenomena, thereby increasing our understanding of all the elements embraced by it.

[3] In popular thinking it is often supposed that science is concerned only with facts. Nothing could be further from the truth. Science involves a constant interplay between theoretical speculation and fact-gathering. Either activity when separated from the other is unprofitable, but the interaction of the two has proven highly profitable in advancing human knowledge. Theory must lead to research, and research must lead back to theory. In our present study, we have reached the point where research must lead back to theoretical considerations.

With these considerations in mind, we propose that religion be defined as a *system of beliefs about the nature of the force(s) ultimately shaping man's destiny, and the practices associated therewith, shared by the members of a group.*[4] This definition is designed in such a way as to include under the heading of religion not only the major theistic faiths such as Christianity, Judaism, and Islam, but also non-theistic faiths such as Hinayana Buddhism, Communism, and even contemporary humanism of the type espoused by such men as Bertrand Russell and Julian Huxley. By classifying these diverse phenomena under a single heading we do not claim that they are all alike in all respects, but we do direct attention to the fact that there are many striking and important similarities among them.

To begin with, all are social phenomena, involving groups of men.[5] Second, all are systems of faith—or more accurately systems of belief accepted on the grounds of faith, not empirical or logical demonstration. Third, all are systems of faith by means of which men seek to cope with the most basic problems of human existence.

Given this definition of religion, it quickly becomes apparent that every normal adult member of any human society is religious. All intelligent human action presupposes assumptions about the nature of the forces which ultimately shape the nature and destiny of man. Only small children and per-

---

[4] We do not claim that belief necessarily precedes practice, in rational fashion. On the contrary, belief may follow practice as a rationalization for already existing patterns of action. See Emile Durkheim, *The Elementary Forms of the Religious Life*, trans. by Joseph Swain (Glencoe: The Free Press, no date).

[5] Some might question whether modern humanists constitute a group in the normal sociological sense of the term. While not as highly organized as most of the more traditional groups, it is clearly not lacking in organization. It has a very loose-knit form of organization geared to modern developments in the field of communication, with its members communicating as often through the mass media as through face-to-face contacts. One may even observe some more traditional, formal organizational nuclei emerging in this group, as in the case of the Unitarian Church or the Ethical Culture movement, but the majority of humanists seem to hold apart from these formal organizational nuclei to a considerable degree.

sons of subnormal intelligence are non-religious in our sense of the term. This is not to say that every person can articulate his faith with any great measure of precision. Sometimes assumptions are half-forgotten as the patterns of action based upon them become sufficiently habitual. Even when basic assumptions have not been lost sight of, those with limited education may have difficulty articulating them, but they are present nonetheless.[6]

Religion as a social phenomenon

Because the core of every religious system involves a set of assumptions about the nature of *ultimate* causation, these assumptions must be taken on faith. But men are seldom content to "bet their lives" on assumptions which are unsupported by some greater authority. Hence, the great majority of men turn to others for guidance and direction in these matters, thereby laying the foundation for the formation of religious groups. While logicians and historians long ago demonstrated that forty million Frenchmen can be wrong, there is unquestionably intellectual security in numbers. If others also believe, this can reduce one's anxieties about the validity of one's own beliefs. More than that, if some of the others who believe are men of demonstrated competence and authority in some sphere of human endeavor, such as President Eisenhower or Lord Russell, this further relieves anxieties. In short, even though the logic which underlies the social character of religion is faulty, the psychology is sound.

The need of the believer for certainty is but one of the forces which give rise to the formation of religious groups. If there is to be any public cultus, this requires religious specialists, and the presence of specialists implies a division of labor and social organization. Yet another factor which gives rise to religious groups is the desire of men to propagate their own beliefs and put down the pernicious doctrines of others. This

[6] There are some people, of course, who profess to be agnostics, but any examination of their patterns of action reveals that all agnostics *act as though* they accepted one or another of the competing systems of belief. Human existence *compels* men to act on unproven and unprovable assumptions, and it makes no exceptions.

latter may not be a universal tendency, but at the very least it seems present in all of the higher religions which contain the elements of hope and promise. Thus Christianity and Communism alike seem leading examples of faiths which give rise to a missionary spirit and thus promote the formation of formal organization.

When new religious movements are formed, they typically possess spontaneity and enthusiasm, both qualities which attract converts who are disenchanted with the routinized and unexciting older faiths. Spontaneity is an inevitable by-product of the newness of the movement and the absence of established routines. Enthusiasm is also a by-product of the nature of the enterprise, involving as it does the discovery (or rediscovery) of "truths" about matters of profound importance to humanity. In many cases a new faith is also linked with the breaking of established behavior patterns—a process which often has an exhilarating effect. Finally, enthusiasm is frequently generated by the personal qualities of the leader, since leadership in such a movement presupposes extraordinary personal qualities.

Much of the modern sociological understanding of new social movements in general, and new religious movements in particular, stems from Weber's pioneering analyses of social organization, and more especially his work concerning the sociology of charisma and charismatic authority.[7] As Weber and his successors make clear, spontaneity and enthusiasm inevitably lose their position of dominance in social movements which survive for any period of time, and the processes of institutionalization and routinization gain the ascendancy. As a consequence, a formal association gradually develops: an association characterized by officeholders, rituals, rules, forms, structures, all designed originally to facilitate the transmission and diffusion of the truths possessed by the group.

Sometimes, especially in the modern world, leaders of newer religious movements intend to create only an association, and not a separate subcommunity. They expect members of their group to participate fully in the social, economic,

[7] See especially *From Max Weber: Essays in Sociology*, op. cit., Chapters 9 and 10, and *The Theory of Social and Economic Organization*, op. cit., Part III, Sections 4–6.

political, and other institutional systems of the secular community, and only to separate themselves from the community at large for specifically religious purposes, such as worship.

This is not easy to accomplish. The great majority of people find it impossible to live entirely in a world of impersonal, secondary relationships. They require in addition the more intimate and personal relationships which only primary groups provide. Since primary groups tend to be rewarding to the degree that those involved share common values, men are disproportionately drawn to others who share their faith.

In this way a network of informal, primary relations comes to be established among the members of every religious association. This network of primary relations, which we have called the religious subcommunity, vastly increases the degree of interaction among group members. It greatly facilitates the indoctrination of the young in the norms and standards of the association, and contributes to their enforcement among adults. This is a matter of great importance in the religiously divided modern metropolis, where individuals are exposed to so many influences which are alien to the spirit of their church.

Failure to perceive the existence of these subcommunities was chiefly responsible for the failure of the last generation of American sociologists to recognize the importance of religious groups in the life of the larger society. To them religious groups were merely a highly specialized type of association which brought together a minority of the population for an hour or two a week, and therefore they could not be too important. It is only today, as we recognize the existence of the system of subcommunities surrounding and reinforcing religious associations, that we begin to form a more accurate estimate of the impact of religion on contemporary life.[8]

However, religious subcommunities should never be thought of *merely* as structures which reinforce the churches. The *raison d'être* of the church and the subcommunity are not the same, and because they are not, they sometimes pull group members in contradictory directions. Subcommunities

[8] For an earlier discussion of this same subject, see Gerhard E. Lenski, "Religion and the Modern Metropolis," *Review of Religious Research*, 1 (Summer 1959), especially pp. 26–29.

inevitably foster provincialism; churches need not invariably do this. Subcommunities foster pragmatism and expediency; churches sometimes foster idealism. In short, while basically religious associations and subcommunities support one another, there are always overtones of conflict and tension present.)

Socio-religious group subcultures

Just as there is more to the organizational structure of most religious groups than the formal association, the church, so, too, there is more to the subcultures of such groups than church doctrines, rites, and customs.[9] The subculture of a socio-religious group represents the accumulated solutions of the group to the whole range of problems which group members deal with *both in the association and in the subcommunity*. Thus, while many problems of a political or economic character may not concern the association, they may be of great concern to group members and be seriously discussed in the primary groups which constitute the subcommunity.

It may seem that we are saying that the subcultures of religious groups deal with all of the problems of human existence. This is not so, since many problems, especially those of a technical nature, are dealt with exclusively by other types of associational groups: corporations, labor unions, military organizations, and so forth. There is no Catholic norm on how to pave highways, any more than there is a white Protestant norm governing the launching of space probes. Such problems are rarely, if ever, dealt with in the context of either churches or their related networks of primary groups.

However, in these latter groups basic, non-technical problems concerning politics and economics are often discussed. The pros and cons of basic political issues, attitudes toward work, the labor unions, big business, the chances of getting ahead, and a variety of other issues are frequently discussed within the family and among friends. *To the degree that such primary groups form segregated communications networks limited to the adherents of the same faith, they facilitate the*

[9] We use the term "subculture" here to indicate that this culture is essentially a variant of the culture of the total society.

development and transmission of distinctive political and economic norms.

FORCES SHAPING SOCIO-RELIGIOUS GROUP SUBCULTURES

The subculture of every socio-religious group is always profoundly affected by the social situation of the group. The social situation provides, in Toynbee's terms, the challenges to which the group must respond: it provides the problems to which solutions must be found. More than this, it provides many of the elements out of which solutions can be constructed, or in some cases even provides ready-made solutions.

Thus, the subculture developed by a religious group made up exclusively of warriors will almost certainly differ from that of a group made up of peasants or of merchants.[10] Similarly, the subcultures of religious groups in highly productive, urban-industrial societies differ from those of groups in agrarian societies.

However, we cannot hope to predict the character of the subcultures of religious groups solely from a knowledge of the social situation in which the group finds itself at any given time. The economic, political, and other norms of such groups are also influenced by the theology or ideology of the group—the opinions of economic determinists notwithstanding.

Economic determinists typically view all idea systems as mere reflections of the economic "substructure" of society and as epiphenomena on the stage of history. Ideas, they say, change nothing; they are only the froth generated by the impact of the objective realities of the social situation on individuals and groups.[11]

[10] See Joachim Wach, *Sociology of Religion* (Chicago: The University of Chicago Press, 1944), pp. 251–68. See also Max Weber, *Wirtschaft und Gesellschaft* (Tübingen: J. C. B. Mohr, 1925, 2nd edition), Vol. I, pp. 267–78.

[11] It is interesting to note, however, that most of the wiser economic determinists eventually retreat from the extreme position and concede a significant role to ideas. See, for example, the letters of Friedrich Engels assembled by Lewis S. Feuer in *Marx and Engels: Basic Writings on Politics and Philosophy* (Garden City: Doubleday Anchor Books, 1959), p. 395 ff. or Leslie White, *The Science of Culture* (New York: Grove Press, 1949), p. 376 ff., especially pp. 382–83.

To "prove" their point they cite innumerable examples to show how idea systems have changed in response to changing economic conditions. However, they choose to ignore the elements of continuity and stability in idea systems in the face of economic change, just as they choose to ignore ideological change and development during periods of economic stability and stagnation. As with every half-truth, much evidence can be found to support economic determinism, but the evidence is hardly satisfactory in view of its highly selective character.

When we examine the theologies of the major faiths of the modern world, we can hardly help being impressed by their continuity and stability in the face of revolutionary changes in the economic order. Creeds formulated fifteen hundred and more years ago are still accepted as definitive statements of faith by major groups. Scriptures originating two and three thousand years ago continue to be regarded as sacred documents. Conceptions of the nature of God formulated by men more than three thousand years ago continue to find acceptance in urban-industrial societies today. While not denying that theological changes have also occurred, we cannot afford to ignore the equally significant fact of continuity.

From this we can only conclude that the theologies of most contemporary religious groups are more than trivia generated by contact with the hard realities of the current social situation. Rather, they are in large measure a heritage from the past, and *at the very least reflect the exposure of past generations of believers to the social environment of earlier eras.* Otherwise we have no way of accounting for the substantial degree of theological continuity in the face of revolutionary economic change.

From this we might suppose that the theology of any religious association is the accumulated residue of responses to the social environment, both past and present. This gives us a closer approximation to reality, but when we get down to cases we discover that the problem is even more complicated. If, for example, we examine the theological heritage of contemporary Mormonism, we discover that while it reflects the influence of the frontier environment of early nineteenth-century America, it reflects the influence of this environment *as it was experienced by Joseph Smith.* Whatever else we may say of Joseph Smith, he was no ordinary frontiersman of his day. Thus it is a matter of profound consequence that the environmental influences of the early nineteenth-century frontier on Mormonism were mediated through the personality of this unusual man. Unless we are prepared to argue that human personalities are identical transmitters of environmental influences, it is clear that a new factor has been added to the equation—a factor which cannot be reduced to social situational terms, however much we may wish it for the sake of simplicity in analysis.

At the risk of being seriously misunderstood, it may be helpful to invoke an organic analogy at this point.[12] Human organizations, like biological organisms, respond to the simultaneous operation of forces within the unit and forces outside it. Where organisms are involved, we speak of the influence of heredity and environment. Virtually all modern biologists agree that one cannot develop an adequate understanding of the structure, functioning, and change of plants and animals without taking *both* sets of forces into account.

In modern sociological analysis, however, the sociological counterpart of heredity has often been ignored, and analyses of human organizations have frequently been conducted along exclusively environmental lines. This has been especially true in analyses by scholars committed to the theory of economic determinism and also by those primarily concerned with social change.

However, in human organizations, just as in biological organisms, it is clear that the structure and functioning of a given unit cannot adequately be accounted for by its current environment. As we have seen, both display an element of continuity in structure and functioning in the face of changing environmental conditions which contradicts any simple environmental interpretation. When one examines human organizations from the standpoint of continuity (which is fully as valid a perspective as that of change), it becomes evident

12 In the past such analogies have had unfortunate consequences for those who have employed them, chiefly because they have often confused analogy and identity. Having begun with the notion that human organizations are *like* organisms, some have concluded with the thesis that organizations are *nothing but* organisms.

that, just as in organisms, there are forces at work which limit the degree to which organizations are able to adapt to changing environmental conditions. Many organizations are destroyed by changing conditions simply because they cannot adapt themselves; others are seriously weakened and injured. Take for example the Catholic Church in the sixteenth century. By adopting many of the radical doctrines propounded by Luther and the other reformers, it might have preserved its organizational unity and political power. But this was impossible given the commitments already made by the organization, and the internalization of these commitments in the personalities of large numbers of its members, especially its top leaders. Rather than yield, the organization stood firm, even though it lost many millions of adherents as a consequence.[13]

In plants and animals genes serve as the basic stabilizing force giving continuity to the form and behavior of individual organisms, and apparently also control their maturation. Because of the existence of genes, puppies do not become cattle, and calves do not become trees, regardless of environmental conditions.

What then are the sociological counterparts of genes in human organizations? Clearly there is no biological mechanism at work producing stability and continuity in human groups. However, there appear to be other types of "mechanisms" which have similar consequences. One of these is the pattern of organizational staffing. In large and enduring organizations, such as many religious groups, there is a constant replacement of personnel. Older members die or withdraw and are replaced by new members who come into the group by birth or conversion. In the earlier and more dynamic stages of organizational growth, the rate of replacement may be quite high, but as the organization matures, this slows down to the point where the annual turnover often represents no more than 2 to 5 per cent of the personnel. Hence all the factors producing stability and continuity in the behavior and per-

---

[13] We do not suggest that this is a *sufficient* explanation for the reluctance of Catholic authorities to compromise with the Protestant Reformers, but we do maintain that this was one important factor substantially reducing the possibilities of compromise.

sonality of individuals[14] contribute to stability and continuity in the structure and functioning of the organizations which these individuals create and staff. Older members of the group typically try to preserve the character of the organization which has satisfied their needs in the past so effectively. By virtue of the slow rate of turnover in mature social organizations, the "command posts" (to use Mills' apt phrase) tend to be dominated by older persons who are psychologically the most committed to stability and continuity.

In their efforts to maintain this stability and continuity group leaders are greatly aided by written records. These become, in effect, a means by which former generations exercise a continuing influence on the organization. This is especially true in the case of ideological organizations, as contrasted with pragmatic organizations like the modern corporation. In pragmatic organizations, there is nothing sacred about the beliefs of the founder or the organizational forms established by him and his immediate successors. However, in ideological organizations—of which religious organizations seem the best example—the teachings of the founder and the organizational patterns established by him and his immediate successors are of considerable importance and cannot readily be ignored. Hence, Christian leaders today constantly find it necessary to justify existing patterns of organization and action by reference to the Scriptures. In this way the first generations of Christians exercise, through the written word, a continuing impact on contemporary Christian churches. This influence of earlier generations makes itself felt not only through the Scriptures, but also through early church creeds and through the writings of the early church fathers and later theologians and church leaders such as Augustine, Aquinas, Luther, Wesley, and others. Thus the written records of the churches perform a stabilizing and continuity-preserving function comparable in many respects to that performed by the genes in biological organisms.

Finally, since the older generation socializes each succeeding generation, verbal communication serves as yet another stabilizing force. By virtue of the inevitable dependence of

[14] See E. Lowell Kelly, "Consistency of the Adult Personality," *American Psychologist,* 10 (November 1955), pp. 659–81.

children on their elders for the basic satisfactions of life, parents and teachers are able to internalize in the young a great many social norms which are not easily discarded. In an area such as religion basic patterns of action are linked with beliefs about the nature of the forces which ultimately control human destiny. These beliefs are not subject to empirical demonstration but are accepted on faith. Hence patterns of action handed down from one's parents, and therefore associated with an important source of authority and satisfaction, persist for a long time even in hostile environments.

The social heritage of religious organizations is not only a source of continuity and stability; it is also a source of change and development. In other words, there is an organizational counterpart to the biological phenomenon of *maturation*. In religious organizations there is almost always a movement from spontaneity to routinism, from charismatic leadership to officialdom, from enthusiasm and fervor to propriety and order. Later, when this process has run its course, a phase of reaction normally sets in—a phase in which idealists in the organization come into conflict with the realists who normally control the key administrative offices. Idealists demand a return to the charismatic era with its enthusiasms and ideals; realists defend the institutionalized realities as practical necessities. Schism is typically the outcome. After the schism, the parent group typically evolves new institutional arrangements to prevent the recurrence of such conflicts.

None of these changes are *caused* by environmental change. External conditions may speed or retard the process of organizational maturation. They may also prevent many religious movements from successfully negotiating the difficult transition from charismatic infancy to institutionalized maturity. But current environmental factors are not the cause of the maturation process in human organizations any more than in biological organisms. This process takes place in response to forces within the unit itself.

Much more might be said on this subject, but we have said enough to show why it is inadequate to regard the patterns of action associated with a given religious group as nothing but reflections of the current social situation. Religious organizations also respond to forces generated by the life of the organization itself—forces which are the counterparts of heredity and maturation. Religious organizations are constantly responding to their social heritage, which is perpetuated by their written records and in the memories of older members in key leadership positions. They also respond to a "maturational" process which generates internal change. Because of the operation of these factors, religious organizations are much less responsive to contemporary environmental pressures than environmentally oriented theorists usually imagine.[15]

Religion's impact on secular institutions

Just as religious institutions must adapt to influences originating in secular institutions, so, too, the latter are obliged to adapt to influences originating in religious institutions. These influences take two distinct forms.

On the one hand, from time to time the leaders of religious associations embark on campaigns to reform some aspect of the secular world which they find objectionable. Occasionally these efforts are successful: more often they are not. Because of this, many have concluded that religious groups have little influence on secular institutions.

[15] Not all aspects of the organizational structure of socio-religious groups are equally resistant (or responsive) to environmental change. Our analysis suggests that the formal association —the church—is far more resistant than the subcommunity. The association has formal leadership and written records; its activities are planned and directed by officials who have been specially indoctrinated in the norms of the group and who are usually highly committed to them. All these things increase its powers of resistance. But the subcommunity lacks these advantages and is more vulnerable to external influences. Thus, we would expect to find popular, or folk, theology changing much more rapidly in response to environmental influences than the official theology of the church, or even what might be called the "working theology" of the association.

On first inspection this distinction may seem highly academic since, as we have seen, nearly all socio-religious groups involve both associational and communal elements. However, as we found in the second chapter, groups vary considerably in the relative vitality of these two aspects of their structure, and hence we would expect them to vary also in the degree of their resistance to current environmental influences.

This conclusion is unwarranted, however, since it ignores the second type of religious influence. Far more important than these calculated, organized campaigns to reform society are the daily actions of thousands (or millions) of group members whose personalities have been influenced to greater or lesser degree by their lifelong exposure to the group and its subculture. Through their continuous participation in political, economic, educational, and kinship institutions, they powerfully influence the character of these institutions.

Although contemporary society encourages compartmentalization of thought and action, the findings of psychology and sociology alike make it clear that there are limits to which this is possible. Basic traits of personality established in early childhood tend to persist throughout life and influence actions in a variety of institutional contexts. This is equally true of goals, values, beliefs, and action patterns acquired later: though acquired in one institutional context, they frequently manifest themselves in others.

Although it is often convenient for the social scientist to think in terms of "political man" or "economic man," these are, at best, fruitful abstractions from a more complex reality. It is "the whole man" who pulls the voting lever or purchases a new car, and the whole man usually finds it difficult to maintain consistently for any period of time the boundaries between politics, economics, religion, and family life. Job performance can be seriously impaired by family strife even though the place of work is far from the place of residence. Elections can be greatly affected by "politically irrelevant" considerations such as the socio-religious group membership of candidates. Of course, so, too, religious activities and commitments may be influenced by promotion on the job or political pressures.

If complete compartmentalization of thought and action were possible, it would make little difference whether the workers in a plant or the members of a political party were Protestants, Catholics, Jews, Muslims, Communists, positivists, or anything else. But because this is not possible, it makes a difference. *What is possible, what is probable, and what is inevitable in any given secular organization is a function, in part, of the characteristics of the individuals who staff them;*

and this in turn is a function, in part, of the socio-religious groups to which they belong.

To understand the power of socio-religious groups it is essential to recognize their capacity to absorb primary groups as subunits in their organizational system. Because of this, the norms of socio-religious groups are constantly reinforced in these intimate, highly valued social relationships which are so crucial in the shaping of personality.

By contrast with the daily actions of the masses of group members, the deliberate efforts of church leaders to induce change pale into insignificance. The latter are much less influential, except perhaps in "clerically controlled" or "theocratic" states such as Calvin's Geneva or Lenin's Russia, and there is reason for thinking that "clerically controlled" states are exceptions to the rule in highly urbanized and industrialized societies.

III. APPLICATION OF
OUR THEORETICAL PERSPECTIVE

If we apply the foregoing analysis to the religious scene in contemporary American society, we arrive at a picture which differs significantly from many of the currently popular images, but which is highly consistent with the findings of recent empirical research, our own included. Basically, our theory leads us to think of contemporary American religious groups not only as associations, but as subcommunities as well; not merely as the carriers of religious norms in any narrow sense, but as the carriers of complex subcultures relevant to almost all phases of human existence. Also, our theory leads us to see these religiously based subcultures not merely as the products of present environmental influences, but equally as the products of the social heritage of the group—which, as we have seen, involves the influence of both former environments and of former personnel.

Given this perspective, one would certainly expect the four socio-religious groups we studied to differ significantly, not merely in theology, but in a wide range of matters relating to the more mundane aspects of daily life. More than that, since these groups involve communal as well as associational elements, we would expect these differences to manifest themselves in the patterns of thought and action of the many millions of persons who are not highly active in church or synagogue. In these respects we have not been disappointed.

Because of the relative size of the groups, and the problems encountered in controlling relevant variables, some of our best documented differences are those involving the white Protestant and Catholic groups. We have repeatedly observed important differences on a wide range of matters. *Our overall impression is that Catholics and Protestants alike have assimilated the materialistic values of contemporary society to the point where they equally value a good job with high income, and are equally likely to aspire to such a position. However, Catholics seem to be at a disadvantage in the competition because of a series of values to which they apparently become committed as a result of their involvement in the Catholic Church and subcommunity.* For example, they seem to become more strongly attached to the kin group than Protestants, and therefore less able to make the break with home and family that is required in many of the more demanding, and hence better-paid, positions in contemporary American society. Also, involvement in the Catholic group apparently fosters a de-emphasis of intellectual independence which is ill-adapted to the more creative and responsible positions in our rapidly changing social order. In addition, involvement in the Catholic group leads to higher than average fertility, which certainly creates difficulties in securing higher education, and which may also have some effect on I.Q., or problem-solving ability, hence further handicapping Catholic youth.

None of these peculiarities of the Catholic group seem to spring solely from current environmental differences between the groups. While it is true that Catholics currently are located somewhat more often in the working class than white Protestants, the differences are not great.[16] Even more im-

---

[16] In addition to the evidence presented in this study, see Donald J. Bogue, *The Population of the United States* (Glencoe: The Free Press, 1959), pp. 688–709; Liston Pope, "Religion and the Class Structure," in *The Annals of the American Academy of Political and Social Science*, 256 (March 1948), pp. 84–91; and

portant, controls for class differences do not appreciably reduce the size of the differences on these points. Furthermore, some of the biggest differences occur in the middle and upper-middle classes, where they matter most to society as a whole.

The differences between contemporary Catholics and Protestants reflect far more the social heritages of the organizations to which they belong. Protestantism came into being in large measure as a sectarian revolt against the massive institutionalization of medieval Catholicism. While the *success* of this revolt was undoubtedly dependent on peculiar features in the economic and political environment of sixteenth-century Europe, the revolt itself seems to have had its origins in the maturation process of the Catholic Church.

From the tenth century on, despite many changes in the economic and political situation, the Catholic Church in western Europe suffered from constant internal conflict. The basic source of the conflict was the contrast between first-century Christianity and medieval Christianity—a contrast both in form and functioning. These inevitably develop in a religious organization which survives beyond its charismatic origins, but which continues to regard those origins as sacred. The contrast between the highly institutionalized and worldly patterns of medieval Catholicism and the simplicity, spontaneity, and fervor of first-century Christianity was bound to evoke conflict between realists and idealists. From the Cluniac reform movement in the tenth century to the Protestant Reformation in the sixteenth, internal ferment and controversy were a continuing feature of the life of the church and a succession of reform movements sprang up. Because of unfavorable environmental conditions none of these came to full flower

Bernard Lazerwitz, "A Comparison of Major United States Religious Groups," *Journal of the American Statistical Association,* 56 (September 1961), p. 574. Each of these reports summarizes the findings of thousands of survey interviews gathered by The National Opinion Research Center of the University of Chicago, The American Institute of Public Opinion (the Gallup poll organization), and the Survey Research Center of The University of Michigan. All show that while there are substantial differences in the class distribution of different Protestant denominations, there are only modest differences in the class distribution of Protestants *as a whole* and Catholics.

until the Protestant movement of the sixteenth century. Then the internal forces generating religious controversy combined with the external forces creating political cleavage to produce a massive schism in Western Christendom which persists to the present day.

Because the Protestant reformers were the idealists in the controversy, and because they were challenging established authority, they could be expected to stress the sectarian elements in the Gospel—those elements which call men to break with the existing social order and create a new community of the elect.

As Troeltsch and Weber noted, these sectarian tendencies in early Christianity, with their radical potentialities, had apparently been safely domesticated in early medieval Catholicism through the institution of monasticism. However, with the Protestant Reformation these tendencies broke loose once again and formed an integral element in all of the new Protestant groups—especially those groups which failed to gain control of the existing machinery of church and state. Hence the radical sectarian orientation was much more pronounced among the Anabaptists, Puritans, Pietists, Methodists, and English Presbyterians than among the Lutherans and Anglicans. However, in order to establish themselves it was necessary for all of these groups to encourage intellectual autonomy to some degree. Only by breaking the older, authoritarian orientation in the religious realm could the new groups hope to establish themselves.[17]

[17] One might well ask at this point why the Buddhist break with Hinduism, a movement with a number of significant parallels with Protestantism, did not have a similar effect and thus generate a spirit of capitalism two thousand years earlier. Apart from technological difficulties, it must be noted that, as Weber and others have indicated, the development of intellectual autonomy was a necessary, but not a sufficient, cause for the rise of capitalism. Buddhism, unlike Protestantism, inherited from Hinduism a profoundly pessimistic view of this world and human activity in it. Hence, Buddhist rationalism was harnessed to the task of fleeing this world rather than transforming it. Protestantism, by contrast, inherited from medieval Catholicism, and even more from the Gospels, a more optimistic outlook on the world and human endeavor. Whereas the religions of the East were consistently pessimistic about this world, Judaism, Christianity, and probably Islam

If the Reformation fostered the growth of intellectual autonomy among Protestants, it had exactly the opposite effect among Catholics. Being in control of the ecclesiastical system, and being the defenders of the *status quo,* Catholic leaders naturally made their appeals to obedience and discipline. In this troubled era, faithfulness to ecclesiastical discipline became one of the best indicators of organizational loyalty.

Ironically, the success of the Protestant Reformation became "proof" to each side that its position was the right one. It proved to Catholic leaders that one cannot trust individual judgment in matters of great weight and importance, and to Protestant leaders that one can. As a result, one by-product of the Reformation was a weakening of the tendencies toward intellectual autonomy found in medieval Catholicism and exemplified in men like Erasmus. Such tendencies came increasingly to be identified with Protestantism and heresy, thus permanently altering the social heritage of Catholicism and creating a difference between Protestants and Catholics which survives to the present day.

As we noted, the sectarian tendencies in Protestantism also helped to weaken family and kin group ties, thereby freeing more of the energies of individuals for the world of work. By weakening the hold of the family on the individual, Protestants have undoubtedly gained a substantial advantage in the competition for economic advancement.

Given the differences between Catholicism and Protestantism in intellectual autonomy and kinship ties, and given the much longer exposure of Catholicism to agrarian environments, the probabilities were certainly greater that the Catholic Church would oppose birth control more vigorously than the Protestant churches. In most agrarian societies childlessness has long been viewed as a sign of divine disfavor. The childless peasant couple was always at a serious economic disadvantage, especially in old age. By contrast, large families were typically seen as a sign of divine favor, and surely represented a substantial economic advantage. Given the traditionalistic tendencies of Catholicism it was probable that as

as well, have always been at the least ambivalent, a distinction of no small importance. See Weber, *The Religion of India,* op. cit., Chapter 10.

large families ceased to be an economic advantage, and as new methods of limiting family size were discovered, the Catholic Church would oppose contraception, and the Protestant churches favor it. The present pattern was certainly not inevitable, but from an actuarial standpoint it was far more likely than the opposite.

In view of the social heritage of contemporary Catholicism, it seems unlikely that in the foreseeable future any devoutly Catholic state will become a leading industrial nation—one in the forefront of economic development and progress. Catholicism seems to contain too many elements which are incompatible with such a role. As an extension of this proposition, it would appear that as the Catholic segment of a pluralistic nation increases, this will tend to reduce the rate of economic growth. These are very sweeping generalizations which will almost certainly be challenged, but there is considerable evidence to support them. None of the predominantly and devoutly Catholic nations in the modern world can be classified as a *leading* industrial nation. Some Catholic nations—such as France, Italy, Argentina, Brazil, and Chile—are quite highly industrialized, but none of them are leaders in the technological and scientific fields, nor do they seem likely to become so.[18] Recently some Brazilian Catholic social scientists compared their country's progress with that of the United States and concluded that the chief factor responsible for the differential rates of development is the religious heritage of the two nations. Within the boundaries of the United States it may even be that the rapid growth of Catholic population in New England in the last century has contributed to the decline of that region as the center of economic progress and advance, though clearly other factors have played the major role.

From the standpoint of a materialistic system of values, this

[18] The case of West Germany poses a peculiar problem. Catholics constitute a substantial percentage of the population of this nation which is clearly in the forefront of economic development and progress. However, the German cultural heritage since Luther's day has been predominantly Protestant, and still today Protestants constitute a majority of the population of the society as a whole even if not of its western segment. West Germany is clearly not in the same category as France, Italy, Argentina, etc.

will appear as a damning indictment of Catholicism. However, it should be recognized that the Catholic Church has never claimed to be concerned primarily with materialistic values. On the contrary, it has asserted that its chief concern is with spiritual values: the worship and service of God, the salvation of souls, the preservation and strengthening of home and family, the propagation of the faith, and the cultivation of charity. Catholic leaders have repeatedly warned their followers against the evils and dangers of a materialistic orientation. It would thus be most surprising if any strongly Catholic nation were in the forefront of economic development and progress. No social system can be all things to all men.

The noted Catholic scholar, and more recently premier of Italy, Amintore Fanfani has made this same basic point in his book, *Catholicism, Protestantism, and Capitalism*.[19] While criticizing many aspects of Weber's analysis of the influence of religion on the rise of capitalism, Fanfani states that "Anyone who strives to understand exactly the respective positions of Catholicism and capitalism cannot be surprised to find the two ideals in conflict. . . . The Catholic *ethos* is anti-capitalistic."

Then what can we say of Protestantism? Surely it does not elevate material values above spiritual? Yet Protestant nations have generally enjoyed great material progress, and if the findings of this study are at all reliable and generally applicable, the Protestant churches have made a significant contribution to this end.

So far as can be judged from available evidence, the contributions of Protestantism to material progress have been largely *unintended by-products* of certain distinctive Protestant traits. This was a central point in Weber's theory, though many of his critics and disciples alike have been unwilling or unable to understand it.[20]

[19] Op. cit., p. 159.
[20] See, for example, Weber's comparison of Confucianism and Puritanism in *The Religion of China* (p. 248), where he wrote, "the world, as promised, fell to Puritanism because the Puritans alone 'had striven for God and His justice.'" For a prominent example of a gross misunderstanding of Weber on this matter, see H. M. Robertson, *Aspects of the Rise of Economic Individualism* (Cambridge: The Cambridge University Press, 1933).

This same point was made much earlier by John Wesley. In his later years he wrote:

> How then is it possible that Methodism . . . though it flourishes now as a green bay tree, should continue in this state? For the Methodists in every place grow diligent and frugal; consequently they increase in goods. Hence they proportionately increase in pride, in anger, in the desire of the flesh, the desire of the eyes and the pride of life. So, although the form of religion remains, the spirit is swiftly vanishing away. Is there no way to prevent this —this continual decay of pure religion? We ought not to prevent people from being diligent and frugal; we must exhort all Christians to gain all they can, and to save all they can; that is in effect to grow rich. What way then can we take, that our money not sink us into the nethermost hell?

Wesley saw only one solution to this problem: Christians should give more as they gain more, and thus lay up for themselves treasures in heaven, rather than on earth. But Wesley's solution has never found wide acceptance among Protestants for the simple reason that most Protestant leaders have never even recognized the problem.

In an earlier era, Protestant asceticism and dedication to work, as noted both by Wesley and Weber, seem to have been important patterns of action contributing to economic progress.[21] Both facilitated the accumulation of capital, so critically important to the economic growth and development of nations.

Today other factors seem to be of greater weight. Asceticism is rare among modern Protestants, and the distinctive Protestant doctrine of "the calling" has been largely forgotten. However, the Protestant concern for intellectual autonomy seems to play an increasingly important role, facilitating scien-

[21] As Weber noted, these patterns were especially evident among the left-wing Protestant groups, the Puritans, the German Pietists, the Methodists, and so forth. They were much less evident in the Anglican and Lutheran groups, except insofar as the latter contained pietist groups which never split off from the mother church.

tific and technical advance. The Protestant small family norm (a relatively recent innovation) provides a new aid to capital formation, since when families are large, more of the income must be spent on consumer goods. The extrafamilial orientation of Protestants seems to facilitate the channeling of energies into the world of work. In short, although the primary concern of Protestantism (like Catholicism) is the attainment of spiritual values, material advance continues to be a by-product of the Protestant effort.

However, as Wesley shrewdly anticipated, Protestantism has had to pay a price for the material success its members have achieved. Protestantism has come more and more to be identified with the middle class and middle-class values. This can be seen, for example, in the relative inability of the Protestant churches to attract nominal Protestants who have not been especially successful in the job world. Among white Protestants in Detroit, nearly twice as many of those earning $8000 or more a year attend church every Sunday as those earning less than $5000 (38 vs. 20 per cent). The situation is very different in the Catholic Church, and the discrepancy negligible (75 vs. 72 per cent).

More serious even than the failure to attract low-income groups is the fact that so many people are confused about the precise nature of Protestantism. Protestantism has become so identified with economic success, respectability, and middle-class virtues that large numbers of the clergy and laity alike appear to have lost sight of basic spiritual goals.[22] If our analysis is correct, this is a problem for which there is no simple solution: it is an endemic disease from which mature Protestantism will always suffer so long as it retains its basic character and is allowed to develop free from governmental or ecclesiastical repression.[23]

[22] For an excellent discussion of this, see Peter Berger, *The Noise of Solemn Assemblies* (Garden City: Doubleday, 1962).

[23] By *mature* Protestantism we mean third and subsequent generations of Protestants. As Wesley noted, it takes time for the Protestant progression from piety to pride to run its course. In the first generation of converts to Protestantism in a non-Protestant environment the identification of Protestantism with economic success, respectability, and middle-class virtues is normally absent. In the second generation, it appears, but is not dominant. But in a

The Negro Protestant group is in an especially interesting situation, sharing as it does much of the theological heritage of white Protestantism, but existing in a totally different environment. For roughly the first two thirds of its existence, Negro Protestantism was a religion of slaves in an agrarian setting. Currently it is becoming the religion of a depressed urban proletariat. In short, it has been obliged to exist in environments which provided minimal opportunities for development. In many ways Negro Protestantism resembles a tree growing on a mountain close to the timber line, and hence having characteristics which do not reveal its potentialities.

By and large, the subculture of contemporary Negro Protestantism has much in common with that of white Catholicism. Fertility rates are high, obedience rather than intellectual autonomy is stressed, a restrictive approach to freedom of speech widely endorsed, and strong support given to the Democratic Party and the welfare state. But, as we have seen, when we control for some of the environmental factors which are operative, there are indications that Negro Protestants more closely resemble white Protestants. Such controls are not easily established, however, owing to the overwhelming concentration of Negroes in the lower working class.

While there is much that is speculative in this judgment, it looks as if the current subcultural similarities between the Negro Protestant and white Catholic groups are the end products of rather different sets of forces, like the equations that result from adding 95 and 5 or 50 and 50. In each case the results are the same, though elements in the two equations are different.

In the case of contemporary American Catholicism it appears that its subculture has been influenced by its associational heritage to a much greater degree than in the case of Negro Protestantism. By contrast, the subculture of contemporary Negro Protestantism seems to be shaped much more by current environmental forces.

As we noted previously, environmental conditions which

free society where Protestant advance is not obstructed by church or state, the pattern seems to be highly visible from the third generation on.

persist for an extended period can ultimately affect the social heritage of a group. It is probable that this has already happened to some degree among Negro Protestants. Even if all current environmental limitations on the development of this group were removed, it is unlikely that it would become identical with the white Protestant group. Three centuries of slavery and economic exploitation have almost certainly left their mark, especially when those centuries were the first three in the group's history. So long as Negro Protestants remain socially segregated from white Protestants, it is likely that they will also remain culturally different to some degree, even though environmental disadvantages may be removed. If environmental differences continue (as seems likely), the Negro Protestant subculture may continue to resemble that of the Catholic group, though still because of a different constellation of influences.

The Jewish group also has many striking points of similarity with the white Protestants, yet nonetheless it diverges sharply in several important areas. Most notable in this connection is the strong political identification of the Jewish group with the Democratic Party and the strong commitment of Jews to the principles embodied in the welfare state. Also noteworthy are the differences in the strength of the kinship bond and the degree of attachment of the individual to the subcommunity.

The distinctive subculture of the Jewish group seems no more explicable merely in terms of current environmental influences than the subcultures of the other groups. One might argue that many Jewish behavior patterns are distinctly middle class in character, a fact highly consistent with the present economic situation of the group. However, this explanation overlooks the fact that many of these same behavior patterns were prevalent in the group a generation or two ago when its members were nearly all recent immigrants concentrated in the working classes—a situation quite similar to that of the Catholic group of the period. These facts suggest that much of the Jewish subculture today can only be fully understood when the social heritage of the group is taken into account.

Like Catholicism and Protestantism, Judaism possesses an extensive literature by means of which men of the past have effectively influenced subsequent generations. This influence was greatly magnified by environmental forces which eventually destroyed Jewish national sovereignty and finally even destroyed the geographical unity of Jewish society. These developments seem to have stimulated Jewish interest in the Scriptures, and other written records, as a means of explaining the disastrous sequence of events which destroyed the Jewish state, and as a source of hope for the future. Thus environmental developments strengthened the influence of the social heritage.

However, environmental influences modified the social heritage of Judaism. Obliged to live as foreigners, or as a pariah people, in nations controlled by others, the Jews were limited severely in their way of life. Many types of activity were closed to them for centuries, especially those related to government, politics, military activity, and landowning. As a result, Jews were driven into urban vocations, notably those of merchant and craftsman. Cut off from opportunities to rise in the major institutional systems of the larger society in which they lived, but of which they were not a part, the vocation with the greatest prestige came to be that of the scholar-rabbi, the man learned in Torah and Talmud. Learning and scholarship rather than power or even wealth came increasingly to be the measure of a man in the ghetto communities.[24] Life as a despised, and frequently victimized, pariah people may also have fostered the rise of dual ethical standards, with one set applicable to the in-group and the other applicable to the out-group.[25] But this same experience seems also to have developed an enduring concern with social justice.

These aspects of Jewish history, so briefly recounted, seem to have played a major role in shaping the social heritage of modern Judaism. They provided modern Jews with a set of skills, values, and intellectual orientations likely to maximize their chances of upward mobility in modern urban-industrial societies, once the economic and educational institutions of

[24] Sombart, op. cit., pp. 178–83.
[25] See Max Weber, *Ancient Judaism*, op. cit., Chapter 13, especially Section 2. In Weber's opinion, the ethical dualism of Judaism had pre-Exilic origins, but it was the first destruction of Jerusalem and the Exile, with the resulting increase in interaction with foreigners, which speeded its development.

these societies were secularized (i.e., made religiously neutral). Fortunately for the Jewish group, the secularization of these key institutions roughly coincided with the period of heavy Jewish immigration. Hence, their economic successes seem to reflect an opportune combination of the forces of environment and social heritage.

The timing of these events may have been especially important for the Jewish group in view of the serious weakening of the associational aspects of Judaism in modern times. If our earlier hypothesis is correct (see footnote 15), the weakening of the associational side of Judaism may make the subculture of that group more vulnerable to environmental influences than it has been in the past. If this had happened when American Jews were heavily concentrated in the working classes, and if the situation had then persisted over three or four generations, the end result might well have been the proletarianization of the Jewish subculture. Today, however, with the majority of American Jews concentrated in the middle classes, it seems likely that the weakening of the hold of synagogue and temple will have a very different set of consequences.

However, as we observed in Chapter 4, the economic successes of the Jews have not been accompanied by a comparable rise in status, and this has important consequences for the Jewish subculture. For one thing, it has kept alive and active the traditional Jewish concern for social justice and humanitarian values. It has also given rise to Jewish support for the principles of welfare statism, a characteristic which on first inspection seems so incompatible with their commitment to many of the values of capitalism. In this respect environmental influences seem to have strengthened commitment to one element in the social heritage of the group which might otherwise have become neglected as a result of economic success.

IV. WEBER IN RETROSPECT

Since this study has drawn so heavily upon the work of Max Weber, it is only fitting in this concluding chapter that we examine the relevance of our findings for Weber's theory.

As is evident, we have not attempted to test his *historical hypothesis* concerning the relationship between Protestantism and the emergence of the spirit of modern capitalism. Rather, we have sought to extract from his many writings on religion the *basic underlying assumption,* and then test it in an analysis of the contemporary scene in one of the major metropolitan communities of the United States. This is the assumption that each of the major religions of the world develops its own distinctive orientation toward all of the major phases of human activity, and thus comes to exercise an influence on the development of other major institutional systems in society, an influence which cannot be accounted for merely in economic terms. In addition, we sought to utilize many of Weber's specific hypotheses pertaining to differences between Catholic and Protestant orientations toward the economic institutions of society.

Our study has provided striking support for Weber's basic assumption—at least as far as it applies to the major religious groups in contemporary American society. As the findings presented in Chapters 3 to 7 make clear, the four major socioreligious groups differ significantly from one another with respect to a wide range of phenomena affecting economic, political, kinship, educational, and scientific institutions. Furthermore, these differences cannot be accounted for in terms of the economic position of either the individuals involved or the groups.

Our findings also support a number of the specific hypotheses on Protestant-Catholic differences in economic behavior which Weber developed for an earlier era. First, our study indicates that Protestants are more likely than Catholics to rise in the economic system, and these differences are especially pronounced at the level of the upper-middle class. Second, it indicates that Protestantism, unlike Catholicism, tends to weaken and undermine the extended family. Third, it indicates that Protestants view work differently from Catholics. Finally, our study provides some indirect support for Weber's hypothesis that Catholics are more inclined to adopt a traditionalistic orientation, while Protestants are more inclined to adopt a rationalistic orientation. This can be seen in the answers to our question concerning the relative importance of a child's learning to think for himself and of learning to obey. Although earlier we interpreted these responses in terms of their relevance for intellectual autonomy, it seems clear that they also have a relevance for Weber's distinction between the rationalistic and traditionalistic orientations. Traditionalism assumes that the answers to life's problems are known, and therefore those who are wise and good will accept them, and obey the precepts derived from them. Given a traditionalistic orientation one would expect people to stress the importance of obedience.[26] Given a rationalistic orientation one would expect people to stress the importance of a child's learning to think for himself. By contrast, the rationalistic orientation assumes that all the answers to life's important problems are not yet known, but that they, or a reasonable approximation of them, can be discovered by rational means. In short, our findings in this area are consistent with Weber's hypothesis.

In some respects, however, our data have *not* supported certain popular extrapolations of Weber's hypotheses. For example, we have not found much evidence that the doctrine of "the calling" is a vital force in contemporary American Protestantism. Neither does our evidence suggest that present-day Detroit Protestants are strongly committed to economic asceticism. It should be understood that these findings are no refutation of Weber, since he explicitly limited his analysis to the era of the rise of capitalism.

Our findings cast an interesting light on Weber's important concept, "the Protestant Ethic." They suggest that this concept is one which is *temporally limited*. That is to say, the Protestant Ethic was a constellation of characteristics which occurred in conjunction with one another at a particular period in history. But like astronomical constellations, some of the elements involved have slowly drifted apart so that the constellation has lost its original character. In the case of the cultural configuration known as the Protestant Ethic, the elements of the calling and of economic asceticism seem to have drifted apart from the rest and are no longer part of the con-

---

[26] Once again see O'Dea, *American Catholic Dilemma, op. cit.*

stellation.[27] Simultaneously, new elements have entered the picture. In view of the substantial changes which seem to have occurred (we are here assuming the accuracy of Weber's portrait of the sixteenth, seventeenth, and eighteenth centuries, which some have questioned), it is doubtful whether Weber's concept, "the Protestant Ethic," is one which can be fruitfully applied in analyses and descriptions of *contemporary* American society. It may well be that the confusions which its use creates are now so great that the term might be better abandoned except in analyses of earlier centuries.

Perhaps the best way to summarize Weber's contribution to the understanding of the influence of religion on contemporary society is to say that his writings continue to be immensely stimulating and provocative, but they cannot be considered definitive. As we stated in the first chapter, Weber suggests important problems which are relevant in every generation. There is perhaps no greater contribution which any man can make to a field of knowledge.

V. IMPLICATIONS FOR THE FUTURE

The changing composition of the American population

This study has many implications not only for general sociological theory, but also for our understanding of American society and its future course of development. In this final section it may be well if we briefly examine some of the latter.

To begin with, it should be noted that the religious composition of this country is constantly changing. At the beginning of Washington's first term as president, the white Protestant group constituted from three quarters to four fifths of the population.[28] The Negro group constituted about one fifth,

[27] It is perhaps significant that economic asceticism is far less important today as a means of personal economic advance than it once was. In a day and age of big business, men are more apt to rise on the basis of occupational skills used in large corporations than on the basis of capital accumulation via small private enterprises.

[28] This is not to say that three quarters or four fifths of Americans were churchgoers or even church members. Then, as now, large numbers of Americans were not active in religious associations.

while Catholics and Jews combined made up no more than one per cent of the American population.[29] Since Negroes were disenfranchised, white Protestants constituted 98 per cent of the electorate.

Today the situation is radically changed. In 1957 the U. S. Bureau of the Census found that among Americans aged 14 and over only 58 per cent belonged to the white Protestant group. Negro Protestants accounted for only another 9 per cent. White Catholics, by contrast, had increased to the point where they constituted 27 per cent of the total, and Jews 3 per cent. [30]

Of equal significance was the finding that in the large metropolitan communities of this country (i.e., urbanized areas with populations of 250,000 or more) white Protestants constituted only 39 per cent of the population. In these same areas Catholics now constitute 38 per cent of the population, Negro Protestants 11 per cent, and Jews 8 per cent. In short, in these influential centers of our society the white Protestant group, which once formed a large and effective majority of the population, now barely enjoys a tiny plurality.

To a considerable degree this transformation of the religious composition of the American population occurred in the interval between 1825 and 1925, the era of mass immigration from Europe. During this period large numbers of Catholic and Jewish immigrants came to this country, settling chiefly in the urban centers of the North. However (on the basis of research carried out by the present writer in another context), it appears that the process of population composition change is still going on today, though at a slower rate than in the period before the First World War.[31] For example, it appears that since 1920 the Catholic segment of the

[29] See, for example, Gerald Shaughnessy, *Has the Immigrant Kept the Faith?* (New York: Macmillan, 1925).

[30] U. S. Bureau of the Census, *Current Population Reports: Population Characteristics,* Series P-20, No. 79, February 2, 1958.

[31] A preliminary report on this other study was read as a paper at the annual meeting of the American Sociological Society in Washington, D.C., in 1957. It was entitled, "The Growth of Catholic Population in the United States Since 1920." Similar conclusions are suggested by an analysis of the age pyramids of the major groups based on the 1957 census report, ibid.

population has grown by about one percentage point per decade, due both to continuing immigration and high rates of fertility. Since World War I there has been little change in the relative sizes of the Negro Protestant and Jewish groups. Hence, the growth of the Catholic population has been accompanied by a corresponding decline in the relative size of the white Protestant group, reflecting both low fertility rates and limited immigration. Available evidence indicates that these trends are likely to continue for the foreseeable future.

If this is true, this means that behavior patterns linked with the Catholic group are likely to become somewhat more prevalent while patterns linked with the white Protestant group are likely to become less common. More specifically, we may expect these gradual changes in population composition to encourage many, or most, of the following developments:

1. Rising rates of church attendance in American society;
2. Strengthening of religious group communalism;
3. Strengthening of both the nuclear and extended family systems;
4. Declining emphasis on intellectual independence;
5. Increasing support for welfare state policies;
6. Increasing support for the Democratic Party;
7. Shifting focus of interest from work group to kin group;
8. Slowing rate of material progress, and perhaps also of scientific advance;[32]
9. Rising birth rates;
10. Narrowing latitude for exercise of the right of free speech;
11. Increasing restraints on Sunday business and divorce, and possibly birth control;
12. Declining restraints on gambling and drinking.

It should be understood that *we are not predicting that*

[32] It seems much less likely that the gradual growth in numbers in groups which are weak in the qualities required for success in science will slow scientific advance, since the numbers of scientists who make the really creative breakthroughs are small and these could easily be recruited from other segments of the population in ample numbers, if society as a whole continues to provide the necessary financial support.

these developments will *occur, but only that these are developments which are likely to be encouraged by the growth of the Catholic segment of the American population and the decline of the white Protestant segment.* Major social changes are seldom attributable to the influence of any single factor. Rather, such changes usually represent society's response to the workings of multiple forces, many of which largely cancel out each other. Therefore, the changes which occur represent the net balance which remains. Our concern here is to identify some of the more important pressures likely to be generated by one significant factor in American life: the slow but steady alteration of the socio-religious composition of the population.

Drift toward compartmentalization?

Among the possible trends cited above, one deserves special comment both because of its far-reaching implications and because many of these implications have received so little attention from the general public. This is the possible trend toward increased religious group communalism. As we noted in Chapter 2, communalism along socio-religious group lines seems to have been gaining in strength in recent years, and promises to continue to gain in the foreseeable future.

This development is one which has been greatly hastened by the rapid decline of the older ethnic subcommunities in recent years—a development noted by Herberg and others. Until about a generation ago, the American population was sharply divided into a rather large number of relatively small ethnic subcommunities which, in the northern part of the country at least, served as basic points of reference for the masses of Americans. These groups, however, were unable to preserve their organizational integrity in the face of the powerful and pervasive pressures to Americanize the immigrant, and intermarriage across ethnic lines has now become quite common.[33] As a result, loyalties to the various ethnic sub-

[33] See especially Ruby Jo Reeves Kennedy, "Single or Triple Melting Pot? Intermarriage Trends in New Haven, 1870–1940," *American Journal of Sociology*, 49 (January 1944), pp. 331–39. Her findings concerning the mid-twentieth century situation are confirmed by Detroit Area Study findings which are as yet largely unpublished. However, see our data concerning intermarriage in

communities cannot be maintained. The successor to the ethnic subcommunity is the socio-religious subcommunity, a group united by ties of race and religion. As our own and various other studies have shown, while intermarriages across ethnic subcommunity lines are occurring with increasing frequency, there is no trend toward increasing intermarriage across socio-religious group lines. Hence, while Poles now marry Irish with greater frequency, these are marriages of Catholics with Catholics. Even where religious intermarriages occur, our study has shown they lead increasingly to the conversion of one partner or the other, and hence the re-establishment of religious unity within the family.

These facts are especially significant in view of Weber's important distinction between classes and status groups, and subsequent work relevant to this distinction.[34] In classical Marxian theory, the chief units of social organization are classes. In Marx and Engels' famous phrase, "The history of all hitherto existing society is the history of class struggles."[35] By this they meant not merely that classes and class struggles are ubiquitous features of human history, but rather that classes and class struggles alone *make history*.

In reacting against this theory of social change, Weber developed the thesis that societies are organized not merely in terms of classes, but also in terms of status groups. These units are differentiated from one another on the ground of social honor or prestige rather than (like classes) on economic grounds. Furthermore, Weber maintains that they are normally communal groups characterized by distinctive subcultures, whereas classes are not. While there is usually some relationship between the class system of a society and its system of status groups, the two are by no means the same.

There seems little doubt that socio-religious groups are rapidly replacing ethnic groups as the basic units in the system of status groups in American society. Of the four major

---

Chapter 2. See also John C. Leggett, *Working Class Consciousness in an Industrial Community* (unpublished doctoral dissertation, The University of Michigan, 1962), p. 141.

[34] *From Max Weber,* op. cit., pp. 180–94.

[35] Karl Marx and Friedrich Engels, *Manifesto of the Communist Party,* 1848.

socio-religious groups, the white Protestants enjoy the greatest social honor, Catholics rank second, Jews third, and Negro Protestants fourth.[36] As the position of the Jewish group indicates, status-group rank by no means parallels class position.

In recent years sociologists have increasingly recognized the importance of status and status groups in the life of industrialized societies.[37] More especially, they have come to recognize that political controversy in modern industrial societies has a tendency to change in character from one decade to the next. Sometimes the basic controversies are between classes; other times they are between status groups. Class-based controversies normally dominate politics in periods of economic crisis, while controversies involving status groups tend to dominate in periods of prosperity.[38]

If our analysis is correct up to this point, it indicates that in

[36] This fact has been demonstrated numerous times in studies of social distance. For example, see Emory S. Bogardus, *Immigration and Race Attitudes* (Boston: Heath & Co., 1928), or Daniel Katz and Kenneth Braly, "Racial Stereotypes of 100 College Students," *Journal of Abnormal and Social Psychology*, 28 (1933) pp. 280–90. More recently the author together with Werner S. Landecker conducted a study of the status of ethnic groups in Detroit which reconfirmed earlier findings.

[37] In addition to the vast literature on the American caste system (referring to the racial cleavage), there is a growing literature on the tripartite religious division among whites. In addition to Herberg's classic analysis, there is Ruby Jo Reeves Kennedy's pioneering work, op. cit., A. B. Hollingshead's article, "Trends in Social Stratification: A Case Study," *American Sociological Review*, 17 (December 1952), especially pp. 685–86, and Mhyra S. Minnis' article, "Cleavage in Women's Organizations: A Reflection of the Social Structure of a City," ibid., 18 (February 1953), pp. 47–53 to cite but a few. It is perhaps significant that much of the literature on this subject comes from the New England area where the Catholic proportion of the American population is greatest and the white Protestant proportion the smallest. If population trends are as our research indicates, and if the drift toward compartmentalization is stimulated by these trends, other sections of the country can be expected to display more of the pattern which is now relatively marked in that one section of the country.

[38] See, for example, S. M. Lipset, "The Sources of the 'Radical Right,'" and Richard Hofstadter, "The Pseudo-Conservative Revolt," in Daniel Bell, ed., *The New American Right* (New York: Criterion Books, 1955), pp. 166–235 and 33–55 respectively.

the foreseeable future we can expect that economic prosperity will be accompanied by heightened tensions between socio-religious groups, and political controversies during such periods will be closely linked with the hopes, fears, and aspirations of these groups. Only severe economic and international crises seem likely to alter the situation. In short, the controversies surrounding John Kennedy's candidacy in 1960 may well mark the beginning of a new era in American life, not the end as many people imagine.

The findings of this study force us to consider the possibility that American society is moving (though admittedly slowly) towards a "compartmentalized society" of the type found in contemporary Holland and Lebanon, to cite but two of the more prominent examples. In these societies most of the major institutional systems are obliged to take account of socio-religious distinctions. Hence, political parties, families, sports teams, and even business establishments are often identified with one or another of the major groups. The Dutch even have a word, *verzuiling*, to describe this kind of social arrangement. Literally translated it means "columnization," since society is organized like a series of parallel columns or pillars.[39]

American society has a long way to go before it will even approach the degree of compartmentalization attained by Holland or Lebanon, but the trend itself is a matter of importance. The old American ideal of a great melting pot out of which would someday emerge a new, unified nation seems to have been abandoned, and increasingly we hear discussions about "pluralistic society." "Pluralistic society" may be a real alternative to "compartmentalized society," but present-day

[39] For a discussion of the Dutch pattern see David O. Moberg, "Religion and Society in the Netherlands and in America," *American Quarterly*, 13 (Summer 1961), pp. 172–78. See also J. A. A. Van Doorn, "Verzuiling: Een Eigentijds Systeem van Sociale Controle," *Sociologische Gids*, 3 (1956), pp. 41–49; I. Schöffer, "Verzuiling, Een Specifiek Nederlands Probleem," ibid., 3 (1956), pp. 121–217; or see the special issue of *Socialisme en Democratie* devoted to the subject of *verzuiling*, January 1957, all cited by Moberg. See also John W. Dykstra, "Holland's Religious Segmentation," *Christian Century*, October 19, 1955, pp. 1207–8 and the special issue of *Social Compass*, 9 (1962) on "vertical pluralism."

proponents of pluralism do not seem greatly concerned with making the distinction. This suggests that "pluralistic society" may turn out to be merely another term, a polite euphemism, for "compartmentalized society," or at best a steppingstone leading to it.

It may well be that compartmentalization along socioreligious group lines is the best we can hope for in a society which is religiously divided as ours is, if at the same time we are to preserve the values linked with the various subgroups. However, if given the group loyalties of Americans, compartmentalization is the best arrangement we can achieve, it would seem desirable that this alternative be chosen *after rational exploration and consideration of the alternatives.* Currently we seem merely to be drifting into a type of social arrangement which Americans of all faiths might well reject if they became fully aware of all it entails.

This problem should be of special concern to religious leaders. Our current drift toward a "compartmentalized society" could easily produce a situation where individuals developed a heightened sense of religious group loyalty combined with a minimal sense of responsibility for those outside their own group. In a more compartmentalized society there is good reason to fear a weakening of the ethical and spiritual elements in religion and a heightening of the ever dangerous political elements. Such a development would be a serious departure from the basic ideals of all of the major faiths in America, sharing as they do in the Biblical tradition. Hence, on both religious and political grounds, Americans might do well to study more critically than they yet have the arguments advanced by advocates of pluralistic society.

Appendix I

SAMPLING ERROR AND
STATISTICAL SIGNIFICANCE

The sample used in the 1958 Detroit Area Study was basically a simple random sample of the population of the metropolitan area. Among the many advantages of this type of sample is the fact that it affords the investigator a basis for estimating the probability that his findings are the result of sampling error. In any study of a population based on observations of a sample, some differences between the sample and the population universe from which the sample is drawn are bound to occur. With most types of samples it is difficult, or impossible, to calculate the probable magnitude of these errors. However, when truly random samples are employed, such calculations can be made with ease. This is not to say that we can determine that a given set of observations of the sample are 2 percentage points too high in a given instance. But we can determine that the probability of an error of 2 percentage points or more is of a certain magnitude. In other words, where random samples are used, we can make valid estimates of the probable magnitude of the errors resulting from reliance on observations of only a sample of the total population.

This fact has given rise to the widespread use by social scientists of what are known as tests of significance. The term "significance" is something of a misnomer, since these are tests designed to determine how likely it is that a given percentage difference between two subgroups in a sample (e.g., Jews and Catholics) could be entirely due to sampling error. If the probability is .90 or .95 that the difference in question could not be accounted for on the grounds of sampling error, most social scientists today accept as valid the conclusion that the observed difference in the sample reflects a real difference in the population universe.

Unfortunately, in the social sciences in recent years many serious abuses have grown up around the use of these tests of statistical significance.[1] Frequently it has been assumed that statistical significance is a measure of *social significance.* Sometimes degree of statistical significance has been assumed to be the same as degree of association. But more serious than any of these is the tendency for researchers and their readers to use tests of significance as *substitute for thought* in the formation of judgments concerning the validity and generalizability of sample findings. Too often researchers and readers have adopted the view that if a test of statistical significance shows that a given relationship found in a sample would not have occurred more than 5 times in 100 because of sampling error therefore it also exists in the population universe, and if the relationship could have occurred more than 5 times in 100, therefore it does not exist in the population universe.

Tests of significance should be recognized for what they are: merely one of the tools available to social scientists to aid in the formation of judgments concerning the validity and generalizability of findings based on observations of samples. At best, tests of significance are a poor substitute for the test of *replication.* Judgments about social relationships are far more reliable when based on the findings of two, three, four, or more independent samples than when based on any single sample of the same size and quality.

It is for this reason that in the text proper we have constantly cited the findings of other studies dealing with comparable relationships. It is also for this reason that we have so often supplemented the findings of the 1958 survey with findings from other surveys conducted by the Detroit Area Study. When three or four well-designed surveys yield findings which consistently conform to a pattern predicted by theory,

---

[1] For a good summary of some of the more serious abuses see Leslie Kish, "Some Statistical Problems in Research Design," *American Sociological Review,* 24 (June 1959), especially pp. 335–38.

even though the individual findings may not always meet some specified level of statistical significance, the probabilities are great that the relationship exists in the universe from which the samples were drawn.

In this connection it may be well to emphasize the importance of *patterns* in findings, and especially patterns which become evident when the findings of separate and independent samples are compared. By this term "patterns" we mean not merely relationships between two specific variables which are consistent in direction and reasonably consistent in magnitude (e.g., studies invariably show that northern white Protestants are much more likely to be Republicans than northern white Catholics), but also relationships among a goodly number of variables with comparable theoretical significance (cf., e.g., the many variables which involve attitudes toward the union movement). As statisticians have long noted, if one simply examines enough relationships, some are certain, by virtue of the laws of probability, to prove statistically significant at some impressive level. By focusing on items *out of context* one can easily come to very misleading conclusions. Similarly, by ignoring the larger context it is possible to overlook a particular relationship on the grounds that it is not statistically significant, when in fact it may be socially quite significant, and furthermore, part of a consistent pattern of findings.

In view of these facts, and also for the sake of making the text more readable, it was decided to emphasize the patterning of relationships rather than tests of statistical significance in the book proper, and place the materials necessary for calculating sampling errors in this appendix. The materials required for making the necessary calculations are provided in *Tables 51 to 54.*

Table 51 indicates the number of respondents in each of the major subgroups in the four surveys examined in this study. Such figures are necessary in making calculations of probabilities of sampling error, since such probabilities vary inversely with the size of the population being considered. Where other subgroups are compared in the text, we have provided the necessary data on the number of cases in these subgroups, using the notation (N=37), with the symbol "N" referring to the number of cases on which the reported percentage was based.

Table 52 provides the information required for determining the confidence intervals around the various statistics presented in this study. To illustrate its use, let us take the finding that 21 per cent of the respondents in the total 1958 sample

Table 51

NUMBER OF RESPONDENTS IN VARIOUS SUBSAMPLES OF 1958, 1957, 1953, AND 1952 SURVEYS

Subsample	White Protestants	White Catholics	Negro Protestants	Jews
1958 Survey: Total	267	230	100	27
Middle class	117	92	13	19
Working class	150	138	87	8
Some college education	54	44	12	7
No college education	213	186	88	20
Age 21–34	95	90	35	8
Age 35–49	92	73	35	11
Age 50 and over	79	67	30	8
1st or 2nd generation	105	151	—	24
3rd or more generation	146	68	—	0
Father: middle class	51	53	12	15
Father: working class	161	135	42	11
Father: farmer	47	32	37	0
Male	116	111	46	12
Female	151	119	54	15
Associational involvement: high	76	174	41	2
Associational involvement: low	190	53	57	25
Communal involvement: high	80	82	55?	20
Communal involvement: low	183	144	45?	6
Devotionalism: high	76	104	67	2
Devotionalism: low	183	118	32	23
Orthodoxy: high	82	137	37	—
Orthodoxy: low	185	87	62	—
1957 Survey: Total	358	262	125	21
Middle class	143	84	18	17
Working class	215	178	107	4
Associational involvement: high	135	205	46	0
Associational involvement: low	221	57	78	21

Subsample	White Protestants	White Catholics	Negro Protestants	Jews
1953 Survey: Total	237	217	52	14
Middle class	87	75	9	10
Working class	150	142	43	4
Associational involvement: high	85	168	22	0
Associational involvement: low	152	49	30	13
1952 Survey: Total	328	254	74	32
Middle class	123	85	7	22
Working class	205	169	67	10
Associational involvement: high	80	179	30	3
Associational involvement: low	245	74	44	29

(N=656) described themselves as Republicans. If one checks under the column headed "700" and on the Sample Percentage row for "20 or 80 per cent," it may be seen that sampling errors of up to 3 percentage points can be expected at the .90 level. This means that if one were to take repeated random samples of about 700 persons in the population of the community, 90 per cent of the time the values obtained in these samples would be within plus or minus 3 percentage points of the true value for the population universe.

In most instances in this study we were not so much concerned with single figures as with relationships between figures. For example, we were less concerned with the percentage of Republicans in the total population than with the *relative* percentage of Republicans in the various socio-religious groups. Here our concern was with the question of the

Table 52

APPROXIMATE SAMPLING ERRORS FOR 1958 DETROIT AREA STUDY (P=.90)

Sample Percentage	Sample size							
	700	500	300	200	100	75	50	25
50%	3	4	5	6	8	9	12	17
30 or 70%	3	3	4	5	8	8	11	15
20 or 80%	3	3	4	5	7	8	9	13
10 or 90%	2	2	3	4	5	6	7	10
5 or 95%	1	2	2	3	3	4	5	8

probabilities that specific differences between the groups might be due merely to sampling error. To answer this question it is necessary to examine *Tables* 53 *and* 54.

Table 53

SAMPLING ERRORS OF DIFFERENCES: ONE-TAIL $P=.10$*

Sample size	300	200	100	75	50	25
	For percentages from 35 to 65 per cent					
300	5	6	7	8	10	14
200		7	8	9	10	14
100			9	10	11	14
75				10	12	15
50					13	16
25						18
	For percentages around 20 and 80 per cent					
300	4	5	6	7	8	
200		5	6	7	8	
100			7	8	9	
75				9	10	
50					10	
	For percentages around 10 and 90 per cent					
300	3	4	4	5		
200		4	5	5		
100			6			

* When the percentage-point difference between two subgroups in the sample (e.g., white Catholics and Protestants) is of the magnitude indicated in the appropriate cell, or greater, and when the difference is one which *was predicted*, the probability is .10, or less, that the observed difference between the subgroups was due to sampling error.

Table 53 indicates the number of percentage points which must separate two groups being compared if there is to be no more than one chance in ten that the difference observed is due to sampling error, *provided the direction of the difference observed was that predicted in advance.* For example, on the basis of past research and theory it was predicted that white Protestants would be Republicans more often than white Catholics, with class position controlled. Among middle-class white Protestants in the 1958 survey, 51 per cent were Republicans ($N=117$). Among middle-class white Catholics the comparable figure was 32 per cent ($N=92$). If one reads down the column headed "100" and across the row labeled "100" to the section for "percentages from 35 to 65 per cent," the figure 9 will be found. This means that the probability is more than .90 that the difference observed in the sample was not due merely to sampling error, since the difference in the sample was greater than 9 percentage points.

In cases where the difference under consideration is one which was *not predicted*, Table 54 must be used.[2] As the

Table 54

SAMPLING ERRORS OF DIFFERENCES: TWO-TAIL P=.10*

Sample size	300	200	100	75	50	25
	For percentages from 35 to 65 per cent					
300	7	8	9	11	13	17
200		8	10	11	13	17
100			12	13	14	18
75				13	15	19
50					17	20
25						23
	For percentages around 20 and 80 per cent					
300	5	6	8	8	10	
200		7	8	9	11	
100			9	11	12	
75				12	12	
50					13	
	For percentages around 10 and 90 per cent					
300	4	5	6	7		
200		5	6	7		
100			7			

* When the percentage differences between two subgroups in the sample is of the magnitude indicated in the appropriate cell, or greater, and when the difference is one which *was not predicted*, the probability is .10, or less, that the observed difference between the subgroups was due merely to sampling error.

[2] In the text we have not always indicated when each of the findings was predicted in advance for fear of becoming tedious. However, the reader will readily recognize that on the basis of past theory and research there are grounds for predicting that Protestants would conform to the spirit of capitalism (in all of its various manifestations) more often than Catholics, but no basis for predicting the reverse. *Table 54* should be used when past theory and research provide no basis for expecting either of the

reader will observe, the values shown in *Table 54* are always somewhat larger than the comparable values in *Table 53*. The reason for this is that when the null hypothesis is being tested (i.e., the hypothesis that the difference in question is merely due to sampling error), it is only half as likely that differences of a given magnitude *and in a predicted direction* will be found as that differences of the same magnitude without regard to the direction of the relationship will be found. For example it is only half as likely that middle-class white Protestants will be Republicans 9 percentage points more often than middle-class Catholics, as that a 9-point difference on party preference will divide the two groups, but without specification as to which group will be more often Republican.

In these tables we have made use of the .90 level of probability rather than the more common .95 level. The primary reason for this is the size of our original sample, and our use of a multivariate mode of analysis. Under these circumstances, we are often obliged to make comparisons between rather small subsamples. The smaller the subgroups being compared, the larger the difference in percentage points required to "pass" the test of statistical significance. Under the circumstances, it seemed that the .90 level was amply rigorous. In our opinion there is as much or more danger of rejecting socially significant data when small samples are involved and overly rigorous levels of statistical significance employed than of accepting as valid relationships which are merely due to sampling error. This is an aspect of the problem which many ignore, but which we feel should not be.

Some readers who are unfamiliar with tables such as 53 and 54 may find it impossible to keep in mind the many figures included, and inconvenient to keep checking back. For their benefit especially, we would like to note some rough rules of thumb which may prove useful. When dealing with *predicted* differences between *all* white Protestants and *all* white Catholics in the 1958 survey, any difference of 6 percentage points or more is always statistically significant at the .90 level. If the differences involve very large or very small percentages (e.g., figures around 10 or 90 per cent), the dif-

---

groups being compared to display the characteristic in question more than the other.

ference required to achieve statistical significance drops to 4 points. If the differences involved are *not predicted*, the comparable figures are 8 and 5 points.

If the comparisons involve only the *middle-class* white Protestants and Catholics, a difference of 9 points would be required if it was in the predicted direction and if it was in the middle range of percentages (i.e., from 35 to 65 per cent). If the difference was not predicted it would have to be a little higher (12 points), or if it was predicted, but in an extreme range of percentages, it could be a little lower (7 points) and still be significant at the .90 level. If the comparisons involve *working-class* members of these two groups, all the figures would be slightly smaller, since the working class is larger than the middle class.

If the comparisons should involve a group as small as the Jews, and they are compared with the white Protestants, a difference of 14 points would be required to achieve the .90 level if the percentages involved were in the middle range and if the difference was predicted. If the difference was one which was not predicted, a difference of 17 points would be required. If the comparison involved only middle-class members of the two groups, differences of 20 or 25 points are required to reach the .90 level, with the former figure applying to predicted differences, and the latter to unpredicted.

One further point should be kept in mind in forming judgments about statistical significance. When a relationship appears in the same form in two or more separate subsamples (e.g., a relationship which is found in *both* the middle and working classes) the probability that this relationship is due merely to sampling error is less than the probability for either subsample. A simple rule of thumb which may be followed to make allowance for this is to add together the number of cases in the two subsamples and use the smaller (or smallest) percentage-point difference as the basis for calculation. For example, in *Table 38* there is a 20-point difference between upper-middle-class Catholics and Protestants, a 9-point difference between lower-middle-class members of these groups, a 15-point difference at the upper-working-class level, and a 9-point difference at the lower-working-class level. An examination of *Table 53* reveals that the two larger differences are statistically significant, but not the two smaller. This might seem to leave in doubt the important question of whether there is, or is not, a statistically significant difference between the two groups with respect to intellectual autonomy. However, if one adds together all of the Catholics (N=228) and all of the white Protestants (N=258), and takes the smallest percentage difference found at any of the four levels (9 points), it quickly becomes evident that the over-all relationship is statistically significant at the .90 level. In fact, a difference of 6 or 7 points would be statistically significant with this number of cases. It should be noted that this technique always yields a *conservative* estimate of statistical significance. The greater the discrepancy between the figures in the subsamples, the more conservative the estimate.

In a few instances in the text we have subdivided our socio-religious groups into four or more subcategories (as in the instance cited above). When this has been done one can also calculate statistical significance on the basis of the binomial expansion. The probability that the same pattern will emerge, as predicted, in all four subcategories being compared is $(\frac{1}{2})^4$, or .07. The probability that the same pattern will emerge in all of *five* subcategories is $(\frac{1}{2})^5$, or .03. For the reader's benefit we have usually included such probability figures in footnotes in the text.

In conclusion, the reader is again urged to use these materials on statistical significance as merely one of the aids available for forming judgments concerning the validity of the interpretations proposed, and not as a technique to be substituted for thought and reflection on the whole range of evidence set forth.

Appendix II

THE CROSS-SECTION INTERVIEW SCHEDULE

1. One of the first things we are interested in is the kind of work Detroiters do. What is your job at the present time?

(IF RETIRED, LAID OFF, OR UNEMPLOYED)

1a. What was your last job?

2. What kind of business is that in? (e.g., bank, steel mill)

3. Do (did) you work for yourself or are (were) you employed by someone else or some company?

(IF EMPLOYED BY SOMEONE ELSE)

3a. About how many people are (were) employed by the company you work(ed) for?

3b. Are (were) you a member of a labor union?

(IF YES)

3c. Which union is (was) that?

3d. Have you ever been a steward or held any other union office?

3e. Did you ever have a business of your own or work for yourself?

(IF YES)

3f. What type of work did you do?

(IF R[1] NOW HOUSEWIFE)

4. Have you ever held a full-time job outside the home?

(IF YES)

4a. For how long a period was this all told?

4b. What type of work did you last do?

(ALL RESPONDENTS)

5. Some people tell us that they couldn't really be happy unless they were working at some job (or keeping house). But others say that they would be a lot happier if they didn't

---

[1] R is an abbreviation for respondent in the schedule.

have to work and could take life easy. How do you feel about this?

    5a. Why is that?

6. Would you please look at this card (SHOW CARD I) and tell me which thing on this list you would most prefer in a job (would want most for your husband's job)?

CARD I

1. High income
2. No danger of being fired
3. Working hours are short, lots of free time
4. Chances for advancement
5. The work is important and gives a feeling of accomplishment

    6a. Which comes next?

    6b. Which is third most important?

    6c. Which is least important?

7. All things considered, do you think that science is, or is not, a good field for a young man to go into today?

    7a. Why do you feel that way?

8. Changing the subject a bit, do you think it's a good idea or a bad idea to buy things on the installment plan?

    8a. Why do you feel that way?

9. Some people tell us that they try to keep careful records of how much they spend on everything, while others tell us they don't. Do you do this (in your family)?

    9a. What kind of records do you keep?

10. Do you (or your husband) have a savings account, own government bonds, or save in any other way?

11. Do you think every family should save a part of its income every month, or not?

(IF YES)

    11a. How important do you feel this is—should people save even if it means doing without some things they could really use, or should they save only when they can do it without trouble?

    11b. Why do you feel saving is important?

12. While we're on the subject of money, when you go to some big store where the clerks are busy, they sometimes make mistakes in figuring your change. When you get a few

cents more change than you're supposed to, do you think it's worth the bother to return the few pennies involved?

13. If you were driving in another state and got a ticket for parking just a few minutes overtime while getting your lunch, would you bother to pay the fine?

(IF YES)

13a. Would you pay it even if you were in a big hurry and knew that the police in that town would never bother you if you didn't pay the fine?

14. Some people say the government should do more than it has in connection with problems such as housing, unemployment, education, and so on. But others say the government is already doing too much along these lines. *On the whole,* would you say that what the government is doing now is too much, about right, or not enough?

(IF NOT ENOUGH)

14a. Would you like to see the government go so far as to take over and run the big industries in this country such as the railroads, or the steel industry, or would you not be in favor of this?

15. Do you consider yourself a Republican or a Democrat?

(IF NEITHER)

15a. In general, do you consider yourself closer to the Republican Party or the Democratic Party?

(IF REP. OR DEM.)

15b. Why are you a (Republican-Democrat)?

15c. Do you usually vote the straight party ticket when you vote, or do you usually split your ticket between the parties?

15d. Have you always considered yourself a (Republican-Democrat)?

16. When you were growing up, did your father consider himself a Republican or a Democrat?

17. Many people tell us they didn't vote in the last presidential election. Do you remember if you happened to vote in that particular election?

(IF VOTED)

17a. Did you vote for Eisenhower or Stevenson?

17b. In the election for Michigan's governor that same year (1956), did you vote for Cobo or Williams?

18. Looking ahead, we're interested in finding out what sort of man Detroiters would most like to see in the White House when President Eisenhower's term is up. Would you prefer a man who bases his campaign on his belief in God and the American way of life, or one who bases his campaign on a discussion of political and economic problems?

19. Would you prefer a man who gets things done by never letting governmental rules and regulations stop him, or one who takes longer to get most things done but generally abides by the rules and regulations?

20. Would you prefer a man who spends a great deal of time studying every problem carefully, or one who seems to have a sixth sense which he depends on?

21. In our country the Constitution guarantees the right of free speech to everyone. In your opinion, does this include the right for someone to make speeches criticizing what the President does?

22. In your opinion, does the right of free speech include the right for someone to make speeches against religion?

23. In your opinion, does the right of free speech include the right for someone to make speeches in favor of Fascism or dictatorship?

24. In your opinion, does the right of free speech include the right for someone to make speeches in favor of Communism? (i.e., speeches only)

(WHITE RESPONDENTS ONLY)

25. Personally, do you think white students and Negro students should go to the same schools, or separate schools?

26. Would you be at all disturbed or unhappy if a Negro with the same income and education as you, moved into your block?

(IF YES OR UNSURE)

26a. What would make you disturbed or unhappy?

(ALL RESPONDENTS)

27. How much thought have you given to world problems —things such as our country's relations with England, France, Russia, and other countries?

28. Some people say we are spending too much to help other countries and that we shouldn't spend a penny abroad except when we have to in the interest of national defense. Do you agree with them or not?

29. Do you think it was a good idea, or not, for the United States to join the United Nations?

30. If a workable plan could be developed for a single government for the whole world, would you like to see the United States join it, or not?

(IF YES)

30a. Why is that?

31. How much chance do you think there is of our country getting involved in an all-out atomic war with Russia during the next ten or twenty years?

32. Here are several statements which you sometimes hear people make, and I'd like to find out how you feel about them. After each one you can tell me whether you agree with it or not. You'll probably find you agree with some, and disagree with others. In each case, just give me your first reaction—don't spend any time on them. The first statement is: Most public officials are not really interested in the problems of the average man.

32a. These days a person doesn't really know whom he can count on.

32b. Every American family should be required by law to own a flag.

32c. Children born today have a wonderful future to look forward to.

33. While we're talking about children, would you please look at this card (CARD II). If you had to choose, which thing on the list would you pick as *the most important* for a child to learn to prepare him for life?

CARD II

1. To obey
2. To be well liked or popular
3. To think for himself
4. To work hard
5. To help others when they need help

33a. Which comes next?
33b. Which comes third?

33c. Which is least important?

34. Do you have a religious preference? That is, are you either Protestant, Catholic, Jewish, or something else?

(IF PROTESTANT)

34a. What specific denomination is that, if any?

(IF JEWISH)

34b. Do you consider yourself Orthodox, Conservative, Reform, or none of these?

(IF ANY PREFERENCE)

34c. Have you always been a (name denomination)?

(IF NO)

34d. What was your religious preference previously?

34e. What were your reasons for changing?

34f. When did you make this change?

35. What is (IF DEAD: was) the religious preference of your father? (GET SPECIFIC DENOMINATION)

35a. Was this the religion in which he was raised?

(IF NO)

35b. What was he originally?

36. When your father was about your age, was he more religious than you are, about as religious, or would you say he was less religious than you are?

37. What is (IF DEAD: was) the religious preference of your mother? (GET SPECIFIC DENOMINATION)

37a. Was this the religion in which she was raised?

(IF NO)

37b. What was she originally?

38. When your mother was about your age, was she more religious than you are, about as religious, or would you say she was less religious than you are?

39. About how often, if ever, have you attended religious services in the last year? (CARD III)

CARD III

1. Once a week or more
2. Two or three times a month
3. Once a month
4. A few times a year or less
5. Never

(IF EVER)

39a. Which of the reasons on this card (CARD IV) is the main reason you attend church?

CARD IV

> 1. Because I've always gone
> 2. To meet my friends
> 3. Family or friends expect it
> 4. To worship God or pray
> 5. God expects it
> 6. To hear sermon
> 7. To learn how to be a better person
> 8. Makes me feel better
> 9. Other (specify)

39b. Which church (synagogue, temple) do you usually attend?

39c. About how long does it usually take for you to travel there?

39d. Are you a member of that congregation or parish?

39e. How long have you been going there?

39f. What was the last Detroit area church (synagogue, temple) you attended before this one?

39g. Do you take part in any of the activities or organizations of your church (synagogue, temple) other than attending services?

(IF YES)

39h. What sorts of activities or organizations are these?

39i. How often have you done these things in the last year? (SHOW CARD III)

40. Would you say you attend religious services more often, about the same, or less often than you did ten or fifteen years ago?

(IF CHANGE)

40a. What has been the reason for the change?

41. All things considered, do you think you are more *interested,* about as interested, or less interested in religion than you were ten or fifteen years ago?

(IF CHANGE)

41a. What has been the reason for this?

42. Some people wonder whether there is a God. How do you feel—do you believe there is a God, or not?

(IF NO)

42a. Did you ever believe in God?

(Q. 43–56 ASKED ONLY IF R BELIEVES IN GOD)

43. Do you think God is like a Heavenly Father who watches over you and helps you, or do you have some other belief?

44. Do you believe that God answers people's prayers, or not?

(IF YES)

44a. Do you believe that God will always give people what they ask for in their prayers, or not?

44b. How often do you pray?

45. Do you believe in a life after death, or not?

(IF YES)

45a. Do you believe that in the next life some people will be punished and others rewarded by God, or not?

(IF YES)

45b. Do you believe that God judges people on the basis of whether they had faith and trust in Him, or on the basis of the kind of lives they led?

46. Do you believe that, when they are able, God expects people to worship Him in their churches and synagogues EVERY week, or not?

47. Some religious groups teach that the world is *soon* coming to an end. Do you believe this, or not?

48. Are you at all afraid of God, or not?

48a. Why is that?

49. Do you think God is more concerned with the way people treat their fellow men, or with their attendance at Church or synagogue, or would you say these things are equally important to Him?

50. Do you think that God is more pleased when people try to get ahead, or when people are satisfied with what they have and don't try to push ahead?

51. Do you think the work you do is as important in God's eyes as the work of ministers and priests (rabbis), or not?

52. What do you believe about Jesus? Do you believe that Jesus was God's only Son sent into the world by God to

save sinful men, or do you believe that he was simply a very good man and teacher, or do you have some other belief?

53. Have you ever doubted that there is a God?

(IF YES)

53a. What caused you to doubt?

53b. What caused you to give up your doubts?

54. Do you feel that someone who doesn't believe in God can be a good American, or not?

55. When you have decisions to make in your everyday life, do you ask yourself what God would want you to do—often, sometimes, or never?

56. Do you feel that you have the right to question what your church teaches, or not?

(RESUME QUESTIONS FOR ALL RESPONDENTS)

57. Which of the people or things on this card (CARD V) has had the *greatest* influence on your religious beliefs?

CARD V

1. Friends
2. Teachers
3. Husband, wife, or children
4. Parents
5. Ministers, priests, or rabbis
6. Books
7. TV or radio

57a. Which has had the next greatest influence?

58. Have your religious beliefs ever had any effect on your political beliefs?

(IF YES)

58a. In what ways? (INVITE MAXIMUM DETAIL)

59. Do you think that religious leaders ought to take a *public* stand on questions such as whether white and colored children should go to the same schools?

60. Do you think religious leaders ought to take a *public* stand on questions such as whether the government should provide doctors and medical care for people?

61. Do you think religious leaders ought to take a *public* stand for or against some candidate for public office?

62. Here are four statements which have been made about the Bible and I'd like you to tell me which is *closest* to your own view. (1) The Bible is God's Word and all it says is true. (2) The Bible was written by men inspired by God, and its basic moral and religious teachings are true, but because the writers were men, it contains some human errors. (3) The Bible is a valuable book because it was written by wise and good men, but God had nothing to do with it. (4) The Bible was written by men who lived so long ago that it is of little value today.

63. I have here the names of several people mentioned in the Bible whom we've found are not too well known. Would you tell me if you recognize any of these names, and if so, tell me briefly anything you know about them: (*a*) Moses, (*b*) Samuel, (*c*) Peter, (*d*) Barnabas, (*e*) Noah.

64. Have you read any part of the Bible in the last year?

(IF YES)

64a. How often have you read the Bible in the last year?
64b. What are your reasons for reading the Bible?

(IF NO)

64c. Have you ever read any part of the Bible?

(IF YES)

64d. When was the last time?

65. Do you ever watch TV programs or listen to radio programs that are about religion or are sponsored by religious groups?

66. Do you feel there are any disagreements between what science teaches and what your religious group teaches?

(IF YES)

66a. Would you say that these disagreements are—very serious, somewhat serious, or not very serious?

(IF R EMPLOYED)

67. Would you say that you talk about religion with any of the people where you work often, sometimes, or never?

(IF EVER)

67a. Have these talks ever had any effect on your religious beliefs in any way?

(IF YES)

67b. In what ways?

68. Are most of the people you work with Protestant, Catholic, or Jewish?

68a. Would (do) you prefer to have most of the people you work with be of the same faith as yourself, or doesn't this make any difference?

(IF R HOUSEWIFE OR RETIRED)

69. Would you say that you talk about religion with any of your neighbors often, sometimes, or never?

(IF EVER)

69a. Have these talks ever had any effect on your religious beliefs in any way?

(IF YES)

69b. In what ways?

70. Are most of the people in your neighborhood Protestant, Catholic or Jewish?

70a. Would (do) you prefer to have most of your neighbors be of the same faith as yourself, or doesn't this make any difference?

(PROTESTANT RESPONDENTS ONLY)

71. Of those relatives you feel really close to, what proportion are Protestants? (CARD VI)

CARD VI

1. All of them
2. Nearly all of them
3. More than half of them
4. About half of them
5. Less than half of them
6. None of them

72. As a general rule, do you think it is wiser for Protestants to marry other Protestants, or not?

73. As a general rule, do you think it is wiser for Protestants to choose other Protestants as their really close friends, or not?

74. Thinking of *your* closest friends, what proportion are Protestants? (CARD VI)

75. If for some reason you decided to become a Catholic some day, do you think *any* of your friends or relatives would try to *discourage* you, or not?

(IF NO)

75a. Do you think any of your friends or relatives would feel *at all unhappy or disturbed* about it, or not?

76. Compared with Protestants, do you think Catholics as a whole are more tolerant, as tolerant, or less tolerant of the religious beliefs of other people?

77. Compared with Protestants, do you think that Catholics as a whole are more fair, as fair, or less fair in their business dealings?

78. Do you feel that Catholics have been trying to get too much power in this country, or not?

79. Compared with Protestants, do you think Jewish people as a whole are more tolerant, as tolerant, or less tolerant of the religious beliefs of other people?

80. Compared with Protestants, do you think that the Jewish people as a whole are more fair, as fair, or less fair in their business dealings?

81. Do you feel that the Jewish people have been trying to get too much power in this country, or not?

82. Would you like to see your own denomination merge, or join together, with any other Protestant group?

(IF YES)

82a. Which groups would you like to see it merge with?
82b. Are there any Protestant groups you would *not* like it to merge with?

(IF YES)

82c. Which groups are these?

At this point there followed a series of questions for *Catholic* respondents similar to those for Protestants, except with appropriate changes in wording. No question comparable to Q.82 was asked of Catholics, but the following were added for Catholics only.

94. Do you believe that the Catholic Church is the only true church established by God Himself, and that other churches were only established by men?

95. Do you think that the ministers of other churches should be allowed to teach publicly, as on the radio, things that are contrary to Catholic teaching? For example, should

they be allowed to teach publicly that it is never a sin to practice birth control, or should they not be allowed to do this?

At this point there followed a series of questions for *Jewish* respondents similar to Q.75–81 for Protestants. In addition, several special questions were asked of Jewish respondents.

101. Do you generally observe any of the following customs? On the last Passover, did you have a Seder in your own home or attend one elsewhere?

102. Does your family generally light Friday night candles?

103. Last Hanukkah did you light Hanukkah candles?

104. Do you use separate dishes for meat and dairy foods?

Next followed a series of questions for members of the Eastern Orthodox faith similar to Q.71–81.

(RESUME QUESTIONS FOR ALL RESPONDENTS)

117. On the whole, which mean more to you, your ties with your relatives, or your ties with your friends?

118. If you were to join a different (some) religious group, which one do you think you'd be most likely to join?

119. How do you feel about gambling? (SHOW CARD VII) From the moral standpoint, would you say it is always wrong to gamble, usually wrong, sometimes wrong, or never wrong?

CARD VII

| 1. Always wrong |
| 2. Usually wrong |
| 3. Sometimes wrong |
| 4. Never wrong |

(IF ALWAYS OR USUALLY)

119a. Do you think the government should have laws against gambling?

120. From the moral standpoint, would you say that it is always wrong for a married couple to practice birth control, usually wrong, sometimes wrong, or never wrong? (CARD VII)

(IF ALWAYS OR USUALLY)

120a. Do you think the government should have laws against birth control?

121. From the moral standpoint, would you say that *moderate drinking* is always wrong, usually wrong, sometimes wrong, or never wrong? (CARD VII)

(IF ALWAYS OR USUALLY)

121a. Do you think the government should have laws against drinking?

(IF NEVER OR SOMETIMES)

121b. Do you think *heavy drinking* is always, usually, sometimes, or never wrong? (CARD VII)

122. From the moral standpoint, do you think it is always wrong, usually wrong, sometimes, or never wrong for business to remain open on Sunday? (CARD VII)

(IF ALWAYS OR USUALLY)

122a. Do you think the government ought to have laws against this?

123. From the moral standpoint, how do you feel about divorce? (SHOW CARD VII)

124. Here are a few more of those statements you sometimes hear people make, and I'd like to find out whether or not you agree with each of them. The first statement is: Most people don't really care what happens to the next fellow.

124a. It's hardly fair to bring children into the world the way things look for the future.

124b. Nowadays a person has to live pretty much for today and let tomorrow take care of itself.

125. If you had to choose, would you say that you are in the middle class or would you say the working class?

126. All told, about how much would you estimate that your family (you) gave to church and charity last year?

127. Compared with other families (persons) in this country, would you say your family (you) have been more fortunate than average, about average, or less fortunate than average with respect to serious illness, accidents, and death?

128. From the economic standpoint, would you say your family (you) have been more fortunate than average, about average, or less fortunate than average?

129. Are you married, single, divorced, separated, or widowed?

(IF WIDOWED OR DIVORCED)

129a. How long were you married?

129b. How many children have you had altogether, including any who died after birth?

(ASK ONLY IF R MARRIED OR SEPARATED)

130. Is this your first marriage?

(IF NO)

130a. How many years were you married to your first husband (wife)?

130b. Did your first marriage end by death or divorce?

131. Is this your wife's (husband's) first marriage?

(IF NO)

131a. How many years was she (he) married to her (his) first husband (wife)?

131b. How many children did she (he) have in her (his) first marriage?

132. How long have you been married to your present wife (husband)?

133. How many children have you had altogether, including any who died after birth?

(IF R 45 YEARS OLD OR OLDER)

134. Looking back now, if you could start your married life over, how many children would you want to have by the time you were 45 years old?

(IF R LESS THAN 45 YEARS OLD)

135. Do you expect to have any (more) children?

(IF NO)

135a. If you could start your married life over again, and choose to have just the number you would want by the time you were 45, how many would that be?

(IF YES)

135b. How many children do you expect to have altogether?

135c. (SAME AS 135a; IF R MARRIED TWO YEARS OR MORE)

(IF MARRIED LESS THAN TWO YEARS)

135d. Now, if you could choose to have just the number you want by the time you are 45, how many would that be?

(FOLLOWING QUESTIONS ASKED ONLY
OF PERSONS WITH CHILDREN)

136. In the case of your children, have (will) you and your wife (husband) give(n) them any kind of religious training at home?

(IF YES)

136a. What kinds of training?

137. Do you feel that a 12-year-old child should be allowed to decide for himself whether he will go to church or Sunday school, or should his parents decide this?

138. Do (did, will) you encourage your children to pray, or not?

139. Do (did, will) your children attend the public schools, or do (did, will) they attend parochial schools?

140. In your family do you ever say a prayer before meals?

(IF YES)

140a. How often is this done—quite often, or just on special occasions?

141. In what denomination have (did, will) you raise(d) your children?

(IF R HAS CHILDREN AGED 20 AND OVER)

141a. Are all your grown children still members of that group?

(IF NO)

141b. How many have changed, and what church have they joined, if any?

(THE FOLLOWING QUESTIONS ASKED ONLY
IF R MARRIED, SEPARATED OR WIDOWED)

142. What is (was) your husband's (wife's) job?

(IF SPOUSE RETIRED, LAID OFF, OR UNEMPLOYED)

142a. What was his (her) last job?

143. What kind of business is (was) that in? (e.g., bank)

144. Does (did) your husband (wife) work for himself (herself) or was he (she) employed by someone else or some company?

(IF EMPLOYED)

144a. About how many people are (were) employed by the company your husband (wife) works(ed) for?

144b. Is (was) he (she) a member of a labor union?

(IF YES)

144c. Which union is (was) that?

144d. Has he (she) ever been a steward or held any other union office?

144e. Did he (she) ever have a business of his (her) own or work for himself (herself)?

145. Did he (she) get any of his (her) education in parochial schools or other schools run by his (her) church?

(IF YES)

145a. How many years did he (she) attend church schools?

146. What is (was) your husband's (wife's) religious preference?

(IF PROTESTANT)

146a. Which denomination is (was) that?

147. Did your husband (wife) ever change his (her) religious preference?

(IF YES)

147a. What was he (she) previously?

147b. Why did he (she) change?

147c. When was that approximately?

148. How often does (did) your husband (wife) attend religious services? (SHOW CARD III)

149. Do (did) you and your husband (wife) see eye-to-eye on religious matters, or not?

150. Does (did) your husband (wife) consider himself (herself) a Republican or a Democrat?

151. Did your husband (wife) ever change his (her) party preference?

(DO NOT ASK THE FOLLOWING QUESTIONS OF NEGROES)

152. What is the original nationality of his (her) family on his (her) father's side?

153. Was his (her) father born in the United States?

154. What is the nationality of his (her) family on his (her) mother's side?

155. Was his (her) mother born in the U.S.?

CENSUS DATA QUESTIONS ASKED OF ALL RESPONDENTS

1. Race (BY OBSERVATION)
2. Sex (BY OBSERVATION)
3. Age?
4. Relationship of respondent to head of household?
5. Marital status?
6. What was the highest grade of school you completed?
7. Did you get any of your education in parochial schools or other schools run by your church?

(IF YES)

7a. How many years did you attend church schools?

8. How long have you lived in the Detroit area? (i.e., Wayne, Oakland, and Macomb counties)

(IF NOT NATIVE)

8a. Where were you born?

9. Do you own this home, or are you renting?
10. About how many other houses or apartments have you lived in here in the Detroit area?

(IF ANY)

10a. How long have you lived at this address?

Questions 11–22 were a series of questions concerning use of telephone service and were unrelated to this study.

23. What was your father's usual occupation while you were growing up?

(DO NOT ASK THE FOLLOWING QUESTIONS OF NEGROES)

24. What is the original nationality of your family on your father's side?
25. Was your father born in the United States?
26. What is the original nationality of your family on your mother's side?
27. Was your mother born in the United States?
28. Were any of your grandparents born in the United States?

(IF YES)

28a. How many were born in the United States?

29. What was your total family income in 1957, considering all sources such as rents, profits, wages, interest, and so on? (SHOW CARD VIII)

CARD VIII

1. $0-999	5. $4,000-4,999	9. $8,000-9,999
2. $1,000-1,999	6. $5,000-5,999	10. $10,000-14,999
3. $2,000-2,999	7. $6,000-6,999	11. $15,000 or more
4. $3,000-3,999	8. $7,000-7,999	

29a. How much of your total family income was the income of the head of the family?

Appendix III

DETAILED TABLES ON SELECTED TOPICS

The variables shown in *Table 55* are a representative sample of the many variables used in this study, and were not selected for any reason other than their importance. While there are some differences in this table which are rather large, these differences seldom fall into any meaningful pattern. For example, an examination of Column I reveals that middle-class Lutherans advocate intellectual autonomy more often than members of any of the other groups, but working-class Lutherans are next to last in this respect. Or, as shown in Column B, middle-class Episcopalians are the most often opposed to installment buying, but working-class Episcopalians are the least often opposed.

A second type of problem arises when we look for patterns involving two or more dependent variables. For example, an examination of Columns C and D reveals that middle-class Lutherans rank second in the proportion of Republicans in their ranks, but they also rank second in the relative strength of their commitment to the principles of the welfare state.

Finally, at certain points where it appeared that a significant difference might exist, *the application of a single control would eliminate the difference entirely.* For example, working-class Baptists had an unusually small percentage of Republicans in their ranks. However, the application of a control for region of birth proved that most of this difference was simply a function of the fact that so many Baptists were southern-born.

In short, with rare exceptions, the data failed to reveal any

Intra-Protestant Comparisons

Table 55

DENOMINATIONAL DIFFERENCES WITHIN THE WHITE PROTES-
TANT GROUP FOR SELECTED VARIABLES, WITH CLASS CON-
TROLLED, IN PERCENTAGES

Class: Denomination	Selected Variables:*									No. of Cases**
	A	B	C	D	E	F	G	H	I	
Middle Class:										
Episcopalian	40	64	89	25	73	18	9	64	82	11
Presbyterian	10	28	65	12	80	28	25	63	84	25
Lutheran	25	47	70	19	59	13	6	47	86	32
Methodist	40	31	69	0	63	31	25	75	81	16
Baptist	33	45	50	11	45	36	30	45	55	11
Working Class:										
Episcopalian	—	38	33	58	38	23	15	54	62	13
Presbyterian	0	44	50	32	28	39	33	39	78	18
Lutheran	-10	40	42	33	31	33	8	56	57	36
Methodist	-33	67	27	40	44	50	16	53	44	18
Baptist	36	43	17	28	49	49	35	54	63	35

* The variables reported above are as follows:

A. Percentage of males with positive attitude toward work *minus* percentage with negative attitude;

B. Percentage believing installment buying wrong or unwise;

C. Percentage of those with party preference who are Republicans;

D. Percentage believing government has not yet done enough *minus* percentage believing government has done too much already;

E. Percentage believing Constitution should be interpreted to permit people to speak against religion;

F. Percentage favoring segregated schools;

G. Percentage believing moderate drinking always or usually wrong;

H. Percentage believing Sunday business always or usually wrong;

I. Percentage believing it more important for child to learn to think for himself than to learn to obey.

** The number of cases shown in the right-hand margin is the total number of members of each group in the class indicated. In some instances the number of cases on which the percentages were calculated were smaller than this owing to some respondents failing to reply, or to limitation of the respondents (e.g., item A is limited to males).

meaningful differences among white Protestants which could be clearly traced to the influence of denomination.[1] It is possible, of course, that with a larger sample and smaller sampling errors, significant differences would emerge. Also, it is possible that an examination limited to persons who were lifelong, and active, members of the various denominations would reveal differences not now evident. Our sample was much too small to permit any such detailed analysis as this.

Doctrinal orthodoxy

Table 56

PERCENTAGE GIVING ORTHODOX RESPONSES TO THE VARIOUS QUESTIONS USED IN DEFINING DOCTRINAL ORTHODOXY, BY SOCIO-RELIGIOUS GROUP

Question	White Catholics	White Protestants	Negro Protestants
Believe in God? (Q. 42)	98	97	99
God like a loving Heavenly Father? (Q. 43)	95	85	97
God responds to men's prayers? (Q. 44)	90	87	97
Believe that in life after death some will be punished? (Q. 45 and 45a)	72	45	52
Jesus God's only Son? (Q. 52)	93	82	89
God expects men to worship Him *every* week, if able? (Q. 46)	82	54	71

[1] Among the exceptions one may note the following: (a) Lutherans were less critical of moderate drinking than other white Protestants, while the Baptists were the most critical; (b) Episcopalians objected to gambling less often than other white Protestants; and (c) Lutherans are much less likely than members of other groups to express the view that Catholics are trying to get too much power, and somewhat less likely than other groups to say this of the Jews.

Doctrinal orthodoxy, devotionalism, and other variables

Table 57

PERCENTAGE OF RESPONDENTS DOCTRINALLY ORTHODOX AND DEVOTIONALLY ACTIVE, BY SOCIO-RELIGIOUS GROUP AND SELECTED VARIABLES SUGGESTIVE OF TRENDS

Socio-religious Group: Selected Variables	PERCENTAGE IN EACH CATEGORY WHO ARE:	
	Doctrinally Orthodox	Active Devotionally
White Catholics:		
Third generation	71	53
First and second generations	61	46
Middle class	62	54
Working class	61	44
College-educated	64	45
No college experience	61	47
White Protestants:		
Third generation: non-southern	29	26
1st and 2nd generations: non-southern	30	34
Middle class	28	33
Working class	33	26
College-educated	22	25
No college experience	33	30
Negro Protestants:		
Northern-born	29	59
Southern-born	39	69
Middle class	8	50
Working class	41	70
College-educated	25	64
No college experience	39	68

$$
\begin{array}{r}
2 \\
25 \\
25 \\
\hline
125 \\
50 \\
\hline
625 \\
150 \\
\hline
775
\end{array}
\qquad
\begin{array}{r}
3 \\
25 \\
6 \\
\hline
150
\end{array}
$$

INDEX TO AUTHORITIES CITED

INDEX TO SUBJECT MATTER

ANCHOR BOOKS

SOCIOLOGY

Sociology (continued)

Sociology (continued)

ANCHOR BOOKS

RELIGION

ANCHOR BOOKS

PHILOSOPHY

* Modern Studies in Philosophy Series

Philosophy (continued)

THE GENESIS OF TWENTIETH CENTURY PHILOSOPHY: The Evolution of Thought from Copernicus to the Present—Harry Prosch, A536

HEGEL: A Reinterpretation—Walter Kaufmann, A528a

HEGEL: Texts and Commentary—Walter Kaufmann, A528b

THE HUMAN CONDITION—Hannah Arendt, A182

* HUME—ed. by V. C. Chappell, AP2

INDIVIDUALS—P. F. Strawson, A364

THE INTELLECTUAL HISTORY OF EUROPE, Vol. I: The Beginnings of Western Civilization to Luther—Friedrich Heer, A610a

THE INTELLECTUAL HISTORY OF EUROPE, Vol. II: The Counter-Reformation to the 20th Century—Friedrich Heer, A610b

IRRATIONAL MAN—William Barrett, A321

* KANT: A Collection of Critical Essays—Robert Paul Wolff, ed., AP4

* LOCKE AND BERKELEY: A Collection of Critical Essays—David M. Armstrong and C. B. Martin, AP6

LOGIC AND LANGUAGE—Antony Flew, ed., A449

MAN IN MODERN AGE—Karl Jaspers, A101

MARX IN THE MID-TWENTIETH CENTURY: A Yugoslav Philosopher Reconsiders Karl Marx's Writings—Gajo Petrović, A584

MARXISM AND EXISTENTIALISM—Walter Odajnyk, A443

THE MARXISM OF JEAN-PAUL SARTRE—Wilfrid Desan, A507

THE METAPHYSICAL FOUNDATIONS OF MODERN SCIENCE—Edwin Arthur Burtt, A41

MODERN SCIENCE AND MODERN MAN—James B. Conant, A10

MYSTICISM AND LOGIC—Bertrand Russell, A104

THE ONTOLOGICAL ARGUMENT—Alvin Plantinga, ed., A435

PATTERNS OF ANARCHY—Leonard I. Krimerman and Lewis Perry, eds., A501

PERCEIVING, SENSING AND KNOWING—Robert J. Swartz, ed., A460

THE PHILOSOPHY OF HISTORY IN OUR TIME—Hans Meyerhoff, ed., A164

PHILOSOPHIES OF JUDAISM—Julius Guttman, A509

THE PHILOSOPHY OF TIME—Richard Gale, ed., A573

PRAGMATIC PHILOSOPHY—ed. by Amelie Rorty, A538

PSYCHE AND SYMBOL—C. G. Jung, A136

SELECTIONS FROM THE WRITINGS OF KIERKEGAARD—Lee M. Hollander, ed. and trans., A210

SOCIALIST HUMANISM: An International Symposium—ed. by Erich Fromm, A529

* Modern Studies in Philosophy Series

Philosophy (continued)

* Modern Studies in Philosophy Series